COOPERATION, COMITY, AND COMPETITION POLICY

COOPERATION, COMITY, AND COMPETITION POLICY

EDITED BY
ANDREW T. GUZMAN

OXFORD
UNIVERSITY PRESS

OXFORD
UNIVERSITY PRESS

Oxford University Press, Inc., publishes works that further Oxford University's objective of excellence in research, scholarship, and education.

Oxford New York
Auckland Cape Town Dar es Salaam Hong Kong Karachi Kuala Lumpur Madrid Melbourne Mexico City Nairobi New Delhi Shanghai Taipei Toronto

With offices in
Argentina Austria Brazil Chile Czech Republic France Greece Guatemala Hungary Italy Japan Poland Portugal Singapore South Korea Switzerland Thailand Turkey Ukraine Vietnam

Published by Oxford University Press, Inc.
198 Madison Avenue, New York, New York 10016

Library of Congress Cataloging-in-Publication Data

Cooperation, comity, and competition policy/edited by Andrew T. Guzman
p. cm.
Includes bibliographical references and index.
ISBN 978–0–19–538770–4 (hardback : alk. paper)
1. Conflict of laws–Antitrust law. 2. Antitrust law–International cooperation.
3. Antitrust law (International law) I. Guzman, Andrew T.
K3850.5.C668 2010
343'.0721–dc22 2010015509

Note to Readers

This publication is designed to provide accurate and authoritative information in regard to the subject matter covered. It is based upon sources believed to be accurate and reliable and is intended to be current as of the time it was written. It is sold with the understanding that the publisher is not engaged in rendering legal, accounting, or other professional services. If legal advice or other expert assistance is required, the services of a competent professional person should be sought. Also, to confirm that the information has not been affected or changed by recent developments, traditional legal research techniques should be used, including checking primary sources where appropriate.

(Based on the Declaration of Principles jointly adopted by a Committee of the American Bar Association and a Committee of Publishers and Associations.)

CONTENTS

I. COUNTRY REPORTS

II. POLICY PROPOSALS

PART ONE

COUNTRY REPORTS

1. COOPERATION, COMITY, AND COMPETITION POLICY
United States

EDWARD T. SWAINE*

I. INTRODUCTION

The United States pioneered the extraterritorial enforcement of antitrust law, but its role was assumed slowly and with evident misgivings. The principal source of federal antitrust law, the Sherman Antitrust Act, declares illegal "[e]very contract, combination in the form of trust or otherwise, or conspiracy, in restraint of trade or commerce among the several States, or with foreign nations."[1] This licensed, on its face, very broad application to foreign parties and practices. Nevertheless, in the Supreme Court's first major inquiry into extraterritoriality, a 1909 decision known as *American Banana*,[2] Justice Oliver Wendell Holmes wrote that it was "surprising" to assert that the Sherman Act might apply extraterritorially. Applying U.S. law to acts taken abroad, he reasoned, would be "unjust" and violate a "general and almost universal rule," one designed to prevent "interference with the authority of another sovereign, contrary to the comity of nations, which the other state concerned justly might resent."[3] The court upheld dismissal of the complaint because the relevant acts—the seizure by the Costa Rican government of property owned by American Banana, allegedly at United Fruit's behest—took place outside the United States.

Though *American Banana* now appears dated, the opinion and its aftermath illustrate several distinctive features of antitrust extraterritoriality as it has been experienced in the United States. The first is the judiciary's dominant role.

---

* Edward T. Swaine is Professor of Law and Director of the Competition Law Center at George Washington University Law School.

1. 15 U.S.C. §§ 1–2. For space reasons, this chapter will not address the territorial scope of other U.S. antitrust laws, which are frequently delimited in more specific terms. Section 7 of the Clayton Act, for example, applies to any person "engaged in commerce or in any activity affecting commerce." 15 U.S.C. §§ 12, 18. Notwithstanding the apparent difference between this language and the Sherman Act, the U.S. enforcement agencies have stated that they apply the same principles to reckoning the extraterritorial scope of both statutes. U.S. Dep't of Justice & Fed. Trade Comm., *Antitrust Enforcement Guidelines for International Operations* § 3.14 (Apr. 5, 1995), *reprinted in* 4 Trade Reg. Rep. (CCH) 13,107 (1995), 68 Antitrust & Trade Reg. Rep. (BNA) Supp. 1 (1995).

2. American Banana Co. v. United Fruit Co., 213 U.S. 347, 355 (1909).

3. *Id.* at 356.

Just as U.S. courts developed their own understanding of the practices prohibited by the Sherman Act, in order to construe "every" restraint on trade more judiciously, they also interpreted the Act's geographic scope more narrowly than every such restraint on "trade or commerce . . . with foreign nations." Eventually, the Sherman Act was amended through the Foreign Trade Antitrust Improvements Act (FTAIA),[4] but as noted below, the FTAIA's peculiarities themselves left considerable room for judicial construction.

One consequence of this common law method—especially given the diffuse nature of judicial authority in the United States—has been the difficulty of discerning which, if any, legal standards prevail. The overruling of *American Banana*'s holding on extraterritoriality, for example, was first acknowledged, indirectly, just over eighty years later—nearly thirty years after its supposed reversal, which had for all practical purposes occurred even before that.[5] The Court's first explicit endorsement of the "effects" test for extraterritoriality then occurred in 1993, though it had been first ventured over fifty years beforehand.[6] Space considerations preclude an account of this tangled history, even as to extraterritoriality, but it suffices to say that prevailing norms are often not apparent until well after the fact.[7]

A second feature is the tangled relationship between jurisdiction over extraterritorial matters and comity. Like Justice Holmes, courts continue to invoke comity as a basis for reading narrowly the prescriptive scope of the Sherman Act. Other courts, however, have understood comity as speaking to the subject-matter jurisdiction of courts or, as yet another option, as relating to the exercise of judicial discretion in cases over which they properly have jurisdiction and as to which the Sherman Act applies. The differences often seem formalistic, but they appear to affect the willingness of courts (and other actors) to venture abroad, and confound any rigid distinction between the subjects. Accordingly, this chapter will distinguish between the use of comity in construing the antitrust statutes' extraterritorial scope and its use (chiefly, but not exclusively, by the courts) in addressing particular fact patterns.

A third notable feature of *American Banana* involved the diversity of actors and controversies that it suggested. That suit concerned two American corporations,

---

4. 15 U.S.C. §§ 6a, 45(1)(3).

5. W.S. Kirkpatrick & Co. v. Envtl. Tectonics Corp., Int'l, 493 U.S. 400, 407 (1990) (citing Continental Ore Co. v. Union Carbide & Carbon Corp., 370 U.S. 690, 704–05 (1962)).

6. Hartford Fire Ins. Co. v. California, 509 U.S. 764, 795–96 (1993) (citing post-*American Banana* authorities).

7. For more comprehensive discussions, see Int'l Competition Policy Advisory Comm. (ICPAC), U.S. Dep't of Justice Final Report (2000); WILBUR L. FUGATE, FOREIGN COMMERCE AND THE ANTITRUST LAWS (5th ed. 1996); JEFFREY L. KESSLER & SPENCER WEBER WALLER, INTERNATIONAL TRADE AND U.S. ANTITRUST LAW ch. 4 (2006); CHRIS NOONAN, THE EMERGING PRINCIPLES OF INTERNATIONAL COMPETITION LAW ch. 8 (2008); 1 SPENCER WEBBER WALLER, ANTITRUST AND AMERICAN BUSINESS ABROAD ch. 6 (3d ed. 1997).

with one allegedly assisted by a foreign government, relating to acts taken abroad but derived from a conspiracy transpiring in the United States. That there was more than one possible locus of wrongdoing and more than one sort of wrongdoer is a complication common to any nation's experience. What is more distinctive is that there was more than one kind of plaintiff who might have initiated a U.S. suit, and that the lawsuit in question sought a private remedy of treble damages. To understand extraterritoriality and comity in the U.S. system, it is essential to grasp that their principles and practices have been developed in response to very different stimuli: the propriety of enforcement may depend on whether suit has been initiated by private, state, or federal plaintiffs; and the availability of relief against foreign conduct—and the means for achieving cooperation—may depend on whether injunctive relief, treble damages, or criminal punishment are being pursued.[8]

II. THE REACH OF THE LAW

A. Extraterritoriality

1. *The "effects" test.* In 1945, Judge Learned Hand—like Justice Holmes, a leading common law jurist—substantially reversed the course charted by *American Banana*, opining that "any state may impose liabilities, even upon persons not within its allegiance, for conduct outside its borders that has consequences within its borders which the state reprehends . . . ."[9] His decision in *Alcoa* is widely credited with developing the "effects" test, which looked past the location of the conduct alleged to have violated U.S. antitrust law to focus instead on the conduct's consequences. It did so in a case that, like *American Banana*, involved civil antitrust claims, but this time was commenced by the United States government—something that might have increased the risk of international acrimony while at the same time disposing the court to defer with respect to comity considerations.

In describing this approach in its much later *Hartford Fire* decision, the Supreme Court stated that "it is well established by now that the Sherman Act applies to foreign conduct that was meant to produce and did in fact produce some substantial effect in the United States."[10] This artfully avoided addressing the difficult questions that had plagued, and continue to plague, the effects test. The basic problem is that *Alcoa* and *Hartford Fire*, and the case law in between,

---

8. For a lengthy discussion, see Edward T. Swaine, *The Local Law of Global Antitrust*, 43 Wm. & Mary. L. Rev. 627 (2001).

9. United States v. Aluminum Co. of Am., 148 F.2d 416, 443 (2d Cir. 1945) (citing cases). Because the Supreme Court lacked a quorum to decide that case, the Second Circuit was empowered to act as the court of last resort. 15 U.S.C. § 29.

10. Hartford Fire Ins. v. California, 509 U.S. 764, 796 (1993).

have focused on developing sufficient, rather than necessary, conditions. *Alcoa,* for example, avoided holding that actual effect within the United States must always be demonstrated, suggesting that the intent to have such an effect might by itself be sufficient;[11] in contrast, it regarded proof of intent to affect U.S. markets as indispensable to avoiding "international complications."[12] Subsequent decisions, in contrast, treated the effect on the United States as the more significant factor, leaving the intent element—and its capacity to protect comity considerations—unclear.[13] Until recently, it was apparently unresolved whether any version of the effects test applied to criminal prosecutions under the Sherman Act.[14] And it remains uncertain how "foreign" a matter must be in order to trigger application of the effects test—a question of some importance, since if a matter is domestic in character, no effects test of any kind need be satisfied.[15]

On the whole, though, cases applying the effects test have evolved toward greater restrictions on extraterritoriality. *Hartford Fire,* for example, appears to have reaffirmed the place of intent, and the Court also clarified that "substantial" effect in the United States is required. The increased stringency suggested by recent cases may express a prior conviction – occasioned, perhaps, by increasingly adventurous claims – or signal a shift in judicial receptiveness.[16]

---

11. 148 F.2d at 443–44.

12. *Id.* at 443.

13. Dee-K Enterprises, Inc. v. Heveafil Sdn. Bhd., 299 F.3d 281, 288 (4th Cir. 2002) (describing how, following *Alcoa,* courts and commentators "disagreed as to whether antitrust jurisdiction over foreign conduct requires both 'an effect' on United States commerce and an 'intent to affect United States commerce,' or just effect or just intent, and as to the magnitude of any effect."); Daniel T. Murphy, *Moderating Antitrust Subject Matter Jurisdiction: The Foreign Trade Antitrust Improvements Act and the Restatement of Foreign Relations Law (Revised)*, 54 U. Cin. L. Rev. 779, 806 (1986) (noting case law describing an "effects only test, a direct or substantial effects test, a direct and substantial effects test, and a some effects, regardless of whether they are intended or substantial, test."); *see, e.g.*, Matsushita Elec. Indus. v. Zenith Radio Corp., 475 U.S. 574, 582 n.6 (1986) (describing the Sherman Act as "reach[ing] conduct outside our borders, but only when the conduct has an effect on American commerce").

14. United States v. Nippon Paper Indus. Co., 109 F.3d 1, 8–9 (1st Cir. 1997).

15. *See Dee-K Enterprises*, 299 F.3d at 294 (concluding that for these purposes, "a court should consider whether the participants, acts, targets, and effects involved in an asserted violation are primarily foreign or primarily domestic").

16. A decision rendered while this chapter was in galleys suggests that this stringency is not limited to antitrust extraterritoriality – indeed, the Supreme Court distinguished earlier case law that explored the reach of the Sherman Act in applying a robust presumption against extraterritoriality in the securities context. Morrison v. National Australia Bank Ltd., No. 08-1191, slip op. at 22 n.11 (U.S. June 24, 2010). The *Morrison* decision arguably suggested, in any event, that the Court would not be eager to expand any exceptional indulgence toward antitrust extraterritoriality.

2. *The FTAIA*. At least marginal progress in clarifying the U.S. approach has been afforded through legislative intervention. In 1982, Congress adopted the Foreign Trade Antitrust Improvements Act (FTAIA),[17] which was intended to reduce tensions over the extraterritorial application of U.S. antitrust law and to clarify the standards to be used by U.S. courts.[18] Toward these ends, the FTAIA established—for "conduct involving trade or commerce (other than import trade or import commerce) with foreign nations"—a threshold requirement that any such conduct have a "direct, substantial, and reasonably foreseeable effect" on domestic, import, or export trade or commerce.[19] Absent such an effect, the FTAIA excluded cases that otherwise might have been cognizable under the Sherman Act.

Unfortunately, the confused drafting of the FTAIA has meant that little was resolved by the text itself, including with regard to the effects test. In theory, the statute left two jurisdictional tests for foreign commerce cases: first, the one subsequently articulated in *Hartford Fire*, which would apply to foreign import commerce; second, the FTAIA test, which would apply in non-import cases.[20] Whether there is any daylight between these approaches remains unresolved. The FTAIA standard specifies not only that the U.S. effect must be "substantial" (which later became incorporated in the *Hartford Fire* version of the effects test), but also that the effect be "direct" in character;[21] while these might suggest a more restrictive approach, its requirement that the effect be "foreseeable" rather than intended probably expands the range of foreign conduct that can be reached.[22]

---

17. 15 U.S.C. § 6a (1982).

18. Not incidentally, the FTAIA was also supposed to immunize U.S.-based joint export activities from antitrust scrutiny. See H.R. Rep. No. 97-686, at 2 (1982), reprinted in 1982 U.S.C.C.A.N. 2487, 2487; *Foreign Trade Antitrust Improvements Act: Hearings on H.R. 2326 Before the Subcomm. on Monopolies and Commercial Law of the H. Comm. on the Judiciary*, 97th Cong., 2 (1981) 2 (statement of Rep. Rodino).

19. 15 U.S.C. § 6a(1).

20. 1995 International Guidelines, § 3.1. Some cases, however, suggest more generally that the FTAIA "provides the guiding standard for jurisdiction over foreign restraints of trade," seemingly even in case involving foreign import commerce. United States v. LSL Biotechnologies, 379 F.3d 672, 679 (9th Cir. 2004).

21. There is room for disagreement as to whether this really changed the preexisting standard—indeed, this was a point of disagreement between the majority and dissenting opinions in *LSL Biotechnologies*. *Id.* at 680 n.6.

22. H.R. Rep. No. 97-686, at 9 (1982), *reprinted in* 1982 U.S.C.C.A.N. 2487, 2494 ("An intent test might encourage ignorance of the consequences of one's actions, which in this context, would be an undesirable result."). In *Hartford Fire* itself, the Supreme Court thought it unclear whether the FTAIA sought to change or enshrine the *Alcoa* effects test, or whether it applied to the case at hand (which involved, in essence, a refusal to sell services into the United States). Rather than resolving those questions, the Court simply

The case law suggests, however, that the FTAIA will be interpreted in keeping with comity. Assuming the requisite effect on domestic U.S. commerce, the FTAIA also requires that it is this effect that "gives rise" to a claim under the Sherman Act. Courts differed as to whether this permitted suit when significant foreign anticompetitive conduct had adverse domestic and foreign effects, but only the foreign effects had given rise to the plaintiffs' claim—for example, because foreign cartel activity raised prices both in the United States and abroad, but (supposedly) independently of one another, and a claim by foreign consumers was in question. The Supreme Court, in *F. Hoffman-LaRoche Ltd. v. Empagran S.A.*,[23] found that Congress did not intend to expand the Sherman Act and would have considered such claims inadmissible under the prior law.[24] Moreover, it invoked the principle that ambiguous statutes should be interpreted so as "to avoid unreasonable interference with the sovereign authority of other nations," such as by reaching foreign conduct causing purely foreign harm. The specific concerns the Court cited were instructive: it noted, for example, that U.S. antitrust law sometimes differed from what was permitted under foreign law; that even when U.S. and other laws agree, as with respect to price fixing, "they disagree dramatically about appropriate remedies"; and, finally, that the governments of Canada, Germany, and the United States believed that permitting treble-damages actions could undermine the incentive for defendants to cooperate with foreign government prosecutors in exchange for amnesty.[25] To the Court, these reinforced "principles of prescriptive comity," according to which the FTAIA should be construed, and the proposed alternative of considering comity on a case-by-case basis was both too modest and "too complex to prove workable."[26]

It may be useful to summarize the state of affairs following *Empagran*. First, that decision—like *American Banana* and *Alcoa* before it—suggests that U.S. courts will employ comity-like considerations as an important ingredient in construing the reach of U.S. statutes, offering (in theory) the prospect of greater clarity and generality as to those statutes' extraterritorial reach. Whether that clarity is achieved, and the ends of comity well served, is open to question. *Empagran* tackled a relatively abstract situation unlikely to occur often, insofar as it presupposed a complete separation between domestic and foreign effects;

---

assumed that the FTAIA standard would be satisfied in any event, and future cases may find it expedient to equate the two approaches. *Hartford Fire*, 509 U.S. at 796 n.23.

23. 542 U.S. 155 (2004).

24. *Id.* at 169–73.

25. *Id.* at 163–68.

26. *Id.* at 168–69. It noted, for instance, competing submissions even in that "relatively simple price-fixing case" as to the effect of permitting private claims on effective antitrust enforcement—a debate, however, on which the Court seemed to take sides in its more general FTAIA analysis.

it did not address circumstances in which "the conduct's domestic effects . . . help bring about that foreign injury,"[27] which one may imagine will be alleged more frequently in its wake. It is less likely that a court will construe the FTAIA to categorically exclude these more integrated claims, or successfully isolate a discrete subcategory of them, and *Empagran* does not provide any tools for addressing such a circumstance. Technically, the Court rejected a case-by-case approach to comity only as a *substitute* for its form of "prescriptive" comity, and did not explicitly foreclose the supplementary use of such an approach, but that possibility had already been marginalized by its earlier decision in *Hartford Fire*—discussed in greater detail below.

Second, the only question in these cases was what Congress intended; none establishes any absolute restriction on extraterritoriality. Under the Commerce Clause of the U.S. Constitution, the national government may regulate conduct in or affecting interstate or foreign commerce, irrespective of its location; this is considerably more permissive than any effects test that has been employed in the antitrust area, and would not in any event limit the states, which have for the most part been successful in maintaining a parallel and overlapping set of antitrust laws. Due process, on the other hand, does require that foreign defendants have minimum contacts with the federal or state jurisdiction and that maintaining jurisdiction is consistent with "traditional conception[s] of fair play and substantial justice";[28] in theory, this entails consideration of comity-like factors, but the bar for exclusion is set considerably higher.[29] Thus, if one puts to one side the practical barriers to extraterritorial actions (such as evidence gathering, service of process, and the enforcement of judgments), U.S. law poses little obstacle to enacting legislation that reaches extraterritorially to the full extent permitted by international law—and, if Congress acts clearly, well beyond.

B. Comity

The use by U.S. courts of comity-based considerations to limit the application of U.S. antitrust statutes—beyond its more general application in reckoning the prescriptive scope of those statutes, as enacted by Congress in the first place—struggled along for less than twenty years before being immolated in

---

27. *Id.* at 173.

28. Burger King v. Rudzewicz, 471 U.S. 462, 476–77 (1985) (internal quotation omitted).

29. The latter considerations may include "the burden on the defendant," "the forum State's interest in adjudicating the dispute," "the plaintiff's interest in obtaining convenient and effective relief," "the interstate judicial system's interest in obtaining the most efficient resolution of controversies," and the "shared interest of the several States in furthering fundamental substantive social policies." World-Wide Volkswagen Corp. v. Woodson, 444 U.S. 286, 292 (1980).

Hartford Fire. A brief review of the doctrine's history is appropriate before turning to the present state of the law.

1. *Judicial comity.* Prior to the FTAIA, at least, the effects test—as actually applied by U.S. courts—served very little function in restraining extraterritoriality. According to one widely cited estimate, as of 1973, none of nearly 250 foreign-focused antitrust actions brought by the U.S. Department of Justice had been dismissed for lack of jurisdiction.[30] In lieu of U.S. self-restraint, other nations adopted "blocking" statutes to frustrate discovery, statutes requiring foreign courts to refuse recognition of treble-damages awards and statutes permitting foreign defendants to "clawback" judgments made against them via their home courts. One commentator opined in 1981 that "there have been five diplomatic protests of U.S. antitrust cases for every instance of express diplomatic support, and three blocking statutes for every cooperation agreement."[31]

During this period, U.S. courts developed a doctrine designed to moderate the application of U.S. jurisdiction. The leading case, *Timberlane Lumber Co. v. Bank of America National Trust & Savings Association,*[32] involved allegations somewhat reminiscent of those involved in *American Banana*—namely, that American and foreign defendants had conspired with foreign government officials against another U.S. company, this time to prevent it from milling Honduran lumber and exporting it to the United States. Accepting Judge Hand's invitation in the *Alcoa* case to approach Sherman Act jurisdiction in light of custom, the court of appeals held that "some" effect ("actual or intended") on U.S. foreign commerce was merely the first step in a three-part inquiry; in addition, after "a greater showing of burden or restraint" was established to demonstrate the kind of injury to the plaintiffs that could be redressed under the antitrust laws, "there is the [third] question which is unique to the international setting of whether the interests of, and links to, the United States including the magnitude of the effect on American foreign commerce are sufficiently strong, vis-à-vis those of other nations, to justify an assertion of extraterritorial authority."[33] Other lower courts also seized the doctrinal reins. Superficially, at least, the differences among their approaches were significant. *Mannington Mills, Inc. v. Congoleum Corp.*, for example, indicated that comity analysis was not part of a threshold inquiry into whether the conduct fell within the Sherman Act, but instead was more of a discretionary factor according to which courts could abstain from proceedings.[34] *Mannington Mills* also added several new factors to those already articulated

---

30. Wilbur L. Fugate, Foreign Commerce and the Antitrust Laws, app. B, at 498 (2d ed. 1973).

31. Joel Davidow, *Extraterritorial Antitrust and the Concept of Comity,* 15 J. World Trade L. 500, 502 (1981).

32. 549 F.2d 597 (9th Cir. 1976).

33. *Id.* at 613.

34. Mannington Mills, Inc. v. Congoleum Corp., 595 F.2d 1287, 1294–95 (3d Cir. 1979).

in *Timberlane* and varied meaningfully in the expression of those they had in common.[35]

In the wake of these initial decisions, the influential American Law Institute, in its Restatement (Third) of Foreign Relations Law of the United States, developed a similar set of principles. The Restatement (Third) sided with *Timberlane* in linking the comity inquiry to prescriptive jurisdiction. It also elaborated its own set of factors to be considered whether the exercise of jurisdiction was "unreasonable":

> (a) the link of the activity to the territory of the regulating state, i.e., the extent to which the activity takes place within the territory, or has substantial, direct, and foreseeable effect upon or in the territory; (b) the connections, such as nationality, residence, or economic activity, between the regulating state and the person principally responsible for the activity to be regulated, or between that state and those whom the regulation is designed to protect; (c) the character of the activity to be regulated, the importance of regulation to the regulating state, the extent to which other states regulate such activities, and the degree to which the desirability of such regulation is generally accepted; (d) the existence of justified expectations that might be protected or hurt by the regulation; (e) the importance of the regulation to the international political, legal, or economic system; (f) the extent to which the regulation is consistent with the traditions of the international system; (g) the extent to which another state may have an interest in regulating the activity; and (h) the likelihood of conflict with regulation by another state.[36]

All this proved problematic, however. For one, the kitchen sink approach suggested by the courts and by the Restatement (Third) was a challenge to

---

35. In *Timberlane*, the Ninth Circuit Court of Appeals provided a nonexclusive list of factors that included:

> the degree of conflict with foreign law or policy, the nationality or allegiance of the parties and the locations or principal places of businesses or corporations, the extent to which enforcement by either state can be expected to achieve compliance, the relative significance of effects on the United States as compared with those elsewhere, the extent to which there is explicit purpose to harm or affect American commerce, the foreseeability of such effect, and the relative importance to the violations charged of conduct within the United States as compared with conduct abroad.

549 F.2d at 615. In *Mannington Mills*, the Third Circuit court suggested considering also the availability of a remedy abroad and whether any proceedings were pending, the potential harm to U.S. foreign policy from asserting jurisdiction and ordering relief, whether the U.S. proceeding was likely to yield an effective order, whether the United States would accept an order for relief if made by the foreign nation under comparable circumstances, and whether there were any treaties governing the complained-of conduct. 595 F.2d at 1297–98.

36. Restatement (Third) of Foreign Relations Law of the United States §§ 401, 403 (1987).

administer. *Mannington Mills*, for example, was not the most complicated of antitrust cases: it involved a relatively limited number of parties and claims by one manufacturer that a second had fraudulently procured foreign patents. Nonetheless, the lower court was charged with the daunting task of applying a ten-factor test in 26 different contexts, given that (as the court of appeals indicated) each of the states concerned might have different laws, policies, and effects on U.S. commerce.[37] Even in *Timberlane*, which involved only one foreign jurisdiction, it took another eight years before the dismissal on comity grounds was finally affirmed.[38] The approach was also subject to more fundamental challenges. Another leading decision countered that judicial invocation of comity-based concerns lacked any legal basis and inappropriately refused congressionally conferred jurisdiction. The result, predicted the court, was that comity "ha[d] not gained more than a temporary foothold in domestic law."[39]

That prediction was more or less vindicated in *Hartford Fire*, though for different reasons. That case involved an action brought by private persons and by 19 U.S. states against domestic and foreign insurance and reinsurance companies. Allegedly, these companies had conspired to restrict insurance coverage by virtue of, among other things, an agreement among London-based companies to provide reinsurance to American companies only on jointly agreed terms.[40] But the London reinsurers argued—with support from the British government—that their behavior was entirely legal under British insurance law, which comprehensively regulated the conduct in question. A divided Supreme Court, satisfied that the alleged conduct satisfied the effects doctrine,[41] was willing to assume *arguendo* the power to dismiss the claim on comity grounds and to be guided by the Restatement (Third). Nonetheless, the Court held that "[n]o conflict exists"—and thus, in its view, no comity-based concerns—"'where a person subject to regulation by two states can comply with the laws of both.'" Because British insurance regulations did not compel the violation of U.S. antitrust law, comity did not require dismissal.[42]

---

37. *Id.* at 1298.

38. Following proceedings on remand from the Ninth Circuit's decision, it took another eight years before the complaint was ultimately dismissed on comity grounds. Timberlane Lumber Co. v. Bank of America, 749 F.2d 1378, 1384 (9th Cir. 1984) (Timberlane II), *cert. denied*, 472 U.S. 1032 (1985).

39. Laker Airways Ltd. v. Sabena, Belgian World Airlines, 731 F.2d 909, 950 (D.C. Cir. 1984).

40. The insurance business has always presented problems for antitrust law, and the Court expended some effort before concluding that the conduct in question was not immunized under the McCarran-Ferguson Act. McCarran-Ferguson Act, 59 Stat. 33 (1945), as amended, 15 U.S.C. §§ 1011–1015.

41. Hartford Fire Ins. Co. v. California, 509 U.S. 764, 796 (1993).

42. *Id.* at 799 (quoting RESTATEMENT (THIRD) OF FOREIGN RELATIONS LAW, § 403 cmt. e).

The decision was unsound in light of its stated premises. First, the majority framed comity not as a jurisdictional question, but solely as a doctrine according to which a court could decline authority given it by Congress—which, as the dissent observed, was inconsistent with the majority's own authorities and certainly put the doctrine in a less flattering light.[43] Second, the majority's perception that comity was germane only when a party was subject to two irreconcilable requirements was simply a misunderstanding, given that the cited authority, the Restatement (Third), clearly indicated that its multifactored "reasonableness" test was supposed to govern in cases like *Hartford Fire*.[44]

Whatever its merits, *Hartford Fire*'s reasoning was thought to be a sea change in the U.S. approach to comity, insofar as it offers little to antitrust defendants beyond what is already afforded by the foreign compulsion defense.[45] Such pessimism is probably unwarranted. For one thing, it may overstate the comity doctrine's prior significance. In practice, few courts actually dismissed actions in the teeth of a substantial effect on U.S. markets—putting aside instances in which there were, in fact, true conflicts between U.S. antitrust law and foreign law—and they were yet more reluctant when the plaintiffs were American.[46] The lengthy and difficult proceedings that the comity doctrine entailed also meant that the burden of U.S. jurisdiction could be reduced, but not minimized.

Moreover, American courts will continue to find ways to assimilate comity-like concerns. *Empagran* subsequently indicated that the Supreme Court is receptive to comity when presented as a tool for statutory construction. Lower courts, too, may apply the effects test more vigorously, and comity considerations may play into the evaluation of conduct falling within the geographic scope of the Sherman Act.[47] Probably the most enduring context will involve procedural and evidentiary questions, where U.S. courts have sometimes shown sensitivity to foreign interests—no doubt mindful both of prior diplomatic contretemps and the practical difficulty of enforcing orders abroad.[48] *Intel Corp. v. Advanced Micro Devices, Inc.*, another recent decision, suggests that they will continue to have that discretion.[49] Advanced Micro Devices sought an order compelling Intel to produce documents previously involved in a U.S. antitrust action—in theory, to

---

43. *Id.* at 812–13 (Scalia, J., dissenting).

44. *Id.* at 818–21 (Scalia, J., dissenting).

45. As the Restatement (Third) makes plain, that defense should be considered quite separate from comity. RESTATEMENT (THIRD), § 403 cmt. e (citing §§ 441, 442).

46. Noonan, *supra* note 7, at 242–43 (reviewing cases).

47. For an extreme example, see *Metro Industries, Inc. v. Sammi Corp.*, 82 F.3d 839, 844–45 (9th Cir. 1996) (indicating that whenever "a Sherman Act claim is based on conduct outside the United States, we apply rule of reason analysis to determine whether there is a Sherman Act violation," even in instances of alleged international price-fixing otherwise considered a per se violation).

48. For further discussion, see ANTITRUST LAW DEVELOPMENTS (6th ed. 2007), ch. XII.

49. Intel Corp. v. Advanced Micro Devices, Inc., 542 U.S. 241 (2004).

use in competition proceedings it had initiated before the European Commission, though the Commission had previously refused to seek the documents itself. Intel argued that even if the Commission was a "foreign tribunal" of the kind triggering a court's discovery authority, production should never be permitted unless the documents were discoverable in the foreign jurisdiction—invoking, in part, the Commission's concern that U.S. plaintiffs would start European proceedings in order to conduct stateside fishing expeditions.[50] Rejecting that argument, the Supreme Court reasoned that foreign entities (and even the Commission itself) might sometimes desire judicial assistance from U.S. courts, and that lower courts could always consider the nature of the foreign proceedings and "the receptivity of the foreign government or the court or agency abroad to U.S. federal-court judicial assistance."[51] Unlike *Empagran*—whose author, Justice Breyer, dissented—the *Intel* majority favored a case-by-case approach over any broader-brush conclusions about the scope of U.S. law, perhaps in part because the potential for implications in diverse areas of law beyond antitrust was more apparent.

2. *Enforcement comity.* Another reason to qualify the impact of *Hartford Fire* is that the evaluation of comity considerations by U.S. enforcing agencies has always been substantially independent of that conducted by U.S. courts. Their position, which has never been repudiated by the courts,[52] is that once the United States determines to commence an antitrust action, courts lack any discretion to dismiss on comity grounds.[53] This means that one of the chief irritants to foreign governments was not subject to judicially imposed comity limits at all.

The flip side to this autonomy, however, is that the agencies may maintain a broader approach to comity than would now be licensed by the Supreme Court. According to their International Guidelines, the agencies continue to take "full account" of the comity factors described by the Restatement (Third), regarding

---

50. Brief of Amicus Curiae the Commission of the European Communities Supporting Reversal, *Intel Corp. v. Advanced Micro Devices, Inc.*, 542 U.S. 241 (2004) (No. 02-572). The Commission also argued, inter alia, that sufficient mechanisms for obtaining information had been established by antitrust cooperation agreements between the United States and the European Communities, discussed below.

51. 542 U.S. at 264.

52. To the contrary, see *United States v. Baker Hughes, Inc.*, 731 F. Supp. 3, 6 n.5 (D.D.C.) (stating, in reaction to diplomatic note from Finland opposing the blocking of a merger, that "[i]t is not the Court's role to second-guess the executive branch's judgment as to the proper role of comity concerns under these circumstances"), *aff'd*, 908 F.2d 981 (D.C. Cir. 1990).

53. U.S. Dep't of Justice, Antitrust Enforcement Guidelines for International Operations, § 5 n.167, 4 Trade Reg. Rep. (CCH) ¶ 13,109.10 (1988); 1995 International Guidelines, § 3.2. Their position with respect to the deference owed decisions by the Federal Trade Commission, which is an independent agency not part of the executive branch, is more circumspect.

Hartford Fire as addressing just one of those factors—the conflict with foreign laws and policies[54]—even if courts might hesitate to refashion *Hartford Fire* along similar lines.[55] Their independence from jurisprudential changes, however, does not necessarily connote internal stability. A case in point is the fluctuating policy toward the exercise of export jurisdiction. While the agencies' 1977 International Guidelines stated that U.S. antitrust enforcement was designed in part to "protect American export and investment opportunities against private imposed restraints," the 1988 version explained that the United States would, as a matter of discretion, forego pursuing foreign restraints that only harmed U.S. exports without affecting U.S. consumers; that reassurance was dropped but four years later, to the great dissatisfaction of many foreign governments.[56] The present guidelines indicate only that action against restraints on U.S. exports would be taken in "appropriate cases" and, if the conduct violated the foreign country's antitrust laws, to defer to prosecution by its authorities if they were better situated.[57]

Absent judicial constraint, another possible source of constraint on the agencies' independent appreciation of comity may be bilateral arrangements. Following the development of a cooperation scheme between the United States and Canada, the Organisation for Economic Co-Operation and Development (OECD) began in 1967 to recommend that its member countries consider limiting their enforcement actions in light of legitimate foreign interests—in what became known as "traditional" or "negative" comity—and later began emphasizing "positive" comity, which involves a duty to at least consider requests by other states to pursue enforcement actions.[58] After some fits and starts, the United States began in earnest to enter into bilateral antitrust cooperation agreements

---

54. 1995 International Guidelines, § 3.2.

55. *Cf. Hartford Fire*, 509 U.S. at 799 (suggesting that "[t]he only substantial question in this case is whether 'there is in fact a true conflict between domestic and foreign law'") (internal citation omitted).

56. Antitrust Div., U.S. Dep't of Justice, Antitrust Guidelines for International Operations, [Jan.–June] Antitrust & Trade Reg. Rep. (BNA) No. 799, at E-5 (Jan. 16, 1977); 1988 International Guidelines, *supra*; U.S. Dep't of Justice, April 3 Statement of Enforcement Policy, 62 Antitrust & Trade Reg. Rep. (BNA) 483 (Apr. 9, 1992); Noonan, *supra* note 7, at 259–69.

57. 1995 International Guidelines, *supra*, § 3.122 ("[I]f the conduct is unlawful under the importing country's antitrust laws as well, the Agencies are also prepared to work with that country's authorities if they are better situated to remedy the conduct, and if they are prepared to take action that will address the U.S. concerns, pursuant to their antitrust laws.").

58. *See, e.g.*, OECD, Revised Recommendation of the Council Concerning Cooperation Between Member Countries on Anticompetitive Practices Affecting International Trade, Doc. No. C(95)130/FINAL (July 27, 1995), 35 I.L.M. 1313, 1314–16 (1996).

with its foreign partners—to date, with Australia, Brazil, Canada, the European Communities, Germany, Israel, Japan, Mexico, and Russia.

As a threshold matter, a party to one of these agreements is supposed to notify the other when the first party's enforcement activity might affect the second party's important interests. Principles of traditional or "negative" comity then suggest that the first, enforcing party should consider those interests in deciding whether to initiate an investigation or proceeding, in establishing the scope, and in deciding what remedies should be sought. Among the factors to be considered are the relative significance of the anticompetitive activities within the two parties' territories, the effect on any reasonable expectations, the undertakings resulting from such activities, and the conflict or consistency between the enforcement activities and the second party's laws or defined economic policies.[59] Later agreements began explicitly to incorporate positive comity, which contemplated the situation in which one party asks the other to address anticompetitive behavior occurring in the second party's jurisdiction, and violating that second party's laws and regulations, where that behavior affects the first party's interests.[60]

These agreements have been widely hailed in the antitrust community as a means of improving the efficiency of antitrust enforcement and avoiding disputes. It is difficult, however, to assess their practical impact, since—due in part to the confidentiality of intergovernmental discussions—the failures are likely to be far more conspicuous than the successes.[61] On the former front, the failure of the European Commission to cede the GE/Honeywell or Boeing/McDonnell Douglas mergers to U.S. authorities is well known.[62] On the latter front, U.S.

---

59. Agreement Regarding the Application of Competition Laws, Sept. 23, 1991, U.S.-E.C., *reprinted in* 4 Trade Reg. Rep. (CCH) 13,504 (1998), 1991 O.J. (L 95) 45, corrected at 1995 O.J. (L 131) 38.

60. Agreement Between the Government of the United States of American and the European Communities on the Application of Positive Comity Principles in the Enforcement of their Competition Laws, Mar. 6–Apr. 6, 1998, E.C.-U.S., 37 I.L.M. 1070.

61. Roundtable Conference with Enforcement Officials, ABA Section of Antitrust Law Spring Meeting (Apr. 20, 2007), *in* The Antitrust Source, June 2007, at 1, 21 ("Absolutely there is cooperation on non-merger conduct matters. I asked the General Counsel's Office whether I was allowed to tell you which ones, and they said no.") (remarks of Deborah Platt Majoras, Chairman, Federal Trade Commission).

62. The literature on these matters is legion. For overviews in the form of case studies, see THOMAS L. BOEDER, *The Boeing-McDonnell Douglas Merger*, *in* ANTITRUST GOES GLOBAL 139–44 (Simon J. Evenett et al. eds., 2000); ELEANOR J. FOX, *GE/Honeywell: The U.S. Merger that Europe Stopped—A Story of the Politics of Convergence*, *in* ANTITRUST STORIES 311–30 (Eleanor M. Fox & Daniel A. Crane eds., 2007). The most recent Microsoft proceedings, in which the European Commission successfully pursued additional and rather far-reaching remedies concerning Windows Media Player and Microsoft server protocols, might also be cited, but the extent to which the U.S. government sought to change the course of the Commission proceedings is unclear. There were also silver linings over the

officials have cited as an example of negative comity the Oracle/PeopleSoft case, in which the European Commission delayed their investigation until the completion of U.S. proceedings—which the U.S. government lost.[63] With respect to positive comity, the tried and true example is the Sabre investigation, in which the United States sought the Commission's assistance in investigating allegations that a computerized reservation system managed by European airlines was discriminating against U.S. airlines.[64]

It is frequently urged that more should be made of these arrangements, but there too the payoff is unclear.[65] Few discussions offer any clear depiction of how past disputes could have been resolved under the comity protocols—without, that is, wishing away divergent political and economic interests and substantive disagreements. As a legal matter, moreover, antitrust cooperation agreements essentially formalize what might otherwise be managed informally. Finally, a gap in the existing law of comity will remain no matter what: namely, treble-damages

---

longer term: the United States and Europe cooperated successfully during the period when the Justice Department was on the warpath (*see* Robert E. Litan, *The First Microsoft Case*, in ANTITRUST GOES GLOBAL, *supra*, at 174–76), and later on a federal district court quashed Microsoft's attempt to obtain evidence to use in its European competition proceeding—fulfilling the opening left by the Supreme Court's *Intel* case. *In re* Microsoft, 428 F. Supp. 2d 188, 195–96 (D.D.C. 2006) (stating, inter alia, that permitting Microsoft discovery would "pit[] this Court against the Commission, rather than fostering cooperation between them, and would violate established principles of comity, under which 'United States courts ordinarily refuse to review acts of foreign governments and defer to proceedings taking place in foreign countries'") (internal citation omitted).

63. 2007 Roundtable Conference, *supra*, at 22 (remarks of Thomas O. Barnett, Assistant Attorney General, Antitrust Division, U.S. Department of Justice). The European Commission also noted, in clearing the merger, that it had cooperated closely with the Department of Justice (though it did not say in what regard), and that it had taken into account evidence that had emerged during trial in the United States. Press Release IP/04/1312, Commission Clear's Oracle's Takeover Bid for PeopleSoft (Oct. 26, 2004); Case COMP/M.3216, Oracle/PeopleSoft, 2005 O.J. (L 218). Its final decision probably took into account the fact that the Justice Department's attempt to block the merger failed (*see* United States v. Oracle Corp., 331 F. Supp. 2d 1098 (N.D. Cal. 2004)), and could be read as suggesting deference to the ultimate application of U.S. law—particularly given the Justice Department's decision not to appeal—but probably also took the development as bearing on its own likelihood of success.

64. 2007 Roundtable Conference, *supra*, at 22 (remarks of Neelie Kroes, European Commissioner for Competition); *see also* Swaine, *supra*, at 653 n.97 (discussing result). For a sympathetic but skeptical appraisal of positive comity provisions, see ICPAC, *supra*, at 226–41.

65. *See, e.g.*, Antitrust Modernization Commission: Report and Recommendations, April 2007, at 221 (providing, in recommendation 41, that "[t]he United States should pursue bilateral and multilateral antitrust cooperation agreements that incorporate comity principles with more of its trading partners and make greater use of the comity provisions in existing cooperation agreements").

suits brought by private parties in cases posing no general issue of how the antitrust statutes should be interpreted, but which nevertheless raise issues as to the proper scope of U.S. antitrust jurisdiction over foreign conduct. The U.S. government may, in some circumstances, weigh in with respect to foreign policy consequences, but it lacks the capacity to pretermit proceedings initiated by private individuals or the U.S. states under federal or state antitrust law. For the time being, defendants to such actions may have to relate comity-type values to other defenses, like foreign sovereign compulsion, that survive *Hartford Fire.*

III. COOPERATION

Given the episodic U.S. appetite for extraterritoriality, and the limits to judicial and enforcement comity, the potential for more cooperation—efforts by antitrust authorities to assist one another in fulfilling their independent objectives, such as by obtaining evidence and persons—is relatively substantial. In many ways, cooperation has succeeded comity as the focus of international antitrust efforts.

Some of this cooperation is facilitated by instruments with broader application, like mutual legal assistance treaties (MLATs) and extradition treaties.[66] While progress requires pursuing initiatives outside of the antitrust realm and achieving agreement on the international plane, application in the antitrust context also requires changes in the domestic laws of foreign states. Thus, for example, the United States persuaded the United Kingdom to remove the previous exclusion of competition matters from their bilateral MLAT,[67] and the two subsequently ratified a new extradition treaty that may facilitate extradition for competition-related offenses.[68] But the critical development was the United Kingdom's

66. For a comprehensive guide to these and other cooperation agreements, see ABA Section of Antitrust Law, International Antitrust Cooperation Guide (2004).

67. Treaty with the United Kingdom on Mutual Legal Assistance in Criminal Matters, U.S.-U.K., Jan. 6, 1994, S. Treaty Doc. No. 104-2; *see* Agreement Concerning the Application of the Treaty on Mutual Legal Assistance in Criminal Matters of January 6, 1994, U.S.-U.K., Apr. 30, 2001, S. Treaty Doc. No. 01-65 (stating that the United Kingdom "no longer sees any reason for refusing to entertain requests for information in criminal anti-trust or competition law cases," and thus "in the future . . . will be prepared to offer assistance in respect of requests from the United States of America made pursuant to the Treaty for assistance in anti-trust and competition law investigations, subject to the normal scrutiny process applied to all other such requests").

68. Extradition Treaty Between the Government of the United States of America and the Government of the United Kingdom of Great Britain and Northern Ireland, U.S.-U.K., Mar. 31, 2003, S. Treaty Doc. No. 108-23.

adoption of a new statute criminalizing certain antitrust offenses.[69] Other MLATs continue to be encumbered by the explicit exclusion of competition matters or because of dual criminality requirements;[70] given the still-relative rarity of criminal antitrust sanctions, the proportion of extradition treaties that can be employed for antitrust offenses is yet smaller.[71]

Antitrust-specific agreements have their own, equally substantial obstacles. The International Antitrust Enforcement Assistance Act (IAEAA), adopted with some fanfare in 1994, allows the United States to enter into agreements (termed Antitrust Mutual Assistance Agreements) to facilitate the exchange of confidential business information obtained during antitrust investigations—though normally that would be prohibited by law. In theory, this permits countries to conduct joint or at least coordinated antitrust investigations without the need to seek waivers from the parties supplying the information. But the benefits are largely theoretical, since only one such agreement—with Australia—has been entered into under the IAEAA. One deterrent has been provisions that appear to require foreign partners to consent to the use of shared information for noncompetition matters as well, which they may be unwilling or even legally barred from doing.[72] Changing this may be a precondition to finalizing any more such agreements, though other bases for resistance are likely to remain.[73]

---

69. This was highlighted by a high profile case in which the extradition of a U.K. national to face prosecution in the United States for antitrust offenses was stymied by British courts on grounds that the alleged conduct preceded its criminalization—though the government appears to continue to support extradition on lesser charges that overlap to a greater degree with the prior law.

70. *International Competition Network, Cartels Working Group, Co-Operation Between Competition Agencies in Cartel Investigation: Report to the ICN Annual Conference,* May, 2007, at 15–16.

71. J. William Howley et al., *Increasing the Bite Behind the Bark: Extradition in Antitrust Cases,* The Antitrust Source, April 2007, at 1.

72. 15 U.S.C. §§ 6211(2) (requiring that agreements be on a "reciprocal basis," thereby suggesting that stipulations as to U.S. sharing must be mirrored), 6211(2)(E) (providing that agreements will contain "[t]erms and conditions that specifically require using, disclosing, or permitting the use or disclosure of, antitrust evidence received under such agreement or such memorandum only" not merely for purposes of administering the foreign antitrust laws involved, but also "with respect to a specified disclosure or use requested by a foreign antitrust authority and essential to a significant law enforcement objective," if prior written consent is provided by the Attorney General or the Federal Trade Commission and certain other conditions are fulfilled). *But see, e.g.,* R.S.C. 1985, c. C-34, § 30.01(d)(ii) (limiting agreements to those in which a foreign state has undertaken to use any evidence provided by Canada solely for the purpose for which it was requested).

73. Antitrust Modernization Commission, *supra,* at 39–40 (recommending that Congress clarify that the IAEAA does not require provisions allowing noncompetition uses of information); *id.* at 219 & n.58 (conceding that other countries have laws

As a result, the vast majority of cooperation in competition-related matters occurs through informal channels. Such cooperation is probably facilitated by antitrust cooperation agreements, which encourage cooperation above and beyond that indicated by traditional and positive comity; such agreements do not have the force of law within the United States (and thus are not liberated from other legal restraints, such as those relating to the handling of confidential business information), and on the international plane are understood to be closer to "soft law" than treaties.[74] The United States has also been in the forefront of "soft" multilateral cooperation, including through the International Competition Network. The upshot, in any case, is that the U.S. enforcement agencies and their foreign counterparts apparently communicate on a near-daily basis about antitrust matters of mutual interest. By popular account, cartel investigations and mergers are the most frequent subjects of these exchanges, though it is difficult to say much about either in the absence of more public information.[75]

While cooperation and comity may be addressed within the same legal instruments, and are frequently examined together in studies of international antitrust regimes, it is worth noting that they can be at loggerheads with one another: facilitating the enforcement of national laws, such as through information exchange, may well enable actions that are ultimately the source of international discord. The theory behind U.S. international antitrust efforts—sometimes made explicit, but more often assumed—seems to be that cooperation will promote convergence toward U.S.-style antitrust analysis, which will in turn diminish the frequency of disagreements about extraterritorial enforcement.[76] However optimistic this theory, it may be defended as a pragmatic assessment of the alternatives.

---

preventing information-sharing agreements for reasons above and beyond the noncompetition uses question).

74. ABA SECTION OF ANTITRUST LAW, INTERNATIONAL ANTITRUST COOPERATION HANDBOOK 5–6 (2004).

75. Roundtable Conference, *supra*, at 21 (remarks of Thomas O. Barnett) ("I do think that the most extensive degree of cooperation that we see on a day-to-day basis, while we do see it on the cartel enforcement front, really is mergers. It can happen on other fronts, but it has become routinized. I mean our staffs talks to each other daily."). For a survey of cooperation efforts in the cartel area, relying on input from the United States and other antitrust agencies, see *Co-operation Between Competition Agencies in Cartel Investigations*, *supra*, at 18–19.

76. *See, e.g.*, Antitrust Modernization Commission, *supra*, at 213–14; ICPAC, *supra*, at 42; J. Thomas Rosch, *The Three Cs: Convergence, Comity, and Coordination*: Speech before the St. Gallen International Competition Forum, May 10–11, 2007 (remarks by a Commissioner, Federal Trade Commission).

2. EXTRATERRITORIALITY, COMITY, AND COOPERATION IN EU COMPETITION LAW

DAMIEN GERADIN, MARC REYSEN, AND DAVID HENRY*

I. INTRODUCTION

The EU competition law regime, with the European Commission ("the Commission") at the apex of its enforcement structure, has steadily evolved to become one of the most mature regimes in the world. Its core provisions, namely Articles 101 and 102 TFEU, do not, however, explicitly indicate whether they apply extraterritorially. The extent to which these provisions apply to foreign activity, therefore, is determined by other legal constructs. Three doctrines, in particular, are relevant. These are the "economic entity" doctrine, the "implementation" doctrine and the "effects doctrine". The first two doctrines are established doctrines of EU law, as recognized by the Court of Justice ("CJ"). In the absence of formal recognition by the CJ, however, it remains unresolved whether the "effects doctrine" enjoys the same status. In the vast majority of cases, however, the fact that the "effects doctrine" has not been formally recognized by the CJ will have no bearing on the ability to assert subject-matter jurisdiction over non-EU undertakings located outside the EU.[1] The economic entity and implementation doctrines should be more than adequate in this respect.

The assertion of extraterritorial jurisdiction can lead to what some nations regard as an impingement on their sovereignty. One consequence of this view is the promulgation and/or activation of domestic blocking statutes. These are not, however, the only costs attributable to the review of economic activity by multiple antitrust authorities. Overlapping jurisdiction of this sort can also generate

* Damien Geradin is Professor of Competition Law and Economics at Tilburg University and a partner at Howrey LLP, Brussels; Marc Reysen is a partner at Howrey LLP, Brussels; and David Henry is an associate at Howrey LLP, Brussels.

1. A discussion of enforcement jurisdiction is beyond the scope of this paper. Subject-matter jurisdiction is the right which States or institutions possess to make their laws applicable to the activities, relations, or status of persons, and to the interests of persons in property. Such jurisdiction is exercised by the enactment of legislation, such as Articles 101 and 102 TFEU, or by the laying down of rules by administrative agencies or by courts. Enforcement jurisdiction, on the other hand, is the power of a State or body such as the EU to induce or compel compliance or to punish noncompliance. *See* Butterworths Competition Law (Loose Leaf), Vol. 3, Issue 71, para. XII/2.

undesirable substantive outcomes, such as divergent results. In order to temper the effects of the unilateral assertion of extraterritorial jurisdiction, comity principles have come to the fore.[2] Primary EU legislation is silent on the principle of comity, however. Comity does form an integral part of the EU's bilateral antitrust cooperation agreements with the United States, Canada, and Japan. Unfortunately, comity provisions in those agreements remain weak. Beyond those arrangements, comity is only deemed to come into play in those circumstances in which the conduct in question is compelled in the relevant third country. Indeed, one can go so far as to say that where there is a real conflict between competition authorities, each will very likely seek to claim an overriding interest in enforcement and disregard comity.

Against the backdrop of comity's lack of mandatory effect, and in order to achieve more effective antitrust enforcement on a European and global level, the Commission has placed itself at the heart of a network of cooperative arrangements. It cooperates closely with Member State national competition authorities ("NCAs") through the European Competition Network ("ECN") and is party to a series of cooperative arrangements with third countries. In addition, the Commission is closely involved in multinational antitrust forums which provide for a platform for discussion of practical competition policy enforcement and policy issues, and for disseminating best practices and encouraging procedural and substantive convergence. Avoidance of conflict is another reason for entering into cooperative arrangements. Conflict does, however, continue to subsist not for want of cooperative effort but invariably because of stark differences in the manner that allegedly anticompetitive conduct is appraised. In this respect, witness the Commission's decisions in *Microsoft* and *GE/Honeywell* with regard to refusal to license and tying, and conglomerate effects respectively.[3] In the greater scheme of things, however, such conflicts are rare occurrences, and cooperation between the European Union and the United States, for example, has been a great success.

In view of the above, the purpose of this paper is to provide the reader with a brief overview of the EU competition law regime (Part II) and to demonstrate how its provisions are used to assert subject-matter jurisdiction over non-EU

---

2. According to the OECD, the concept of *positive comity* describes "a voluntary policy calling for a country to give full and sympathetic consideration to other countries' important interests while it is making decisions concerning the enforcement of its own competition law." *Negative comity*, on the other hand involves "a country's consideration of how it may prevent its law enforcement actions from harming another country's important interests." *See* OECD, *Committee on Competition Law and Policy Report on Positive Comity* (1999), para 5.

3. *See* Commission Decision, COMP/C-3/37.792, Microsoft, nyp (Mar. 24, 2004) and Commission Decision 2004/134/EC, General Electric/Honeywell, 2004 O.J. (L 48) 1 (July 3, 2001).

undertakings located outside the EU, which engage in alleged violations of EU competition law (Part III). The subject of comity will then be looked at with the discussion essentially focusing on the comity provisions found in the EU/US cooperation agreements (Part IV). The EU's internal and external cooperative arrangements will then be examined (Part V). Finally, a short conclusion will be provided (Part VI).

II. THE EU COMPETITION LAW REGIME

The antitrust set-up within the EU is based on a two-tier system whereby the Commission and NCAs have parallel competence to apply Articles 101 and 102 TFEU in a particular case.[4] Article 101(1) TFEU prohibits agreements between undertakings, decisions by associations of undertakings, and concerted practices which restrict or distort competition and which may affect trade between Member States.[5] Article 101(3) may render the Article 101(1) TFEU prohibition inapplicable on the fulfillment of a narrow category of cumulative criteria.[6] Cartels will very rarely find exemption under Article 101(3), because such practices are presumed to have negative market effects and thus fall within the ambit of an almost per se prohibition pursuant to Article 101(1) TFEU.[7] Article 102 TFEU prohibits the abuse by one or more undertakings of a dominant position within the common market or in a substantial part of it insofar as it may affect trade between

4. *See* Council regulation (EC) No 1/2003 of Dec. 16, 2002, on the implementation of the rules on competition laid down in Articles 81 and 82 of the Treaty, (2003) O.J. L1/1 ("Regulation 1/2003").

5. A concerted practice has been described as "a form of coordination between undertakings which, without having reached the stage where an agreement properly so called has been concluded, knowingly substitutes practical cooperation between them for the risks of competition" *See* judgment of the Court of Justice, Case 48/69, Imperial Chemical Industries Limited v. Commission [1972] E.C.R. 619, para. 64.

6. Article 101(1) may be rendered inapplicable where an anticompetitive agreement or practice contributes to improving the production or distribution of goods or to promoting technical or economic progress, while allowing consumers a fair share of the benefit, and does not (a) impose on the undertakings concerned restrictions which are not indispensable to the attainment of these objectives and does not (b) afford such undertakings the possibility of eliminating competition in respect of a substantial part of the products in question.

7. *See* recital 18 of the Commission's Guidelines on the applicability of Article 81 of the EC Treaty to horizontal cooperation agreements, (2001) O.J. C 3/2.

Member States.[8] An abuse is characterized by the exploitation of customers and/or the exclusion of competitors.[9]

Completing the Commission's competition law toolkit is the EU Merger Regulation ("EUMR").[10] A concentration with a Community dimension falls within the Commission's exclusive remit, such remit being triggered on the meeting of the relevant turnover thresholds.[11] Concentrations that do not have a Community dimension fall to be assessed by the Member States' merger regimes.[12] Once a merger has been notified to the Commission, it is examined to see if it would significantly impede effective competition in the EU.[13]

III. EU COMPETITION LAW AND EXTRATERRITORIALITY

Articles 101 and 102 TFEU are silent as to whether they apply extraterritorially, a result of which has been that their extraterritorial application has been developed by Commission decisional practice and a court-created corpus of case law. Indeed, it is now established that Articles 101 and 102 TFEU apply no matter

---

8. Dominance has been defined in relation to "a position of economic strength enjoyed by an undertaking which enables it to prevent effective competition being maintained on the relevant market by giving it the power to behave to an appreciable extent independently of its competitors, customers and ultimately of its consumers." *See* judgment of the Court of Justice, Case 27/76, United Brands v. Commission [1978] E.C.R. 207, para. 65. A presumption of dominance arises where an undertaking has a market share of 50 percent. *See* judgment of the Court of Justice, Case C-62/86, AKZO v. Commission [1991] E.C.R. I-3359, para. 60. Additional factors are also taken into account in order to establish dominance, especially where an undertaking holds a market share of less than 50 percent. Such factors include ownership of intellectual property rights (*see* judgment of the General Court, Case T-30/89, Hilti v. Commission [1991] E.C.R. II-1439, para. 93) and superior technology (*United Brands, supra*, paras. 82–84).

9. In particular, the following types of conduct are deemed to be an abuse if engaged in by a dominant undertaking: (a) the direct or indirect imposition of unfair purchase or selling prices or other unfair trading conditions; (b) the limitation of production, markets, or technical development to the prejudice of consumers; (c) the application of dissimilar conditions to equivalent transactions with other trading parties, thereby placing them at a competitive disadvantage; and (d) making the conclusion of contracts subject to acceptance by the other parties of supplementary obligations which, by their nature or according to commercial usage, have no connection with the subject of such contract.

10. Council Regulation (EC) No. 139/2004 of 20 January on the Control of Concentrations Between Undertakings, (2004) O.J. L24/1, and Commission Regulation (EC) No. 802/2004 of Apr. 7, 2004, Implementing Council Regulation No. 139/2004 on the Control of Concentrations Between Undertakings (2004) O.J. L 133/1.

11. *See* Article 1(2) of the EUMR.

12. *See* Article 21(2) and (3) of the EUMR. Notification becomes compulsory on meeting the relevant turnover thresholds.

13. *See* Articles 2(2) and 2(3) of the EUMR.

where an undertaking has its headquarters or where the agreement has been concluded.[14] In assessing whether the long jurisdictional arm of Articles 101 and 102 TFEU applies to undertakings located outside the EU, three legal theories have been propounded. The first is the "economic entity" doctrine, which has its underpinnings in the nationality principle (A).[15] The second is the "implementation" doctrine, which is based on the territoriality principle (B),[16] and the third is the "effects doctrine," which extends subject-matter jurisdiction to all situations where the economic effects in the EU of anticompetitive actions taken abroad are immediate, reasonably foreseeable, and substantial (C).[17]

A. The "Economic Entity" Doctrine

Dyestuffs represents the seminal EU case as far as the economic entity doctrine is concerned.[18] On the basis of the nationality principle, jurisdiction was asserted over non-EU parent undertakings by attributing liability to them for the illegal price-fixing of dyestuffs by their subsidiaries located in the EU over which the non-EU parent undertaking exercised control. The CJ held that the fact that a subsidiary has separate legal personality is not sufficient to exclude the possibility of imputing its conduct to the parent company. The CJ went further by holding that such may be the case in particular where the subsidiary, although having separate legal personality, does not decide independently upon its own conduct on the market but carries out in all material respects the instructions given to it by the parent company (i.e., the parent undertaking exercises decisive influence over the subsidiary).[19]

---

14. *See* para. 100 of the Guidelines on the effect on trade concept contained in Articles 81 and 82 of the Treaty, (2004) O.J. C 101/81.

15. On the basis of the nationality principle, the Commission has jurisdiction *ratione personae* over the activities of undertakings having their seat in the EU.

16. The territoriality principle allows a nation to subject to its jurisdiction conduct which has a sufficiently close link to its territory. *See* L. Ritter, W. David Braun, & F. Rawlinson, *European Competition Law: A Practitioner's Guide,* KLUWER LAW INTERNATIONAL 62 (2d ed. 2000).

17. Judgment of the General Court, Case T-102/96, Gencor v. Commission, [1999] E.C.R. II-753, para. 90. The "effects doctrine" is derived from the territoriality principle. *See id.*

18. See Imperial Chemical Industries Limited v. Commission, *supra* note 5.

19. In *Dyestuffs,* the applicant was able to exercise decisive influence over the policy of the subsidiaries as regards selling prices in the EC and in fact used this power. For example, the applicant sent its subsidiaries in the EC telex messages ordering them to charge a certain price and to apply other conditions of sale vis-à-vis their customers. More recently, the Commission has held:

> a parent company can be held liable for the conduct of its subsidiaries, if it exercised or is presumed to have exercised (and the presumption is not reversed) decisive influence over the *general commercial* policy of the latter (i.e. if the parent company determines or is presumed to have determined the basic orientation of the commercial strategy and operations of the strategy), regardless of whether such influence

Similar reasoning is to be found in the CJ's *Continental Can* judgment.[20]

According to the *Dyestuffs* line of case law, therefore, the nub of the issue is to check the extent to which a non-EU parent undertaking controls its subsidiaries located in the EU in order to establish a single economic entity. In the eyes of the CJ, control is to be assessed against, inter alia, the shares that the parent undertaking has in the subsidiary.[21] A finding that there is a single economic entity brings a non-EU undertaking within the scope of the EU competition law provisions. Though the effects of the relevant practices were briefly alluded to by the CJ, a response on the application of the "effects doctrine" was shied away from, preference being accorded to handing down a judgment based on the established doctrine of a single economic entity.[22] The CJ's coy stance vis-à-vis the effects doctrine, however, could be attributed to the fact that Europe's political elite at that time vociferously criticized the doctrine when employed by the U.S. antitrust authorities.[23]

B. The "Implementation Doctrine"

The implementation doctrine represents an alternative legal construct as far as the extraterritorial application of EU competition law is concerned, its advent reflecting the inherent limitations of the economic entity doctrine in that it could not be stretched to catch purely non-European players.[24] Pursuant to the implementation doctrine, which is based on the territoriality principle, agreements and practices fall within the purview of Articles 101 and 102 TFEU irrespective of where they find their geographic origin, if they are *implemented* within the European Union and trade between Member States is affected. According to the CJ in its *Woodpulp* judgment:[25]

> consisted specifically in encouraging the illegal behaviour or in imposing such behaviour upon the subsidiaries. For the same reasons, when the said presumption applies, the undertaking concerned cannot reverse it by simply stating that the parent company was not directly involved in or was not even aware of the cartel.

See Commission Decision, COMP/F/38.443, Rubber Chemicals, nyp, para. 256 (Dec. 21, 2005). Therefore, if a parent undertaking can establish that the subsidiary was in reality an autonomous entity and rebut the aforementioned presumption with regard to the exercise of decisive influence over a subsidiary, it will be able to escape liability.

20. *See* Judgment of the Court of Justice, Case 6/72, Europemballage Corporation & Continental Can Company Inc. v. Commission, [1973] E.C.R. 219, para. 15.

21. *Supra* note 5, para. 136.

22. *Id.* para. 126.

23. *See* J.J. Friedberg, "The Convergence of Law in an Era of Political Integration: The Wood Pulp Case and the Alcoa Effects Doctrine," Research Paper 9017, p. 10.

24. *Id.* p. 13.

25. See judgment of the Court of Justice, Joined Cases 89, 104, 114, 116, 117, and 125 to 129/85. A. Ahlström Osakeyhtiö and others v Commission [1988] E.C.R. 5193.

> It should be observed that an infringement of Article [101 TFEU], such as the conclusion of an agreement which has had the effect of restricting competition within the common market, consists of conduct made up of two elements, the *formation* of the agreement, decision or concerted practice and the *implementation* thereof. If the applicability of prohibitions laid down under competition law were made to depend on the place where the agreement, decision or concerted practice was formed, the result would obviously be to give undertakings an easy means of evading those prohibitions. The decisive factor is therefore the place where it is implemented. The producers in this case implemented their pricing agreement within the common market. It is immaterial in that respect whether or not they had recourse to subsidiaries, agents, sub-agents, or branches within the Community in order to make their contacts with purchasers within the Community. Accordingly the Community's jurisdiction to apply its competition rules to such conduct is covered by the territoriality principle as universally recognized in public international law.[26]

According to *Woodpulp*, therefore, the criterion as to the implementation of an agreement is satisfied by mere sale within the European Union, no matter the location of the sources of supply and the production plant and where the anticompetitive arrangement was entered into. A corollary of this is that EU jurisdiction is triggered by the simple fact that products are directly sold to purchasers within the EU. One commentator has indeed argued that the triggering of EU jurisdiction on the basis of direct sales to EU purchasers sits uneasily with public international law as "it does not constitute a sufficiently close and relevant link with the regulating State that is compelling enough to justify jurisdiction on its part."[27] Despite such misgivings, however, the Commission recently made explicit reference to the *Woodpulp* judgment in order to assert jurisdiction over a global price-fixing cartel for lysine involving undertakings from third countries.[28]

C. The "Effects Doctrine"

A third triggering doctrine for the purposes of asserting extraterritorial jurisdiction is based on the economic effects felt within the EU. Though the effects doctrine has been recognized and accepted by the Commission, testimony of which is borne by dicta in various Commission decisions and in Commission Notices,[29] the CJ has never handed down a judgment explicitly affirming the

---

26. *Id.* paras 16–18.

27. W. Van Gerven, *EC Jurisdiction in Antitrust Matters: The Wood Pulp Judgment* Fordham Corp. L. Inst. 470 (1989).

28. Commission Decision of June 7, 2000, *Amino Acids*, (2001) O.J. L 152/24, para. 182.

29. *See, e.g.*, Commission Decision of July 24, 1969, *Dyestuffs*, (1969) O.J. L 195/11, para. 28 and para. 100 of the Effect on Trade Guidelines, *supra* note 14.

doctrine, preferring to rely on the more politically uncontroversial economic entity and implementation doctrines. In *Wood Pulp*, for example, the Commission held that the relevant pulp producers and trade associations had infringed Article [101(1) TFEU], all of which had their registered offices outside the EU with only few having some kind of representation, such as a subsidiary, within the EU. The Commission explicitly made reference to the effect of the agreements and practices on prices announced and/or charged to customers and on resale of pulp within the EU in order to assert jurisdiction.[30]

On appeal, Advocate-General Darmon espoused the effects doctrine, reflecting a belief among several Advocate-Generals that the doctrine should become an established concept of EU law.[31] In particular, he opined that "there is no rule of international law which is capable of being relied upon against the criterion of the direct, substantial and foreseeable effect."[32] Despite the Advocate-General's fervent view that the effects doctrine should become a cornerstone of EU competition law when applying it extraterritorially, the CJ subsequently relied on the implementation doctrine (see above) to assert jurisdiction over undertakings located outside the EU.

In the field of merger control, the General Court ("GC") would seem to have endorsed the effects doctrine. In *Gencor*, the territorial scope of the EUMR vis-à-vis a proposed concentration notified by undertakings whose registered offices and mining operations were outside the EU was at issue.[33] The applicants challenged the Commission's assertion of jurisdiction before the GC. The GC held, using language evocative of that of Advocate-General Darmon, that the "application of the [Merger] Regulation is justified under public international law when it is foreseeable that a proposed concentration will have an immediate and substantial effect in the Community."[34] The application of such a test is open to criticism, however, in that not all mergers that must be brought to the attention of the Commission based on the relevant turnover thresholds produce foreseeable, immediate, and substantial effects.[35]

---

30. *See* Commission Decision of December 19, 1984, *Wood pulp*, (1985) O.J. L 85/1, para. 79.

31. Advocate-Generals assist the CJ in its decision-making through the giving of opinions. Such opinions are not binding on the CJ, however.

32. *See* Opinion of Advocate-General Darmon of May 25, 1988 in joined cases 89, 104, 114, 116, 117, and 125–129/85 [1988] E.C.R. 5214 para.57. The effects doctrine was also recognized by Advocate-General Mayras in the *Dyestuffs* case. *See* Opinion of Advocate-General Mayras of May 2, 1972 in cases 48, 49, and 50–57/69 [1972] E.C.R. II-665, pp. 693–94.

33. *See supra* note 17.

34. *Id.* para. 90.

35. *See* A. Jones and B. Sufrin, "EC Competition Law: Text, Cases and Materials", 2d ed., Oxford, 2004, p. 1262.

In the vast majority of cases, however, the fact that the "effects doctrine" has not been formally recognized by the CJ will have no bearing on the ability to assert jurisdiction extraterritorially. The economic entity and implementation doctrines should be more than sufficient.[36] In this regard, whether one applies the implementation doctrine or the effects doctrine, similar outcomes should normally be reached, although it is arguable that the latter doctrine is wider in scope. Indeed, as noted by one commentator, the effects doctrine and the implementation doctrine reach diverging outcomes in some cases. Such would be the case where a cartel of U.S. producers decides not to purchase goods from EU producers as such a decision cannot be said to have been implemented within the EU.[37] The fact, however, that the CJ has thus far fudged on handing down an unequivocal ruling on the effects doctrine as such means that the effects doctrine as a concept of EU law remains unresolved.

IV. COMITY

With anticompetitive practices increasingly taking on an international hue, and more competition authorities claiming jurisdiction over allegedly illicit activity, comity principles have been at the forefront of administrative authority and judicial consideration. The recent *Microsoft*, *Intel*, and *Empagran* cases bear testimony to this.[38] A system of overlapping review by different antitrust authorities, however, without taking into account the other parties' interests, leads to undesired consequences such as forum hopping,[39] divergent results, duplicate

---

36. Other commentators are of the same conviction. *See* R. WHISH, COMPETITION LAW 437 (5th ed. 2003).

37. *See* J.P. Griffin, *Foreign Governmental Reactions to U.S. Assertions of Extraterritorial Jurisdiction*, 19 ECLR 68 (1998). On the other hand, Alexander Schaub, former Director-General of DG Competition within the Commission, has stated that "where Community companies are prevented by cartels in third countries from exporting certain goods and where this may even have an indirect influence on the flow of trade in the Community, I submit that the Community has the power to exercise jurisdiction." *See* speech by A. Schaub, "Scope of application of the competition rules of the European Union," Tokyo, Nov. 22, 1995.

38. See Microsoft, supra note 3, where the Commission imposed a fine of EUR 497 million on Microsoft, which was later upheld by the General Court in Judgment of the General Court, Case T-201/04, Microsoft Corp. v. Commission, nyp. At the time of the Commission Decision, however, Microsoft had already reached settlement in U.S. proceedings, F. Hoffman-LaRoche Ltd. v. Empagran S.A., 542 U.S. 155 (2004) and Intel Corp. v. Advanced Micro Devices, Inc., 542 U.S. 241 (2004).

39. See R. Hewitt Pate, Current Issues in International Antitrust Enforcement, Remarks Before the Fordham Corporate Law Institute 31st Annual Conference on International Antitrust Law and Policy (Oct. 7, 2004), available at http://www.usdoj.gov/atr/public/speeches/206479.pdf.

sanctions, and a misallocation of administrative resources and can have detrimental effects on other legal systems.[40]

Primary EU legislation is silent on the principle of comity, however. The principles of comity and positive comity do, nonetheless, form an integral part of the first generation EU/US Agreements of 1991 and 1998,[41] and, though voluntary in nature, have frequently been accorded considerable importance as tenets of EU cooperation with third countries.[42] According to Article VI of the 1991 EU/US Agreement, which deals with the avoidance of conflicts over enforcement activities, each party has made a commitment to take into account the important interests of the other party, making sure that it considers factors such as the relative significance of the anticompetitive activities and conduct within the enforcing party's territory in comparison to conduct within the other party's territory, or the degree of conflict or consistency between the enforcement activities and the other party's laws or articulated economic policies.

Conversely, Article V of the 1991 EU/US Agreement incorporates a positive comity provision whereby if a party believes that anticompetitive activities carried out on the territory of the other party are adversely affecting its important interests, the first party may notify the other party and may request that the other party's competition authorities initiate appropriate enforcement activities.[43]

The EU/US positive comity instrument was later reinforced in 1998 in view of a perceived imbalance between the extensive territorial jurisdiction asserted

---

40. In this respect, the Commission has on various occasions expressed fears to the U.S. courts regarding the production of documents in the United States that had been submitted to it in conjunction with European enforcement proceedings. Such fears concerned, for example, the chilling effect that such production would have on the latter's leniency program. In this context, see, for example, *In re Rubber Chemicals Antitrust Litigation*, 486 F. Supp. 2d 1078 (N.D. Cal. 2007). Furthermore, failing to take into account principles of comity may force upon other jurisdictions remedies that have been explicitly rejected in that other jurisdiction, e.g., treble damages in the United States which the EU is reluctant to introduce. In this context, see T.F. Bush, *Coming to America: A group of claimants are currently trying to enforce claims under European competition rules in a U.S. court*, COMPETITION LAW INSIGHT 8 (2008).

41. *See* the 1991 EU/US Competition Cooperation Agreement, (1995) O.J. L 95/47 and the Agreement between the European Communities and the Government of the United States of America on the application of positive comity principles in the enforcement of their competition laws, (1998) O.J. L 173/28. The latter agreement supplements the former.

42. *See, e.g.*, Mario. Monti, "The EU Views on Global Competition Forum," ABA meetings, Washington, Mar. 29, 2001, Speech/01/147.

43. In this context, see also Articles V and VI of the Agreement between the EU and Japan concerning cooperation on anticompetitive activities, (2003) O.J. L 183/12 and the Agreement between the European Communities and the Government of Canada regarding the application of their competition laws, (1999) O.J. L 175/50.

by the United States and the less far-reaching jurisdiction claimed by the EU.[44] Pursuant to Article III:

> The competition authorities of a Requesting Party may request the competition authorities of a Requested Party to investigate and, if warranted, to remedy anti-competitive activities in accordance with the Requested Party's competition laws. Such a request may be made regardless of whether the activities also violate the Requesting Party's competition laws, and regardless of whether the competition authorities of the Requesting Party have commenced or contemplate taking enforcement activities under their own competition law.

Article IV(1) of the 1998 EU/US Agreement provides that the parties *may agree* that the requesting party will defer or suspend pending or contemplated enforcement activities during the pendency of enforcement activities of the requested party. Article IV(2) creates a *presumption* that the competition authorities of a requesting party will normally defer or suspend their own enforcement activities in favor of enforcement activities by the competition authorities of the requested party in a defined set of circumstances.[45] Such a presumption exists, for example when, inter alia, the anticompetitive activities at issue (a) do not have a direct, substantial, and reasonably foreseeable impact on consumers in the requesting party's territory or where the anticompetitive activities do have such an impact on the requesting party's consumers, they occur principally in and are directed principally towards the other party's territory, and (b) the adverse effects on the interests of the requesting party can be and are likely to be fully and adequately investigated and, as appropriate, eliminated or adequately remedied pursuant to the laws, procedures, and available remedies of the requested party.[46] Article IV is of considerable importance in the context of

---

44. K. Van Miert, *International Cooperation in the Field of Competition: A View from the EC*, Fordham 24th Annual Conference, Oct. 16, 1997. This assertion regarding the scope of each authority's exercise of jurisdiction is very much open to dispute, however, given the broad jurisdictional scope of the EU implementation doctrine discussed above. The 1998 Agreement is to be seen as a "commitment on the part of the United States and the European Union to co-operate with respect to antitrust enforcement rather than seeking to apply their antitrust laws extraterritorially." *See* Commission Communication to the Council concerning the Agreement between the European Communities and the Government of the United States on the application of positive comity principles in the enforcement of their competition, June 18, 1997, at 5.

45. According to some commentators, it is open to debate whether multinationals are able to invoke a "right to deference." *See* C. Canenbley and M. Rosenthal, *Co-operation between Antitrust Authorities In—and Outside the EU: What Does it Mean for Multinational Corporations?—Part 2*, 26 ECLR 181 (2005).

46. *See* OECD Report on Positive Comity, *supra* note 2, for a full discussion. According to Article II(4)(a) of the 1998 EU/US Agreement, the EU merger control rules do not fall within its ambit.

EU-US cooperation. but it is an intrinsically weak provision. Words like "may agree," "presumption," and "normally" only serve to highlight its lack of binding effect.

Since the promulgation of the 1991 EU/US Agreement, the positive comity instrument has rarely been invoked. For example, in the *Sabre/Amadeus* case, the U.S. Department of Justice requested that the Commission investigate, under the EU competition rules, alleged anticompetitive conduct by four European carriers that were accused by Sabre, a computer reservation system owned by American Airlines,[47] of failing to provide it with the same comprehensive and timely flight information as they provided to the European system known as Amadeus, and their failure to offer Sabre the same technical possibilities such as online confirmation of bookings.[48] Though the Commission later initiated formal Article [102 TFEU] proceedings against Air France, as one of Amadeus's parent carriers, the need to render a decision became superfluous in view of the conclusion of a "code of good behavior" between Sabre and Air France.[49] Conversely, in the *Boeing/McDonnell Douglas* case, the Commission requested, pursuant to Article V of the 1991 Agreement, that the U.S. Federal Trade Commission (FTC) take account of the EU's important interests in safeguarding competition in the market for large civil aircraft.[50] One of the Commission's primary concerns related to Boeing's twenty-year exclusive supply contracts with American, Delta, and Continental.[51] The U.S. authorities, however, considered the exclusive supply contracts as business arrangements that preceded the merger as a result of which they were not relevant to how the merger might change competition and prices.[52]

In the context of comity, the question arises whether the Commission would rule on the merits of the case in circumstances similar to those pertaining to the U.S. *Hartford Fire* case or whether it would refrain from exercising jurisdiction.[53]

---

47. For a good discussion of the political and legal underpinnings in relation to comity of the *Sabre/Amadeus* case, see B. Zanettin, COOPERATION BETWEEN ANTITRUST AGENCIES AT THE INTERNATIONAL LEVEL 195–96 (Hart Publishing 2002).

48. *See* Commission Press Release IP/00/835 (July 25, 2000), "Commission acts to prevent discrimination between airline computer reservation systems."

49. *See* the Study to Assess the Potential Impact of Proposed Amendments to Council Regulation 2299/89 with regard to Computerised Reservation Systems of October 2003 as prepared for the European Commission by The Brattle Group and Norton Rose, p. 6.

50. Commission Decision of July 30, 1997, *Boeing/McDonnell Douglas*, (1997) O.J. C 136/3, para. 11.

51. *Id.* para. 43 et seq.

52. *See* speech by D.A. Valentine, "Building a Cooperative Framework for Oversight in Mergers—The Answer to Extraterritorial Issues in Merger Review," George Mason Law University, Oct. 10, 1997.

53. Hartford Fire Insurance Co. v. California, 509 U.S. 764 (1993). For a good discussion of the *Hartford Fire* case and the issues concerning extraterritoriality, see W.S. Dodge,

To recap, the defendants in *Hartford Fire* were private re-insurers based in London who conspired to restrict the terms of coverage of commercial general liability insurance available in the United States. The U.S. Supreme Court held that the Sherman Act was applicable to the U.K. re-insurers,[54] and laid down the principle that considerations of comity were confined to situations of contradiction in which the foreign sovereign *compelled* an alleged anticompetitive practice rather than simply *permitted* it. Jurisdiction could be asserted over the activity of the U.K. undertakings because the conduct was permitted under the laws thereof as a consequence of which no conflict between the two jurisdictions arose.[55]

In the EU, a similar distinction is drawn between *compulsion* and *permission*. As mentioned above, the *Wood Pulp* saga involved allegedly anticompetitive behavior by pulp producers and trade associations, all of which had their registered offices outside the EU. The U.S. applicants in this case, who were members of an export cartel registered in 1952 under the Webb Pomerene Act, argued that by applying its competition rules, the EU had acted in breach of the principle of noninterference.[56] The CJ made short shrift of such a line of argumentation. It held that there was no contradiction between the conduct required by the United States and that required by the EU since the relevant U.S. law merely exempted the conclusion of export cartels from the application of the U.S. competition laws, but imposed no obligation to conclude such cartels.[57] Similarly in *Gencor*, the GC, in response to the applicant's grievances regarding the GC's assertion of jurisdiction over a South African merger, held "suffice it to note that there was no conflict between the course of action required by the South African Government and that required by the Community given that . . . the South African competition authorities simply concluded that the concentration agreement did not give rise to any competition policy concerns, without requiring that such an agreement be entered into."[58]

Gencor is a good illustration of when comity principles should come to the fore. Indeed, this raises the question of whether comity has ever stopped EU or U.S. authorities, for example, from meddling in a transaction or taking issue with a certain line of conduct because the other party is better placed to deal with it. In our opinion, the answer is that it has not. Whenever there is a real conflict,

---

Extraterritoriality and Conflict-of-Laws Theory: An argument for Judicial Unilateralism, 39 HARV. INT'L L.J. 101 (1998).

54. Judge Souter in *Hartford Fire* for the majority held that "it is well established by now that the Sherman Act applies to foreign conduct that was meant to produce and did in fact produce some substantial effect in the United States." 509 U.S. at 796.

55. For a good discussion of comity considerations from a U.S. perspective, see S.W. Waller, *The Twilight of Comity*, 38 COLUM, J. TRANSNAT'L L. 563 (2000).

56. *Supra* note 25, para. 19.

57. *Id.* para. 20.

58. *Supra* note 17, para 103.

the authorities will very likely seek to claim an overriding interest in enforcement and disregard comity.[59] The recent *Microsoft* decision bears witness to this where conflict stemmed from differences in the philosophical approach to certain types of conduct.[60]

V. COOPERATION

Since the EU structure is composed of 27 Member States, cooperation takes on both an internal and external dimension. From an internal perspective, the Commission and the NCAs in all EU Member States actively cooperate with each other through the ECN.[61] The ECN deals with cooperation on the application of Articles 101 and 102 TFEU, providing an effective platform for the exchange of information and assistance in investigations.[62] The Commission and the NCAs also cooperate in the field of merger control pursuant to, for example,

---

59. With regard to the assailability of the principle of comity, see *Laker Airways v. Sabena, Belgian World Airlines*, 731 F.2d 909, (D.C. Cir. 1984), where it was held:

> [T]here are limitations to the application of comity. When the foreign act is inherently inconsistent with the policies underlying comity, domestic recognition could tend either to legitimize the aberration or to encourage retaliation, undercutting the realization of the goals served by comity. No nation is under an unremitting obligation to enforce foreign interests which are fundamentally prejudicial to those of the domestic forum.

731 F.2d at 937.

60. *See supra* note 3. Appraisals of unilateral behavior reflect perhaps most clearly the level of divergence between the EU and the U.S., for example. In this context, see speech by J.B. MacDonald, Deputy Assistant Attorney General, *Section 2 and Article 82: Cowboys and Gentlemen*, presented at the second annual conference of the Global Competition Law Centre, College of Europe, June 16 & 17, 2005. More recently, the Commission and the U.S. Department of Justice have issued guidance on single firm conduct from which it remains clear that differences continue to subsist insofar as some types (e.g., predation) are appraised. *See* respectively *Communication from the Commission: Guidance on the Commission's Enforcement Priorities in Applying Article 82 EC Treaty to Abusive Exclusionary Conduct by Dominant Undertakings, COM* (2008) and the *U.S. Dep't of Justice Competition and Monopoly: Single Firm Conduct Under Section 2 of the Sherman Act* (2008).

61. The Commission also cooperates with the national courts of each Member State insofar as the application of Articles 101 and 102 TFEU is concerned. The principles governing such cooperation are found in the Commission Notice on the cooperation between the Commission and the courts of the EU Member States in the application of Articles 81 and 82 EC, (2004) O.J. C 101/54. In this context, also see Council Regulation (EC) No. 1206/2001 of May 28, 2001 on cooperation between the courts of the Member States in the taking of evidence in civil or commercial matters, (2001) O.J. L 174/1.

62. The ECN has also, for example, recently launched a Model Leniency Programme in order to facilitate the handling of parallel leniency applications in the ECN. *See* http://ec.europa.eu/comm/competition/ecn/model_leniency_en.pdf.

the pre-notification referral mechanism provided for in the EUMR.[63] From an external perspective, the EU has entered into bilateral relations on competition issues with third countries and engages in multilateral cooperation on competition policy in various forums.[64]

A. Internal Cooperation

The core provisions dealing with cooperation between the Commission and the NCAs and the NCAs *inter se* are found in Article 11 of Regulation 1/2003 and the Commission's Notice on Cooperation within the Network of Competition Authorities ("Network Notice").[65] This part discusses how (i) cases are allocated and (ii) information shared between the Commission and the NCAs and the NCAs between themselves.

1. Case Allocation Within the ECN The Commission's Network Notice provides for case allocation principles in order to ensure both an efficient division of work between the Commission and the NCAs and the NCAs *inter se* and an effective and consistent application of EU competition rules.[66] According to paragraph 8 of the Network Notice, an NCA is considered to be well placed to deal with a

---

63. In the context of merger review and cooperation, NCAs can avail themselves of the pre-notification mechanism provided for in the EUMR. Pursuant to Article 4(4) of the EUMR, prior to the notification of a concentration, an undertaking may inform the Commission, by means of a reasoned submission, that the concentration may significantly affect competition in a market within a Member State that presents all the characteristics of a distinct market and should therefore be examined, in whole or in part, by that Member State. The referral apparatus provided for in Article 4 of the EUMR is further elaborated upon in the Commission Notice on Case Referral in respect of concentrations. *See* Commission Notice on Case Referral in respect of concentrations, (2005) O.J. C 56/2. The referral notice provides general guidance on the appropriateness of an envisaged referral. Unlike the case with the ECN, however, NCAs in the context of cooperation in merger control cannot exchange confidential information unless they are either entitled to do so under national law or have been given waivers by the relevant parties.

64. For a discussion of cooperation between the Member States in their own right and the U.S. authorities, see ABA Section of Antitrust Law, International Antitrust Cooperation Handbook (2004).

65. *See* Commission Notice on cooperation within the Network of Competition Authorities, (2004) O.J. C 101/43. According to Article 11(1) of Regulation 1/2003, "the Commission and the competition authorities of the Member States shall apply the Community competition rules in close cooperation." A Commission Notice does not bind NCAs. All NCAs of the 27 Member States have, however, signed a declaration that they will abide by the principles set forth in the Network Notice. For a further, more comprehensive discussion of the Commission's Network Notice, see C. Gauer, L. Kjolbye, D. Dalheimer, E. de Smijter, D. Schnichels and M. Laurila, Regulation 1/2003 and the Modernisation Package fully applicable since May 1, 2004, 2 Competition Policy Newsletter 1 (2004).

66. The system has so far been working effectively. Between May 1, 2004, and April 30, 2008, the Network was informed of 876 case investigations. *See* European Competition

case if the following three cumulative conditions are met: (a) the agreement or practice has substantial direct actual or foreseeable effects on competition within its territory and is implemented within or originates from its territory, (b) the authority is able to effectively bring to an end the entire infringement, and (c) it can gather, possibly with the assistance of other authorities, the evidence required to prove the infringement.

Though it is preferred that cases be dealt with by a single authority,[67] parallel action by two or three NCAs is also foreseen in the event that an agreement or practice has substantial effects on competition mainly in their respective territories and the action of only one NCA would not be sufficient to bring the entire infringement to an end and/or to sanction it adequately.[68] In the event of such parallel action, however, the authorities are encouraged to coordinate their work and are advised to designate a lead authority.[69]

On the other hand, the Commission is particularly well placed if one or several agreement(s) or practice(s), including networks of similar agreements or practices, have effects on competition in more than three Member States (cross-border markets covering more than three Member States or several national markets).[70] Moreover, the Commission is particularly well placed to deal with a case if it is closely linked to other EU law provisions that may be exclusively or more effectively applied by the Commission, if the Community interest requires the adoption of a Commission decision to develop competition policy when a new competition issue arises or to ensure effective enforcement.[71] Article 11(6) of Regulation 1/2003 reflects the fact that the Commission sits at the pinnacle of the ECN in that pursuant to this provision, where the Commission initiates proceedings for the adoption of a decision, this relieves the NCAs of their competence to apply Articles 101 and 102 TFEU. This may arise, for example, where the NCAs between themselves fail to agree on which of them should assess a given case.[72] Though the Commission can relieve NCAs of their competence, it remains

---

Network Statistics, *available at* http://ec.europa.eu/comm/competition/ecn/statistics.html.

67. *See* recital 18 of Regulation 1/2003, *supra* note 4.

68. *Supra* note 65, para. 12.

69. *Id.* para. 13.

70. *Id.* para. 14. In this context. see the U.K.'s Office of Fair Trading's referral of a complaint concerning Apple's iTunes service to the Commission. The OFT decided that the Commission was better placed to consider this matter, especially since Apple iTunes operated in more than three EU Member States. *See* http://www.oft.gov.uk/news/press/2004/itunes.

71. *Supra* note 65, para. 15.

72. W. Wils, *Regulation 1/2003: A Reminder of the Main Issues, in* Modernisation and Enlargement: Two Major Challenges for EC Competition Law 47, ¶ 115 (D. Geradin ed., 2004).

open to requests for consultation by NCAs on the application of EU law.[73]

2. Information Sharing Within the ECN The abovementioned principles of allocation are complemented by provisions on the passing on of information in relation to new cases, thus facilitating cooperation and allowing for a seamless reallocation of competition authority should the circumstances so require.

In order to facilitate the detection of multiple procedures and to ensure that cases are dealt with by a well-placed competition authority, the members of the network must be informed at an early stage of the cases pending before the various competition authorities. Article 11(3) of Regulation 1/2003 requires NCAs, when acting under Article 101 or 102 TFEU, to inform the Commission before or without delay after commencing the first formal investigative measure. Such information is also to be made available to the other members of the ECN.[74] Furthermore, in accordance with Article 11(4), no later than thirty days before the adoption of a decision, for example, NCAs must inform the Commission providing the latter with a summary of the case or the envisaged decision or, in the absence thereof, any other document indicating the proposed course of action. Such information may also be made available to the other NCAs.

Article 12(1) of Regulation 1/2003 offers the possibility for the Commission and the NCAs to provide one another with and use in evidence any matter of fact or law, including confidential information. Indeed, the sharing of information is obviously of fundamental importance to cooperation within the ECN but represents an issue that should be approached with care in view of the patchwork of penalties available for infringements of Articles 101 and 102 TFEU within the different Member States.[75] Some caveats do apply, however. For example, information that is exchanged is only to be used for the purpose of applying Articles 101 and 102 TFEU and in connection with the subject matter for which it was collected by the transmitting authority. Furthermore, information exchanged can only be used in evidence to impose sanctions on natural persons when the law of the transmitting authority foresees sanctions of a similar kind in relation to infringements of the EU competition rules.

Article 12 is of considerable importance since an NCA or the Commission may, pursuant to Article 22 of Regulation 1/2003, request another NCA to carry

---

73. Article 11(5) of Regulation 1/2003, *supra* note 4.

74. Empirical evidence suggests that this system is working effectively. According to statistics for 2008, the total number of case investigations which the ECN members were informed of amounted to 159 cases. *See* European Competition Network Statistics, *available at* http://ec.europa.eu/competition/ecn/statistics.html.

75. In the U.K., custodial sentences may be imposed, pursuant to the U.K. Enterprise Act 2002, on individuals who dishonestly engage in cartel conduct. In Spain, on the other hand, Law 16/1989 on the Defence of Competition does not provide for criminal sanctions for antitrust infringements.

out an inspection or other fact-finding measure on its behalf. Articles 11(3), 22, and 12 of Regulation 1/2003 in combination allow for simultaneous inspections to be carried out in different Member States and then for information to be passed on to another authority. Such a possibility will often prove essential in detecting and later punishing cartel operators.[76]

B. External Cooperation

Cooperation with third countries has become a must in view of the globalized nature of trade and the multi-jurisdictional effects of cartels, unilateral conduct, and mergers. Furthermore, cooperation can and does obviate the need to promulgate and/or activate blocking statutes,[77] and more generally serves to avert conflict between authorities, which continues to arise occasionally despite commitment to comity principles. For trade purposes, it is in the interest of the EU and other jurisdictions to have a real competition culture diffused throughout the globe. In view of that, the following section provides a brief overview of (i) bilateral arrangements entered into by the EU with third countries and (ii) the multinational forums in which the Commission is closely involved.

1. **Bilateral Arrangements** As mentioned above, the EU has dedicated cooperation agreements on competition policy with the United States, Canada, and Japan.[78] In addition to provisions pertaining to coordination of enforcement

---

76. The uncovering and punishment of the recent Flat Glass cartel serves as a good example of coordination between the Commission and the NCAs. *See* Commission Press Release IP/07/178, Commission Fines Flat Glass Producers € 486.9 Million for Price Fixing Cartel (Nov. 28, 2007).

77. *See, e.g.*, the U.K. Protection of Trading Interest Act 1980 and France's Statute No. 80-538 of 1980.

78. *See supra* notes 41 and 43. Similar provisions on cooperation are found in all three agreements. For a good discussion of the EU/US Competition Cooperation Agreement, see A. Riley, *The Jellyfish Nailed? The Annulment of the EC/US Competition Co-operation Agreement*, 3 ECLR 185 (1995). Cooperation between the United States and the EU has overall been very successful with only very few high profile exceptions. *See, e.g.*, the *McDonnell Douglas* merger, *supra* note 50, or *GE/Honeywell*, *supra* note 3. Examples of successful cooperation abound. *See, e.g.*, Procter & Gamble's $57 billion acquisition of Gillette where the U.S. FTC and the Commission coordinated their efforts to achieve compatible remedies in oral health care products. Federal Trade Commission, Bureau of Competition, Antitrust Enforcement Activities Report, Fiscal Year 2002 - March 15, 2006 (*available at* http://www.ftc.gov/reports/aba/abaspring2006.pdf) and the recent *Reuters/Telerate* merger in which suitable remedies were accepted to address competition concerns for financial market data platforms and following which Competition Commissioner Neelie Kroes stated, "we are very pleased with this outcome, which follows close cooperation with the U.S. Department of Justice and coordinated efforts to find a suitable remedy that fully resolves the Market Data Platforms competition problem." *See* Commission Press Release IP/05/596, Mergers: commission conditionally clears Reuters' acquisition of competitor Telerate (May 24, 2005. Recently, the EU-US air transport agreement was

activities, these agreements provide for exchanges of information between the different jurisdictions.[79]

In furtherance of the commitment to cooperate, the EU and the United States have also agreed on an Administrative Arrangement on Attendance (AAA). The AAA sets forth administrative arrangements between the respective competition authorities allowing for reciprocal attendance at certain stages of the procedures in individual cases.[80] In the field of merger review in particular, the EU and United States have set up a Merger Working Group, the principal objective of which is to enhance transatlantic cooperation in the control of global mergers. Within the framework of that working group, a set of best practices on cooperation in reviewing mergers that require approval in both the EU and United States was agreed upon. The best practices address issues pertaining to, inter alia, coordination on timing and consistency in the imposition of remedies.[81]

---

signed, and it has been applied since March 30, 2008. The agreement envisions cooperation between the Commission and the U.S. Department of Transportation in the field of competition law and policy in the air transport sector. In particular, the agreement contains provisions pertaining to, inter alia, consultation, regular meetings, notification of proceedings, and the disclosure of confidential information between the two authorities. *See* Annex 2, Article 4 of the Air Transport Agreement between the United States of America, of the one part, and the Member States of the European Union, and the European Community, of the other part, (2007) O.J. L 134/4. For a discussion of this agreement, see M. Gremminger, *New EU-US cooperation agreement in air transport*, 2 COMPETITION POLICY NEWSLETTER 27 (2007).

79. For example, Article II of the 1991 EU/US Competition Cooperation Agreement establishes that each party is to notify the other whenever its competition authorities become aware that their enforcement activities may affect important interests of the other party. Article III of the 1991 Agreement provides for regular bilateral meetings between the two jurisdictions to share information on current enforcement activities and priorities, while Article VII of the same agreement sets out the relevant provisions pertaining to bilateral consultation. Article VII of the 1991 Agreement and Article V of the 1998 EU/US Agreement deal with the exchange of information, including confidential information.

80. The AAA was used for the benefit of the Commission in, for example, the *Worldcom MCI/Sprint* case, where an EU official was able to attend a meeting between the DOJ and the merging parties. *See* Report from the Commission to the Council and the European Parliament on the application of the agreements between the European Communities and the Government of the United States of America and the Government of Canada regarding the application of their competition laws, COM(2002)45 final.

81. *See* US-EU Merger Working Group: Best Practices on Cooperation in Merger Investigations, *available at* http://www.usdoj.gov/atr/public/international/docs/200405.htm. For a good example of the successful use of these best practices, see the *GE/Instrumentarium* merger (Commission Decision of September 2, 2003, *GE/Instrumentarium*, (2004) O.J. L 109/1), as discussed by D.P. Majoras, Principal Deputy Assistant Attorney General, Antitrust Division, U.S. DOJ, in her speech of October 23, 2003, *Vigorous Antitrust Enforcement Covering the Waterfront: An Update from the Antitrust Division*, *available at* http://www.usdoj.gov/atr/public/speeches/201435.htm.

Softer bilateral cooperative arrangements exist between the EU on the one hand and Korea and China on the other. With Korea, for example, the EU has established a permanent forum for consultation whereby the respective competition authorities share their experience and views on competition policy. Provisions on information exchange and notification also exist but are given only fleeting treatment.[82] With China, the Commission has agreed on a structured dialogue to share experience and views on competition matters and provide technical and capacity-building assistance to China.[83] The EU is also party to a number of Free Trade Agreements with third countries that incorporate provisions treating basic aspects of cooperation in competition matters.[84] In addition, the EU has committed itself to cooperating on competition matters with the African, Caribbean, and Pacific countries pursuant to the Cotonou Agreement,[85] and is also currently providing competition-related assistance to Croatia, which has been granted EU candidate country status, pursuant to the Stabilisation and Association Agreement.[86] Though agreements such as the Cotonou agreement are soft in nature, the negotiations in relation to Croatia's accession to the EU on the other hand require that the former undertake far-reaching and mandatory reforms before they are concluded. Indeed, in line with the "Copenhagen criteria," Croatia, as in the case of other EU candidate countries, must show that it has laid down competition laws—mirroring those found

82. Memorandum of Understanding on cooperation between the Korean Fair Trade Commission and the Commission's DG Competition (2004). At the time of writing, the possibility of concluding a more far-reaching intergovernmental cooperation agreement between the two parties was being mooted.

83. *See* the Terms of Reference of the EU-China competition policy dialogue (2004). In the context of this structured dialogue between the EU and China, a EU-China Competition Policy Dialogue took place in Beijing in September 2007. *See* Commission Press Release MEMO/07/338, EU Competition Commissioner Neelie Kroes to visit China to strengthen competition policy cooperation (Aug. 31, 2008).

84. *See, e.g.*, Article 41 of the Euro-Mediterranean Agreement establishing an Association between the European Community and its Member States, of the one part, and the People's Democratic Republic of Algeria, of the other part, (2005) O.J. L 265/2.

85. *See* Article 45(3) of the Partnership Agreement between the Members of the African, Caribbean, and Pacific Group of States of the one part, and the European Community and its Member States of the other part, (2000) O.J. L 317/3. *See also* Council Decision 2005/599/EC of June 21, 2005 concerning the signing, on behalf of the European Community, of the Agreement amending the Partnership Agreement between the members of the African, Caribbean, and Pacific Group of States, of the one part, and the European Community and its Member States, of the other part, signed in Cotonou on June 23, 2000, (2005) O.J. L 209/26.

86. See the Stabilisation and Association Agreement between the European Communities and their Member States, of the one part, and the Republic of Croatia, of the other part, (2005) O.J. L 26/3.

in the *acquis communautaire*—that a competent national competition authority has been set up and that a credible enforcement record has been instituted.[87]

2. **Multinational Forums** In parallel with the ECN, the NCAs and the Commission participate in the association of European Competition Authorities (ECA) alongside the competition authorities of Norway, Iceland, Liechtenstein, and the EFTA (European Free-Trade Association) Surveillance Authority.[88] The ECA serves as, among other things, a forum for discussion on the application and enforcement of competition rules and is made up of various working groups, one of which concerns cooperation in multi-jurisdictional mergers.

On a more general level, the Commission, as a founding member and policy driver, takes part in the International Competition Network (ICN), which also sets up a platform for discussion of practical competition policy enforcement and policy issues and for spreading best practices and encouraging procedural and substantive convergence.[89] The ICN is also made up of working groups in the fields of, inter alia, cartels, mergers, and more recently, unilateral conduct, the latter of which could not be set up at a more opportune time in view of the considerable divergence that exists between, for example, EU and U.S. appraisal of such conduct in contrast to cartels.[90] The ICN cartel working group organizes an annual cartel workshop while the merger working group has adopted a set of nonbinding "guiding principles and recommended practices" which competition

---

87. For a further discussion of the EU accession criteria in relation to competition policy, see D. Geradin & D. Henry, *Competition Law in the New Member States, Where do we come from? Where do we go? in* Modernisation and Enlargement: Two Major Challenges for EC Competition Law 273 (D. Geradin ed. 2005). According to latest reports, Croatia has made progress in this field, but work still remains to be done. *See* Commission Report COM(2006) 649 final-SEC(2006) 1385.

88. *See* the Agreement on the European Economic Area, (1994) O.J. L 1/3. The EEA agreement contains specific competition provisions, namely Articles 53 to 64, which are identical to those of found in the TFEU.

89. *See* http://www.internationalcompetitionnetwork.org/. For background reading relating to the ICN, see M. Todino, *International Competition Network: The State of Play after Naples*, 26 World Competition 283 (2003). *See also* the speech by N. Kroes of May 30, 2007, *The International Competition Network—Achievements and Goals, available at* http://europa.eu/rapid/pressReleasesAction.do?reference=SPEECH/07/345&format=HTML&aged=1&language=EN&guiLanguage=en.

90. The ICN is currently working hard to iron out the impediments to international cooperation in cartel cases. Such impediments relate to, inter alia, the exchange of confidential information between agencies and the absence of waivers of confidentiality by leniency applicants. *See* the recent ICN report, *International Competition Network Cartels Working Group Subgroup 1–General Framework–Cooperation between competition agencies in cartel investigations*, May 2007.

authorities are encouraged to adhere to when carrying out an analysis of mergers that touch upon several jurisdictions.[91]

The Commission also plays a prominent role in various bodies of the Organisation for Economic Co-operation and Development (OECD). For example, the Commission is on the OECD Competition Committee and takes part in peer reviews of OECD member countries.[92] The OECD Competition Committee, which is an important forum for discussion of competition law issues, frequently holds roundtables on competition matters.[93] Furthermore, the OECD has been very active in fostering international cooperation in competition law matters.[94] In 2005, for example, the OECD adopted best practices for the formal exchange of information between competition authorities in hard-core cartel investigations.[95]

Outside the OECD, the Commission is also involved in the workings of the United Nations Conference on Trade and Development (UNCTAD). The Commission actively participates in the UN Review Conference assessing the United Nations Set of Principles on Competition.[96] On an annual basis, the Commission also takes part in the Intergovernmental Group of Experts on Competition Law and Policy, which gets together to seek ways of improving global cooperation on competition policy implementation and furthering convergence through the medium of dialogue.[97]

While it is true that further progress is necessary,[98] the work carried out by the abovementioned soft law antitrust institutions has proved fruitful. The high-level discussions on contemporary and pressing competition law issues have led to the adoption of numerous (nonbinding) recommendations and best practices

---

91. More recently, the ICN has adopted Recommended Practices on the Assessment of Dominance, Substantial Market Power and the Application of Unilateral Conduct Rules to State-Created Monopolies.

92. In the context of peer reviews, in January 2006, the OECD published a report reviewing competition law and policy in the European Union. *See* http://www.oecd.org/dataoecd/7/41/35908641.pdf.

93. For more information on the OECD and its work in the field of competition, see http://www.oecd.org/topic/0,3373,en_2649_37463_1_1_1_1_37463,00.html.

94. *See* http://www.oecd.org/dataoecd/60/42/21570317.pdf.

95. *See* Best Practices for the Formal Exchange of Information Between Competition Authorities in Hard Core Cartel Investigations, section II B, *available at* http://www.oecd.org/document/38/0,3343,en_2649_40381607_2474918_1_1_1_1,00.html.

96. The UN Set is a multilateral agreement on competition policy that (a) provides a set of equitable rules for the control of anticompetitive practices, (b) recognizes the development dimension of competition law and policy, and (c) provides a framework for international co-operation and exchange of best practices. *See* http://www.unctad.org/Templates/Page.asp?intItemID=4106&lang=1.

97. *See* http://www.unctad.org/Templates/Page.asp?intItemID=4068&lang=1. The EU has also been a driving force behind an international framework for international competition rules within the WTO. Such an agreement remains dead in the water, however.

98. *See supra* note 90.

providing a useful point of reference for both practical enforcement of competition laws,[99] and cooperation between a large number of competition authorities and their respective interlocutors.[100] Indeed, the OECD's successive recommendations on cooperation between competition agencies underpin the vast majority of international cooperation agreements.[101] Moreover, these institutions have proved to be a very useful medium through which valuable technical assistance can be channeled to nascent or less sophisticated antitrust regimes. With regard to the latter point, witness the robust competition law arrangement in Korea which, though a long-time recipient of, inter alia, OECD assistance, now provides technical assistance to other Asian countries.[102]

Another useful yardstick against which the impact and success of these multilateral forums should be assessed is the extent to which they have provided a stimulus for legislative change in member countries. In this regard, evidence indeed suggests that the principles and best practices that have emanated from the forums alluded to above have had a direct bearing on substantive and procedural changes in domestic competition laws. Australia, Brazil, and Japan can be cited as examples of nations that amended their leniency programs following ICN efforts,[103] while almost half of the ICN member jurisdictions, such as Estonia and Belgium, have sought to align to a greater degree their merger control laws with ICN recommended practices.[104]

VI. CONCLUSION

With many commercial activities having a global impact, dealing with alleged antitrust violations no longer remains the exclusive preserve of a single regulator.

---

99. Examples of cases where best practices and recommendations have underpinned antitrust enforcement abound. To cite one such example, the Japanese Fair Trade Commission has recently made use of the Manual on Anti-Cartel Enforcement Techniques in relation to Digital Evidence Gathering. *See* International Competition Network, *A Statement of Achievements*, June 2006–May 2007.

100. *See* speech by P. Lowe of September 5, 2006 at the 4th Seoul International Competition Forum, *International Cooperation Between Competition Agencies: Achievements and Challenges.*

101. *See* ICN Report, *supra* note 90. In this regard, see in particular the OECD's *Recommendation of the Council concerning Cooperation between Member Countries on Anticompetitive Practices Affecting International Trade*, July 27, 1995 - C(95)130/FINAL.

102. Recently, the OECD-Korea Policy Centre was set up with a view to assisting competition authorities in the Asian region to develop and implement effective competition law and policy.

103. *See* D. D. Sokol, *Monopolists without Borders: The Institutional Challenge of International Antitrust in a Global Gilded Age*, 4 BERKELEY BUS. L.J. 115 (2007).

104. *See supra* note 99.

Indeed, the Commission often finds itself having to appraise, in tandem with other antitrust authorities, allegedly anticompetitive conduct by undertakings that do not necessarily have any link whatsoever with the EU. In order to be able to deal with non-EU undertakings whose allegedly anticompetitive activities originate outside the EU, a series of legal theories, namely the "economic entity," "implementation," and "effects doctrines" have been set forth. In the absence of a categorical CJ judgment affirming the "effects doctrine," however, it remains unsettled whether it is a universally recognized concept of EU law. The consequences of the uncertainty surrounding its legal status should not be overplayed, however. The scope of the "implementation" and "economic entity" doctrines should be more than sufficient to assert subject-matter jurisdiction over purely non-European undertakings involved in allegedly illicit activity that has an effect in the EU.

Though noble in its cause to bring an end to anticompetitive conduct, the Commission's unilateral exercise of extraterritorial jurisdiction over conduct, which is being simultaneously appraised by third-country antitrust authorities, is liable to lead to unsatisfactory outcomes characterized by conflict, divergent results, and the attendant misallocation of resources. As a result, the principles of comity and cooperation have come to play a prominent role—the latter perhaps more so than the former. With regard to comity, the Commission has concluded cooperation agreements with the United States, Japan, and Canada containing comity provisions. Their lack of binding effect and their infrequent invocation make them somewhat of a damp squib, however. Furthermore, and in line with the U.S. stance toward comity, the Commission, when examining a case, only takes comity into consideration in circumstances where the relevant conduct is mandated in the third country. Moreover, whenever there is a real conflict, the Commission will very likely seek to claim an overriding interest in enforcement and brush aside comity.

As a result, cooperation has become a much more useful and productive tool to ensure that allegedly anticompetitive conduct, which touches upon several jurisdictions, is dealt with efficiently and optimally. In this regard, the Commission has set up a robust framework for cooperation with the EU Member States and has concluded bilateral cooperation agreements with a number of third countries. Furthermore, it is a driving force behind antitrust cooperation in multi-national antitrust forums, a corollary of which is the steady yet effective spread of best practices. In view of the philosophical gulf between how certain conduct—especially in the field of unilateral conduct—is assessed, conflict does sometimes arise. Examples of successful cooperation abound, however, and the move toward even deeper antitrust cooperation is to be strongly welcomed.

3. THE INTERNATIONAL REACH OF CANADIAN COMPETITION LAW

EDWARD M. IACOBUCCI*

I. INTRODUCTION

In a small, open economy like Canada's, it would be plainly incomplete to think of antitrust law and policy as involving only domestic interests. This has always been true, but of course has become even more essential to appreciate with growth in international trade. In this chapter, I map out the international contours of Canadian competition law and practice. First, I consider the extraterritorial reach of Canadian competition law. There are three relevant dimensions of extraterritorial application that I consider. Does Canadian law reach domestic conduct that affects foreign markets? Does Canadian law reach foreign conduct that affects domestic markets? Finally, does Canadian law reach foreign conduct that affects foreign markets?

In discussing extraterritoriality, the central issue is whether Canadian law has jurisdiction over the relevant conduct. But even if it does have jurisdiction, it may decline to assume jurisdiction on grounds of international comity. The second section outlines the role of comity in Canadian attitudes to the extraterritorial reach of its statutes.

Setting aside substantive law, cross-border antitrust also involves potential questions of cooperation and conflict between domestic and foreign antitrust enforcers. The third section outlines Canada's stance on international cooperation with other antitrust enforcement agencies. While the mandate of this chapter is simply to describe the law in Canada, in the fourth section, I briefly evaluate Canada's attitude toward international antitrust matters, concluding that while there is much to admire, there are some concerns as well.

Before embarking on the substantive discussion, it is worth emphasizing some features of the Canadian institutional landscape which render some of the legal assertions in what follows open to debate. While Canada has had a long history of antitrust law, dating back to the first statute in 1889, many aspects of Canadian competition policy, such as merger review and abuse of dominance, were not active in any meaningful way until the modern Competition Act ("the Act") was passed in 1986. Even matters that were more actively governed, like conspiracy, were of much more limited importance until the 1986 Act and

* Edward M. Iacobucci is Osler Chair in Business Law and Professor of Law at the Faculty of Law, University of Toronto.

the creation of the Competition Bureau. This relatively short history of vigorous antitrust enforcement has naturally limited the stock of relevant case law that clarifies open interpretive questions. Moreover, there are relatively limited private rights of action for damages under the Competition Act: under Section 36, plaintiffs may only sue for single damages, and only where there has been a criminal violation of the Act. The limited scope for private actions helps explain the smaller number of litigated cases in Canada, even on a proportionate basis, compared to those in the United States.

Perhaps as a consequence, there are elements of the law as it relates to cross-border matters that have not been tested in Canadian courts. We have not had our *Alcoa,*[1] *Hartford Fire,*[2] and *Empagran*[3]; nor, for that matter, have we had our *Wood Pulp.*[4] In lieu of definitive leading cases, there are three sources that I rely on to ground my opinions of the law. First, there is the Competition Act itself. On some matters, the statute is explicit about cross-border issues; on other matters, the statute offers at least implicit guidance. Another source is agreements that Canada has signed with various trading partners that concern cross-border antitrust issues. Finally, there are some "soft law" sources. For example, in part because of the dearth of case law, the Canadian Competition Bureau has issued a series of guidelines that, while not a definitive source of law, indicate the Bureau's opinion of the law. Moreover, Bureau officials make speeches from time to time that also indicate the views of the Bureau. While courts may ignore the Bureau's views, and indeed the Bureau itself may ignore its past statements,[5] these sources are at least presumptively influential, particularly given the broad carriage of antitrust matters with which the Competition Act entrusts the Bureau.[6]

II. EXTRATERRITORIALITY

There are two basic questions that inform analysis of extraterritorial application of law: Where did the relevant conduct take place? And where were the effects

---

1. United States v. Aluminum Co. of America, 148 F.2d 416 (2d Cir. 1945) (U.S. antitrust law applies to foreign conduct with effects in the United States).

2. Hartford Fire Ins. Co. v. California, 509 U.S. 764 (1993) (comity principles bar the application of U.S. antitrust law to foreign conduct having an effect in the United States only if this would create an unavoidable conflict with foreign law).

3. F. Hoffman-LaRoche Ltd. v. Empagran S.A., 542 U.S. 155 (2004) (foreign plaintiffs cannot collect under U.S. antitrust law for damages arising in a foreign country).

4. Dec. 85/202 [1985] OJ L85/1 (EU law applies to conduct taking place outside the EU that has an effect in the EU).

5. In *Canada (Commissioner of Competition) v. Superior Propane Inc.*, [2001] F.C.J. No. 455, for example, both the Federal Court of Appeal and the Bureau rejected the Bureau's previously issued Merger Enforcement Guidelines.

6. *See* M. Trebilcock & E. Iacobucci, *Designing Competition Law Institutions,* 25 World Competition 361 (2002).

of the conduct felt? Domestic law obviously covers the case where domestic conduct affects domestic markets, but other cases will be considered in turn: domestic conduct affects foreign markets; foreign conduct affects domestic markets; and foreign conduct affects foreign markets.

A. Domestic Conduct Affects Foreign Markets

There are several indicators in the Competition Act suggesting that conduct by Canadian producers that affects foreign markets is outside the scope of Canadian competition policy. As a preliminary matter, there is the preambular provision setting out the purpose of the statute that stresses the domestic objectives of Canadian competition law:

> 1.1 The purpose of this Act is to maintain and encourage competition in Canada in order to promote the efficiency and adaptability of the Canadian economy, in order to expand opportunities for Canadian participation in world markets while at the same time recognizing the role of foreign competition in Canada, in order to ensure that small and medium-sized enterprises have an equitable opportunity to participate in the Canadian economy and in order to provide consumers with competitive prices and product choices.

Not only does the primary objective—maintaining and encouraging competition *in Canada*—exclusively mention domestic concerns, but three of the four supporting motivations for this objective cited in the section also single out Canadian concerns. (With respect to the fourth supporting motivation, given the somewhat inelegant repetition elsewhere in the provision, perhaps it was viewed as redundant to cite prices and choices facing "Canadian consumers" specifically.) Even without the particular examples elsewhere in the Act that I outline shortly, it is apparent that the Act is directed only at conduct that may affect Canadian markets; local conduct with foreign effects is outside the scope of the Act. It is worth noting that Section 1.1 has been treated as central in courts' analysis of other interpretive controversies, such as the question of consumer versus total welfare in interpreting the efficiencies defense to mergers in Section 96 of the Act.[7]

Section 1.1 provides a strong indication that domestic conduct that affects foreign markets is outside the scope of the Act. In addition, there are specific provisions that focus only on domestic effects on competition that provide further support for this conclusion. For example, export cartels are not illegal under the Act. While Section 45(1) generally criminalizes conspiracies, Section 45(5) provides:

> (5) No person shall be convicted of an offence under subsection (1) in respect of a conspiracy, agreement or arrangement that relates only to the

7. *See Superior Propane, supra.*

> export of products from Canada, unless the conspiracy, agreement or arrangement
>
> (a) has resulted in or is likely to result in a reduction or limitation of the real value of exports of a product;
>
> (b) has restricted or is likely to restrict any person from entering into or expanding the business of exporting products from Canada; or
>
> (c) is in respect only of the supply of services that facilitate the export of products from Canada.

There are no reported cases discussing Section 45(5), but it is notable that a case involving a misleading advertising provision in the Competition Act, Section 52, cited it in reaching a conclusion that the phrase "to the public" in s. 52 means 'to persons in Canada.'"[8] Throughout the reasoning in *R. v. Stucky*, the court refers to the "'Canadiancentric' roots and aspects" of the Competition Act.[9]

Some civil provisions also specifically mention Canadian markets. For example, in order to find an abuse of dominance, there must be a finding pursuant to Section 79(1)(a) that the firm in question "substantially or completely control[s], throughout Canada or any area thereof, a class or species of business."

There is thus support for the conclusion that the Competition Act in Canada does not address domestic conduct that has extraterritorial effects.

B. Foreign Conduct Affects Domestic Markets

While no cases have been litigated expressly on the matter in the competition area, it is apparent that Canadian competition law assumes jurisdiction over foreign conduct that has an impact in Canadian markets. The preamble in Section 1.1, as well as specific provisions in the Act, stress scrutiny of conduct that affects Canadian markets and does not distinguish whether the conduct takes place locally or abroad. Moreover, in connection with cartels, Section 46 expressly provides that a corporation doing business in Canada that acts on instructions from a foreign corporation (presumably a foreign parent) that have the effect of implementing a conspiracy in Canada is guilty of an indictable offense, even if the corporation doing business in Canada has no knowledge of the conspiracy.

There have been no convictions of foreign corporations for conspiracy without guilty pleas, so the boundaries of potential liability are not set. But there have been a number of guilty pleas and substantial fines in connection with foreign cartels with local effects. In these cases, the Bureau has been emphatic in stressing its jurisdiction over conduct that affects local markets, wherever that conduct takes place. Consider the following clear statement by the then Commissioner of Competition in a press release marking the settlement with a Hoffman-La Roche executive who admitted to being personally involved in an international vitamin cartel that affected Canadian markets:

---

8. *R. v. Stucky* (2006), 216 C.C.C. (3d) 148 (Ont. S.C.J).
9. *Id.* at para. 54.

> "It is the Bureau's policy to pursue executives who engage in anticompetitive activities that affect the Canadian market," said Konrad von Finckenstein, Q.C., Commissioner of Competition. "It does not matter whether these individuals are Canadian citizens or foreign nationals, residents or non-residents in Canada, we will go after them to the full extent of the law."[10]

The most recent case relying on Section 46 involved an international conspiracy in graphic electrodes, in which a number of companies affiliated with foreign corporations involved in a conspiracy registered guilty pleas.[11] Interestingly, SEC Carbon of Japan paid a fine of $250,000 for agreeing *not* to operate in Canada, which represents a relatively expansive (though clearly justifiable from a policy perspective, and probably justifiable from a statutory perspective) conception of competitive effects in Canada. Until there is litigation, some of these boundary issues will remain unclear.

On the civil side, the willingness of Canadian authorities to assume jurisdiction over foreign conduct that has effects in Canada is perhaps best demonstrated in the context of mergers. Procedurally, merging parties must notify the Competition Bureau of a merger if they meet certain size thresholds both with respect to the value of their assets and with respect to their sales in Canada. Thus, entirely foreign companies have pre-notification obligations if they have a significant presence in Canada. Substantively, the Competition Bureau on a number of occasions has reviewed foreign mergers that have an impact in Canada. For example, AkzoNobel (Netherlands) acquired ICI Paints (U.K.) and agreed to divestiture and conduct undertakings with the Bureau to alleviate Canadian competition concerns.[12]

To be sure, the Bureau takes seriously the role of parallel review of a merger by foreign antitrust authorities, but it is nevertheless willing to intervene to protect competition in Canadian markets. I will discuss comity in greater detail below, but the following captures the attitude of Canadian authorities: the Bureau is willing to sit on the sidelines if foreign agencies' actions remedy concerns about competition in Canada, but not if there is idiosyncratic concern about competitive conditions in Canada. The Mergers Remedies Guidelines state:

> To resolve competition concerns within Canada, the Bureau may either take specific action or it may determine that action beyond what will be taken in foreign jurisdictions is not required. While enforcement decisions are made on a case-by-case basis, the Bureau is more likely to formalize negotiated

10. Competition Bureau Press Release, Former Roche Executive Convicted and Fined for International Conspiracies under the Competition Act (Oct. 27, 1999). *See also* Press Release concerning the guilty plea of Bayer AG to conspiracy charges: "The Competition Bureau will not hesitate to prosecute any business, whether in Canada or abroad, that participates in price fixing cartels in the Canadian market."

11. *See, e.g., R. v. Mitsubishi Corp.* (2005) 40 C.P.R. (4th) 333 (Ont. S.C.J.), in which Mitsubishi pleaded guilty and paid a fine of $1 million.

12. *See* http://www.competitionbureau.gc.ca/epic/site/cb-bc.nsf/en/02544e.html.

> remedies within Canada when the matter raises Canada-specific issues, when the Canadian impact is particularly significant, when the asset(s) to be divested reside in Canada, or when it is critical to the enforcement of the terms of the settlement. In contrast, the Bureau may rely on the remedies initiated through formal proceedings by foreign jurisdictions when the asset(s) that are subject to divestiture, and/or conduct that must be carried out as part of a behavioural remedy, are primarily located outside of Canada. However, the Bureau will do so only if it is satisfied that the actions taken by foreign authorities are sufficient to resolve the competition issues in Canada.[13]

It is clear from this passage that while Canadian authorities will rely on foreign solutions to problematic international mergers where this addresses Canadian competitive conditions, they will act on their own to seek remedies to protect otherwise unprotected Canadian competitive concerns. Canada clearly assumes jurisdiction over foreign conduct that has an effect in Canada.

An exception to the general rule that the competition case law in Canada has not addressed cross-border matters arose in *Director of Investigation & Research v. Hillsdown Holdings (Canada) Ltd.*[14] In *obiter dicta* in that case, Madam Justice Reed questioned the Competition Bureau's Merger Enforcement Guidelines' (MEGs) approach to the efficiencies defence in Section 96 of the Competition Act. This provision establishes that a merger whose efficiencies are greater than its anticompetitive effects is permissible. The problem is that "anticompetitive effects" is undefined. The MEGs (at the time of the *Hillsdown Holdings* decision) took a total welfare approach: anticompetitive effects are deadweight losses, and transfers from consumers to producers from higher prices are socially neutral. Reed J. wondered whether such an approach would be appropriate in cases in which "the dominant firm which charges supra-competitive prices is foreign-owned so all the wealth transfer leaves the country."[15] As we have seen, foreign mergers that affect domestic consumers are addressed by the Competition Act, but in considering these mergers, foreign and domestic producers may be treated differently, with greater laxity under s. 96 for domestic merging parties.

Madam Justice Reed did not answer the question of whether foreign producers should be treated differently from domestic producers under Section 96. Nor unfortunately did the later *Superior Propane* case. This case turned on the efficiencies defense, unlike *Hillsdown*, but lengthy litigation resulted in a decision from the Federal Court of Appeal, which held that the Competition Tribunal should not be categorical about the appropriate approach to Section 96, but rather should consider how to approach "anticompetitive effects" depending on

---

13. Competition Bureau, Information Bulletin on Mergers Remedies in Canada, Part VII, International Coordination and Cooperation, Sept. 22, 2006.

14. [1992] 41 C.P.R.3d 289 (Reed J.).

15. *Id.* at 343.

the context. The *Hillsdown* query is thus unanswered; in any given case, it is open to argue that the fact that foreigners realize the gains from a merger may be reason to treat transfers from consumers as a negative factor.[16]

The efficiencies defense turns the question of foreign conduct affecting Canadian markets on its head. In competition matters, the ordinary focus is on consumer welfare, and hence it is natural for Canadian authorities to concern themselves with Canadian consumers. Section 96 invites consideration of producer welfare. The provision does not draw an explicit distinction between foreign and domestic producers in assessing "anticompetitive effects,"[17] but there are at least hints that courts may treat foreign producers differently from domestic producers. The Federal Court of Appeal left important matters under Section 96 to the Tribunal's case-by-case judgment in *Superior Propane*; and the Tribunal indicated in *Hillsdown* a view that foreign producers ought to be treated differently. The efficiencies defense favoring approval of a merger that harms domestic consumers is potentially available to domestic producers, but it may not be available to foreigners. Only further litigation will clarify the matter.

C. Foreign Conduct Affects Foreign Markets

Canada will not intervene in cases where foreign conduct affects competition outside Canada. It is probably sufficient to reach this conclusion to reiterate the observations above about the local focus of the Competition Act: given that the concern of the Act is competition in Canada, there is no provision in the Act for grounding complaints about conduct that harms foreign consumers. But in addition, there are explicit relevant observations by the Canadian government about the *Empagran* case. Canada took a position that aligns clearly with that of the U.S. Supreme Court, and not the D.C. Circuit Court of Appeals, in *Empagran*.

In that case, the question was whether U.S. courts would assume jurisdiction over foreign cartels affecting foreign consumers. The U.S. Supreme Court concluded that foreign conduct harming foreign consumers was not subject to antitrust sanction under U.S. law. In reaching this conclusion, the Court had the benefit of the Canadian government's view of the subject in an amicus curiae brief.[18] Various arguments were made against the result reached by the

16. *See* Stephen F. Ross, *Afterword: Did the Canadian Parliament Really Permit Mergers that Exploit Canadian Consumers So the World Can Be More Efficient?* 65 ANTITRUST L.J. 641 (1997).

17. There is reference in Section 96 to the goal of maximizing the value of exports, but this does not logically imply that foreign gains should not be accounted for in making the efficiencies trade-off.

18. Hoffman-La Roche, Ltd. v. Empagran, S.A., 542, U.S. 155 (2004). *See* Brief for the Government of Canada as Amicus Curiae Supporting Reversal, 2004 WL 226389 (Feb. 3, 2004).

Court of Appeals, including those invoking comity, a matter I consider in more detail below. Following U.S. law, particularly *Hartford Fire,* the brief first asks whether U.S. courts have jurisdiction over the conduct in question, and then asks whether comity requires the courts to decline jurisdiction. On the first question, the brief notes some substantive differences between U.S. and Canadian law. For example, treble damages are not available in Canada, and at the time, there was a requirement of a showing of an undue lessening of competition to find a cartel.[19] The brief states at p. 14:

> The conflict with Canadian antitrust regulation and the intrusion on Canadian sovereignty would perhaps be most direct in the case of cartel behavior by Canadian companies in Canada that injured Canadian nationals. A sovereign's interests are most immediately involved in enforcing its own laws against its own nationals for actions within its own territory. Yet if the cartel behavior had some unrelated effect on U.S. commerce, the respondents' proposed construction of the FTAIA would result in U.S. jurisdiction over foreign nationals and wholly foreign transactions. In comparison to Canada's interests, the interests of the United States would be meager, and the effect of upholding U.S. jurisdiction would be to make the courts of the United States the de facto forum of choice for any plaintiff anywhere in the world who could identify some effect of the anticompetitive behavior on U.S. commerce.

There have been no cases seeking to rely on Canada as a jurisdiction to hear a dispute over foreign conduct affecting foreign consumers. Given that plaintiffs have historically faced more onerous requirements in cartel cases in Canada (the undue lessening of competition requirement) and only single damages, it is not surprising that *Empagran* arose in the United States and not Canada. But it is clear from the statute, and from the Canadian government's position in *Empagran,* that foreign conduct that affects foreign consumers is not a matter that the Canadian authorities address.

III. COMITY

Canada has committed to respecting the principle of comity in its interactions with foreign jurisdictions over antitrust matters. There are two ways in which this is manifested. First, Canadian authorities rely on comity as a general matter in dealing with potential international conflicts. Second, Canada has signed agreements with several countries over competition matters, which agreements specifically contemplate a significant role for comity. I consider these matters in turn.

---

19. Recent amendments to the Competition Act, Section 45, which took effect in March 2010, treat naked price-fixing as per se illegal.

As a general proposition, respecting comity is an integral part of Canadian conflicts of law jurisprudence. As the brief of the Canadian government in the *Empagran* case stated:

> The courts of Canada, like those of other nations, have also recognized these principles. "Greater comity is required in our modern era when international transactions involve a constant flow of products, wealth and people across the globe." Hunt v. T & N p.l.c., [1993] S.C.R. 289, 322 (Can.). The Supreme Court of Canada also has recognized restrictions on "the exercise of jurisdiction over extraterritorial and transnational transactions," and that a Canadian court may exercise jurisdiction "only if it has a real and substantial connection with the subject matter." Tolofson v. Jensen, [1994] S.C.R. 1022, 1049 (Can.) (internal quotation omitted). See also, Morguard Invs. (same); Amchem Prods., Inc. v. British Columbia Workers' Comp. Board, [1993] S.C.R. 897 (Can.) (same).

Morguard Investments Ltd. v. De Savoye, [1990] S.C.R. 1077, 1096 states that:

> "Comity" in the legal sense, is neither a matter of absolute obligation, on the one hand, nor of mere courtesy and good will, upon the other. But it is the recognition which one nation allows within its territory to the legislative, executive or judicial acts of another nation, having due regard both to international duty and convenience, and to the rights of its own citizens or of other persons who are under the protection of its laws.

These statements about the importance of comity suggest a broader view of the obligations that it creates than those found in the majority opinion in *Hartford Fire Insurance*, which seemed to conclude that comity only applied in the face of irreconcilable conflicts. In the *Hartford Fire* fact situation, in which U.K. firms "conspired" in a manner that was entirely consistent with U.K. law, it is at least a possibility that the "recognition" of foreign law that comity invites would lead Canadian courts to decline jurisdiction over the U.K. firms. That is, the more robust view of comity expressed in Canadian cases than that of the majority in *Hartford Fire* might well lead to the approach taken by the dissent in that case.

Comity also finds expression in bilateral agreements. For Canada, the most important antitrust agreement is that which it has with the United States. Canada and the United States are the largest bilateral trading partners in the world, and Canada's economy especially is disproportionately affected by activities in the United States.[20] In 1995, Canada and the United States entered into an

20. The Canadian brief in *Empagran* at p. 17 reviews the importance of the relationship: "Canada and the United States share the world's largest trading relationship with approximately US$1.2 billion in goods crossing the border each day. *See* Canada Department of Foreign Affairs and International Trade, Trade and Economic Analysis Division, *Fourth Annual Report on Canada's State of Trade* (May 2003). The United States

"Agreement between the Government of Canada and the Government of the United States of America Regarding the Application of Their Competition and Deceptive Marketing Practices Laws" (the "1995 Agreement"). The 1995 Agreement contains two provisions that explicitly contemplate comity between the nations on antitrust matters. Article VI establishes mutual obligations on the countries to avoid or at least minimize conflicts in their application of antitrust law:

> Avoidance of Conflicts
>
> 1. Within the framework of its own laws and to the extent compatible with its important interests, each Party shall, having regard to the purpose of this Agreement as set out in Article I, give careful consideration to the other Party's important interests throughout all phases of its enforcement activities, including decisions regarding the initiation of an investigation or proceeding, the scope of an investigation or proceeding and the nature of the remedies or penalties sought in each case.
> 2. When a Party informs the other that a specific enforcement activity may affect the first Party's important interests, the second Party shall provide timely notice of developments of significance to those interests.
> 3. While an important interest of a Party may exist in the absence of official involvement by the Party with the activity in question, it is recognized that such interest would normally be reflected in antecedent laws, decisions or statements of policy by its competent authorities.
> 4. A Party's important interests may be affected at any stage of enforcement activity by the other Party. The Parties recognize the desirability of minimizing any adverse effects of their enforcement activities on each other's important interests, particularly in the choice of remedies. Typically, the potential for adverse impact on one Party's important interests arising from enforcement activity by the other Party is less at the investigative stage and greater at the stage at which conduct is prohibited or penalized, or at which other forms of remedial orders are imposed.
> 5. Where it appears that one Party's enforcement activities may adversely affect the important interests of the other Party, each Party shall, in assessing what measures it will take, consider all appropriate factors, which may include but are not limited to:

---

is the destination of more that 81% of Canadian exports and the source of 70% of its imports. *Id.* The market for U.S. goods in Canada is larger than the market for such goods in the fifteen nations of the European Union combined and more than three times as large as the Japanese market for U.S. goods. U.S. Dep't of Commerce, Bureau of Economic Analysis, *U.S. Int'l Trade in Goods and Services*, Ex. 14 (Jan. 14, 2004). Through November 2003, Canada took in almost 24% of all U.S. exports for the year. *Id.*"

(i) the relative significance to the anticompetitive activities involved of conduct occurring within one Party's territory as compared to conduct occurring within that of the other;

(ii) the relative significance and foreseeability of the effects of the anticompetitive activities on one Party's important interests as compared to the effects on the other Party's important interests;

(iii) the presence or absence of a purpose on the part of those engaged in the anticompetitive activities to affect consumers, suppliers or competitors within the enforcing Party's territory;

(iv) the degree of conflict or consistency between the first Party's enforcement activities (including remedies) and the other Party's laws or other important interests;

(v) whether private persons, either natural or legal, will be placed under conflicting requirements by both Parties;

(vi) the existence or absence of reasonable expectations that would be furthered or defeated by the enforcement activities;

(vii) the location of relevant assets;

(viii) the degree to which a remedy, in order to be effective, must be carried out within the other Party's territory; and

(ix) the extent to which enforcement activities of the other Party with respect to the same persons, including judgments or undertakings resulting from such activities, would be affected.

Article VI(5) in particular essentially commits the significant elements of traditional comity analysis to a formal agreement: a party must account for the extent of an activity's connection to their territory, as well as the interests of the other party, in determining the extent of its enforcement approach to that activity. Article V of the 1995 Agreement goes further, as illustrated by its common description as the "positive comity" provision. Under this provision, there is an obligation on each party to consider a request by the other party to investigate and perhaps sanction domestic anticompetitive activity that is harming the other party. The Article provides:

Cooperation Regarding Anticompetitive Activities In The Territory Of One Party That Adversely Affect The Interests Of The Other Party

1. The Parties note that anticompetitive activities may occur within the territory of one Party that, in addition to violating that Party's competition laws, adversely affect important interests of the other Party. The Parties agree that it is in their common interest to seek relief against anticompetitive activities of this nature.
2. If a Party believes that anticompetitive activities carried out in the territory of the other Party adversely affect its important interests, the first Party may request that the other Party's competition authorities initiate appropriate enforcement activities. The request shall be as specific as possible

about the nature of the anticompetitive activities and their effects on the interests of the Party, and shall include an offer of such further information and other cooperation as the requesting Party's competition authorities are able to provide.

3. The requested Party's competition authorities shall carefully consider whether to initiate enforcement activities, or to expand ongoing enforcement activities, with respect to the anticompetitive activities identified in the request. The requested Party's competition authorities shall promptly inform the requesting Party of its decision. If enforcement activities are initiated, the requested Party's competition authorities shall advise the requesting Party of their outcome and, to the extent possible, of significant interim developments.
4. Nothing in this Article limits the discretion of the requested Party's competition authorities under its competition laws and enforcement policies as to whether to undertake enforcement activities with respect to the anticompetitive activities identified in a request, or precludes the requesting Party's competition authorities from undertaking enforcement activities with respect to such anticompetitive activities.

This article gained more specific meaning in a follow-up 2004 agreement, the Agreement between the Government of Canada and the Government of the United States of America on the Application of Positive Comity Principles to the Enforcement of Their Competition Law. Article I, the Scope and Purposes section of the 2004 Agreement states:

1. This Agreement applies where the competition authorities of a Party satisfy the competition authorities of the other Party that there is reason to believe that the following circumstances are present:
   (a) Anticompetitive activities are occurring in whole or in substantial part in the territory of one of the Parties and are adversely affecting the important interests of the other Party; and
   (b) The activities in question may be subject to penalties or other relief under the competition laws of the Party in whose territory the activities are occurring.
2. The purposes of this Agreement are to:
   (a) Help ensure that trade and investment flows between the Parties and competition and consumer welfare within the territories of the Parties are not impeded by anticompetitive activities for which the competition laws of one or both Parties can provide a remedy, and
   (b) Establish cooperative procedures to achieve the most effective and efficient enforcement of competition law, whereby the competition authorities of each Party will normally avoid allocating enforcement resources to dealing with anticompetitive activities that occur principally in and are directed principally towards the other Party's territory, where the

> competition authorities of the other Party are able and prepared to examine and take effective sanctions under their law to deal with those activities.

The 2004 Agreement goes on to clarify more precisely the mutual obligations to respond to a request by the other party. Article III, labelled "Positive Comity," provides:

> The competition authorities of a Requesting Party may request the competition authorities of a Requested Party to investigate and, if warranted, to remedy anticompetitive activities in accordance with the Requested Party's competition laws. Such a request may be made regardless of whether the activities also violate the Requesting Party's competition laws, and regardless of whether the competition authorities of the Requesting Party have commenced or contemplate taking enforcement activities under their own competition laws.

Thus, there is no obligation to undertake enforcement activities in accordance with the requesting party's laws, but there is a commitment to investigate and possibly remedy domestic anticompetitive activities that are problematic under domestic law that have an effect on the foreign requesting party. Interestingly, the requesting country need not have laws in place that would address the behavior if domestic. Returning to the *Hartford Fire* fact situation, suppose that the roles were reversed and that U.S. firms were conspiring and thereby affecting U.K. markets. Even if the U.K. did not prohibit such activity (as the U.K. did not in fact in *Hartford Fire* itself), it could ask the United States to investigate and possibly sanction the conspiracy.

I have focused on the Canada-U.S. agreement because it is overwhelmingly the most important agreement that Canada has. But other agreements also contain bilateral comity obligations. For example, the 1999 Agreement between the Government of Canada and the European Communities Regarding the Application of Their Competition Laws, as well as the 2001 Agreement between the Government of Canada and the Government of the United Mexican States Regarding the Application of Their Competition Laws, contain comity provisions similar to those in the U.S.-Canada 1995 Agreement. Canada also has bilateral agreements with explicit comity provisions with Australia and New Zealand, Costa Rica, Chile, Japan, and the U.K.

IV. COOPERATION

The Canadian Competition Bureau interacts in a number of standard ways with other competition authorities around the globe. Perhaps the most significant of these interactions is its participation in the International Competition Network. But of greater importance to international legal relations are the bilateral cooperation agreements Canada has entered into with some significant trading partners. Again, the agreement with the United States is of paramount importance given the intimate connection between the two economies. As the Canadian brief in *Empagran* notes, "Canada and the United States share a long history of cooperation in investigating and prosecuting international cartels dating back to the early 1900s when they jointly investigated and prosecuted a cartel involving newsprint that operated in both countries." More recently, two prominent agreements foster cooperation between the countries' competition authorities. First, the 1990 "Mutual Legal Assistance Treaty" allows either country to call on the other to provide assistance in enforcing criminal laws, including criminal antitrust laws.

Second, the 1995 Agreement described above with respect to comity also includes a number of provisions addressing cooperation. The comity provisions themselves contemplate cooperation between the countries, with, for example, each party able to request action by the other if its interests are adversely affected by conduct in the other party's territory. But other provisions go to cooperation directly. Article II of the Agreement sets out a number of notification obligations, the foundational obligation in Article II(1) requiring each party to notify the other country "with respect to its enforcement activities that may affect important interests of the other Party." The 1995 Agreement elaborates a number of specific obligations, including, for example, a duty to notify the other party with respect to information requests of persons in the other's territory. Article III of the 1995 Agreement is aptly entitled "Enforcement Cooperation" and establishes a number of mutual assistance duties. It essentially requires each party, to the extent compatible with each country's laws, to share information with the other. Article III provides:

1. (a) The Parties acknowledge that it is in their common interest to cooperate in the detection of anticompetitive activities and the enforcement of their competition laws to the extent compatible with their respective laws and important interests, and within their reasonably available resources.
   (b) The Parties further acknowledge that it is in their common interest to share information which will facilitate the effective application of their competition laws and promote better understanding of each other's enforcement policies and activities.
2. The Parties will consider adopting such further arrangements as may be feasible and desirable to enhance cooperation in the enforcement of their competition laws.
3. Each Party's competition authorities will, to the extent compatible with that Party's laws, enforcement policies and other important interests,
   (a) assist the other Party's competition authorities, upon request, in locating and securing evidence and witnesses, and in securing voluntary compliance with requests for information, in the requested Party's territory;

(b) inform the other Party's competition authorities with respect to enforcement activities involving conduct that may also have an adverse effect on competition within the territory of the other Party;
(c) provide to the other Party's competition authorities, upon request, such information within its possession as the requesting Party's competition authorities may specify that is relevant to the requesting Party's enforcement activities; and
(d) provide the other Party's competition authorities with any significant information that comes to their attention about anticompetitive activities that may be relevant to, or may warrant, enforcement activity by the other Party's competition authorities.

4. Nothing in this Agreement shall prevent the Parties from seeking or providing assistance to one another pursuant to other Agreements, treaties, arrangements or practices between them.

The caveat that the obligations are restricted by domestic law in Subsection 3 may be significant in some circumstances. Section 29 of the Canadian Competition Act forbids the Bureau to share confidential information with third parties, with four exceptions: the Bureau may disclose confidential information to Canadian law enforcement agencies; may disclose information that has become public; may disclose information with the authorization of the source; and, more sweepingly, may disclose confidential information for the "purposes of the administration or enforcement of the Act." The last exception is relevant to international cooperation obligations. The Bureau issued an enforcement bulletin in 2007 entitled "Confidentiality and Mutual Assistance in Enforcing Competition Laws" in which it sets out its views of its confidentiality obligations, particularly those under Section 29. Section 4.2.2 begins:

> 4.2.2.1 With the increasing globalization of business activities, including actions that raise competition law issues in both the criminal and civil fields of competition law, cooperation with foreign counterparts has become crucial to the effective enforcement and administrative activities of competition authorities around the world. To this end, the Bureau is committed to enhancing the effectiveness of Canadian enforcement efforts through cooperation with foreign authorities enforcing similar legislation. In conducting these cooperative activities, the Bureau may need to communicate confidential information to a foreign authority either on its own initiative or on that of the foreign authority. The decision to communicate confidential information to foreign authorities is not taken lightly.
>
> 4.2.2.2 While respecting the requirements of section 29, the Bureau may communicate information in specific circumstances to foreign authorities to address a matter under the Act. In all cases where confidential information is communicated to a foreign authority, the Bureau seeks to maintain the confidentiality of the information through either formal international instruments or assurances from the foreign authority. The Bureau also requires that use of

the confidential information by the foreign authority will be limited to the specific purposes for which it is provided.

The Bureau further stresses the importance of cooperation agreements, stating that, "Generally, where there is no bilateral or multilateral cooperation instrument in force, the Bureau does not communicate information protected by section 29 unless it is fully satisfied with the assurances provided by the foreign authority with respect to maintaining the confidentiality of the information and the uses to which it will be put."

In summary, while Canada and the United States mutually agree to share information, there are potentially significant confidentiality restrictions that suggest that Canadian authorities will be cautious in sharing. But if conditions are right, the authorities will share.

Another important aspect of the Canada-U.S. 1995 Agreement concerns coordination of enforcement over related matters. Article IV establishes an obligation on each country's authority to consider coordinating with the other's authority over related matters. Article IV.2 provides that:

2. In considering whether particular enforcement activities should be coordinated, either in whole or in part, the Parties' competition authorities shall take into account the following factors, among others:
   (a) the effect of such coordination on the ability of both Parties to achieve their respective enforcement objectives;
   (b) the relative abilities of the Parties' competition authorities to obtain information necessary to conduct the enforcement activities;
   (c) the extent to which either Party's competition authorities can secure effective relief against the anticompetitive activities involved;
   (d) the possible reduction of cost to the Parties and to the persons subject to enforcement activities; and
   (e) the potential advantages of coordinated remedies to the parties and to the persons subject to the enforcement activities.

While the U.S.-Canada Agreement is the most important agreement on cooperation that Canada has entered, there are several other bilateral agreements. The 2001 Canada-Mexico Agreement mentioned above is similar in relevant dimensions to the U.S.-Canada 1995 Agreement. Canada has also entered into agreements that include many similar cooperation obligations with Europe, the U.K., Japan, the Republic of Korea, New Zealand, Australia, Chile, and Costa Rica.

V. CONCLUSION

In this section, I focus on the desirability of the regime concerning cooperation that Canada has established. While I develop the basis for this premise elsewhere, my starting point for this analysis is that international agreements should not seek to abrogate local sovereignty, but rather should seek only to address strategic choices by countries seeking to benefit themselves at the expense of their trading partners and global welfare.[21] Given that economic circumstances vary across countries, and that there are many unresolved—probably irresolvable—disagreements over fundamental values, as well as debate over different laws' efficacy, it would not be desirable to short-circuit local choice through a harmonization agenda. On the other hand, there is genuine concern about self-interested domestic laws that exploit foreigners because of trade.

For the most part, the Canadian approach to extraterritoriality is consistent with an emphasis on local sovereignty. Canada applies its antitrust laws to producers, be they domestic or foreign, who act anticompetitively in Canadian markets. It does not, for example, apply its laws to foreigners who allegedly harm other foreigners. This gives space for Canadian sovereignty over its markets, but not over foreign markets.

There are, however, anomalies in the law and international agreements that lead to concerns over parochialism on Canada's part. International agreements provide that Canada may have an obligation to apply its laws to conduct within its territory at the request of a foreign jurisdiction. But Canada is only obliged to investigate conduct illegal under its Act. Unfortunately, the Act explicitly treats foreigners and locals differently in a couple of provisions. Most notably, as mentioned above, Canada explicitly creates an exemption from its conspiracy laws with respect to export cartels.[22] Thus, if the United States were to request that Canada investigate a cartel among Canadian producers whose cartel pertains only to a cartel exporting to the United States, query whether Canada would have any grounds to investigate, seeing that such behavior is permissible under the Act. The United States may apply its laws on an extraterritorial basis to address the problem of a Canadian export cartel, but given the investigative advantage of Canada, this is not a perfect substitute for a Canadian investigation. Thus, the statute and the Agreement allow some effect from undesirable discrimination between foreign and domestic producers and consumers.

Another concern arises from the approach to positive comity found in several agreements, the most important for Canada being the 1995 Agreement with the United States. Under these provisions, a country may ask the other to investigate conduct in the other country even if the conduct in question does not contravene the law of the requesting country. This allows the requesting country potentially

---

21. *See* Edward Iacobucci, *The Interdependence of Trade and Competition Policies* 21 World Competition 5 (1997); Michael Trebilcock & Edward Iacobucci, *National Treatment and Extraterritoriality: Defining the Domains of Trade and Antitrust Policy, in* Competition Laws in Conflict: Antitrust Jurisdiction in the Global Economy (R. Epstein & M. Greve, eds., 2004).

22. As another example, the positive effect of a merger on exports is explicitly a consideration in evaluating that merger. Section 92.

to enjoy a strategic advantage in making such requests. In essence, the Canadian statute reflects policy trade-offs, as does U.S. law, and there is a danger that in a given case, an authority may prefer the foreign rule and can selectively adopt it by making a request of the foreign authorities pursuant to their agreements. Because they do not internalize all the effects, there may be attempts by either country to realize the upside of a policy trade-off without the downside.

For example, Canada has not adopted per se, or partial per se, treatment of tying as in the United States, but rather requires a showing of a substantial lessening of competition. The divergent approaches presumably reflect divergent perceptions in each country of the costs and benefits of tying. Under the 1995 Agreement, however, Canadian authorities could request that U.S. authorities investigate tying by a U.S. firm with apparent market power in a North American market under the American per se rule. Canada might make such a request not because tying particularly harms or benefits Canadian consumers—that is, not because tying substantially lessens competition in Canada—but rather because tying harms a Canadian competitor. While Canada would not take such a producer-oriented approach when all the effects of tying arise in Canada, the per se rule in the United States and the 1995 Agreement allow Canada to protect Canadian producers by requesting that American authorities intervene in this case. Canada can stick to its chosen policy trade-off on tying for domestic conduct, but on cross-border matters may realize parochial benefits for Canadian producers. As this example demonstrates, while in general the international regime appropriately focuses on procedural cooperation and avoids substantive harmonization, the Agreements are open to criticism as allowing some self-interested behavior in the form of opportunistic and selective enforcement.

4. JURISDICTION, COOPERATION, COMITY, AND COMPETITION POLICY IN BRAZILIAN INTERNATIONAL ANTITRUST LAW

LUCIANO BENETTI TIMM*

INTRODUCTION

Today's information society is characterized by the speed of the exchange of information and by the rapid flow of goods and services. A global economy tends to increase the level of international economic transactions among companies and countries. Moreover, globalization is characterized by transnational firms, which are present in several countries. As a result, some transactions and business practices can exert more influence on countries halfway around the world than on the original country. This creates new problems in the area of competition law, since the marketplace no longer has a territorial base. Some type of coordination among States is necessary to tackle these new antitrust problems. And this coordination depends on policies adopted by those States, which in turn depend on the understanding of laws and policies of the main parties involved. Nevertheless, groups will not always share the same interests, and cooperation among them might not always be an efficient or simple process.

The purpose of this paper is to present the current state of international jurisdiction and cooperation in Brazilian antitrust law, in order to orient strategies and policies related to international competition law issues. Due to the specific focus of this paper and the limitation of space, mainly pragmatic issues will be addressed, setting aside some academic discussions.

Briefly, Brazilian antitrust law admits the extraterritoriality of its substantial rules based on the effects doctrine. Those rules are to be applied both by the judicial and administrative branches of the Brazilian government pursuant to procedural norms regarding the power to adjudicate foreign defendants. There is no clear limitation for that substantial and procedural extraterritoriality under black letter law or case law. There are striking differences between judicial

* Luciano Benetti Timm is Professor at Catholic University from Rio Grande do Sul (PUCRS) and at Universidade do Vale dos Sinos (UNISINOS). The author would like to thank Leticiá Hecktheuer, an intern at CADE who helped with materials and research. Leticiá Hecktheuer was part of the Law and Economics Group of Pontificia Universidade Catolica, RS, Brazil, 2008. Thanks also to Professor Andrew Guzman, who made important comments from the perspective of a common lawyer and an international law scholar.

procedure and administrative proceedings in the application of antitrust law, including forms of cooperation with foreign countries.

Cooperation in the judicial area is regulated by the Brazilian Code of Civil Procedure and International Conventions. In the administrative scenario, the Brazilian antitrust agency, the Administrative Council for Economic Defense/*Conselho Administrativo de Defesa Econômica* (CADE), and the investigatory governmental body, Economic Law Secretariat/*Secretaria de Direito Econômico* (SDE), have entered into cooperation agreements with some of Brazil's major economic partners, such as the members of Mercosur (the Southern Common Market, inspired by the European Community Market (ECM) and including Brazil, Argentina, Paraguay, and Uruguay), the United States, Canada, and Portugal.

Understanding Brazilian extraterritorial jurisdiction rules requires some comprehension of the Brazil's national antitrust law system. Competition oversight by means of regulation and litigation in Brazil is a blend of the American antitrust system (Sherman and Clayton Act) and the European system (the Treaty of Rome). As is true in the United States, private parties can bring tort (or even injunction) lawsuits against companies that violate the Federal Antitrust Law (FAL), Federal Law 8884 of 1994. These cases are adjudicated by state courts.[1] District attorneys may also bring collective law suits (class actions) in courts, but the dictrict attorneys are generally not very active, at least compared to U.S. government antitrust litigation.

As in Europe, however, private parties can file a complaint with the antitrust agency. In this case, the procedure is merely administrative and conducted before the Secretaria de Direito Econômico (SDE), an inquisitorial body related to the Ministry of Justice. The outcome varies from the imposition of a fine to an injunction order issued by CADE (an administrative adjudication body). The SDE may also, without provocation from a private party, investigate the violation of the FAL and send the results to be adjudicated by CADE. Since CADE is a federal agency, its decision, like that of any other administrative proceeding, is subject to judicial review before a federal court.

With regard to substantive law, Brazilian competition rules do not vary significantly from those of the United States. Antitrust law tackles the illegal conducts of players in the marketplace, such as vertical and horizontal restraints, abuse of economic power, and deals with mergers approvals.

---

1. The Republic of Brazil is a Federation of (relatively) independent States. The major issues are regulated by federal law, such as the Civil Code, the Penal Code, and the Civil Code of Procedure. Brazil's judicial system is organized between state and federal courts. Federal courts adjudicate cases where the Federal Union is directly or indirectly interested in disputes, such as those involving federal crimes, federal taxes, an so forth. All other disputes are handled by state courts.

This paper will be presented in two parts. The first part, Section I, will be dedicated to the extension of Brazilian antitrust laws and the second (Section II) to cooperation policy with respect to competition.

I. THE EXTENSION OF BRAZILIAN ANTITRUST LAWS

In the first part of this section (A), the paper will discuss in which situations and circumstances Brazilian competition laws apply to conduct that occurs abroad (such as abuse of economic power or a cartel) and when a merger or acquisition (an act of concentration of firms) occurs elsewhere.

The second part of this section (B) will address so-called "comity," i.e., the circumstances under which Brazilian authorities refrain from the application of its laws or even the exercise of its jurisdiction over a case.

A. Extraterritoriality of Brazilian Antitrust Laws

According to Brazilian legal scholars, extraterritoriality can be related either to legislative (or substantive) extraterritoriality and procedural (truly jurisdictional) extraterritoriality.[2] This division is important in this context since it seems that U.S. legal scholars and courts do not make such a distinction. It appears that the assumption is that U.S. courts and agencies will have the power to adjudicate a case if it is determined that U.S. law (e.g., antitrust law) applies to a particular case. The effects test of extraterritorial jurisdiction, such as in the *Hartford Fire* decision[3] will define when that is the case.[4] In Brazil, however, the distinction between power to adjudicate and substantive law has always been defined in the international law literature. Nonetheless, this distinction became partially blurred in Brazilian competition law because of the influence of U.S. antitrust law.

Thus, Brazilian antitrust legislation (substantive rules passed in Brazilian congress) can potentially apply to noncitizens or even to companies and persons not domiciled in Brazilian territory, which defines the extraterritoriality of Brazilian substantive legislation. A second aspect of the problem is the extent, in terms of procedural jurisdiction, of CADE and of Brazilian court decisions to parties domiciled outside Brazilian territory (extraterritorial procedural jurisdiction[5]). Therefore, the problem of extraterritoriality is twofold: (1) when do

---

2. Lima e Silva, Valéria G. de. "Direito Antitruste—Aspectos Internacionais." Curitiba: Juruá, 2006, p. 351.

3. Hartford Fire Insurance Co. v. California, 509 U.S. 764 (1993).

4. William Dodge, *An Economic Defense Of Concurrent Antitrust Jurisdiction*, 38 Tex. Int'l L.J. 27 (2003).

5. As a matter of fact, Brazilian general theory of procedure has long established that only the judicial branch has *jurisdictio* (the power to interpret and declare the law) because of the separation of powers. The executive branch does not have this power. However, this

Brazilian courts or agencies have jurisdiction over the case (no matter what substantive law applies, including foreign law), and (2) when does Brazilian legislation apply to citizens living outside the country (theoretically, in this case, Brazilian law can be adopted by an international or foreign court as the applicable legal system).

1. **Extraterritoriality of Brazilian Courts and Antitrust Agencies** The first question of extraterritoriality is whether a Brazilian court or agency does in fact have the power to adjudicate the case. This is a fundamental issue because the application of Brazilian antitrust substantive law aimed at the foreign conduct of firms (such as cartels and abuse of economic power) depends de facto on the extraterritorial jurisdiction of CADE and Brazilian courts, since these are the only governmental bodies in the world dedicated to applying Brazilian substantive laws. Naturally, these jurisdictional issues are presented to adjudicate conduct and assess mergers, as explained previously.

Extraterritorial procedural jurisdiction of Brazilian investigative and adjudicative antitrust authorities is divided into two main categories: (a) administrative proceedings before SDE and CADE and (b) litigation before the courts. This distinction is important because administrative proceedings are more effective in Brazil and bring about different results, related especially to applicable procedural rules.

(a) International Jurisdiction of Brazilian Courts in Antitrust Matters The FAL does not have a specific provision on procedural jurisdiction of Brazilian courts. It simply states:

> Section 2. Without prejudice to any agreements and treaties to which Brazil is a party, *this Law applies to acts wholly or partially* performed within the Brazilian territory, or *the effects of which are or may be suffered therein.*
> Sole Paragraph. Foreign companies that operate or have a branch, agency, subsidiary, office, establishment, agent or representative in Brazil shall be deemed domiciled in the Brazilian territory. (emphasis added)

This is a provision on applicable substantive law. The subject of the power of courts or agencies to adjudicate a case, which is a procedural issue, is not explicitly mentioned. It is well established that in Brazil, applicable substantive law is a matter of Conflict of Law rules, and the power to adjudicate is a procedural law issue.

Unlike the U.S. jurisdictional text of "minimum contacts" of the *International Shoe*[6] and *Helicopteros Nacionales de Colombia (Helicol)*[7] cases, the principles of civil international procedural jurisdiction of Brazilian courts rely on the Brazilian Federal Code of Civil Procedure (BCCP) and on international conventions and

---

ongoing theoretical discussion will not be raised here. We will assume here that any kind of adjudication, be it in court or in CADE, represents the exercise of jurisdiction.

6. International Shoe Co. v. Washington, 326 U.S. 310 (1945).

7. Helicópteros Nacionales de Colômbia S.A. v. Hall, 466 U.S. 408 (1984).

treaties signed by Brazil, such as those related to the Inter-American Specialized Conferences on Private International Law from the Organization of the American States (OAS). These legal documents are known in Portuguese and Spanish as CIDIP, and they are dedicated inter alia to service of process, as well as to taking of evidence abroad.[8]

The procedural jurisdiction over civil cases is thus defined in Sections 88 (concurrent jurisdiction)[9] and 89 (exclusive jurisdiction)[10] of the Brazilian Code of Civil Procedure. Essentially, Brazilian courts might concurrently adjudicate civil cases in which an international contract was performed in Brazil (for instance, a distributorship agreement in which the agent sells the products in Brazil and wishes to bring an action against the manufacturer seated in Miami), the defendant is domiciled within Brazil (even if he is not a Brazilian citizen), or if the conduct occurred in Brazil (such as an accident occurring within Brazilian territory caused by a foreign citizen). Lastly, disputes dealing with real estate properties located in Brazil must be adjudicated exclusively by Brazilian courts.

According to legal scholars, the above circumstances of Section 88 that designate concurrent procedural jurisdiction of Brazilian courts over international disputes are not extensive (*numerus clausus*). Under the influence of European cases on procedural jurisdictional tort law matters,[11] jurists argue (based on a broader meaning of the text of Section 88, CCP) that another test rendering civil concurrent jurisdiction to Brazilian authorities should be considered—the effects doctrine, by which Brazilian courts must have concurrent procedural jurisdiction over events that occur outside the national territory but which lead to consequences within the country (e.g., tort and environmental cases occurring elsewhere, but in which the harm is inflicted in Brazil). This is precisely the case of antitrust law (FAL), since conducts and mergers might bring different effects in distinct territories.[12]

Thus, even though FAL does not have a specific provision regarding procedural jurisdiction, the effects doctrine has been advocated by legal scholars as the proper means to turn Section 2 of the FAL into practice. Indeed, if Brazilian antitrust substantive law is to be applied to conduct and mergers occurring

8. David Caron, Reading Materials for Resolution of Private International Disputes (Law 261.2). UC-Berkeley, Boalt Hall School of Law, Fall 2007.

9. Section 88 of the Brazilian Civil Procedure Code states that Brazilian courts are empowered to hear a case whenever: a) the defendant, of any nationality, is domiciled in Brazil; b) the obligation is performed in Brazil; or c) the cause of action is referred to a fact happened or practiced in Brazil.

10. Lawsuits dealing with real estate goods located in Brazil must necessarily be filed before a Brazilian court.

11. Handelskwekerij G.J. Bier B.V. v. Mines de Potasse D'Alsace S.A (Rec CJCE, 21/76,1976); e Dumez France & Tracoba v. Hessische Landesbank e outros(CJCE, C-220/88,1990).

12. Lima e Silva, *supra*.

elsewhere, consequently affecting the Brazilian market, then the only practical means of enforcing the law is through Brazilian courts and agencies. This point of view might be considered pragmatic. It is based on the principle derived from ancient Roman Law which states that if the legislation provides you with the ends, it might also provide you with the means.

Moreover, there is also an analogical argument. There is a provision in Section 70 of the Criminal Code of Procedure which states that criminal procedural extraterritorial jurisdiction is based on the result of a criminal action and is not justified only by the territorial test of the place where the act itself occurred.[13] The idea is simple; there is fiction that assumes that the result was part of the action initiated elsewhere. As a result, the court with the power to adjudicate conduct has the same power to adjudicate its consequence. Thus, for instance, if a group of foreign private reinsurers (who sell reinsurance to primary insurers) is conspiring to restrict the terms of coverage of commercial insurance available in Brazil, Brazilian courts would have the power to adjudicate the case and exercise procedural jurisdiction.

Unfortunately, there is no Brazilian case law applying Brazilian antitrust rules (or even tort or environmental substantive rules) to conduct or events that occurred abroad, even though Brazilian judges are well paid (in comparison with the developed world), and the judicial sector is significantly corrupt or biased (Brazilian judges are not nominated or elected, and they work independently pursuant to several constitutional guarantees to).[14]

As mentioned earlier, this occurs because Brazil, like Europe, tends to rely more administrative proceedings than direct court litigation, though in contrast to Europe, the latter is not forbidden. Private parties, SDE, and the Ministry of Justice do not usually go to court, preferring to rely on the expertise of CADE (administrative proceedings). Actually, there is only one leading antitrust case from the Federal Superior Court of Justice, and it deals exclusively with domestic issues.[15]

The general district attorney's office does not have the experience and the specific knowledge for prosecuting based on securities and antitrust law (though this is rapidly changing in keeping with Brazil's growing economy). Another chapter still to be written concerns private litigation, since law firms do not have

---

13. Section 70 of the Code of Criminal Procedure (CCrP) states: "Jurisdiction will be determined by the place where the crime was committed . . . [however] . . . the magistrate's court where the crime has had partial effects or in which effects should have been felt has jurisdiction over the case."

14. Dakolias, M. Court performance around the world: a comparative perspective. World Bank Technical Paper, n.430, 1999. *See also* Castelar Pinheiro, Armando; Saddi, Jairo. Direito, Economia e Mercados. Rio de Janeiro: Elsevier, 2005; R.D. Cooter & D.L. Rubinfeld, *Economic Analysis of Legal Disputes and their Resolution*, 27 J. ECON. LITERATURE 1067 (Sept. 1989).

15. Superior Court of Justice, Special Recourse 261155—from São Paulo, published at the homepage www.stj.gov.br.

the expertise for large antitrust law suits. Lately, the only antitrust litigation arising in courts is that related to the judicial review of CADE's decisions in domestic matters.[16]

Finally, problems due to lack of efficiency and forum shopping among competing jurisdictions abroad, along with lack of procedural instruments like discovery, cross-examination, anti-suit injunctions, and other trends of the adversarial U.S. legal system, might also affect the intent of the parties so as to avoid litigation in Brazil.

(b) International Jurisdiction of Brazilian Antitrust Agencies There is no specific provision in Brazilian law with respect to extraterritorial power of governmental agencies to hear and decide cases. The fact that CADE has been dominated by economists, with a nonlegal and a more pragmatic approach to antitrust issues, and is probably influenced by U.S. antitrust law, has made it easier for the agency to overcome procedural disputes that normally supersede any substantive legal debate in Brazil.[17] So, unburdened by CCP rules, CADE can assert its concurrent procedural jurisdiction in any case to which FAL applies (that is to say, the effects test).

We say "concurrent" because there is no argument that CADE (as in court litigation) has procedural jurisdiction over subject matter, excluding foreign jurisdictions. The few cases brought before CADE are based on the assumption that a different conduct or merger might have different effects under distinctive markets and shall be assessed domestically.

Unfortunately, SDE and CADE (executive branch) have not had much opportunity to handle competition law violations occurring outside Brazilian territory, nor do they possess the structure and know-how to do so. SDE has investigated only three incidents outside Brazil, mainly due to the fact that it had information about convictions in the United States of cartels involving companies that were also engaged in business activities in Brazil.

As a matter of fact, the first case was filed by a private party, Union Carbide Química Ltda., Administrative Proceedings # 08012.007412/99-93, against several national and multinational chemical companies accused of conspiring outside the territory, consequently promoting dumping in the exportation of product HEC and predatory pricing in Brazil. Even though the investigations began in 2000, the case is still not over.

The second case investigated by the SDE is Administrative Proceedings # 08012004897/00-23, filed by the Brazilian Ministry of Finance (Secretaria de

---

16. An example is the law suit brought by Nestlé (the Swiss-based food company) to set aside CADE's decision against the acquisition of Garoto (a Brazilian chocolate factory). The case is still pending a final decision in Federal District Court.

17. Schuartz, Luis Fernando. "A desconstitucionalização do direito da concorrência." Unpublished. Paper presented at the I Annual Meeting of the Brazilian Law and Economics Association at Pontificia Universidade Catolica do Rio Grande do Sul, 2008.

Acompanhamento Economico) against ADM Exportadora e Importadora S.A. and others. The case was initiated because the Brazilian government became aware that a group of multinational companies doing business in Brazil had been convicted in the United States for the formation of a cartel between 1992 and 1995 in order to restrain and control the offer of a chemical product called "lysine." The goal of the ongoing investigations is to determine the effects of the cartel in Brazil, such as a price increase or falling competition. This case is also not over yet.

A third case deals with vitamins (Administrative Proceedings #8012004599/9918). SDE and the Brazilian Ministry of Finance learned that the transnational companies BASF and Roche formed a cartel in the United States in order to fix prices; they were consequently convicted. SDE is still trying to determine the effects of this cartel on the Brazilian market. The case is still open.

So far, the antitrust agencies have not issued any guidelines on extraterritoriality. They have merely signed a few cooperation agreements in exchange for information and with regard to other issues, which will be explained in the following part of the essay.

It is important to mention that CADE might serve a foreign company by means of its affiliated company, its agent, or any kind of domestic representative in Brazil for conduct that occurs overseas but which affects the domestic market.[18]

In reality, the foreign mergers and acquisitions oversight of CADE are probably more effective than investigations of conduct such as cartels because they rely on the parties, and they are somewhat spontaneous, since the parties must notify the agency of any merger or acquisition (Brazilian law call it "concentration act"). This means that companies that engage in businesses in Brazil and become involved with mergers overseas automatically inform to CADE of their operation not only because the approval is mandatory, but also because of the interest in preserving their assets due to the existence of a parental or affiliated company in Brazil. Therefore, in those cases, there are more incentives to cooperate with the antitrust agency. On the other hand, there is less incentive for cooperation with the agency from economic agents in cartels. Thus, investigations on cartels overseas require much more investment, knowledge, structure, and a proactive attitude from Brazilian authorities.

2. **Extraterritoriality of Brazilian legislation** With respect to the application of Brazil's competition laws to conduct that takes place outside its territory, the FAL states:

> Article 2. Without prejudice to any agreements and treaties to which Brazil is a party, this Law applies to acts wholly or partially performed within the Brazilian territory, or the effects of which are or may be suffered therein.

---

18. "Article 2. Sole Paragraph. Foreign companies that operate or have a branch, agency, subsidiary, office, establishment, agent or representative in Brazil shall be deemed situated in the Brazilian territory."

> Sole Paragraph. Foreign companies that operate or have a branch, agency, subsidiary, office, establishment, agent or representative in Brazil shall be deemed domiciled in the Brazilian territory.

This is the "de jure standard." Therefore, it is clear that black letter law determines the application of the substantive rules of the FAL to conduct that occurs outside the territory, but that has effects in Brazil. Thus, for instance, as with the example above, if a group of foreign private reinsurers is conspiring to restrict the terms of coverage of commercial insurance available in Brazil, their conduct can be adjudicated according to Brazilian substantive laws.

As a matter of fact, this rule of FAL, because it is based on U.S. antitrust laws, breaks officially with the general principles of Brazilian Conflict of Law stated in the Introductory Law of the Brazilian Civil Code (ILBCC) (which was influenced by German and French law) in which no provision on the effects doctrine can be found. Section 9 of the ILBCC only states that "to qualify and govern obligations, the court must apply the legal system of the country in which they were originated." Therefore, generally speaking, a Brazilian judge applying this rule must enforce U.S. law if a contract was entered into in New York between a Brazilian citizen and an American citizen. Similarly, black letter law would require the application of foreign law if a tort is committed outside the country against a Brazilian domiciled citizen (a New York newspaper published in the United States with a special report offending the image of the Brazilian President, for example).

In truth, the black letter of the ILBCC has been criticized by legal scholars. They suggest that Brazilian conflict of laws should also adopt the effects doctrine, i.e., the principle by which the applicable substantive law is that of the country where the effect was felt.[19] However, so far this suggestion still has not been adopted by the courts.

Therefore, the FAL breaks with this somewhat dated principle of applying the legal system from which the fact was originated or the conduct was committed. Also, FAL can be applied to events which occurred in other countries that present undesirable effects in Brazil. This is important because Brazilian rules on antitrust might be stricter than those of the other country in question.

One must bear in mind that these examples presume that a Brazilian court or agency would have the power to adjudicate the case (procedural jurisdiction). If the hypothetical case of insurers mentioned above was to be brought before Brazilian authorities, it would be easier for CADE to exercise its extraterritorial procedural jurisdiction than for courts to do the same. CADE already has three

---

19. Araújo, Nádia de. Direito Internacional Privado. Teoria e Prática Brasileira. Rio de Janeiro: Renovar, 2007; Dolinger, Jacob. Direito Internacional Privado. Rio de Janeiro: Renovar, 2006; Rechsteiner, Beat Walter. Direito Internacional Privado: teoria e prática. São Paulo: Saraiva, 2006.

precedents; courts do not. CADE has a more pragmatic interpretation of the law; courts are often bound by procedural discussions.

In addition, mergers and acquisitions outside Brazilian territory affecting and possibly harming the Brazilian market must be approved by CADE. In this case, even though the American antitrust agency might have approved the merger, CADE is free to decide otherwise, since the effects of the operation on the Brazilian market could be different (this is particularly relevant in cases of mergers of parent of foreign companies with subsidiaries doing business in Brazil).

As a matter of fact, CADE has proceeded in this manner in several cases. For instance, in the *Kolynos-Colgate* case (Procedure # 27/1995), Colgate Palmolive (CP) had acquired control over American Home Products (AHP) in the United States. AHP was the owner of the Kolynos trademark rights. The merger was approved in the United States. However, in Brazil, since Kolynos represented a very important share of the toothpaste market (much larger than it had at that time in the United States), CP had to enter into an agreement with CADE not to use the Kolynos trademark in Brazil in order to get for the transaction to be approved.

Any merger, acquisition, or other form of cooperation among companies (e.g., a joint venture) for which the turnover in Brazil of any of the involved companies exceeds 400 million Brazilian reais per year (R$400,000,00)—less US$200 million as of November 2008—must be submitted for review.[20]

B. Comity

According to the Brazilian Constitution (article 5, item XXXV), jurisdiction is a duty of the State. Thus, if the facts of the case are covered by article 88 of the Code of Civil Procedure (conceived originally by taking into account general principles of international comity) or by the provisions of another law (such as FAL) or the doctrinal principle of international jurisdiction, it is difficult for a court to refrain from exercising jurisdiction over the case because of a foreign proceeding or an stronger alien interest. Nothing in the legislation precludes a case from simultaneously being investigated and judged in an overseas tribunal. This form of concurrent jurisdiction would not be viewed as problematic for Brazilian courts.

Indeed, during a trial in Brazil, once the court decides to adjudicate a case, the *lis pendens* defense regarding jurisdiction would not apply[21] (Section 90 of the

20. *See, e.g.*, case 08012.002992-02004-14 from CADE (ACD Telecommunications, Inc. e Krone International Holding Inc.).

21. *Lis pendens* means parallel litigation or "suit pending"; that is, generally speaking, if one of the parties brings a second lawsuit over the same cause of action and with the same parties before a different court, the first trial prevails. According to CCP, this second trial must be immediately dismissed in favor of the first case (priority of the first judge

Code of Civil Procedure[22]). No court in Brazil would issue international anti-suit injunctions, based on any kind of balance of public or private interest, to bar the right of a foreign party to exercise its right to bring a lawsuit before a foreign court when a concurrent jurisdiction case is at stake. The only test to ascertain jurisdiction would be whether there is any legal rationale for the exercise of procedural *and* substantive jurisdiction. If this issue is answered in the positive, then the case should proceed. Because of this, there is no *forum non conveniens* doctrine in Brazil: either the Brazilian authorities have jurisdiction or they do not.

Courts will only decline jurisdiction if a foreign award is recognized within Brazilian territory, that is, after its formal recognition by Brazilian Courts (the principle of res judicata[23]). This procedure would take place in Brazil despite any cooperation agreement or bilateral treaty signed by the countries and would occur when a proper procedure of recognition is brought before the Superior Court of Justice (Section 483 of the Brazilian Code of Civil Procedure).[24]

Following Hans Kelsen's pure theory of law, political balance such as comity in the exercise of jurisdiction is normally considered a pre-legal argument in the Brazilian scholarship tradition. Thus, generally speaking, unless the rule was conceived in a broader context, such as a policy or a principle,[25] political issues are important issues for legislatures, not judges (for instance, if the CCP or FAL had stated that Brazilian courts should have jurisdiction over a case with *predominant effects* in Brazil or only when *reasonable effects* are felt in the territory). Arguments of policy are only accepted in Brazil when they can be explicitly or implicitly derived from the legal system.

Nonetheless, even though the legal system is codified (and also assuming that the language of the rules on jurisdiction were not drafted in broader terms like principles, or general terms so as to give more discretion to judges), courts are not precluded from adjudicating a case based on principles of law and policies rather than mere grammatical interpretation of the norm. This has often been the case in Constitutional cases. Like the United States and unlike Europe, in Brazil, any judge can interpret the Constitution, and the Supreme Court in Brazil serves, normally, as a recourse tribunal, controlling the application of the

---

with jurisdiction over the case). However, in international lawsuits, Section 90 of CCP states the opposite, meaning that there is no such priority of jurisdiction.

22. Section 90: "A lawsuit filed before a foreign court does not imply *lis pendens*, nor impedes that the Brazilian authority adjudicate the same cause of action."

23. Res judicata means a case has already been decided and there is no more pending recourse or discussion.

24. Section 483: "A foreign award will not have legal effects in Brazil before its official recognition before the Superior Court of Justice."

25. Brazilian legislator sometimes use a very broad language such "good faith", "social function of property", "social function of contracts", which give a high degree of judicial discretion in the interpretation of such language.

Constitution *ex post* (with a kind of writ of certiori named Extraordinary Recourse). Subsequently, in "hard cases," the principles of the Constitution that could be construed as the underpinning of the values of the rules established by the CCP or even the FAL on international jurisdiction—such as solidarity and reciprocity among nations—could be used as arguments by courts to limit or broaden the scope of these rules.

The literature agrees to some extent that at least the principles of International Public Law on sovereignty and independence of states are the basis of the rules of the Code, such as Section 483, which deals with res judicata, and also of other treaties signed by Brazil, such as some bilateral treaties on extradition.[26] By the same token, the legal literature argues that issues such as convenience and feasibility create the underpinnings of Articles 88 and 89 of the Code of Civil Procedure.[27] The former is "the interest of a State to regulate or to judge a certain conflict,"[28] and the latter is "efficacy that the judgment potentially may have,"[29] that is, the actual possibility of the judgment to be enforced. Those principles could also be applied in antitrust matters, such as when the FAL is at stake. Because principles and policies can be used as legal reasoning in courts, it is arguable that the ideas of comity, convenience, and efficiency could all be used to solve international jurisdiction conflicts in cases where the mere application of the rules might result in unfairness or unconstitutionality ("hard cases").

Another possible argument to limit the jurisdiction of Brazilian authorities can be found in the principle of the rule of reason behind the FAL. Since Section 2 of the FAL requires effects in Brazil, one might argue that courts or agencies should take into account only significant or reasonable effects. These arguments would bar jurisdiction with the advantage of avoiding the muddy and uncertain problems of the comity test and the problems of the lack of *lis pendens*.

Since there is no leading case in this matter to illustrate how this idea could be presented in court, we can assume, from a theoretical point of view at least, that the best strategy for tackling the problem of the conflict of laws and jurisdictions in antitrust matters would probably be to convince the courts to refrain from the exercise of their constitutional duty to adjudicate in situations where the harm or potential harm to the domestic market is to be considered irrelevant. If the event did not occur in Brazil, or if the effects were not felt in Brazil, then the court simply lacks jurisdiction. It does not mean that by having jurisdiction over the case a Brazilian court would somehow waive its adjudication power to a foreign court because it has more interest in the case. To deny jurisdiction (*non liquet*) or access to justice to a plaintiff would be a problem in Brazil.

---

26. Lima e Silva, *op. cit.*, p. 351.
27. Carneiro, Athos Gusmão. "Jurisdição e Competência." São Paulo: Saraiva, 1993.
28. Lima e Silva, *op. cit.*, p. 351.
29. Lima e Silva, *op. cit.*, p. 351.

Most likely, the second best argument would be to produce evidence that the effectiveness of the judgment is grossly at risk and that no interest of Brazilian authorities is at stake (because there is neither an agent, a representative, nor assets in Brazil, and the chance of recognition of the judgment in a foreign court would be minimal). And probably the most unconvincing argument would be to balance the constitutional principles of access to justice and *non liquet* with specific principles of the Constitution such as solidarity and comity among nations.

The peculiarities of an antitrust lawsuit make the possibility of comity considerations more remote, since each market has it own characteristic and structure. It is difficult to assess in a mere procedural discussion with respect to jurisdiction (without getting to the merits of the case) which market was more affected. Besides, the fact that Microsoft, for instance, settled the case with the U.S. government does not mean that judges in Brazil would take this ruling into consideration. Plus, in Brazil, the subject of antitrust is regarded as a matter of public policy and *ordre publique*. Comity is already a very unusual argument in Brazilian procedural legal culture, but its use by a judge as a basis to bar the exercise of jurisdiction would be near nonsense. So, in our example, if the reinsurers are conspiring in the United States to limit competition in Brazil, it would be difficult to find a judge who would waive his power to adjudicate the case because of the stronger interests of the U.S. government. This analysis would be strikingly odd for Brazilian legal culture. However, the court would dismiss the case because of its lack of significant effects in Brazil, not because of a balance-of-interests test.

Those problems of conflict of jurisdiction would be simpler with respect to administrative agencies (SDE/CADE) since, as we have seen, they are not part of the Brazilian judicial system and thus are not bound by procedural rules such as *non liquet*, access to justice, and other principles (or even dogmas), which were so carefully added to the text of the democratic Constitution of 1988.

It is probably simpler to convince any governmental agency that to investigate a practice that occurred elsewhere with insignificant effects in Brazil is of no interest to the Brazilian government. But again, as stated above, any administrative decision to do so would be subject to judicial review. In addition, we can foresee that it would be easier for a member of the Executive branch (such as SDE/CADE) to hear the Minister of Foreign Affairs, or to find a balance between the consequence of its decision and the foreign policy of the country, or at least to take into account diplomatic or political arguments. The Judiciary could face this situation in the form of lack of impartiality or undue influence of the Executive (compromising the separation of powers and its "checks and balances"). Actually, it is rare for a court to heed the opinion of the Executive branch or some other amicus curiae (though this is changing, especially in environmental class actions).

II. COOPERATION IN INTERNATIONAL JURISDICTION

Again, in this section one must draw a line between judicial proceedings (A) and administrative proceedings (B).

A. Judicial Cooperation in Brazil

In court cases, the Code of Civil Procedure (CCP) provides the legal foundation for cooperation among courts. Article 483 of the CCP permits Brazilian authorities to recognize foreign judgments as long as they comply with certain formal and narrow requirements (essentially, due process of law).[30] Indeed, by recognizing a foreign award (a specific lawsuit must be brought before the Brazilian Superior Court of Justice), the Court would not fully consider the merits of the case; it would simply verify if Brazilian public policy was respected by the foreign court. According to the leading cases, public policy involves looking to certain procedural rules and determining whether the defendant was served in accordance with Brazilian legal system, if both parties had the right to present a defense and to produce evidence, and if the award was issued by a court with jurisdiction over the case. Public policy also means that a foreign judgment should not offend the basic notions of fairness and justice which are normally derived from the Brazilian Constitution, such as the prohibition of capital punishment, life prison sentences, imprisonment in civil cases, and so forth.

Another means of judicial cooperation is to respond to requests from foreign courts. Section 201 of the CCP provides for compliance with letters rogatory issued by foreign courts. A letter rogatory or letter of request is the principle legal means under civil law systems such as Brazil's by which a court may carry out a process outside of its territorial jurisdiction. It is a formal communication between domestic and foreign courts by which a judge requests the cooperation of another court in order to serve a foreign defendant, to produce evidence, or to practice any other kind of procedural act necessary for the advancement of the domestic trial. As a matter of fact, there is no other way to serve a foreign defendant but with a letter rogatory.[31] It has now been accepted that even preliminary injunctions can be executed by means of letters rogatory. The underlying idea is reciprocity. By cooperating with foreign courts, Brazilian courts expect the same treatment.

---

30. Recently, the Superior Court of Justice issued a Resolution # 9 of 2005 to establish the procedure for recognition of foreign awards.

31. U.S. methods of serving foreign defendants, such as giving formal notice by mail or by the lawyer (via affidavit) or by seizure of assets, are not practiced nor accepted in Brazil. Consequently, Brazilian courts may not recognize decisions such as *Banco do Commercio e Industria de Sao Paolo S.A v Esusa Engenharia e Construcoes, S.A.*, 173 A.D.2d 340, 341 (N.Y. App. Div. 1991).

The exchange of documents (letters of request) among courts is normally controlled by the Brazilian Foreign Affairs Department or by the Ministry of Justice, depending on whether Brazil has a Bilateral Cooperation Protocol (BCP) or a Multipart Convention (such as the Inter-American Convention on Letters Rogatory from the Organization of American States, 1975) with the requesting authority. The Ministry of Justice is the central authority for international procedure cooperation in cases where Brazil has the BCP.[32] These BCPs normally have more or less the same language—the best efforts of each nation to cooperate with the other and, among other things, create obligations to help the other authority to serve a party and to produce evidence in favor of a requesting authority. The execution of a letter rogatory *(exequatur)* in Brazil also depends on a formal authorization from the Superior Court of Justice. This is so because Brazilian judges might not cooperate with lawsuits that offend the public policy, as explained above.

Common lawyers must be aware that cooperation will ensue in accordance with Brazilian procedural rules of the CCP. As a result, the production of documents will have a much lesser scope if compared to discovery procedures in the U.S. legal system.[33] Also, depositions of witnesses would be proceed pursuant to the Brazilian CCP. For instance, in Brazil, cross examination is different than in the United States, and Brazilian trial judges have much more control over attorneys (in some cases, judges might not allow direct questions to the witnesses). The use of expert witnesses also works differently in Brazil: experts, as in other civil law systems, are nominated by the court—not by the parties—in order to guarantee impartiality.

This is also the case in antitrust trials. Brazilian courts can be receptive to foreign parties or courts wishing to serve a Brazilian defendant[34] or to produce evidence of facts (testimony, experts) occurring in Brazilian territory, even in cases where there is parallel litigation.

---

32. This is also the case with Portugal, Spain, France, Italy, Argentina, and Uruguay.

33. Section 844 of the CCP states that the party that demands the exhibition of a certain document in possession of the other party or even of a third party might ask for it by means of an injunction to a court. Thus, in Brazil, production of documents in court has a much narrower scope than discovery in the United States. Everything is mediated by the judge, and the party must ask for specific documents to be presented in court. Also, the consequence for failure to produce documents is not as clear in Brazil as it is in the United States in cases of contempt of court.

34. The only acceptable way to serve a foreign defendant according to Brazilian procedural law is by means of a letter rogatory. The methods of service within the U.S. legal system are disregarded in Brazil. If a Brazilian defendant is not duly served by an alien court, the Brazilian Superior Court of Justice will not recognize the foreign award if the Brazilian citizen did not spontaneously present his defense.

B. Cooperation Agreements among Antitrust Agencies

From an international cooperation perspective, administrative proceedings from CADE are regulated not by the Code of Civil Procedure (CCP), but by the Federal Law of Administrative Procedure (Law 9784 of 1999). Thus, the quoted articles of the CCP regarding judicial cooperation on letters rogatory and recognition of foreign awards do not apply directly, but only in a subsidiary form. Since there is no court-to-court relationship based on the CCP or treaties, and because CADE/SDE are part of the Executive Branch of the Government, CADE/SDE must enter into cooperative agreements with other agencies in order to exchange information, evidence, and so forth.

Lately, as the result of the internationalization of the Brazilian economy, CADE and SDE have been investing in a cooperative global approach. Both have joined the International Competition Network (ICN), more specifically the Competition Policy Implementation (CPI) and the Cartels Working Groups.[35] The ICN was created in October 2001 by 14 antitrust agencies worldwide with the goal of not only promoting global convergence in antitrust law, but also of creating an independent forum to discuss competition policies. It resulted from a proposal made by the International Competition Policy Advisory Committee (ICPAC) in the United States, with consent from the EU Commission. Since then, CADE has adopted the merger template suggested by ICN in order to inform economic agents of the procedure of a merger notification.[36] SDE is adopting the ICN cartels template and recently has dedicated much time to tackling cartels (including those formed overseas but with effects in Brazil, as discussed above).

CADE also has been involved in the discussions of the Organisation for Economic Co-operation and Development (OECD) on competition law and policies, and has been making an effort to adopt the recommendations of this international body.[37] Also, CADE is apparently taking into consideration the studies and recommendations of the United National Conference on Trade and Development (UNCTAD) on competition laws and policies.[38]

CADE has also entered into cooperation agreements with Argentina, Portugal, the United States, Canada, and Russia. Basically, they all have the same wording: mutual obligations to share information with respect to procedures and investigations of each antitrust agency that might affect the interest of the other party of the agreement; to exchange information and data; to engage in mutual

---

35. http://www.cade.gov.br/Internacional/ICN.pdf.
36. http://www.cade.gov.br/internacional/ICN_Merger_Template_2005.pdf.
37. http://www.cade.gov.br/Internacional/oecd2008.asp.e.
38. http://www.cade.gov.br/internacional/UNCTAD.pdf.

training; and to attempt to avoid jurisdiction and investigation conflicts among agencies.[39]

For instance, the Cooperation Agreement between Brazil and the United States, which can be considered a template for other agreements signed by Brazilian antitrust authorities (such as the one with Canada), aims to "promote the cooperation among the antitrust agencies of the Parties, including the cooperation in the application of antitrust laws, as well as technical cooperation, and also to make sure that both Parties of the Agreement will assure that reciprocal relevant interests will be taken into account in the application of their competition laws."

The Agreement also requires that the agencies of the Parties promptly notify their investigations about significant conduct occurring in the territory of the other Party, or mergers and acquisitions involving a company incorporated according to the laws of the other Party, or even practices related to or approved by the other Party, among other things.

Its language also states that both Parties agree that "it is in their common interest to cooperate so as to identify anticompetitive practices and to the application of their competition laws, besides of the cooperation to share information that will facilitate the application of these laws and to promote the best understanding of the policies and activities of each Party."

Parties to the Agreement agree to the preservation of their markets from anticompetitive practices. They also acknowledge that they should be protected from conduct occurring in the other Party's territory that might affect the interest of the other Party (in the preservation of its market). If one of the Parties believes that conduct occurring in another Party's territory is affecting its interest, it might demand that the other Party investigate such practices. The agreement provides the procedure for this request. It also states that the Parties will retain jurisdiction over the subject matter in spite of any investigation request to the other Party.

The Agreement provides that the agencies of the Parties will consider the convenience of the coordination activities when interrelated practices are investigated. In any coordinated activity, each Party should take into consideration the objectives of the other. Finally, each Party assumes the obligation to balance the relevant interests of the other Party when investigating a practice connected to the other Party.

On a truly international scale, Brazil, along with other MERCOSUR members, is part of a Competition Law Protocol adopted in 1996 (Fortaleza Protocol[40]). This Protocol aims to regulate the commerce within the MERCOSUR borders. For this purpose, this Protocol created a Competition Defense Committee (CDC)

---

39. *See, e.g.,* http://www.cade.gov.br/internacional/Cooperation_Arrangement.pdf (Canada/Brazil Agreement).

40. http://www.cade.gov.br/internacional/Protocolo_de_Ouro_Preto.pdf.

formed by the antitrust agencies of the four member states and connected to the Commerce Commission of MERCOSUR. The idea was to create a truly regional body of antitrust law within the borders of MERCOSUR to be put in practice whenever the commerce among the Member States is at stake or an abuse of economic power occurs within these countries' relevant markets. In those cases, national antitrust agencies must cooperate with the CDC, investigating the facts according to the instructions of the CDC. After a preliminary report from the national antitrust agency, the CDC must reach a consensual decision. If the CDC does not reach a consensus, the case must be referred to a consensual Directive from the Commerce Commission and then adopted by the Member States. However, this Protocol has not been implemented yet since Paraguay still lacks an antitrust agency to form the CDC.

An example of how the application of all the precedent cooperation agreements by CADE is actually working is Administrative Proceeding # 08012.001885-2007-11, by which CADE refused to approve a merger of Saint Gobain with Owens Corning because of the risks of concentration within the Brazilian market of glass manufacture (and others), in addition to informing the other antitrust agencies from MERCOSUR the outcome of the proceedings before CADE.

Finally, due to the presence of economists on its staff (who often obtain their doctorate degrees in the United States), and because of CADE's specialization in antitrust law (in which the United States plays a prominent role in theory and practice), U.S. precedent (and European, to a lesser extent) might seem highly persuasive; but even so, CADE would not refrain from judging a case adapted to the Brazilian market (normally with less competition than the U.S. market).

On the contrary, experience has shown that SDE relies on U.S. court convictions to open an investigation in order to assess the effects of the conduct on the Brazilian market. Evidence gathered by EU and U.S. agencies has been used as a source and probable alternative to the insufficient number of technicians needed to cover all the necessary investigations abroad, as shown above.

CONCLUSION

Brazilian antitrust law accepts the extraterritoriality of its rules based on the test of the effects doctrine. Those laws can be applied by judicial or administrative proceedings pursuant to the procedural rules of international jurisdiction of domestic authorities. Therefore, conduct overseas that affects the Brazilian market can be investigated, and the foreign companies that are responsible can be sued in Brazil (served by their subsidiaries, agents, or representatives located in Brazil or even served abroad by means of a letter rogatory). Also, mergers that have an impact on Brazil must be approved by the Brazilian antitrust agency, which is particularly relevant for transnational firms with branches in Brazil.

The limitation for this extraterritoriality is not clearly stated by the black letter of the law, nor has it been decided by any relevant precedent or administrative guideline. Theoretically, those limits could either be defended based on the rule of reason test, by which a court or agency should only take into consideration actual or potential harm to the market (therefore irrelevant effects in the Brazilian market could lead to a lack of jurisdiction over the case), or founded on the general principles of international law with some constitutional linkage (such as solidarity among nations) or in some specific doctrinal principles of the Brazilian international jurisdiction rules as developed by legal scholars (such as convenience and viability) that form the theoretical underpinning of the rules on international jurisdiction of Brazilian authorities found in the Code of Civil Procedure.

In a balancing test of national interests and of comity among nations, the best approach is to change the text of federal antitrust law in order to leave its language broader, including some wording on principles of comity.

The Brazilian antitrust agency, the Conselho Administrativo de Defesa Econômica (CADE) and the investigatory governmental body, the Secretaria de Direito Econômico (SDE) have entered into bilateral cooperation agreements with some of Brazil's major economic partners, such as the members of MERCOSUR (the common market of the south involving Brazil, Argentina, Paraguay, and Uruguay), which was inspired by the European Community Market (ECM), the United States, Canada, and Portugal for purposes of exchanging information and maintaining a mutual understanding regarding the relevant interests of all parties whenever applying their competition laws in an international context. However, in any of those bilateral agreements, jurisdiction would be *a priori* constrained. In addition, the same agreementsy are also part of international discussion groups on competition law and policy, such as ICN.

However, more than this exchange of information and bilateral or multilateral commitments, to take into consideration other countries' interest would mean to loose a fraction of sovereignty. For this to happen, a supranational entity that would take that fraction of sovereignty and work in an unbiased way for the sake of commerce—or at least for nondomestic interests—is needed. The difficulty experienced by countries when giving up their jurisdiction was evidenced by the Hague Convention on Choice of Court Agreements (2005), in which "the elephant gave birth to a mouse,"[41]—originally conceived as a treaty on international jurisdiction, the Convention resulted in an agreement concerning the validity of the choice of forum clause.

41. The expression was used by Talpis in Jeffrey Talpis and Nick Krnjevic, *The Hague Convention on Choice of Court Agreements of June 30, 2005: The Elephant that Gave Birth to a Mouse*, 13 Sw. J.L. & Trade Am. 1 at 19, n.102 (2006).

5. COOPERATION, COMITY, AND COMPETITION POLICY

Japan

NAOKI OHKUBO* AND ZENICHI SHISHIDO**

INTRODUCTION

In the United States, whose antitrust laws have been regarded as a point of reference for discussing topics arising under the Antimonopoly Law of Japan (AML),[1] competition law commentators and practitioners start a lively discussion about prescriptive jurisdiction of competition law as soon as they see the word "extraterritorial application." It would be no exaggeration to say that only the prescriptive jurisdiction of U.S. antitrust laws and related matters, including comity, are covered in antitrust law textbooks and casebooks under the heading "extraterritorial application."[2] The authors understand that the focus on prescriptive jurisdiction in the United States is due to the wide authority that U.S. competition authorities are granted with regard to enforcement jurisdiction.[3]

The situation in Japan is somewhat different. In Japan, where actions for damages and injunction suits have been sporadic until recently,[4] the Japan Fair Trade Commission (JFTC) has played the leading role in enforcing the

---

* Naoki Ohkubo is on the Faculty of Law at Gakushuin University.

** Zenichi Shishido is Professor of Law at the Graduate School of International Corporate Strategy, Hitotsubashi University.

1. Act concerning Prohibition of Private Monopolization and Maintenance of Fair Trade. The English translation of the Antimonopoly Law is available at the Web site of the JFTC: http://www.jftc.go.jp/e-page/index.html.

2. *See, e.g.*, Lawrence A. Sullivan & Warren S. Grimes, The Law of Antitrust: An Integrated Handbook Ch. XVIII (2000); Phillip Areeda et al., Antitrust Cases (6th ed. 2004); Mark S. Popofsky, *Extraterritoriality in U.S. Jurisprudence, in* ABA Section of Antitrust Law, Issues in Competition Law & Policy 2417 (2008).

3. Einer Elhauge & Damien Geradin, Global Competition Law and Economics 1015 (2007) states, "Because creating any anticompetitive market effect suffices to create minimum contacts and foreign firms are generally subject to service for other purposes, in practice this is not much of a bar to exercising personal jurisdiction over foreign firms." *See also* Richard Whish, Competition Law 476 (6th ed. 2009).

4. It was only after 2001 that an individual became able to seek injunctions by law against an act in violation of the Antimonopoly Law. Under Article 24, only unfair trade practices, as defined in Article 2(9), can be the subject of an injunction order. An injunction order against private monopolization and unreasonable restraint of trade prohibited under Article 3 is not permitted.

AML.[5] For the JFTC, enforcement jurisdiction—not prescriptive jurisdiction—must be the primary issue when applying the AML to international cases. As explained in one of the sections below, enforcement jurisdiction of the AML before the amendment in 2002 was limited, and the JFTC had to be careful not to overstep the authority entrusted to it. Seen from the perspective of entrepreneurs[6] who are subject to AML regulation, it was much easier to contest and overturn JFTC's holdings with regard to enforcement jurisdiction. Readers could easily find early cases in which the JFTC discontinued the formal proceedings for lack of enforcement jurisdiction.

When enforcement jurisdiction could be established, on the other hand, there was little incentive for entrepreneurs to challenge the arguments put forward by the JFTC about prescriptive jurisdiction because the sanctions imposed on violators under the AML were not so severe. It was the amendment in 1977 that authorized the JFTC to issue surcharge payment orders against entrepreneurs participating in conduct such as cartels or bid-riggings. Prior to the amendment, the JFTC was limited to ordering infringers to cease and desist from illegal conduct. Even after the introduction of the surcharge system, its scope and effectiveness were limited in that only activities such as cartels and bid-rigging were subject to the surcharge, and the amount of the surcharge was no more than 3 percent of the sale price of the relevant goods or services.[7]

Before the administrative procedure was reformed in 2005, the first step the JFTC took when it discovered illegal activities was to recommend that the infringers take appropriate measures to cease the violations.[8] The JFTC would not initiate a formal hearing procedure until the addressee rejected the recommendation. Because of the limited enforcement jurisdiction, foreign companies with critical interests in cases were not necessarily made the addressees. Even when they were addressed, the most rational choice was to accept the recommendation as it stood because surcharge payment—even when imposed—was relatively small, while a formal hearing procedure necessitated time and money. As a consequence, most cases ended with a recommendation decision that substantively the same as the recommendation. No one would insist that legal opinions contained in recommendation decisions are as calculated as judgments written by U.S. judges after hearing a series of arguments and counterarguments.

It should be clear from the foregoing paragraphs that describing only prescriptive jurisdiction is not enough to get the whole picture of extraterritorial

---

5. Many commentators refer to this as "JFTC-centrism."

6. According to Article 2(1) of the AML, the term "entrepreneur" means a person who operates a commercial, industrial, financial, or any other business.

7. The percentage was increased to 6 percent in 1991 and to 10 percent in 2005. As the amount of surcharge payment was increased, the number of entrepreneurs contesting cease and desist orders and surcharge payment orders also increased.

8. Concerning the administrative enforcement system of the AML, see Masako Wakui, Antimonopoly Law 281–93 (2008).

application of the AML. Even if the statement accepting the effects doctrine was contained in a decision, that statement did not necessarily mean that the AML was enforced against foreign companies without any presence in Japan. Therefore, in this paper, the authors would also like to give an account of enforcement jurisdiction.

In Section 1 below, famous cases in the context of prescriptive jurisdiction are introduced and analyzed. Section 2 addresses enforcement jurisdiction, describing how the JFTC's authority had been limited and was expanded by the 2002 amendment. Lastly, we would like to touch upon international cooperative agreements between Japan and other countries.

The focus of all the sections in this paper is what positions the JFTC—not the courts—has taken regarding extraterritorial application of the AML. Until a decade ago, courts played a minor role in enforcing the AML because, as stated above, the addressees of a JFTC's decision rarely filed an appeal with the Tokyo High Court to rescind the decision. In addition, only a handful of people have directly claimed compensation for damages or have sought an injunction against an alleged violation.

I. PRESCRIPTIVE JURISDICTION

This section first explores a topic of interest to competition law practitioners and commentators around the world—that is, under what principle do competition authorities apply competition law to international cases. After clarifying that, we proceed to how comity is taken into account in enforcement of the AML.

A. Principles for Prescriptive Jurisdiction

1. Principles Prevalent in Early Cases In most of the early cases mentioned in Japanese textbooks and casebooks under the heading of extraterritorial application, Article 6 was applied. The article states, "No entrepreneur shall enter into an international agreement or an international contract which contains such matters as fall under unreasonable restraint of trade or unfair trade practices." Article 6(2) prior to the 1997 amendment required entrepreneurs to notify the JFTC when they entered into an international agreement or contract, so it must have been much easier for the JFTC to detect violations.

A bird's-eye view of the early cases suggests that in the early days, the JFTC did not direct its attention whether Japanese customers were adversely affected by the agreement or contract. The JFTC applied the AML to a case in which Japanese companies participated in an agreement or a contract involving more than one territory, such as an agreement between foreign companies or one concerned with the cross-border transfer of goods, services. technologies, capitals, and so forth. In the next two paragraphs, we will analyze the oft-cited early cases.

The 1972 *Rayon Yarn* case[9] is the most well known among the early cases. In that case, the JFTC regulated an international market allocation agreement between three Japanese manufacturers and eleven European manufacturers. The Japanese manufacturers would not export their products to the western part of Europe and vice versa; the Japanese manufacturers and the European ones divided the markets other than Europe, Japan and the United States into several regions, setting the minimum prices in each region. Indeed, this agreement adversely affected the Japanese rayon yarn customers because the agreement kept European manufacturers from supplying their products in Japan. However, the recommendation decision by the JFTC did not express that concern and only stated that the agreement caused a substantial restraint of competition in the field of exporting rayon yarn to the relevant regions. Under this recommendation decision, it would be possible to insist that under the AML, European customers were entitled to claim damages from the participants in Japanese courts.

The *Soda Ash* case in 1983[10] is also worth mentioning. In that case, the JFTC enforced the AML without showing that the conduct in question imposed a harmful effect on the Japanese market. The decision prohibited an agreement that four Japanese manufacturers had reached for the purpose of limiting the amount of soda ash imported from the United States. The JFTC's main concern in the case was that the agreement prevented competitive pricing in the Japanese soda ash market by limiting the supply. However, in the decision, the JFTC did not mention what harmful impact the agreement had on Japanese customers, and only held that the agreement adversely affected transactions with U.S. manufacturers (sellers).

These two cases demonstrate the early approach adopted by the JFTC as to extraterritorial application of the AML: the JFTC applied the AML to cross-border cases as long as Japanese entrepreneurs were involved in those cases, without confirming that Japanese customers were adversely affected by the conduct in question. Later, the AML was sometimes applied based on the same approach, and some commentators are trying to provide the justification for such application. For example, in the famous *Vitamin Cartel* case, the JFTC issued a warning to two Japanese chemical companies based on their suspicion that the two companies had agreed to restrict their participants' output, which had adversely affected customers around the world.[11]

9. Decision on recommendation, Dec. 27, 1972, 19 Shinketsu-shu 124.

10. Decision on recommendation, Mar. 31, 1983, 29 Shinketsu-shu 104. When this decision was issued, the surcharge payment system was already introduced, but agreements between buyers were not subject to surcharge payments. As a result of the amendment in 2005, buyer cartels became subject to a surcharge payment.

11. Warning, Apr. 5, 2001. Unlike the warning itself, an unofficial explanatory note written by some JFTC officials on the case implies that the JFTC was concerned only with

It should be noted that Section 6, which was invoked quite often in the early days, applies in recent cases. Some commentators argue that the application of Section 6 in this context can be justified in terms of international cooperation. Nowadays, the raison d'être for Article 6 is questioned because Article 6 is no different from other main provisions[12] after an international agreement or an international contract containing such matters that fall under unreasonable restraint of trade were made subject to surcharge payments in 1977, and the notification system was abolished in 1997. While it is often argued that Article 6 should be abolished, some commentators point out the significance of Article 6 in the following respect.

According to some commentators, Article 6 is the only provision applicable to a cartel case in which the victimized customers are located outside Japan. The main provisions in the AML, including Section 3, should not be applied to the case because today it is agreed almost all over the world that competition law in each jurisdiction should regulate illegal conduct only when and so long as the conduct adversely affects customers within that jurisdiction (although there is disagreement about whether effects alone are enough for application). On the other hand, however, there is also universal consensus that—under whichever competition law—price-fixing and bid-rigging should be prohibited. Some commentators argue that application of Article 6 in this context demonstrates commitment to the universal consensus without deviating from its application based on effects within the territory.[13]

---

an adverse effect within Japan. The officials stated in the note that the case ended with a warning, and not a formal decision, partly because it was impossible to prove a harmful effect on Japanese customers.

12. The main provisions of the AML are Article 3 and Article 19. These provisions prohibit private monopolization, unreasonable restraint of trade, and unfair trade practices, each of which are modeled after Sections 2 and 1 of the Sherman Act and Section 5 of the Federal Trade Commission (FTC) Act.

13. This argument reminds the authors of an explanation that can be observed in the context of the business combination regulation in the AML.

Some commentators explain that the JFTC investigates whether the business combination in question has a negative impact on the global market. Problematically, these commentators never identify the exact meaning of the term "global market," but some of the commentators imply by this word a market that consists not only of customers within Japan, but also the ones outside Japan. According to this explanation, not only Article 6 but also the business combination regulation address the harmful effects on consumers outside Japan.

However, the authors are of the opinion that this explanation is based on a complete misunderstanding of the relevant documents, including Guidelines to Application of the Antimonopoly Act Concerning Review of Business Combination (May 31, 2004, Japan Fair Trade Commission, revised as of May 1, 2006, revised as of Mar. 28, 2007). The relevant sections of the guidelines state as follows

However, the authors cannot agree with the above argument. As already mentioned, after several amendments, Article 6 is comparable to Article 3 in that both provisions dispense with the notification system and impose surcharge payment obligations on entrepreneurs who engage in conduct that is considered to be unreasonable restraint of trade. We cannot comprehend why application of Article 6 is justified in cases to which Article 3 should not be applicable.

2. Nordion Case (1998) and Thereafter It is generally agreed that recently, the JFTC is concentrating its attentions on an adverse effect caused by illegal conduct within Japanese markets. The *Nordion* case[14] is refereed to as an example in nearly all AML textbooks and casebooks. In other words, this case is often cited for the proposition that the JFTC finally accepted the effects doctrine. The respondent in the case was Nordion Inc., a Canadian corporation. Nordion had concluded contracts with two Japanese companies, which included provisions that all products had to be purchased from Nordion. The JFTC held that this exclusive dealing arrangement violated the AML by restraining competition in the Japanese marketplace. However, it was also recognized that the order stated that the place of the contract was Tokyo. Therefore, it is fair to say that this case still left unanswered the question whether the AML was applicable on the basis of effects on a Japanese market alone.

In the *BHP Billiton and Rio Tinto* case in 2008,[15] the JFTC might have intended to provide a final answer to the question. The JFTC commenced a formal investigation into the proposed acquisition by BHP Billiton of Rio Tinto's shares based on the suspicion that the acquisition would have substantially restrained competition in some fields of trade in Japan. Without relying on the effects doctrine, it must have been difficult for the JFTC to intervene in this case because

---

> If users inside and outside a territory usually purchase a certain product irrespective of whether the geographic location of suppliers is inside or outside the territory, even if the price of the product is raised in Japan, it is possible that the price increase will be prevented because users in Japan can substitute purchases from overseas producers for purchases of the product in Japan. In this situation, the geographic range is defined as crossing national borders.

3 in Part II.

Although the last sentence certainly refers to a possibility that the range of marketplaces may be delineated internationally across the border, if the section is read as a whole, it is clear that it simply refers to a case where foreign suppliers are also taken into consideration when deciding the range of the marketplace if Japanese customers substitute Japanese suppliers with foreign suppliers in case of a price increase. This is completely different from defining the range of the marketplace by taking into account customers both inside and outside the country. The guidelines can also be construed as being in agreement with the position that only Japanese customers are taken into consideration.

14. Decision on recommendation, Sept. 3, 1998, 45 Shinketsu-shu 148.

15. On the JFTC's Web site, readers can view a press release published by the JFTC when it closed its investigation into the proposed acquisition after the relevant parties abandoned the plan. http://www.jftc.go.jp/e-page/pressreleases/2008/December/081203.pdf.

neither BHP Billiton nor Rio Tinto has any footholds in Japan.[16] However, there was no authoritative decision released on the case because the relevant parties abandoned the acquisition plan before the JFTC came to a conclusion. The analysis of this case from the point of enforcement jurisdiction will be covered in the next section.

We would like to conclude this subsection with a topic which is at the center of attention in the United States: what magnitude and type of effect within Japan's territory is necessary in order for competition law to apply to matters involving foreign commerce. If the AML is applicable to international cases based on effects in Japan, the AML must also answer this question.

The authors think the answer to this question is not so complicated as it is in the United States. In Japan, there are no independent provisions prescribing the reach of the main substantive provisions, or specifying that conduct falls within the AML only if the effects on Japanese commerce are "direct, substantial, and reasonably foreseeable." Therefore, the question is inseparable from the question about the meaning of "substantial restraint of competition" under Article 2(5) and 2(6) or "tendency to impede fair competition" under Article 2(9). Whether the relevant cases have an international dimension or not, the conduct is subject to regulation by the AML when the conduct substantially restrains competition or has a tendency to impede fair competition. This is fundamentally the answer to the question in Japan, and we would need an entire treatise to explain the concepts that form the basic answer.

We just add two things to the above answer. First of all, some readers might ask whether the AML is applicable to a case in which the alleged infringer did not expect that the conduct would adversely affect Japanese markets. The classic answer to this question is "yes" as far as enforcement by the JFTC is concerned.[17] It is generally accepted that the intent of cease and desist orders is not to punish the relevant entrepreneurs, but to eliminate the violation in order to ensure fair and free competition. While it is difficult to find the rationale for imposing criminal sanctions on persons without malice or negligence, issuing an administrative order against entrepreneurs who are not at fault can be justified because it certainly fulfills the intent or leads to the elimination of violations whether the entrepreneurs are at fault or not. Therefore, subjective intent is not regarded as a requirement for the JFTC to issue orders.

---

16. The amendment in 1998 made the business combination regulation applicable to "foreign corporations" (Article 9 (2)). Since then, several cases regarding mergers between foreign corporations have been contemplated by the JFTC. However, in those cases, at least one of the relevant parties had established subsidiaries in Japan, so there were no cases in which only a harmful effect arises in Japan.

17. According to the general principles in the Civil Code and the Penal Code in Japan, subjective intent is a requisite for damages claims and criminal punishment.

However, some commentators point out the difficulty of maintaining this traditional answer about surcharge payment orders. Some argue that a surcharge payment order is issued by the JFTC, an administrative body, and not by criminal courts; but because the order to pay a surcharge is no different from punishment, a surcharge should not be imposed on entrepreneurs who do not intend to commit an illegal conduct.

Second, readers must remember that the JFTC is permitted to issue a warning even when the effects produced by the conduct in question do not reach the level required under Article 2(5), 2(6), or 2(9). Although a warning is not accompanied by any sanctions, it can in fact force entrepreneurs who are concerned with their reputation to cease and desist from performing the conduct in question.

B. Comity

We have thus far analyzed the issues that determine whether an international case is within prescriptive jurisdiction of the AML. In this subsection, we will discuss whether the legal system or enforcement activities of a foreign state can influence such decision-making processes. As in other sections, our attention here is focused on enforcement by the JFTC.

As we have stated repeatedly, only a few entrepreneurs have challenged the JFTC's decisions to clarify the basic principle defining the AML's prescriptive jurisdiction, and still fewer have challenged the AML's comity considerations. As far as we know, there are no JFTC orders or judgments addressing comity. Provisions such as those contained in bilateral agreements with the government of the United States[18] are the only statements that can be found in Japan with regard to comity.

The first paragraph of Article 6 in the agreement with the United States specifies as follows: "Each Party shall give careful consideration to the important interests of the other Party throughout all phases of its enforcement activities, including decisions regarding the initiation of enforcement activities, the scope of enforcement activities and the nature of penalties or relief sought in each case." The next paragraph of Article 6(3) identifies the following factors that should be considered carefully: (a) the relative significance to the anticompetitive activities of conduct or transactions occurring within the territory of the country of the enforcing Party as compared to conduct or transactions occurring within the territory of the other country; (b) the relative impact of the anticompetitive activities on the important interests of the respective Parties; (c) the presence or absence of evidence of intent on the part of those engaged in the anticompetitive activities to affect consumers, suppliers, or competitors within the territory of

18. Similar articles are also contained in the agreements with the European Union and Canada.

the country of the Party conducting the enforcement activities; (d) the extent to which the anticompetitive activities substantially lessen competition in the market of each country; (e) the degree of conflict or consistency between the enforcement activities by a Party and the laws of the other country, or the policies or important interests of the other Party; (f) whether private persons, either natural or legal, will be placed under conflicting requirements by both Parties; (g) the location of relevant assets and parties to the transaction; (h) the degree to which effective penalties or relief can be secured by the enforcement activities of the Party against the anticompetitive activities; and (i) the extent to which enforcement activities by the other Party with respect to the same persons, either natural or legal, would be affected.

However, prior to the time the parties entered into agreements containing the above provision, the JFTC sometimes took comity into consideration. In exercising its discretionary power to take on cases in which it will enforce Japanese competition laws and craft the language of its orders, the JFTC does take foreign legal systems into consideration.

For instance, the authors are aware that approximately a quarter century ago (in the mid-1980s)—when Japanese products flooded the global market—Japanese manufacturers, at the request of some of the countries and manufacturers in those countries, entered into an agreement to set the maximum amount they would export to certain countries. Under the principle employed by the JFTC at that time, this agreement restricting competition in the field of export transactions was within prescriptive jurisdiction of the AML. However, to the best of our knowledge, the JFTC did not take any action against these manufacturers. One cannot tell from cases how, when determining the outcome of the cases, the JFTC weighs factors such as those enumerated in the relevant provisions of the cooperative agreement. But it can be argued that sometimes the JFTC does not enforce the AML when the enforcement overlaps with that of other jurisdictions.

II. ENFORCEMENT JURISDICTION

The existence of prescriptive jurisdiction with regard to conduct is a necessary condition for application of the AML, but it is not sufficient. It is generally accepted in public international law that a State is not allowed to enforce the law in question within another State's territory without that State's permission. In one word, the JFTC[19] must have not only prescriptive jurisdiction but also enforcement jurisdiction in relation to international cases. In this section, we

19. Also in this section, we would like to focus our attention on the JFTC. One of the reasons is that, as stated in the Introduction, the role of courts in enforcing the AML has not been so influential. The second reason is that treaties and other rules utilized in court procedures are more developed than the relevant provisions in the AML.

would like to describe how enforcement jurisdiction was limited before the 2002 amendment and how it was expanded in 2002 after the amendment.

1. **Before the 2002 Amendment** In terms of enforcement jurisdiction, there was a fatal flaw in the Antimonopoly Law prior to its amendment in 2002. The AML requires the JFTC to send procedurally important documents to the addressees. For instance, Article 49(2) says: "A cease and desist order shall take effect by serving a transcript of the written cease and desist order to the addressee thereof." Therefore, the service of documents can be characterized as an exercise of the JFTC's enforcement powers. However, before the amendment in 2002, there was no provision regarding the service of documents in other jurisdictions. Article 69(2) of the AML prior to the amendment set forth the provisions regarding the service of documents pursuant to the Code of Civil Procedure, which were to be applied *mutatis mutandis* to the AML, but the article did not mention the provisions concerning the service of documents in a foreign country. Therefore, it was difficult to construe the AML as authorizing the JFTC to service documents outside Japan.

As a result, for example, in 1964, when the JFTC made a decision to commence hearing proceedings against shipping companies (including foreign companies) and sent the decisions to the offices of Japanese agencies of some of the foreign companies, some of those foreign companies argued that they did not authorize their agencies in Japan to receive such legal documents. Eventually in 1972, the JFTC discontinued the proceedings against those foreign companies.[20]

There is a well-known case in which the relevant document was sent directly to a company in the United States. In the *Japanese Microsoft* case,[21] Microsoft Company Limited, in Japan, which was a wholly owned subsidiary of Microsoft Corporation, denied that it had authority to receive service of official documents. Consequently, the warning was sent by post to the parent company in the United States. However, because a warning is classified as a form of administrative guidance and because the service of that warning is not considered an authoritative act, this case has not established precedent.

Before the amendment in 2002, only when foreign entrepreneurs in question have a base located in Japan, can documents be served at that base. In the *Nordion* case cited in the prior section about "prescriptive jurisdiction," Nordion's Japan office was not considered a base because the office had no function. Yet documents were properly served on Nordion's lawyer in Japan as the lawyer was authorized to represent the company, including in the capacity to receive official documents.[22]

---

20. Decision, Aug. 18, 1972, 19 Shinketsu-shu 197.

21. At the time of the Decision on recommendation issued on December 14, 1998, Microsoft headquarters was also warned.

22. Decision on recommendation, Sept. 3, 1998, 45 Shinketsu-shu 148.

There were several cases in which the JFTC intended to mitigate the above-mentioned inadequacies by applying Antimonopoly Law Article 6, as illustrated in the following example. Suppose a foreign enterprise Y, with no bases in Japan, restricts by contract the selling price of Z, a Japanese enterprise. This resale price restriction by Y has a negative impact on consumers in Japan, which should be regulated under the AML. However, as stated above, the JFTC could not serve documents unless Y has a base in Japan. In this circumstance, Article 6 enables the JFTC to initiate a formal hearing against Z. Article 6 does not state that one shall not commit an act of violation but it does state that one shall not be a party to an agreement or contract which contains such matters as fall under unreasonable restraint of trade or unfair trade practices. Company Z, which may be a victim of the violation, is in any event a party to the contract contrary to the AML. Therefore, if Article 6 is applied to this case, and as long as the participation of an enterprise located in Japan is confirmed, the violation can be indirectly rectified by a JFTC order issued to the Japanese enterprise Z. This scenario is based on an actual case that occurred in the past,[23] but since this type of legal action was severely criticized from the viewpoint of procedural due process, today the JFTC would not open a formal hearing procedure against Z under Article 6.

2. After the 2002 Amendment The amendment of the AML in 2002 finally vested the JFTC with the authority to serve documents outside Japan. The new Article 70-17 (the former Article 69(2)) specifies that Article 108 of the Code of Civil Procedure dealing with the service of documents in a foreign state shall apply *mutatis mutandis*. In addition, the 2002 amendment introduced the provisions permitting the JFTC to effect service by posting on the notice board of the Fair Trade Commission (Article 70-18). According to Article 70-18, the JFTC may effect service by public notification in such cases as "[w]hen, after the lapse of six months from the date when a foreign competent authority was commissioned to conduct service pursuant to the provisions of Article 108 of the Code of Civil Procedure as applied mutatis mutandis pursuant to the preceding Article, documents certifying the service are not received."

Under the amended AML, the JFTC investigated BHP Billiton's proposed acquisition of Rio Tinto's shares in 2008. According to some newspaper articles, neither company had any offices or representative agencies in Japan. However, as stated in the previous section, the JFTC held that the acquisition might lead to the lessening of competition in a Japanese market and decided to demand information from the parties. In this case, Article 70-17 was invoked and the service of the order to report was commissioned to the Melbourne consul. When BHP Billiton refused to accept service of the documents, the JFTC affected service by public notification. Without the 2002 amendment, the JFTC was not able to

23. Decision on recommendation, Jan. 12, 1970, 16 Shinketsu-shu 134. Novo Industry, which was in the position of Y, filed a suit to rescind the decision, but the court dismissed the suit due to lack of standing to sue. Supreme Ct., Nov. 28, 1980, 29 Minshu 1592.

address this case, despite the adverse effects of the acquisition on Japanese customers.

Even with the 2002 amendment, there is still a need for improvement. According to Antimonopoly Law Article 70-17, service of documents in a foreign state can be conducted as follows: "a service to be made in a foreign state shall be made as commissioned by the Japan Fair Trade Commission to the competent government agency of that state or the Japanese ambassador, minister or consul stationed in that state." Currently, however, since no country has yet authorized its government agency to serve the documents pursuant to the AML, it should be noted that the only means to effect service of the documents abroad is through the consul or other officials stationed in that country after obtaining the consent of that country, as was done in the *BHP Billiton and Rio Tinto* case. The JFTC recognizes the necessity of international or bilateral agreements that make possible the service of documents through foreign counterparts, which enables the JFTC to enforce the AML against foreign entrepreneurs more efficiently.

At the end of this section, let us mention the latest focus of debate in Japan. Recently, the extraterritorial exercise of enforcement jurisdiction by other jurisdiction has garnered attention. There are cases in which competition authorities in some jurisdictions have sent faxes containing requests for information—not to the Japanese company's branch office in the foreign state—but to an unrelated division of the company's Japanese main office. The fax message sent would be merely a request for the voluntary submission of information, which is different from service, so, strictly speaking, this would not constitute an exercise of public authority. However, if the companies do not respond to such requests in an expedient manner, it is likely that they would suffer drawbacks. For instance, such companies could lose an opportunity to apply for leniency. Therefore, for companies, these requests are comparable to compulsory orders for information, and this raises doubt about whether it is legal to send the documents by fax.[24]

III. INTERNATIONAL COOPERATIVE AGREEMENTS

In general, international cooperative agreements serve two purposes.[25] One purpose is to resolve conflicts that arise between competition authorities. Such conflicts arise when one jurisdiction prohibits conduct that is permitted in other jurisdictions. The other purpose of such agreements is the achievement of a

---

24. This issue is addressed in a report with the title, "Interim Report by the Study Group on International Enforcement of Competition Law" (June 25, 2008). This study group was established by the Ministry of Economy, Trade and Industry in Japan. One of the authors was a member of the study group.

25. Whish, *supra* note 3, at 490.

successful regulation of international cases. For the JFTC, which was entrusted with very limited authority with regard to enforcement jurisdiction, the latter of the two purposes must have been important in that these agreements enable the JFTC to rely on the assistance provided by its foreign counterparts, even when the JFTC is not able to obtain information directly from foreign entrepreneurs.

International cooperative agreements that the JFTC has entered into are divided into two different types. One type is antitrust cooperation agreements, the object of which is to develop cooperative relationships only for the enforcement of competition laws. The other type is economic partnership agreements, the object of which is to develop general economic cooperative relationships, which include the enforcement of competition laws. Economic partnership agreements might seem more important than cooperation agreements, because the former of these two instruments requires the passage of a legislative resolution, while the latter does not. However, some economic partnership agreements simply call for the enforcement of each country's competition laws through appropriate procedures. The others are, at most, as developed as antitrust cooperation agreements. Therefore, we would like to describe here cooperation agreements.

Japan has concluded cooperation agreements with the United States, the EU, and Canada. Negotiations with Australia about such an agreement are currently pending. The agreement with the United States is the first agreement of its kind, and the content of subsequent agreements formed with the EU and Canada largely follows that of the U.S.-Japan agreement.

In addition to Article 6 mentioned in section 2 above, "Enforcement Jurisdiction," the U.S.-Japan agreement consists of the following articles. Article 2 obliges the competition authorities in each jurisdiction to notify each other when they believe their enforcement activities affect an important interest of the other party. Article 3 deals with assistance rendered to each other in enforcement activities, including providing significant information within their possession. Article 4 addresses coordination of enforcement activities and sets forth factors to be taken into account when considering whether particular enforcement activities should be coordinated. Article 5 articulates that if anticompetitive activities carried out in the territory of a Party are believed to adversely affect the important interests of the other Party, the competition authority of the former Party may request that the competition authority of the other Party initiate enforcement activities.

The 2009 amendment[26] adds a new provision (Article 43-2) specifying conditions under which the JFTC is permitted to provide foreign counterparts with information. The new provision, for instance, requires the JFTC to make

---

26. The June 3, 2009, amendment was promulgated in the official gazette on June 10, 2009. Some amendments were implemented on July 10, 2009 and the others on January 1, 2010.

sure that confidential information supplied by the JFTC is kept confidential in receiving jurisdictions to the same extent as under Japanese law.

Assistance and coordination have been channeled through these articles in high-profile cases of Antimonopoly Law violation in recent years.[27] In some cases,[28] JFTC officials publicly announced that the commission had conducted joint investigations with the U.S. and/or EU competition authorities.

CONCLUSION

At the end of this paper, the authors would like to draw reader's attention to the 2009 amendment again. In our opinion, this amendment, though it is mainly unrelated to the topics addressed in this paper, will encourage the sophistication of legal rules with regard to extraterritorial application, especially prescriptive jurisdiction. Under the amended AML, illegal conduct such as discriminatory consideration, unfair low prices, resale price restriction, etc. are made subject to surcharge payment. The amount of the surcharge imposed on these activities is small (1–6 percent of the sales amount of the relevant goods or services) in comparison with that imposed on price-fixing and bid-rigging arrangements (basically 10 percent). However, considering that the AML occupies an important position today and that the failure in complying with the AML can severely damage the reputation of a business, a growing number of entrepreneurs will not accept JFTC cease and desist orders as they now stand. As stated in the above "Enforcement Jurisdiction" section, the amendment in 2002 enabled the JFTC to make foreign firms the respondents of formal proceedings and the addressees of cease and desist orders. Therefore, it is not difficult to predict that the 2009 amendment will bring more foreign companies into an animated discussion with the JFTC about the prescriptive jurisdiction of the AML.

---

27. WHISH, *supra* note 3, at 494 states, "Cooperation between the Commission, the US, Canada and Japan is now a fact of daily life."

28. For instance, the *Vitamin* cartel case mentioned in the note 11 and the merger between Johnson & Johnson and Guidant Corporation (JFTC, M&A Consultation 2005 Case 9) were subject to joint investigation.

6. EXTRATERRITORIAL APPLICATION OF ANTITRUST—THE CASE OF A SMALL ECONOMY
Israel

MICHAL S. GAL*

I. INTRODUCTION

International trade has changed some of the challenges faced by antitrust authorities: it has added an international dimension. While in the past, competition issues were largely domestic, countries now face an increasing prospect that their economies will be harmed by anticompetitive conduct that takes place, at least to some degree, in another jurisdiction. Indeed, more than ever before, companies are seeking expansions or alliances that go well beyond domestic borders, and a large percentage of domestic demand of many countries is supplied by foreign firms. This requires countries to devise tools that enable them to deal with antitrust issues with extraterritorial dimensions. It also implies that countries may need to cooperate in order to effectively regulate international antitrust issues of mutual concern.[1]

Under the current system of international antitrust, the backbone of enforcement is unilateral: each country applies its own tools to deal with international antitrust issues within the constraints imposed upon it by public international law. This enforcement pattern is sometimes coupled with cooperation agreements (bilateral, multilateral, and even international), which are based on the realization that while cooperation among firms might be anticompetitive, this is generally not true for cooperation among countries. Yet such cooperation is often limited to exchange of information, harmonization of antitrust rules, and positive comity rather than to joint efforts of enforcement.[2] Some of the implications of this enforcement system are elaborated upon below.[3]

---

* Professor, Haifa University School of Law; Global Hauser Visiting Professor, NYU School of Law. The author would like to thank Dikla Zarfaty and Hila Nevo for research assistance, Boaz Golan, Asher Goshen, Michal Halperin, Ariel Katz, Ilan Steiner, and David Tadmor for helpful discussions; and the Israeli Science Foundation for funding this project. Any errors or omissions are my own.

1. *See* Michal S. Gal, *Antitrust in a Globalized Economy: The Unique Challenges of Small and of Developed Economies*, 33 FORDHAM INTL. L. J. 1 (2009).

2. Nonetheless, some jurisdictions have entered into regional agreements that involve some degree of joint enforcement on antitrust issues. For elaboration see, e.g., Michal S. Gal, *Regional Agreements: An Important Step in International Antitrust*, 60 U. OF TORONTO L. J. 239 (2010).

3. For elaboration, see Gal, *supra* note 1.

This paper analyzes the tools available to Israel to tackle international antitrust issues. The case of Israel is interesting not only as a stand-alone case study, but mostly because it provides useful insights into the reality of enforcing antitrust in a globalized world by a small economy.[4] As discussed elsewhere, even when they possess the *legal* tools to tackle international antitrust issues, small economies often suffer from serious *practical* deficiencies.[5] Most important, they frequently cannot create a credible threat to large, multinational firms that engage in anticompetitive conduct which harms their economies. They also have limited resources and incentives to deal with international anticompetitive conduct, especially when such conduct is addressed by other jurisdictions. As a result, despite the sometimes severe effects of anticompetitive conduct on their markets, small economies are marginal players in the globalized antitrust regime and are generally passive bearers of the effects of international anticompetitive conduct and of the enforcement actions of larger jurisdictions rather than proactive confronters of such issues and actions. This is well reflected in the Israeli case study.

As discussed below, this observation has important implications for a globalized antitrust regime. Small economies would undoubtedly share some of the benefit from the convergence of competition policies. At the same time, it is far from clear that a negotiated outcome will grant such economies a piece of the total welfare pie that is proportional to their size or contribution to total global welfare.[6] This is because under the current balance of powers, the interests of small economies are routinely overlooked both by international firms and other jurisdictions when a clash of interests exist.

The rest of this chapter is organized as follows. The second section analyzes the current international antitrust regime in Israel. The analysis raises interesting theoretical and practical issues that are relevant to all jurisdictions that apply their domestic laws to foreign firms. Section III analyzes the regime from a wider perspective and focuses on the practical aspects of antitrust enforcement. Section IV analyzes some of the implications of the findings for international antitrust and also briefly suggests some ways that small economies can adopt in order to play a more effective role in the international antitrust arena.

II. THE ISRAELI INTERNATIONAL ANTITRUST REGIME

The ability to contend with antitrust issues with a foreign dimension that affect domestic welfare is based on the existence of a legal basis for application and on

---

4. A small economy is defined as "an independent, sovereign jurisdiction that can support only a limited number of firms in most of its industries." *See* Michal S. Gal, Competition Policy in Small Market Economies ch. 1 (Harv. Univ. Press 2003). As elaborated therewith, small size is influenced by three main factors: population size, population dispersion and openness to trade.

5. Gal, *Unique Challenges*, *supra*, note 1.

6. *Id.*

practical considerations of enforcement. This section seeks to explore the former, whereas the following will focus on the latter.

A. Extraterritoriality

The scope of application of the Israeli Restrictive Trade Practices Law 1988 (the RTPL) to issues with an extraterritorial dimension is anchored both in customary public international law and in specific legal provisions, such as those included in the Israeli Penal Law.

Before analyzing the relevant principles and their application, it is useful to examine the Israeli antitrust system. The Director of the Israeli Antitrust Authority (Director and IAA) is authorized, inter alia, to decide whether a restrictive agreement or an abuse of power exists.[7] Such decisions create a rebuttable presumption for their correctness in any legal procedure, although they do not carry any direct consequences.[8] The Director is also authorized to approve or condition a merger.[9] The decisions of the Director are subject to review by an expert Antitrust Tribunal, in case of an appeal.[10] In addition, antitrust matters may arise in the general court system in civil (mostly damages and contracts) and they might also be subject to criminal proceedings.

Under Israeli law, the rules of customary public international law apply and constitute an integral part of Israeli law, unless express contradictory legislative provision exists.[11] Such law is automatically incorporated, without any need for a formal legislative act.[12] Moreover, where there is a potential conflict between Israeli law and public international law, the court will attempt to interpret Israeli law in a fashion consistent with public international law.[13] Except with regard to merger review, the RTPL does not contain specific contradictory provisions. Indeed, the Director specifically noted that no such contradictory provision exists with regard to restrictive agreements.[14]

---

7. Section 43(a) of the RTPL.

8. Section 43(e) of the RTPL.

9. Section 21 of the RTPL.

10. Section 43(c) of the RTPL.

11. *See, e.g.*, Ruth Lapidot, *The Place of Public International Law in Israeli Law*, 19 MISHPATIM 807 (1990); Yafa Zilberschatz, *The Adoption of the Public International Law into the Israeli Law*, 24 MISHPATIM 317 (1994). For the adoption of this principle in other jurisdictions, see, e.g., L. OPPENHEIM, INTERNATIONAL LAW (9th ed. 1992).

12. *See, e.g.*, Criminal Appeal 174/54 Shtampper v. Attorney General, 10 Court Decisions 5.

13. Bagatz 302/72 Hilou v. The Israeli Government et al., 27(2) Court Decisions 169, 177.

14. Director, *Selective Perfume Market—James Richardson, in* ANTITRUST (Israeli Bar Association, Tova Olshtein ed., 2002) Vol. D ("*James Richardson*").

Public international law includes several principles for the application of domestic laws to persons or enterprises located outside the jurisdiction.[15] An important basis for jurisdiction is territoriality. Israeli law, following international law doctrines, distinguishes between two bases: subjective territoriality, which applies when a person is within the territory of the jurisdiction, and objective territoriality, which applies when the conduct has an effect within the territory of the jurisdiction. The subjective territoriality principle may apply when a firm operates in Israel, for example where an international firm builds a production facility or opens a branch in Israel. In such cases, the RTPL may apply to its actions.

The subjective territoriality principle was applied by the Director in the *EMTA* case.[16] There, the Director declared an agreement among 12 foreign maritime shippers and an Israeli firm to charge a fixed handling charge for shipment to be a "restrictive agreement" under the RTPL. The decision does not mention the effects of the extraterritorial dimension of the agreement on jurisdictional issues. Yet since all the foreign firms had offices in Israel, it was assumed that they were captured under the subjective territoriality principle, which is also part of customary public international law, and which applies when a person is within the territory of the jurisdiction. As noted in the decision, the parties did not dispute the extraterritorial application of Israeli law in that case. Thus, the Director did not see any need to elaborate on this point.

The objective territoriality principle (often called the "effects doctrine") enables a country to apply its domestic laws to foreign persons or enterprises when their conduct has an effect within the domestic jurisdiction. This doctrine thus broadens the application of domestic laws to acts performed outside the territorial boundaries, even if by foreign companies, provided that their conduct influences competition within the jurisdiction.[17] In essence, under this basis for jurisdiction, harm is used as a proxy for territory.

The effects doctrine was applied by the Director as a basis for the application of the RTPL to foreign firms in the matter of *James Richardson*.[18] James Richardson, an Israeli firm, held a franchise to operate a duty-free store at the national airport. It reached agreements with perfume manufacturers with regard to the maintenance of price margins of 30 percent between itself and other stores

15. For exposition of these principles, see, e.g., CHRISTOPHER L. BLAKESLEY ET AL., THE INTERNATIONAL LEGAL SYSTEM ch. 3 (Foundation Press 5th ed. 2001).

16. Director, *Restrictive Agreement Among the Sea Carriers Which are Parties to the EMTA Conference* (Apr. 30, 2003, not published).

17. *See, e.g.*, United States v. Aluminum Co. of America, 148 F. 2d 416 (2d Cir. 1945).

18. *James Richardson, supra* note 13. Although there are no other official decisions that apply the doctrine, the IAA did apply the doctrine in several other cases as well to justify their basis for extraterritoriality. This information is based on discussions with several senior IAA officials and with several lawyers.

located in Israel. The perfume manufacturers, who were party to these agreements, were all foreign companies located overseas. The Director applied the RTPL to the perfume manufacturers by using the effects doctrine as a basis for such application.[19]

The *James Richardson* decision was not appealed and thus was not subject to the scrutiny of the court. However, it is reasonable to presume that the effects doctrine will also be applied by Israeli courts as part of established customary international public law, especially in the area of antitrust. The prospect of such adoption is bolstered in two fundamental ways. First, the effects doctrine—or a relatively similar version of it like the EU implementation doctrine—serves as a basis for the extraterritorial application of antitrust in many industrialized jurisdictions, including the United States and the EU.[20] Israeli courts and quasi-judicial institutions usually look to these jurisdictions for guidance on antitrust issues.[21] Second, the adoption of the effects doctrine furthers the goals of the RTPL, which is to prohibit anticompetitive conduct within Israeli markets. Since Israel is a small jurisdiction, much of the anticompetitive conduct that affects it takes place elsewhere. For example, most of the international cartels that limit competition within Israeli markets are agreed upon and implemented outside its borders. Absent the effects doctrine, the RTPL would generally not apply, and Israel would not be able to limit such anticompetitive conduct.[22]

It is also reasonable to assume that Israeli courts will condition the application of the RTPL on the requirements that are applied elsewhere and that are followed in such a way that they are regarded as customary public international law. All jurisdictions that adopted objective territoriality principles have applied significant limiting factors to their application. Jurisdiction is regularly recognized only if the alleged anticompetitive conduct has "substantial, direct and intentional" anticompetitive effects on competition in the jurisdiction. These conditions were specifically acknowledged in the *James Richardson* decision.[23]

Salt Industries, another decision which involved foreign firms, however, did not mention the effects doctrine. Yet it cannot serve as a basis for an argument that the effects doctrine does not apply in Israel. First and foremost, if the effects doctrine is part of customary public international law, then the Director cannot

---

19. *Id.*

20. The EU doctrine that serves a similar purpose, the implementation doctrine, is in many ways comparable to the effects doctrine, although some minor differences exist. *See* Cases 89, 104,114,16,117 and 125-9/85, A Ahlstrom Oy v Commission [1988] ECR 5193, [1988] 4 CMLR 901. *See, e.g.*, ALISON JONES & BRENDA SUFRIN, EC COMPETITION LAW 1053 (Oxford Univ. Press 2001). The European court applied the doctrine after it evaluated the position under public international law.

21. For example, in the *James Richardson* decision, the Director cited U.S. and EU decisions.

22. See the discussion of the Penal Code below.

23. *James Richardson, supra* note 13.

override it. Rather, he is obliged to apply it in relevant cases. The doctrine would not apply only if an express contradictory legislative provision existed in the RTPL. However, no such provision exists except in the merger context. Moreover, as noted above, where there exists a potential conflict between Israeli law and public international law, the court will attempt to interpret the Israeli law in a fashion consistent with public international law.

In *Salt Industries*, the Director issued an administrative decree which stated that an Israeli firm participated in a cartel between an Israeli and a Cypriot firm.[24] The decision did not mention the extraterritorial dimension of the cartel and its legal implications for the applicability of the RTPL. The decision supplies no explanation. Nonetheless, two possible explanations arise.[25] First, the Director proved a factual basis for significant and intentional harm to competition. She did so despite the fact that the case involved a cartel of a kind that does not ordinarily require proof of anticompetitive effects since a per se presumption of harm is applied. Thus, it might be assumed that since the conditions for the applicability of the doctrine were proven, there was no need to mention its applicability.

Another possible explanation involves the fact that the administrative decree applied only to the Israeli firm. According to the facts set forth in the decree, the Israeli firm aggressively coerced the Cypriot firm into the cartel when the latter attempted to introduce competition into the Israeli salt market. It did so, inter alia, by dumping a huge amount of salt on the Cyprian market, which then had a significant effect on prices there. Thus, the "blame" was mainly on the Israeli firm. It might be that given these circumstances, the Director decided not to declare the Cypriot firm an infringer of the RTPL. Thus, she assumed that it did not have to engage in questions of extraterritorial application.

This explanation raises an interesting set of questions, which are relevant whenever anticompetitive conduct involves both a foreign and a domestic firm. In such cases, if the legal implications are only directed at the domestic firm, should the effects doctrine apply? In other words, does the effects doctrine act as a precondition for a finding of anticompetitive conduct if some of the parties are foreign, or does it apply only if there is a finding of anticompetitive conduct that has direct legal implications for the foreign firm? If indeed the Director did not mention the effects doctrine in *Salt Industries* because the decision was not directed at the foreign firm, then this signifies that the Director adopted the latter proposition. In this sense, the effects doctrine is a precondition for

24. Director, *Israeli Salt Industries Inc.—Party to a restrictive agreement with MP Theodorou (Salt Industry) & Co., Ltd.* (Apr. 2, 2006, not published).

25. It can be assumed that the Director was aware of the doctrine. The Director mentioned in the decision a legal opinion, given to one of the parties, which applied the *James Richardson* decision to an agreement between an Israeli and a Jordanian firm. *Israeli Salt, id,* at n.51.

prosecution of a foreign firm but does not prevent such a finding against a domestic firm. The legality of such a rule would have to be determined in accordance with public international law doctrines. However, given that the decision carries no direct legal implications and consequences for the foreign firm, it might fit with the rationale of the doctrine.[26]

This leads to another interesting set of questions. Many domestic antitrust laws include presumptions of harm (per se rules). Such presumptions would normally apply to domestic firms. Yet the effects doctrine normally requires proof of "a significant and direct" anticompetitive effect. Now, assume that the relevant conduct normally falls under the presumption of harm. Can the presumption then be applied as a proxy for the conditions of the effects doctrine? Can it be applied to the domestic firm but not to the foreign one? Most of these questions have not been directly answered in Israel. Yet the case law and doctrinal considerations suggest that presumptions of harm cannot be used in order to prove the elements of the effects doctrine.

Let us first analyze the doctrinal basis. Some presumptions of illegality, like those contained in the RTPL, are very wide and capture under their wings conduct that does not always significantly harm competition.[27] In such cases, applying a presumption of harm would not necessarily fulfill the requirement that "significant, direct and intentional" anticompetitive effects be proven. Accordingly, applying the presumption in such cases goes against the doctrine's intent. This is because extraterritorial application of a domestic law is an exception to the rule that the laws of a state apply within its boundaries. The balance between the clashing jurisdictional interests is reached by ensuring that laws should be applied extraterritorially only where their application is necessary to prevent conduct with substantial and intentional anticompetitive effects within the jurisdiction. Thus, applying a presumption that does not ensure all the agreements that come under its scope significantly harm competition clashes with the goal of the doctrine. This is especially true in the case of Israel. Beyond the problem created by the extremely wide scope of the presumptions of illegality, another problem arises, which is based on the basic requirements of the law. The RTPL requires only proof of "probable harm to competition." The presumptions of harm included in the RTPL are intended to eliminate the need to prove this element. Since "probable harm" is a much lower standard than "significant harm,"

26. Indeed, this explanation also fits well with the structure of the *James Richardson* decision, as elaborated below.

27. *See, e.g.*, David Gilo, *Is It Appropriate to Open the Dam of Restrictive Agreements and Block It by Ad Hoc Remedies?*, 27 Iyunei Mishpat 751 (2004); David Gilo, *A Restriction Which Harms Competition Between the Party Enjoying It and a Third Party*, 28 Iyunei Mishpat 517 (2004); Michal S. Gal, *Separating the Wheat from the Chaff: Restrictive Agreement in Light of the Supreme Court's Recent Decisions*, 1 Din Udvarim 533 (2004).

it cannot be presumed that the elements of the effects doctrine have been fulfilled even if one decides that the presumptions can apply to foreign firms.

Let us now turn to the case law. In both *James Richardson* and the *Salt Cartel*, the Director applied a presumption of harm. However, it also proved significant anticompetitive effects on the Israeli market. Moreover, in *James Richardson*, the Director specifically recognized the requirements of the effects doctrine and stated that the RTPL "should be applied in the spirit of the effects doctrine."[28] Furthermore, the *James Richardson* decision supports the conclusion that a presumption is not sufficient. There, the Director applied the presumption, analyzed the harm in practice, and, as a last step, applied the effects doctrine. It can thus be assumed that the requirements of the effects doctrine were regarded by the Director as cumulative to those that apply in a case without an extraterritorial dimension.[29] Yet these AAI decisions have limited relevance since regardless of what the Director intended, he cannot deviate from customary public international law doctrines.

In light of the above considerations, it is my view that a presumption of harm under the RTPL cannot be applied in order to fulfill the requirement of the doctrine of "significant harm" to competition. Moreover, the presumption does not prove intentional harm, which must be proven separately. It is noteworthy that in criminal or administrative proceedings initiated by the IAA, these issues have little practical relevance. This is because despite the presumptions, the Authority has never brought a case in which it did not believe there was significant harm to the Israeli market. Nonetheless, these questions may arise in civil matters between private parties, in which one party argues that the agreement is illegal.

Where conduct constitutes a criminal offense under Israeli law, as is the case with cartels, abuse of dominance, and mergers without approval, Chapter C of the *Israeli Penal Law*[30] sets forth several principles for the territorial reach of the law. Chapter C dictates that for Israeli penal laws to apply, some factual element of the offense must take place within Israeli territory.[31] The theoretical application of this requirement in abuse of dominance offenses was recognized by the Director in the matter of *James Richardson*:[32]

> Where a monopolist acts in a way that might reduce competition in business in Israel or might harm the Israeli public—this is an internal offense which may be tried in Israel.

---

28. *James Richardson, supra*, note 13.

29. In the conclusion of the decision, the Director states that a presumption applies. However, I do not think this should be read as rejecting the substantive requirements of the effects doctrine, since it would clash with its statement that the RTPL "should be applied in the spirit of the effects doctrine."

30. Israeli Penal Law, 1977.

31. S. Z. Peller, *Elements of Criminal Law* (1, 5744-1984) 260. *See also James Richardson, supra* note 13, at 43–44.

32. *James Richardson, supra* note 13.

Yet despite the wide scope of the law, criminal cases are rarely brought in Israel. This raises an interesting question: whether Chapter C of the Penal Code determines the scope of the jurisdictional reach of the RTPL in civil or administrative cases that involve conduct which could, potentially, also serve as a basis for a criminal offense, or whether it determines the applicability of the RTPL only in criminal cases. This question has not yet been answered. But should the answer be in the negative, the immediate result is that the practical scope of the application of the Penal Code is quite limited.[33]

It is noteworthy that in the matter of *Tagar*,[34] the District Court in Jerusalem stated, in obiter dicta, that an export cartel between Israeli firms that did not harm competition in Israel may still constitute an offense under Israeli law, if some of the elements of the offense took place in Israel, although it may be exempt if a proper request be made on "public good" grounds.[35] In my view, this wide application of the law is contrary to the goals of the RTPL and should be rejected. Indeed, in the case of *Nesher*, the Tel Aviv District Court stated that an exclusivity agreement between Israeli and Palestinian firms that affected only the Palestinian market was not covered under the RTPL, "which is territorial in its scope."[36]

---

33. In *James Richardson*, for example, the Director mentioned Chapter C of the Penal Code but did not analyze its applicability in his decision.

34. CrimC 385/98 State of Israel vs. Tagar Co. [Apr. 13, 2003, not published] ¶¶ 20–22. *See also* Bagatz 588/84 Kesher Sachar Asbest, Supreme Court Decisions 40(1) 29.

35. In several discussions with market participants, the IAA adopted a similar view, which considerably widens the scope of the application of the RTPL. The IAA separated the question of the jurisdictional scope of the RTPL and the question of public policy—whether the IAA has an incentive to bring suit against foreign firms. In particular, the IAA understood the EU *Gencor* decision (case T-102/96 Gencor Ltd. v. Commission [1999] ECR II-753) as implying that the RTPL applies to any firm that is based in or operates in Israel, even if its conduct does not affect the Israeli market. Thus, an Israeli firm that participated in an international cartel which did not affect the Israeli market (given that the other cartel members' products did not fit demand in the Israeli market) was, under this view, caught under the RTPL. In my view, this wide interpretation should be rejected and would most likely be rejected by the courts. Most important, it does not fit within the purpose of the RTPL, which is to promote competitive conditions in the Israeli market. Put differently, the RTPL has a territorial purpose, rather than maintaining the morality of Israeli firms in foreign markets. Indeed, the purpose of the subjective territoriality principle, which enables countries to apply their laws to firms and individuals within their territorial scope, is to enable countries to prevent conduct which implicitly affects competitive conditions within their jurisdictions. Indeed, the EU *Gencor* decision, on which the IAA relies, involved conduct that significantly affected competition within the EU market. There, the Commission prohibited the merger between two foreign undertakings on the basis that the merger would have created a duopoly in the platinum and rhodium markets, as a result of which effective competition would be significantly impeded in the common market. Richard Whish, Competition Law 483 (Oxford Univ. Press 6th ed. 2008).

36. HP 1407/94 Magrizo vs. Nesher Cement Co. [Aug, 7, 1995, not published].

The decision in *Nesher* was rendered before that in *Tagar*, but in accordance with Israeli law, neither has precedence over the other. The issue has not, as of yet, come before the Supreme Court. Nonetheless, as noted above, it is my view that a purposive interpretation of the RTPL will lead to the recognition that the RTPL should only be applied to conduct that affects the Israeli market, either directly or indirectly.

Accordingly, customary public international law, as well as the Israeli Penal Code, forms the possible basis for the extraterritorial application of the RTPL. An exception exists in merger regulation, which specifically limits the application of the RTPL beyond what would have applied otherwise. Since the RTPL narrows Israeli jurisdiction, there is no conflict with international law principles, since sovereign independence is impinged less, rather than more. A "merger" is defined in the RTPL as a merger among firms that are either registered in Israel or that have a business location in Israel.[37] The first requirement is interpreted to include international firms with local subsidiaries or with other means of direct control over Israeli firms.[38] The second requirement is interpreted widely by the IAA to include foreign firms with significant influence over their local representative (be it a distributor or the holder of another title). The IAA inquires whether the foreign firm can determine the quantity, price, quality, display, or other commercial decisions regarding its imported products. The more control the foreign firm has over these parameters, the more likely that it will come under the purview of the merger provisions.[39] The merger provisions do not cover, however, foreign firms that have not as of yet done business in Israel or firms whose products are sold in Israel through independent importers. Merger law thus excludes mergers among such international firms or even between such international firms and an Israeli one. Accordingly, the IAA does not have jurisdiction to block such mergers or impose any conditions upon them, even if they significantly harm the Israeli economy. Indeed, to give but one example, when KLM and Air France merged, they did not notify the IAA, despite the fact that the merger affected competition in some routes to and from Israel. This application pattern, which might be partly justified by practical enforcement considerations as elaborated upon below, nonetheless creates skewed incentives

37. Articles 1 and 17 of the RTPL.

38. Director of IAA, Conditional Approval of Merger between Osem and Tnuva [Dec. 22, 1996, not published]; IAA Merger Guidelines, pp. 23–24, http://www.antitrust.gov.il/Files/HPLinks/Mergers%20Guidelines.pdf

39. It is noteworthy that this interpretation of the IAA is relatively broad and might clash with the wording of the RTPL. However, it has yet to be challenged in court. This interpretation is still narrower in scope than the effects doctrine.

for Israeli firms to merge with international firms even if a merger among Israeli firms might have been more efficient otherwise.[40]

B. Comity Considerations

Comity is the use of moderation and restraint by a jurisdiction in the extraterritorial application of domestic laws, having due regard both for international duty and convenience and for the rights of its own citizens. Comity thus recognizes certain circumstances in which the interests of another state are sufficient so that the exercise of jurisdiction should be restrained.[41]

As with the effects doctrine, under Israeli law, comity limitations on jurisdiction will apply so long as they are part of established customary international public law, unless a clear provision in the relevant law states otherwise. However, here the case for adoption is weaker, given that comity principles are less established in international law.

Nonetheless, comity principles were recognized in Israel. In *Berman v. TWA*,[42] the district court held:

> Comity principles have significant importance in the modern world and especially in the U.S.-Israel relationship. They imply honoring the sovereignty of foreign countries by limiting, to the extent possible, "invasion" of the domain of a foreign country by giving a judicial decision that has effects outside Israeli borders. These principles point towards the respect of the authority of the jurisdiction in which the foreign firm has its center of business . . . and abstention from interrupting the process by giving conflicting decisions.

Accordingly, although there is no case law dealing with this issue in the antitrust context, an argument can be made that Israeli courts will apply international comity principles in relevant antitrust cases. The language of the RTPL does not limit the applicability of comity considerations.

Yet the scope of comity principles to be applied is questionable, as there is no international consensus with regard to their scope, and thus it might be quite difficult to argue for a specific set of comity principles which constitute customary public international law. For example, in the United States there is an ongoing debate with regard to the scope of comity. In the much-cited *Timberlane* case, a U.S. court of appeals applied a balancing-of-interests test to the extraterritorial reach of the Sherman Act to ensure that the interests of the United States are

40. Michal S. Gal, *Monopolies in Competition: The Balance between Innovativeness and Competition in the Israeli Competition Law*, 2 UNIV. HAIFA L. REV. (DIN UDVARIM) 425 n.155 (2006).

41. *See Timberlane Lumber Co. v. Bank of America*, 549 F. 2d 597 (9th Cir. 1976) and other cases cited in *Hartford Fire Insurance Co. v. California*, 509 U.S. 764 (1993).

42. Pshitat Regel (Tel Aviv) 1255/01 Berman v. TWA, Takdin- Mehozi 2001 (1) 29449, at 29448.

sufficient to support the exercise of extraterritorial jurisdiction.[43] The Restatement has also adopted similar criteria to determine the "reasonableness" of applying the law. Reasonableness is a necessary requirement for existence of a jurisdiction in the first place.[44] The majority in *Hartford Fire*, however, adopted a narrow test for the application of international comity principles.[45] It stated that international comity principles are only relevant if there is a "true conflict" between U.S. and foreign law. The majority held that such a conflict did not exist where a person subject to regulation by two nations can comply with the laws of both, although they involve different requirements and are based on somewhat clashing policy goals. The majority opinion in *Hartford Fire* was much criticized.[46]

Comity and balancing principles were included in the *Agreement Regarding the Application of Their Competition Laws, between the U.S. Government and the Israeli Government*.[47] Article VI of the Agreement, titled "Avoidance of Conflicts," states that "each party shall . . .give careful consideration to the other party's important interests throughout all phases of its enforcement activities, including decisions regarding the initiation of an investigation or proceedings . . . ."[48] The Agreement adopts a balancing test for cases in which the enforcement activities of one party may adversely affect the important interests of another party. Accordingly, section VI(5) of the Agreement states that in such cases, the party assessing the measures it will take shall consider all appropriate factors, including:

(a) The relative significance to the anticompetitive activities involved of conduct occurring within one state as compared to the conduct occurring within that of the other;
(b) The relative significance and foreseeability of the effects of the anticompetitive activities on one Party's important interests as compared to the effects on the other Party's important interests;
(c) The presence or absence of a purpose on the part of those engaged in the anticompetitive activities to affect consumers, suppliers or competitors within the enforcing state;

---

43. *Timberlane, supra*, note 40.

44. RESTATEMENT (THIRD) OF FOREIGN RELATIONS LAW § 403(2), cmt. g, & notes to § 415.

45. *Hartford Fire, supra* note 40. The European ruling in the matter of *Eastern Aluminium* is strikingly similar. *Aluminium Imports from Eastern Europe*, OJ 1985 L92/1, [1987] 3 CMLR 235, sec. 14.7.

46. *See, e.g.*, A. V. Lowe, *Blocking Extraterritorial Jurisdiction: The British Protection of Trading Interests Acts, 1980*, 75 AM. J. INT'L L. 257 (1981); Phillip R. Trimble, *The Supreme Court and International Law: The Demise of Restatement Section 403*, 89 AM. J. INT'L L. 53 (1995); Kenneth W. Dam, *Extraterritoriality in an Age of Globalization: The Hartford Fire Case*, 1993 SUP. CT. REV. 289.

47. Signed on Mar, 15, 1999.

48. *Id.*, Section VI(1).

(d) The degree of conflict or consistency between the first Party's enforcement activities (including remedies) and the other Party's laws and other important interests;
(e) Whether private persons, either natural or legal, will be placed under conflicting requirements by both parties;
(f) the existence or absence of reasonable expectations that would be furthered or defeated by the enforcement activities;
(g) The location of the relevant assets;
(h) The degree to which a remedy, in order to be effective, must be carried out within the other state; and
(i) The extent to which enforcement activities of the other party with respect to the same persons, including judgments or undertakings resulting from such activities, would be affected.

Accordingly, in case the conduct in question violates both U.S. and Israeli competition laws, the Agreement sets out positive comity principles to be applied. Article V states that in such cases, "a party may request that the other Party's competition authorities initiate enforcement activities against anticompetitive activities carried out in the requested State, if the requesting Party believes that such activities adversely affect its important interests."[49] Although Article V states that "nothing in this Article . . . precludes the requesting Party's competition authorities from undertaking enforcement activities with respect to such anticompetitive activities," it seems that if the conduct having "direct, substantial and intended" effect in the Israeli market also violates U.S. law, the IAA should first try to stop the conduct by requiring the U.S. antitrust authorities to apply their own rules domestically, especially if the U.S. authorities are already engaged in such enforcement activity which is liable to remedy anti-competitive conduct problems within the Israeli market as well. This limitation conforms with the purpose of the Agreement, which is "to promote cooperation and coordination between the competition authorities of the Parties, to avoid conflicts arising from the application of the Parties' competition laws and to minimize the impact of differences on their respective important interests."[50] It is noteworthy, however, that the Agreement was never formally rectified. Thus, while it might impact the decisions of the IAA, it does not bind Israeli courts.

Comity and avoidance of conflict provisions are also commonplace in many other bilateral agreements.[51] That is, many jurisdictions have agreed to limit

---

49. *Id.*, Section V, titled "Positive Comity."

50. *Id.*, Section I.1.

51. *See, e.g.*, Agreement between the Government of the United States of America and the Government of the Federative Republic of Brazil (Oct. 26, 1999), secs. IV and VI; Agreement between the Government of the United States of America and the Commission of the European Communities Regarding the Application of their Competition Laws (Sept. 23, 1991), secs. V and VI; Agreement between the Government of the United States of

their enforcement activities when foreign interests are involved. Most important, comity principles were incorporated in the 1995 Recommendations of the Council of the OECD Concerning Cooperation Between Member Countries on Anticompetitive Practices Affecting International Trade.[52] The Recommendations recognize "the need . . . to give effect to the principles of international law and comity and to use modernization and self-restraint in the interest of co-operation in the field of anticompetitive practices." Since Israel recently joined the OECD, it will most likely adhere to these recommendations. Moreover, these agreements may strengthen the case for recognizing comity principles as part of customary public international law.

C. Cooperation with other Jurisdictions

Cooperative agreements are an important tool for tackling international antitrust issues of mutual concern. Indeed, Israel is party to several agreements that are relevant in the antitrust context. It is party to one multilateral convention and several bilateral treaties concerning criminal assistance (with Austria, Germany, the United States, Australia, and Canada).[53] While these agreements are not competition-specific, they can play an important role in international cartel cases as they enable the authority to engage in formal cooperation, including the exchange of information, if the conduct under investigation amounts to a criminal offense.[54] As noted, under the RTPL, restrictive agreements and abuses of dominance are considered criminal offenses. Indeed, Israel received assistance from a foreign jurisdiction in the pre-investigation stage of an international cartel. The foreign jurisdiction provided the IAA with the alleged anticompetitive agreements that it sought.

In addition, free trade agreements usually contain basic provisions on cooperation in competition matters. Israel has concluded such agreements with several countries and organizations. Most notably, The EU-Israel Association Agreement[55]

America and the European Communities on the Application of Positive Comity Principles in the Enforcement of their Competition Laws (June 4, 1998), secs. III and VI.

52. OECD Doc. No. C (95) 130 (July 27, 1995).

53. European Convention on Mutual Assistance in Criminal Matters (signed in Strasbourg in 1959; Treaty for Mutual Assistance in Applying the European Convention on Mutual Assistance In Criminal Matters with Austria (signed in 1975); Treaty for Mutual Assistance in Applying the European Convention on Mutual Assistance in Criminal Matters with Germany (signed in 1975);Treaty for Mutual Assistance in Criminal Matters with the U.S.A (signed in 1998); Treaty for Mutual Assistance in Criminal Matters with Australia (signed in 1994); Treaty for Mutual Assistance in Criminal Matters with Canada (signed in 1999).

54. Any exchange of information concerning private parties is subject to confidentiality rules.

55. Euro-Mediterranean Agreement, signed November 1995 and entered into force in June 2000. O/J/ L 147/3 (June 21, 2000), *available at* http://www.delisr.ec.europa.eu/english/content/eu_and_country/asso_agree_en.pdf.

declares that anticompetitive practices and abuses of a dominant position are incompatible with the agreement if they affect trade between the EU and Israel. It also states that when such a practice arises, "which threatens to cause serious prejudice to the interests of the other party or a material injury to its domestic industry, each party may take appropriate measures after consultation of the Association Committee" or after thirty days of the referral of the matter to the committee. It also contains a provision regarding exchange of information, subject to secrecy limitations.[56]

As noted in the previous section, Israel is also party to a bilateral antitrust agreement with the United States. Under the agreement, competition authorities on both sides exchange information and coordinate their enforcement activities. Each side may ask the other to take enforcement action (positive comity); and each side must take account of the other's significant interests when enforcing competition rules (traditional comity). However, there has not yet been a case in which the IAA was asked to lessen its involvement due to the interests of the U.S. authorities. Thus, in practice, the Agreement so far has had little effect.

The lack of additional cooperation agreements is due, in part, to the fact that their signing requires the cooperation of the Israeli Ministry of Foreign Affairs and the Israeli Ministry of Justice. Due to lack of resources of both the IAA and the aforesaid ministries, the IAA was unable to sign additional agreements.[57] As will be elaborated in the next section, this is also a direct result of the limited effectiveness of such agreements.

By far, the most significant liaison of the IAA, based on both formal and informal relationships, is with the United States. Informal cooperation involves, inter alia, discussing such matters as investigative strategies, market information, and witness evaluations. It also involves long and short visits by IAA members to U.S. antitrust agencies in order to learn firsthand how they handle cases, and sometimes even joint seminars and conferences. Such informal cooperation can be quite useful in advancing investigations.[58]

In addition, Israel regularly discusses competition issues with other countries in multilateral forums such as the International Competition Network (ICN), United Nations Conference for Trade and Development (UNCTAD), and the OECD's Competition Committee as well as in its Working Parties and the Global Forum on Competition. The IAA takes an active role in the ICN and was appointed as a member of its interim Steering Group. It headed the Merger

56. *Id.*, Articles 36–37.

57. IAA, International Cooperation, Including Exchange of Information in Cartel Investigations, submitted to the OECD, 2000.

58. OECD, Hard Core Cartels: Third Report on the Implementation of the 1998 Council Recommendation (2005), *available at* http://www.oecd.org/dataoecd/58/1/35863307.pdf.

Investigation Techniques Subgroup, operating within the ICN's Merger Working Group, which focuses on the development of best practices for the investigation of mergers. Importantly, these forums have created informal and interpersonal ties with many agencies that enable the IAA to informally request assistance on specific issues from other authorities. Such cooperation is mostly case or issue specific. This is due, in part, to the fact that long-term macro cooperation requires investment of resources that the IAA does not have. Most importantly, it cannot spare the personnel to work on such issues when there are insufficient resources to enable it to deal with all domestic anticompetitive issues.

However, all of these relationships have limited effects on international antitrust enforcement in Israel, as they do not solve the two main problems faced by it: limited enforcement resources and a limited ability to create a credible threat, which are discussed below.

III. PRACTICAL OBSTACLES IN APPLYING ANTITRUST TO FOREIGN FIRMS[59]

Conduct that takes place elsewhere can significantly harm Israeli markets. International cartels or abuse of dominance by internationally dominant firms can increase prices and lower quality or quantity. The worldwide Vitamins cartel, for example, affected prices of vitamins in Israel.[60] Similarly, Microsoft's abusive conduct affected the price and quality of operating systems of personal computers for Israeli consumers.[61] Mergers among foreign firms can also significantly affect the Israeli market. One example involves the Unilever/Best Foods merger of a European and an American food producer. The merger was approved by the EU and the United States, as it did not raise anticompetitive concerns in their markets. Yet it substantially lessened competition in Israel, given that it was preceded by the merging of each of the parties with a dominant competitor in some Israeli food markets. The merger raised concerns regarding its effects on competition in Israel—both the strengthening of a food conglomerate as well as the lessening of competition in several specific food markets, such as chocolate and snacks.[62] The large proportion of foreign-produced products that are traded

59. This section is based largely on Gal, *Small Economies, supra* note 3, ch. 6 and Gal, *Unique Challenges, supra,* note 1.

60. For an analysis of the self-nicknamed "Vitamins, Inc." cartel, see, e.g., John M. Connor, Global Price Fixing: Our Customers are the Enemy (2001).

61. U. S. v. Microsoft Corp., 84 F. Supp. 2d 9 (D. D. C. 1999) (findings of fact); 87 F. Supp. 2d 30 (D. D. C. 2000) (conclusions of law); 97 F. Supp. 2d 59 (D. D. C. 2000) (final judgment), *aff'd in part, rev'd in part, remanded in part*; 253 F.3d 34 (D.C. Cir. 2001).

62. Conditioned Approval of the Director of the Merger between Tozeret Mazon Israelit Baam and Unilever N.V. (M/4006) (Director of Israeli Competition Authority, Sept. 27, 2000, not published).

in Israel and the reduced ability of domestic market forces to effectively regulate foreign importers often imply that the anticompetitive conduct of dominant foreign importers will have strong negative effects on Israeli markets with which they trade, without significantly offsetting efficiencies.

Yet, as elaborated elsewhere,[63] the current system of national laws and unilateral enforcement, coupled with limited cooperation on joint enforcement significantly limits the practical ability and the incentives of small economies, such as Israel, to prevent the anticompetitive conduct of foreign firms that has negative effects on their jurisdiction. The unilateral approach is based on the fundamental assumption that extraterritorial conduct that significantly affects the domestic market can be redressed at the national level through national competition laws. This proposition does not hold true for small economies, as they face severe challenges to effective prosecution.

The main problem is that small economies can rarely make a credible threat to prohibit the conduct of a foreign firm, especially if it has positive effects elsewhere that do not result only from the negative effects in the small jurisdiction. Even those small economies that have signed bilateral agreements with large ones are not much better off, as positive comity does not reduce their concerns with regard to extraterritorial conduct with negative effects on their domestic markets that does not infringe foreign law.

Let us take the example of a merger that has no negative welfare effects on a large economy, such as the merger between KLM and Air France. If trade in Israel is only a small part of the foreign firm's total world operation, were the IAA to place costly restrictions on the merging parties, they would, most likely, choose not to fly to Israel and trade only in other jurisdictions. The foreign firm would exit the Israeli market if its loss of revenues from terminating its trade and the possible increase in overall production costs should the firm face scale economies over the whole range of production are smaller than the increase of revenues it anticipates to achieve as a result of the merger elsewhere. Also, the negative welfare effects on Israeli markets of the exit of the foreign firm may well be greater than the negative welfare effects from its continued operation within the economy's borders. Accordingly, Israel usually has limited power or incentives to prevent the merging parties from trading within its borders even if the merger harmed the Israeli economy. The foreign firm, acknowledging this effect, will not take into account, in its merging decision, the effect of its decision on the Israeli market; it will only consider the effects of the merger on its own profits in such a market. In fact, an empirical study conducted on twenty small economies confirmed this result: in no small economy did the antitrust authority attempt to prohibit a merger that had been approved by large ones, except to limit its direct

63. Gal, *Unique Challenges*, *supra* note 1. *See also* Andrew T. Guzman, *Antitrust and International Regulatory Federalism*, 76 N.Y.U. L. Rev. 1142 (2001); Guzman, *Is International Antitrust Possible?*, 73 N.Y.U. L. Rev. 1501 (1998).

consequences within the small jurisdiction.[64] This can have significant consequences, as exemplified by the Unilever/Best Foods merger, noted above. There, the IAA did not interfere in the merger, which was approved by the United States and the EU, despite its significant effects on the Israeli market. Instead, it imposed limited behavioral limitations that applied to the merging parties' Israeli subsidiaries.

Accordingly, in practice, small economies such as Israel act as if they were applying a worldwide total welfare standard, since the large economies that have approved the merger represent a much larger share of consumers than they do. Even if the increase in market power is accompanied by increased efficiencies, these will rarely be realized by the small economy, as in many cases the production facilities are located outside its borders, and more often than not, markets in the small economy are highly concentrated and thus more prone to the realization of market power.

For similar reasons, small economies often face problems in regulating the anticompetitive conduct of multinational firms that serve a large part of their domestic demand. Empirical evidence demonstrates that this is not just an academic concern. Rather, large foreign importers frequently use an explicit or an implicit threat of exit should a small jurisdiction impose upon them limitations which they may agree to if imposed by a large economy.[65] Microsoft, for example, has declined in the past to sign an agreement that limits its conduct in Israel, which contained conditions similar to those included in the agreement it reached with the EU, even though such conditions were necessary in order to address the unique characteristics of the Israeli market.

Political obstacles might also stand in the way of a small economy attempting to prevent a merger or joint venture among foreign firms or even taking a strong stance against an export cartel. If the effects of such conduct are positive in the home jurisdiction or in other jurisdictions (higher taxes, lower unemployment, lower production costs), the small economy might encounter political resistance to its decision, especially because foreign firms have an advantage in shaping public opinion in their home jurisdiction. This consideration is based on a presumption that the small economy's size is positively correlated with its political power.

Add in the limited resources a small economy often has to combat anticompetitive conduct, with the result that small economies often have no incentive or a limited ability to take on international conduct that negatively affects their jurisdiction.

Indeed, the Israeli Authority has chosen not to bring cases even where harm to the Israeli economy might be relatively easy to prove. International mergers

64. Gal, *Unique Challenges, supra* note 1. Some of these jurisdictions are also developing ones, a fact that may further lessen their ability to deal with international issues.

65. *Id.*

that are covered under the RTPL are rarely limited or conditioned. Likewise, international cartel or abuse cases are rarely tackled. Let me provide two recent examples. The United States is currently investigating the international freight cartel. El-Al, which is the largest freight carrier to and from Israel and has limited routes elsewhere, has publicly declared that it has set aside US$20 million to cover possible liability costs arising from the U.S. antitrust suit. Despite this obvious signal that the Israeli economy had suffered some harm resulting from anticompetitive conduct, the IAA decided not to pursue the case. Similarly, Siemens, a large supplier of the Israeli Electricity Company, was declared in a report issued by the EU Commission to be part of the Gas Insulated Switches International Cartel. The Israeli Electricity Company declared that it suffered significant damages from such high prices. Despite this fact, the IAA decided not to bring suit against Siemens.

These examples raise the question of whether the enforcement decisions of the authority are rational. The answer is generally in the affirmative. Proof of an international cartel is long and costly. Since the IAA cannot rely on the findings of a foreign court or an antitrust agency, it would have to prove in court not only the domestic effects of the cartel, but also its existence. Such large cases may well be beyond its means. This is strengthened by the following facts: (a) fines imposed on such cartels in Israel are generally relatively low; (b) the United States often imposes prison sentences on top officials of international cartels (Israel would generally not impose additional imprisonment sentences); (c) the cartels often cease to exist as a result of the enforcement activities of foreign jurisdictions; and (d) the IAA has a limited budget. Given these facts, it might well be rational to decide not to prosecute such cartels.[66] Nonetheless, these considerations should not prevent the IAA from assisting private plaintiffs who bring damage suits against such cartels.

In some cases, suboptimal enforcement levels result from the inability of small economies to obtain the relevant information. For example, the IAA considered bringing a case against the Vitamins cartel after it was prosecuted elsewhere. However, the Authority could not obtain the relevant information as the U.S. Department of Justice was prevented, under its consent agreement with the relevant firms, from transferring the relevant materials to most other jurisdictions. In this case, the U.S. authority made a strategic decision, limiting the number of possible worldwide prosecutions against the cartel in order to ensure that it be brought to trial in a handful of large jurisdictions. Even from a

66. If, however, enforcement costs are reduced significantly, it might then be rational for the IAA to bring such cases. For a suggestion that countries be allowed to rely on the cartel findings of other jurisdictions and only prove the elements of the offense which are unique to it, see Michal S. Gal, *Free Movement of Judgments: Increasing Deterrence of International Cartels through Judicial Reliance* forthcoming, 51(1) VIRGINIA J. OF INT. L. (2010).

worldwide welfare point of view, this might be a sound decision. As discussed below, one of the immediate outcomes of the prosecutorial efforts of large jurisdictions is generally the discontinuation of the international cartel.[67] Thus, small jurisdictions such as Israel can enjoy positive externalities. Yet, this state of affairs is still far from optimal. The main reason is that limited enforcement leads to limited deterrence for future cartelists.[68]

Still, Israel has strong incentives to assist other jurisdictions in bringing down cartels or abusive conduct or prohibiting an anticompetitive merger. Indeed, it provides such assistance unless it is prevented from so doing under domestic laws.[69]

The above factors lead to the following conclusion: Extraterritoriality is an efficient tool for large jurisdictions that possess sufficient power over foreign firms to command obedience. Small ones often lack the requisite power to discipline foreign entities that harm them. It is thus not surprising that most do not have developed doctrines of extraterritoriality and of comity. Rather, small jurisdictions often act as "free riders" on the prohibitive efforts of other jurisdictions in the international arena.

It is not obvious, however, that when a large jurisdiction prevents the continuation of abusive or cartelistic conduct, small jurisdictions also benefit from such prevention. Do the United States and EC findings of a worldwide cartel prevent the operation of a cartel outside their borders? Often the answer is yes. Yet it depends on whether the cartel can operate outside their borders without affecting their domestic welfare. In fact, several cartels have been set up especially so that they will not create negative welfare effects on large economies, such as the Minerals cartel. In addition, such limited cartel enforcement cannot provide sufficient deterrent for firms not to engage in international cartels.[70] Similarly, the prevention of abusive conduct in one jurisdiction does not necessarily create positive externalities on others. Yet in some cases, prohibiting some type of abusive conduct in one jurisdiction has positive externalities on others. For example, when Microsoft was prohibited by U.S. and EU courts from bundling its operating system with its Web browser, it then changed the packages it sold worldwide.[71]

Where domestic effects are significant, they can be dealt with separately, and the cost to the foreign firm is not prohibitive so that it would not result in its exit

---

67. In some cases, however, the cartels will continue to operate in those jurisdictions in which prosecution is unlikely.

68. *See, e.g.*, Gal, *Free Movement, supra* note 65.

69. One example involves the information provided by the IAA to the U.S. Department of Justice in the international cartel case against LSL Biotechnologies Inc., et al. (tomato seed market allocation cartel).

70. *See, e.g.*, Gal, *Free Movement, supra* note 65.

71. This was recognized by the IAA. *See* answer to Bagatz 6623/03 Oded Lavie vs. Director of Antitrust Authority [Sept. 30, 2003]: "It makes no sense to bring a case against a company when as a result of a foreign prohibition it has already refrained from the abusive conduct worldwide.").

from the Israeli market, and the IAA might apply remedies that pertain to Israeli markets. This is exemplified by international mergers. The IAA generally takes changes in the market structures of its large importers as a given. Yet an attempt is sometimes made to regulate the merged entities with regulatory tools that relate to the actions of these foreign firms within their domestic markets, although such tools are generally more costly and less effective than prohibiting the merger from occurring.

One such option is the imposition of structural and behavioral conditions on the merging parties that apply only to their operation within the small economy. In *Unilever/Tami*,[72] for example, the IAA conditioned its approval of the merger between the U.S. and European food companies on limitations of joint business activity between Elite and Tami, the two Israeli food companies that became parts of the same international food conglomerate as a result of the merger. The conditions included limiting information transfer and maintaining a structural and personal division between the two Israeli firms. Similarly, when Unilever next acquired control over Ben & Jerry's, and the merger raised concerns regarding competition in the Israeli ice cream market, the IAA conditioned its approval on the distribution of Ben & Jerry's ice cream in Israel through an independent distributor who would be free to determine prices charged for the products. The Authority also required that the quality or quantity of the products be at least as high as those in the pre-merger situation, and that any new product be made available to the distributor.[73] These are limited remedies since they cannot totally erase the fact that both firms are controlled by the same entity that determines their strategic decisions. At the same time, the IAA often relies on the fact that the international firm will not change its strategic decisions (such as Ben & Jerry's introduction of a new product in world markets) only to reduce competition in it. Moreover, such remedies are applied only in rare cases, in which harm to the Israeli market is considerable, the remedy does not prevent the international firms from merging or does not increase the costs of merging significantly, and the remedy is relatively easy to administer.

IV. SOME IMPLICATIONS FOR INTERNATIONAL ANTITRUST[74]

The obstacles small economies like Israel face in applying their competition laws to combat international antitrust issues have important implications for efforts to reach international cooperative solutions.

---

72. *Tozeret Mazon/Unilever, supra* note 61.

73. Director, Conditions for the Approval of a Merger between Ben & Jerry's Homemade Inc. and Unilever N.V. (Dec. 16, 2001, not published).

74. This section is based, in large part, on Gal, *Unique Challenges, supra* note 1.

The past decade has seen an upsurge in attempts to reach international cooperative solutions. Such efforts are largely concentrated in the International Competition Network (ICN). The ICN is a voluntary, quasi-private association of public actors, based on persuasion and common agreements rather than on coercion and hierarchical mechanisms of control.[75]

Undoubtedly, Israel stands to benefit from international cooperation and coordination. Harmonization reduces the transaction costs of importers that might otherwise find it uneconomical to invest in learning and complying with its laws. Small economic size often implies that there are limited profits to be had. Accordingly, the lower the costs of trade in Israel—including the costs of learning and complying with domestic antitrust laws—the higher the incentives of foreign firms to import their products into it.[76] Likewise, similarity of laws may reduce the export costs of domestic firms.[77] Both effects strengthen one of the most important tools for overcoming the limits created by smallness: expanding the boundaries of the market by export and import.[78]

The creation of global antitrust standards may also assist antitrust advocates in advancing the adoption of welfare-based competition rules. Indeed, it is more difficult for interest groups to put forward a set of rules which significantly diverges from the ICN's recommendations than if such recommendations were absent. Such effects are especially important for small jurisdictions like Israel, in which political and business elites are often intertwined.[79] Moreover, joining forces to prevent anticompetitive worldwide cartels, mergers, and joint ventures will benefit all directly and indirectly, by creating stronger deterrence effects.

Yet the limited ability of small jurisdictions such as Israel to tackle international antitrust issues undoubtedly affects their bargaining position in reaching international cooperative agreements that go beyond voluntary compliance, especially on those issues that matter most to them. Harmonized rules that are likely to emerge from voluntarily negotiated agreements will probably be tilted toward the interests of the large countries. This is because diverse unilateral enforcement levels create different degrees of dependency, which in turn create a pattern of power that affects the negotiations. This is because large jurisdictions have limited motivation to consent to changes in their antitrust policy,

---

75. *See* www.internationalcompetitionnetwork.org. The author has been a nongovernmental advisor to the ICN since its inception.

76. Of course, foreign trade is not without its problems. For example, it exposes economies to the vulnerabilities of fluctuations in worldwide demand levels. *See, e.g.* Lino Briguglio, *Small Island Developing States and Their Economic Vulnerabilities*, 23 World Development 1615 (1995); Commonwealth Consultative Group, VULNERABILITY: SMALL SATES IN THE GLOBAL SOCIETY (London: Commonwealth Secretariat, 1985).

77. Michal S. Gal, *The 'Cut and Paste' of Article 82 of the EU Treaty in Israel: Conditions for a Successful Transplant*, 9 Eur. J. L. Reform 467 (2007).

78. *See* Gal, *Small Economies*, *supra* note 3, ch. 1.

79. *Id.*

which moves them closer to the global optimum but which might reduce their own welfare.[80]

This is especially true with regard to the current ICN cooperation efforts. While no jurisdiction controls the agenda or the final choice, the dynamics of the organization inevitably lead to an outcome that does not significantly change the status quo. Since agreements are voluntary, any rule that changes the current status quo should make all better off.[81] Large jurisdictions would thus not agree to concessions that reduce their benefits from the current situation. The fact that negotiations are generally area-by-area, and even rule-by-rule, strengthens this outcome, since no "trading" on benefits in different areas can be achieved, as Guzman has suggested.[82] This outcome is also strengthened by the fact that generally large or developed jurisdictions head the working groups that prepare the recommendations, since they can spare the resources to take an active part in the ICN. While the importance of international agreements should not be downplayed, a more realistic approach to their possible outcomes is warranted.

Let me provide here one example and refer the reader elsewhere for additional ones.[83] This example involves the use of market shares as indicators of market power in abuse cases.[84] Given the costs involved in a full-fledged market analysis and the fact that in many cases market shares do indeed provide a good estimate of market power, small jurisdictions often use market share indicators.[85] However, the ICN committee on unilateral conduct, which is mostly comprised of agency representatives and nongovernmental advisors from the United States and the EU, reluctantly and only partially acknowledged the benefits of the use of market shares, and at one point, suggestions were made to criticize this practice.[86] Indeed, market shares are imperfect indicators of market power. But requiring the use of much more complicated indicators may imply that in small jurisdictions, no cases of abuse could be brought in practice, given the prohibitively high costs of proof. Thus, while ICN deliberations are based on voluntary

80. For the seminal work on this issue, see Guzman, *International Antitrust, supra* note 62.

81. At least it should result in the strongest negotiators being better off.

82. Guzman, *supra* note 62.

83. Gal, *Unique Challenges, supra* note 1.

84. Another example involves the use of market shares in merger analysis. The ICN recommendations suggest the use of turnover rates and criticizes the use of market shares as prima facie indicators of harm to competition. However, the use of turnovers is highly problematic in small jurisdictions, since a turnover rate that would capture all mergers that harm such economies would also capture a large number of international mergers. ICN Merger Notification Recommended Practices, 2004, part IIB.

85. *See, e.g.*, Gal, *Small Economies, supra* note 3.

86. *See* www.internationalcompetitionnetwork.org. The author is a nongovernmental advisor of the working group on unilateral conduct.

participation and discursive democracy, in reality, small jurisdictions are mostly rule takers rather than rule makers.

Small jurisdictions, however, do have a strong card up their sleeve, should they join forces: their pre-merger notification procedures. This card is worthy not because of how it is used to remedy the problems of each jurisdiction by itself, but because of the sheer number of small jurisdictions that have adopted merger notification requirements. These procedures impose high transaction costs on firms wishing to merge that operate in global markets, which are generally located in large jurisdictions. Thus, small jurisdictions can potentially "trade in" this card, as Guzman suggested, for concessions in other fields of antitrust, such as export cartels and abusive conduct by international firms.[87]

Unfortunately, political considerations prevent Israel from entering into regional joint enforcement agreements on antitrust issues. Such agreements can provide some respite from enforcement problems.[88]

V. CONCLUSION

This chapter has examined the application of Israeli competition law in international antitrust cases. It analyzed both the existing legal regime as well as the practical considerations in applying the RTPL in such cases. It demonstrated that the current system of limited national vision and the unilateral noncooperative and cooperative enforcement approaches that currently predominate international antitrust creates major obstacles to Israel in enforcing its laws on large foreign firms. Moreover, current harmonization efforts hold little promise to resolve these enforcement problems.

---

87. For a general idea of mutual payoffs see Guzman, *Regulatory Federalism, supra* note 62, at 1156.

88. Gal, *Unique Challenges, supra* note 1; Gal, *Regional Agreements, supra* note 2.

7. COOPERATION, COMITY, AND COMPETITION IN CHINA

DONG LING*

INTRODUCTION

On August 30, 2007, the 29th session of the Standing Committee of the 10th National People's Congress passed the Anti-Monopoly Law of the People's Republic of China, which took effect on August 1, 2008. The law, including eight chapters—altogether 56 articles—sets forth the basic systems of the Anti-Monopoly Law, reflects China's competition policy, and constitutes the basic legal foundation for China to carry out its antimonopoly law. Additionally, the content relating to antimonopoly law is incorporated in a series of laws enacted previously, including Law of the People's Republic of China Against Unfair Competition (1993), Price Law of the People's Republic of China (1997), and Law of the People's Republic of China on Tenders and Bids (1999). These laws, together with the Anti-Monopoly Law, have formed China's antimonopoly law system.

The most significant change in this antimonopoly law is that it is a comprehensive, basic law in the antimonopoly sphere which has, for the first time, established an enforcement system for antimonopoly law, as well as pinned down the definition, investigation procedure, and legal liability of monopolistic conduct in a complete and systematic way. Before this law, there was no agency specifically devoted to antimonopoly law enforcement. Instead, it was the responsibility of separate sector regulatory agencies to regulate monopolistic conduct in the form of excluding and restricting competition. Thus, these regulations used to be unsystematic and incomplete. With this antimonopoly law, instead, it will not only regulate economic monopolistic conduct like monopoly agreements, abuse of dominant market position, and undertakings concentration that has the effect of excluding and restricting competition, but it will also regulate conduct that abuses administrative power. This law has both substantial and procedural provisions. For these reasons, I believe that this antimonopoly law is an important step for China in its course of perfecting a market-economy based legal system. Because there is no material difference between this law and its comparables in the West, it has also become the foundation of cooperation between China and other countries on competition law issues.

However, there are some clear problems with this law, including the lack of a unified enforcement agency, resulting in a multichannel enforcement situation

* Dong Ling is a faculty member of the school of law at the University of International Business and Economics (UIBE).

(to be discussed in more detail in following paragraphs). It is neither clear whether the enforcement agencies have exclusive or preferred enforcing power over monopolistic conduct, nor whether there is division or collaboration between these agencies and other sector regulatory agencies. Second, the provisions are not specific enough for direct application, which will unavoidably require a lot of other regulations to complement it. An example is that, for monopolistic conduct involving intellectual property rights (IPR), the law has only provided that "the conducts of undertakings in abusing the IPR to exclude or restrict competition should be subject to this law." In order to be applied, the provision will require further definition by more detailed implementation rules or guidelines.

According to the Anti-Monopoly Law, there is a two-tier enforcement system in China. Article 9 of the Anti-Monopoly Law provides that the Anti-Monopoly Committee under the State Council is in charge of organizing, coordinating, and guiding the antimonopoly efforts. Article 10 provides that the authority designated by the State Council to undertake the responsibilities of antimonopoly enforcement ("Anti-Monopoly Enforcement Authority under the State Council") is responsible for the enforcement of the Anti-Monopoly Law. According to the working rules of the Anti-Monopoly Committee, the Committee performs its duties primarily through the Committee's plenary sessions, Chairman's meetings, and special sessions. It does not step into the shoes of its subordinate member units or departments when executing its administrative responsibilities. The Ministry of Commerce (MOFCOM), the National Development and Reform Commission (NDRC) and the State Administration for Industry and Commerce (SAIC) are responsible for enforcing the Anti-Monopoly Law.[1] The main job of the State Council Anti-Monopoly Committee is enactment of competition policies and other legislative works rather than enforcement of the Anti-Monopoly Law. Enforcement of the law is accomplished jointly by the MOFCOM, NDRC, and SAIC. According to the organization, staffing, and function plan ("the Organization Plan") approved by the State Council, the MOFCOM, SAIC, and NDRC, are respectively responsible for "carrying out antimonopoly review against the concentration between undertakings according to law," "investigation and punishment on illegal pricing behavior and monopolistic pricing behavior," and "antimonopoly law enforcement works including monopoly agreements, abuse of dominant market position, abuse of administrative powers to eliminate or restrict competition (with exception for monopolistic pricing behaviors)."[2]

---

1. *The State Council Approved the Working Rules of the Anti-Monopoly Committee*, People's Daily, Sept. 14, 2008, at p 2.

2. Lu Tianling, *Putting Question Marks Behind the Three Departments Sharing the Power in Antimonopoly Enforcement*, Nanfang Daily, Aug. 26, 2008. It is not clear which department is responsible for the intellectual property license-related antimonopoly cases, and it is not impossible that these kinds of case would be handled by the IP authority. However, judging from the above-mentioned division of enforcement power, it seems

The Organization Plan also provides that the function of the MOFCOM in antimonopoly includes guiding Chinese enterprises to respond to antimonopoly charges in foreign countries and carrying out bilateral and multilateral international exchanges and cooperation with regard to competition policies.

As for the range of application, Article 2 of the Anti-Monopoly Law provides a general guideline that this law is applicable to monopolistic conduct in economic activities within the territory of the People's Republic of China. It also provides that this law is equally applicable to monopolistic conduct outside the territory of the People's Republic of China if such conduct has exclusive or restrictive effects on competition in the domestic market. Other than this, issues concerning the application of some specific antimonopoly systems outside China's territory are also provided for in some regulations. For example, the threshold for when concentrations between undertakings should be reported is set forth in the Provisions of the State Council on Standard for Notification of Concentration between Undertakings (2008).

The Anti-Monopoly Law has only been in effect for a short time, and antimonopoly law enforcement authorities have been established only recently. A few relevant implementation rules or guidelines have been published, and cases that have been enforced according to the Anti-Monopoly Law are mostly about examination of undertakings concentration. Most international cooperations are in the fields of capacity building and information exchanges(for example, inviting foreign experts to research and provide advice on the legislation of the Anti-Monopoly Law). Given these facts, it is very difficult to describe and interpret the extraterritorial jurisdiction of China's Anti-Monopoly Law, the application of the comity principle, or the procedures, forms, and operations in international exchanges and co-operations in connection with competition law.

In this chapter, I can only seek to make tentative jurisprudential predictions about the questions mentioned above and estimate what might be the most probable answers from the Chinese Anti-Monopoly Law enforcement authorities by examining existing legislative materials and related legal documents and news reports in combination with Chinese Anti-Monopoly Law theories. Based on these findings, I will try to provide some constructive suggestions.

The first section discusses the principles of the extraterritorial jurisdiction of China's Anti-Monopoly Law as well as related questions. The second section discusses the application of the comity principle in China's Anti-Monopoly Law. The third section discusses the principles and forms that China might adopt in carrying out competition policies with regard to international corporations. In the conclusion, I summarize the whole chapter.

---

that the State Administration for Industry and Commerce should be responsible for these cases. *See also* http://fldj.mofcom.gov.cn/aarticle/gywm/200809/20080905756026.html.

I. STIPULATIONS ON EXTRATERRITORIAL JURISDICTION IN CHINA'S ANTI-MONOPOLY LAW

A. Doctrines and Standards in Determining the Jurisdiction

In essence, extraterritorial jurisdiction is an issue under international law, which is determined mainly for the purpose of avoiding conflicts in international relationships and which is the traditional mechanism of international law. In this regard, the concepts of sovereignty and the territorial doctrine play a major role in determining other doctrines of jurisdiction, such as the nationality doctrine, protected doctrine, and effects doctrine, which play complementary roles. In the realm of international law, China has had much practical judicial experience,[3] which is undoubtedly of great importance in guiding the determination of the extraterritorial jurisdiction of China's Anti-Monopoly Law.

As mentioned, Article 2 of the Anti-Monopoly Law provides that even if the monopolistic conduct occurs outside the territory of the People's Republic of China, if this conduct has exclusive or restrictive effects on competition in the domestic market, the Anti-Monopoly Law will still apply. This has, in effect, established the effects doctrine[4] with regard to the extraterritorial application of the Anti-Monopoly Law, which is in line with the established doctrine of most countries. In fact, the effects doctrine, which was developed from the territorial doctrine, has long been embodied and enforced in China's legislative and judicial practices. An example is Paragraph 3 of Article 6 of the Criminal Law of the People's Republic of China (revised in 1997), which provides: "If, among the acts or results of a crime, one of them takes place in the territory of the People's Republic of China, it shall be deemed a crime committed in the territory of the People's Republic of China."

According to the effects doctrine, the Anti-Monopoly Law will be applicable to the monopolistic conduct which has or will have restrictive effects on competition in the domestic market of China, regardless of the nationality and residence of the subjects, or the place of origin of the monopolistic conduct. Therefore, if the monopolistic conduct planned or implemented by foreign enterprises outside the territory of China has restrictive effects on the competition in China's domestic market, this conduct will be subject to China's Anti-Monopoly Law. However if the competitive conduct launched by Chinese enterprises in the extraterritorial markets has no effect on the domestic market, this conduct is not subject to China's Anti-Monopoly Law. To be specific, the language of Article 2 of the Anti-Monopoly Law can be restated as follow: First, if both the monopolistic

---

3. China has signed on to or participated in several international treaties, based on which the courts have made some judgments. See the Web site for Chinese commercial and maritime trials involving foreign parties, available at http://www.ccmt.org.cn/dxal.php. *See also* http://en.chinacourt.org/.

4. A country has jurisdiction over such behaviors that (although have taken place overseas) have or will have the effect of restricting competition in the country.

conduct and its results occur in the territory of China, even if the actors are foreigners, the Anti-Monopoly Law is directly applicable, and there is no conflict of law. This is because the Anti-Monopoly Law is based in public policy and therefore is mandatory within the realm of sovereignty. Second, if both the monopolistic conduct and its results occur outside the territory of China, China's Anti-Monopoly Law is not binding, regardless of the actors' nationalities. Meanwhile, pursuant to foreign antimonopoly law, a suit for damages cannot be filed in China. The argument is that the competition policy embodied in the antimonopoly law reflects a nation's basic economic policy. China can neither promote its own economic policy outside its territory, nor does it have the obligation to implement a foreign country's economic policy. Third, if the monopolistic conduct occurs in foreign countries, but the results occur in the territory of China or have restrictive effects on the competition in the domestic market of China, then China's Anti-Monopoly Law has jurisdiction based on the effects doctrine. However, since the provision on the effects doctrine in the Anti-Monopoly Law is very sketchy, and there is no legal precedent on the issue, at present it is still hard to generalize a legal standard for the application of the effects doctrine. Instead, I can explain how the effects doctrine is applied to specific cases.

B. Application of the Effects Doctrine in China's Anti-Monopoly Law

The extraterritorial application of the Anti-Monopoly Law is prominently reflected in the following two respects: the prohibition of international cartels and the antimonopoly review of mergers.

1. International Cartels International cartel refers to competition restriction agreements that have transnational effects. Using the members of a cartel as criteria, international cartels can be classified as cartels between multinational companies, export cartels, import cartels, and so forth.

In "Recommendation Concerning Effective Action Against Hardcore Cartels" passed by the OECD in 1998,[5] the main types of international cartels are labeled "hardcore cartels," which means there is an anticompetitive agreement, anticompetitive concerted practice, or anticompetitive arrangement among competitors to fix prices, make rigged bids (collusive tenders), establish output restrictions or quotas, or share or divide markets by allocating customers, suppliers, territories, or lines of commerce. In recent years, along with the globalization of the world economy and the development of trade liberalization, there has been an increasing number of international cartel cases. An example was given in a report by EU to the World Trade Organization in 2002, which revealed that the graphite electrodes cartel, which had lasted at least seven years and involved products worth a total of about €2.5 billion, had fixed prices at approximately 50 percent above the competitive market price, implying illegal gains for the

5. C (98) 35/FINAL.

cartel members of about €1.2 billion within the European Community alone. Therefore, the fine imposed (about €280 million) represented a relatively small proportion of the gains.[6] In 2001, the European Community had imposed fines totaling €1,836 million on 56 companies, 38 of which were from the EC and 18 of which were from other countries.[7]

According to Article 13 of China's Anti-Monopoly Law, it is illegal for horizontal competitors to carry out the following practices by way of monopoly agreements: (i) fixing or changing the prices of commodities; (ii) restricting the output volume or sales volume of commodities; (iii) dividing sales market or supply market of raw materials; (iv) restricting the purchase of new technologies or new facilities, or restricting the development of new technologies or new products; and (v) concerted boycotting. All of these monopoly agreements can be classified as core cartel. Accordingly, when an international cartel has exerted influence on sales and consumption in China's market through these monopoly agreements, even if the cartel was not formed in the territory of China or its members have no branches in China, in principle, China's Anti-Monopoly Law still has jurisdiction over it.[8] This is evidenced in the case of the patent pool of DVDs, where some scholars believe that even though the patent pool was concluded outside the territory of China, if these agreements have caused serious harm to the benefits of Chinese licensees or consumers, China's Anti-Monopoly Law should have extraterritorial jurisdiction over them.[9] It is worth noting that China's Anti-Monopoly Law does not explicitly provide that the per se illegal rule is applicable to the above-mentioned agreements. However, the illegality of these types of conduct is too evident to circumvent penalties under the Anti-Monopoly Law.

When the jurisdiction over hardcore cartel concerns foreign countries' exporter cartels, the situation is more complicated, since many countries' anti-monopoly laws admit the legality of their exporter cartels. This issue concerns the restriction in application of the effects doctrine and the comity doctrine, which will be discussed further in the latter part of this chapter.

2. Extraterritorial Merger There are two situations where extraterritorial merger may affect competition in domestic markets: one is domestic enterprises carrying out mergers in foreign markets, and the other is foreign enterprises

---

6. *See* Report on the Meeting of July 1–2, 2002, WT/WGTCP/M/18, Sept. 20, 2002.

7. *Id.*

8. The Anti-Monopoly Law clearly provides against: "(iv) restricting purchase of new technologies or new facilities, or restricting the development of new technologies or new products; (v) concerted boycotting," and places the two circumstances side-by-side with the other three circumstance, demonstrating that these activities have the same effects in the law. Moreover, both the Anti-Monopoly Law and the Law on Tenders and Bids prohibit collusive tenders. In another words, "hardcore cartel" in China's Anti-Monopoly Law is a broader definition compared with the OECD's definition.

9. Wang Xiaoye (editor in chief), Detailed Annotation on the Anti-Monopoly Law of the People's Republic of China, p. 22 (Intellectual Property Publishing House 2008).

carrying out domestic or transnational mergers in foreign markets. The same standard applies in both situations in terms of jurisdiction. China's Anti-Monopoly Law established the prior notification requirement for mergers. Article 21 states that where the concentration between undertakings reaches the notification threshold stipulated by the State Council, the undertaking shall file a notification with the Anti-Monopoly Enforcement Authority under the State Council before the concentration. No concentration action shall be implemented without prior notification. The specific notification standards are: (i) the combined aggregate worldwide turnover of all the undertakings concerned is more than 10 billion RMB in the last accounting year, and the aggregate turnover of each of at least two of the undertakings concerned is more than 400 million RMB in the last accounting year in China; and (ii) the combined aggregate turnover of all the undertakings concerned is more than 2 billion RMB in the last accounting year in China, and the aggregate turnover of each of at least two of the undertakings concerned is more than 400 million RMB in the last accounting year in China.[10] These notification standards have incorporated the concept of the lowest turnover of undertakings concerned in China, which can be understood as a specific quantification standard when applying the effects doctrine in extraterritorial mergers. That is, whatever the specific characteristic the extraterritorial merger has, as long as the foreign enterprise that takes part in the merger has already had enterprises in the Chinese market and has reached a certain revenue threshold, it should file merger notification with the Chinese antimonopoly law enforcement authority. Although foreign enterprises' absolute turnover in the Chinese market and the proportion of that against its total worldwide turnover is not large, its extraterritorial merger conduct will undoubtedly have an impact on market competition and consumers in China.

In order to reduce conflicts between countries over extraterritorial merger jurisdiction, the International Competition Network (ICN) published in September 2002 the Recommended Practices for Merger Notification Procedure, which holds that the countries claiming jurisdiction should have an appropriate nexus with the merger under review.[11] If one of the following criterion may be satisfied, then the jurisdiction concerned can require notification because it can be deemed that the merger is likely to have a significant, direct, and immediate economic effect within the jurisdiction concerned: (i) at least two parties to the transaction have significant local activities, and (ii) the acquired business has a significant direct or indirect presence in the local territory, such as local assets or

---

10. Provisions of the State Council on the Standard for Notification of Concentration between Undertakings.

11. Recommended Practices for Merger Notification Procedures, *available at* http://www.internationalcompetitionnetwork.org/uploads/library/doc588.pdf.

sales in or into the jurisdiction concerned.[12] By this standard, the jurisdiction criteria under the Chinese Anti-Monopoly Law has both satisfied the indicator of "having at least two undertakings concerned (i.e., at least two undertakings have reached the minimum sales revenue)" and the indicator of "having significant economic activity (i.e., the sales revenue is over 400 million RMB)," and thus is a clear and simple standard to apply in cross-border mergers when compared with the standard of market share.

The standard has also reflected the development level of China's economy.[13] For example, using this standard, we can assume what will happen if Boeing and Airbus will merge. Because they both have subsidiaries in China, and their annual sales in the Chinese market have far exceeded 400million RMB, even though their main business locations are not in China, such a merger would undoubtedly have a great impact on competition in China, and thus they would have to file notification with China's Anti-Monopoly Law enforcement authority for ratification. Example could be seen in the joint venture case between BHP Billiton and Rio Tinto in early 2010 which is outside China but has been reported to the Ministry of Commerce of China according to China's concentration notification requirement.[14]

C. Review and Comment on the Extraterritorial Effect of China's Anti-Monopoly Law

China's Anti-Monopoly Law has adopted the well-recognized effects doctrine in determining its extraterritorial validity. At present, the difficulty with law enforcement is that the description in the law itself for the effects doctrine is too sketchy, and it lacks the basic conditions for application such as having a "direct, substantial, and reasonably foreseeable effect," as is established under U.S. antitrust law, The description also does not mention the "interest-balancing approach." These deficiencies have made it especially difficult to enforce extraterritorial jurisdiction pursuant to the Anti-Monopoly Law and to determine how to advocate extraterritorial jurisdiction on an international cartel. Against the background of economic globalization, it is hard to claim that international cartels that originate overseas will not have any "effect" on market competition in China. If we

12. *Id.* Comment 1 to paragraph C of Article 1, Nexus to Reviewing Jurisdiction. *See also* Notification & Procedures Subgroup of Merger Working Group of International Competition Network, Setting Notification Thresholds for Merger Review, *available at* http://www.internationalcompetitionnetwork.org/uploads/library/doc326.pdf.

13. Zhang Xinzhu & Dong Weigang, *Estimation of Application Criterion of Enterprises Acquisition*, DONGYUE TRIBUNE, 2007.1.

14. Deng Yao, *Rio Tinto and BHP Billiton have filed notification to the Ministry of Commerce of China for antimonopoly scrutiny on their joint venture plans*, 21CENTURY BUSNISS HERALD, May 5, 2010, *available at* : http://www.21cbh.com/HTML/2010-5-5/xMMDAwMDE3NTYxMw.html.

only focus on effect without limitation, it will lead to a different understanding of what "effect" means, and thus result in an overly broad application of the antimonopoly law or even conflicts of jurisdiction. In fact, since China's antimonopoly law enforcement authority is in a preliminary stage of development, it is too heavy a burden to impose on them the task of overseas jurisdiction even if the condition to use such effects doctrine is relaxed enough. So although it is absolutely necessary to set up objective and practical standards (such as whether the effect is obvious or substantial, whether it is reasonably foreseeable, and whether it is necessary to investigate intent, etc.), in order to avoid conflicts of jurisdiction, we should also consider other elements, including possible conflicts with foreign policies and laws, the primary business location of the undertakings under consideration, the anticipated effect of using the jurisdiction, and the importance of such influences in China when compared with other countries.

In terms of extraterritorial merger notification, the jurisdictional criterion established by the Anti-Monopoly Law is reasonably clear. It can be deemed as the embodiment of the effects doctrine, which is both operational and in line with the development trend of antitrust law. The report threshold for mergers has actually provided an important criterion for applying the effects rule in Chinese Anti-Monopoly Law by "having certain level of sales in the territory of China." If the enterprises that are carrying out monopolistic conduct in foreign countries have business activities in China, and the activities cannot be ignored, then the effects rule can be seen as an important factor for judging whether monopolistic conduct "has exclusive and restrictive effects on domestic market," so as to determine whether the Anti-Monopoly Law has jurisdiction over it. This can, to some extent, reduce the uncertainty in exercising extraterritorial jurisdiction. However, at best, this is nothing more than a logical conclusion. The best way is still to stipulate clearly the conditions for applying the effects doctrine through legislation, which is what the Anti-Monopoly Committee has been doing.

II. INTERNATIONAL COMITY IN THE APPLICATION OF ANTIMONOPOLY LAWS

A. Status and Role of the Comity Principle in Chinese Law

Comity is a concept reflecting mutual respect for sovereignty and interests among nations. Because there are frequent conflicts between governing laws, the comity principle exists in international law to avoid conflict and to resolve disputes. This principle has its basis in the consideration of mutual interest and needs among nations—a nation shall fairly treat others in order to be fairly treated. Because the effects doctrine is widely applied in the antimonopoly laws in most nations—which, if unduly over-applied may result in enforcement according to one nation's antimonopoly law not being recognized in another nation—the reasonable principle and comity theory have generally been adopted as an adjustment and a compliment to the effects doctrine. A good example is the U.S. Antitrust Enforcement Guidelines for International Operations (1995), which provides that "In enforcing the antitrust laws, the Agencies consider international comity . . . in determining whether to assert jurisdiction to investigate or bring an action, or to seek particular remedies in a given case, each Agency takes into account whether significant interests of any foreign sovereign would be affected." The Guidelines also provide that the agencies shall consider eight relevant factors in performing a comity analysis.[15]

Although the comity theory has become the main rationale for solving jurisdictional conflicts and has been a major principle in determining practice, China's international law theories have not explicitly acknowledged a comity principle. The reason is that China's domestic law theories hold that the comity principle involves decisions made by a nation based on its own interests and represented by its own free will, while comity in itself is not a component of international law, nor can it actually solve problems. It also holds that even though some nations developed the international comity principle and made it a concept in their domestic laws by providing for stringent restrictions using express legal standards, when applying this principle in specific cases, final decisions are usually unpredictable and lack consistency because the bodies making the decisions (e.g., a court) are fairly independent, and the mechanism of decision-making is often provisional. Each nation involved in an antitrust conflict may demand that the other side abide by the comity principle, but there is no specific norm to determine which party shall make the concession.

Although China has also adopted a policy of mutual respect among nations as the prerequisite for developing international relationships—which is in line with the comity concept—its international law theories attach more importance to the so-called "five principles of peaceful coexistence" (i.e., mutual respect for territorial integrity and sovereignty, mutual nonaggression, noninterference in each other's internal affairs, equal and mutual benefit, and peaceful coexistence) as the foundation for dealing with international relationships. China uses the international treaties to which it is a party as the basis for its assumption of international obligations and regards the issue of comity as an affair within a nation's sovereignty.

In other words, at present, China does not use comity as a principle in dealing with jurisdictional conflicts, nor does it specify the factors to be considered when dealing with jurisdictional issues. What is clear is that it will use international treaties to which it accedes as authority in dealing with international relationships,

---

15. U.S. Department of Justice and Federal Trade Commission, Antitrust Enforcement Guidelines for International Operations, § 3.2 (April 1995), *available at* http://www.justice.gov/atr/public/guidelines/internat.htm.

while maintaining consistency and coherence in handling issues of international law. Based on past experience, it is foreseeable that in the course of enforcing its antimonopoly rules, China's law enforcement agencies and judiciary will defer to established international law principles (e.g., foreign sovereign immunity) and its international obligations through international treaties, which means that it will neither recklessly determine the scope of application of the Anti-Monopoly Law nor unscrupulously apply the jurisdictional principle specified by this law; rather, it will determine whether to exercise jurisdiction over specific matters on a case-by-case basis, based on the circumstances of each case.

The fact that one of the mandates of the Anti-Monopoly Bureau of MOFCOM is to provide guidance for Chinese enterprises when defending antimonopoly cases abroad shows that China has anticipated complex situations where the extraterritorial reach of different states' antimonopoly laws may result in Chinese enterprises having to defend cases abroad and foreign enterprises having to defend cases in China.

With regard to foreign relationships and international laws for enforcing the Anti-Monopoly Law, it is probable that the Anti-Monopoly Committee (which is in charge of organizing, coordinating, and directing antimonopoly work) will need to render final decisions absent a clear stipulation in the Anti-Monopoly Law. This is not only because the members of that committee are of a high administrative level[16]and many of them are experienced in handling international affairs and thus have a better perspective and more authority, but also because that this will guarantee a unified implementation of foreign relationship policy of the state and avoid possible conflicts due to multichannel management.

If the enforcement of antimonopoly laws raises issues of foreign relations and international laws, it is likely that the Anti-Monopoly Committee will be the final decision maker. When the committee is making decisions, it will consider many factors, including international relationships and legal principles, and so it is actually inevitable that it will consider the rule of "international comity" and other related factors (such as the degree of conflict between laws and policies, the expected effect of exerting jurisdiction, etc.). One could say that this is because there is no material conflict between the "five principles of peaceful coexistence" advocated by China and the "international comity" principle. Instead, it could be that the comity principle is a concrete expression of the "five principles." The difference, however, is that the process of applying the "five principles" and elements of consideration are not open, although the aim of China to avoid diplomatic conflict and be equitable in international affairs could be foreseeable.

16. The chairman of the committee is the vice premier of the State Council, while members are officials from various ministries and departments at the level of at least deputy minister. *See* http://www.caijing.com.cn/2008-09-14/110012362.html.

B. Practical Antimonopoly Issues Possibly Involving Comity

The exercise of extraterritorial jurisdiction over international cartels is likely to be contentious; thus the comity principle needs to be considered. In this respect, the comity principle as described by the U.S. Supreme Court in its *Hartford Fire* decision has been controversial. The *Hartford Fire* case emphasizes that it is necessary to consider the comity issue and exercise a balancing of interests only when there is a true conflict of jurisdiction between the United States and foreign nations. According to this decision, a true conflict demands that the conduct subject to the United States jurisdiction must also violate laws of the foreign state. That is, unless foreign laws "order" the person to violate U.S. antitrust laws, the application of U.S. antitrust law shall not be precluded, even where the foreign state has a strong policy that permits or encourages such conduct.[17] Therefore, the *Hartford Fire* decision has limited the comity principle to special circumstances where foreign laws expressly demand enterprises to act in breach of the Sherman Act so that these enterprises cannot be in a position to simultaneously comply with both domestic laws and U.S. antitrust laws. This decision has abandoned the balance of interests implied by the comity principle, which will inevitably result in de facto demise of the comity principle as defined by the United States.[18]

As mentioned, how China's Anti-Monopoly Law will treat export cartels and import cartels that affect market competition in China is a sensitive issue. From the perspective of domestic policy, since the strict prohibition of cartels in export will be deemed extremely altruistic,[19] many nations allow export cartels, even if they aim to fix export prices or export quantities. By the same token, out of consideration for economies of scale and reducing transaction costs, antimonopoly laws in many nations also recognize the legitimacy of import cartels, even where domestic importers establish an import cartel for the purpose of boycotting the import of foreign goods. Article 15 of China's Anti-Monopoly Law provides that business operators may legitimize export cartels or import cartels by proving that these cartels are established "for safeguarding valid interests in foreign trade and foreign economic cooperation." Although in line with legislations in most countries, this provision makes conflict more possible.

Under the *Hartford Fire* rule, the United States may well hold that Chinese export cartels or import cartels have significant effects on market competition in the United States, and thus U.S. antitrust laws should apply without considering the comity principle, because China's antimonopoly law does not "compel"

---

17. Hartford Fire Ins. Co. v. California, 509 U.S. 764, 798 (1993).

18. Actually, when describing the comity analysis, the Antitrust Enforcement Guidelines for International Operations emphasizes a comprehensive comity analysis other than conflict of laws.

19. Eleanor M. Fox, *International Antitrust and the Doha Dome*, 43 VA. J. INT'L L. 911, 919 (2003).

export or import enterprises to form export cartels or import cartels.[20] On the other hand, it remains to be seen whether China can exert extraterritorial jurisdiction over legal foreign export or import cartels.[21] Since there has not been specific regulation in this regard in China, we can only assume that, according to past practice, China will most likely use reciprocity principles or mutual benefit principles to solve the problem, rather than directly applying extraterritorial jurisdiction of antimonopoly law or merely considering whether there is a conflict of law and the conflict of law is only limited to the situation that the laws of two states cannot simultaneously be followed, as is the case in *Hartford Fire*. Under the reciprocity principle or mutual benefit principles, a competent authority will determine the reasonableness of jurisdiction after balancing interests sufficiently and comprehensively[22] (although it means that for quite a long time, it will be impossible to know from publicly available sources how and to what extent the interests are balanced).

This method is also helpful for China in maintaining certain flexibility on this issue. In this process, antimonopoly penal decisions made by foreign antimonopoly agencies against their domestic enterprises (e.g., the consent decree entered into by Microsoft and the U.S. Department of Justice) naturally will be taken into consideration by Chinese antimonopoly agencies (although the specific weight and extent may vary from case to case) as part of the comprehensive

---

20. Prior to the promulgation of the Anti-Monopoly Law, there were cases where Chinese exporting enterprises were sued in the United States for monopolistic agreements. For example, in June 2005, six Chinese enterprises including Welcome Pharmaceutical (North China Pharmaceutical), Weisheng Pharmaceutical (Shijiazhuang Pharmaceutical), Jiangshan Pharmaceutical, and Northeast Pharmaceutical received summons issued by Rains & Animal Science Products Inc. and served by the U.S. District Court for the Eastern District of New York pursuant to the Hague Convention, alleging that such companies had colluded to manipulate the prices and quantity of Vitamin C exported to the United States and other countries since December 2001 and violated antitrust laws of the United States and California. *See* http://www.in-pharmatechnologist.com/Materials-Formulation/China-s-vitamin-C-makers-ready-for-anti-trust-battle.

21. Actually, there has been precedent for exclusive behaviors exempted from U.S. antitrust laws (e.g., Export Trading Company Act of 1982) being sued for violating antitrust laws in foreign countries under foreign antitrust laws. In the *Woodpulp* case, ECJ pointed out that U.S. antitrust agencies had been notified of this case at the beginning, but they had no opposition to the practice of EC. *See* Woodpulp Cartel v. Commission, (1988) E.C.R. 5193 (E.C.J).

22. For example, whether the foreign country has a comprehensive, sound, and legitimate competition policy system, and the factors mentioned in Section 3.2 of the Antitrust Enforcement Guidelines for International Operations: whether to encourage certain behaviors, whether to enable parties to freely choose different strategies or whether to prohibit some of these strategies, and the impacts of its enforcement activities on relevant enforcement activities of foreign antitrust agencies, these are all considerations when the competent authority is making the decision.

interest-balancing exercise. However, when deciding punishment for domestic enterprises under antimonopoly laws, the Chinese antimonopoly agency may normally not consider possible reactions to a decision by antimonopoly agencies of foreign countries.

C. Comment on the Application of International Comity under China's Antimonopoly Law

At present, China's Anti-Monopoly Law makes no provision for comity analysis in terms of extraterritorial application. In its international law theory, China has acknowledged the "five principles of peaceful coexistence" but does not officially recognize the so-called "comity principle." It is a fact that, in theory, China's Anti-Monopoly Law does not include a comity principle. As one Chinese scholar has pointed out, in the course of the application of antimonopoly laws, it is not appropriate for judges to judge the interests of foreign governments by adjudicating specific cases, because the responsibility of a judge is to analyze and judge issues of law, not to judge issues of foreign affairs, national defense, or international economic policies of foreign governments.[23] Some foreign scholars have expressed similar views that

> a transnational antitrust issue is really a manifestation of a policy conflict between national governments. . . . In such cases resolution should be sought through the normal methods of consultation and negotiation. For one government to seek to resolve the conflict in its favor by invoking its national law before its domestic tribunals is not the rule of law but an application, in judicial guise, of the principle that economic might is right.[24]

But this does not automatically lead to the conclusion that Chinese antimonopoly agencies will not conduct comity analyses in the course of law enforcement. Actually, according to Chinese international law theory, in the case of law application concerning foreign relationships, the decision maker will not only consider the conflict of laws issue, but also comprehensively consider the comity factor advocated by western countries. These "soft" influences will be reflected in the practice of law, when dealing with specific cases. As previously mentioned, China is aware of the complexity of this matter and has appointed a body especially for the purpose of guiding enterprises in defending foreign antimonopoly suits, but China has not shown any intention of enacting blocking statutes to

---

23. Wang Xiaoye, *Regulating Anticompetitive Behaviors of Transnational Enterprises under Antimonopoly Law*, *in* New Developments of Competition Law in the Economic Globalization Era 294 (Wang Xiaoye ed.).

24. J.S. Stanford, *The Application of the Sherman Act to Conduct outside the United States: A view from Abroad*, 11 Cornell Int'l L.J. 195, 213 n.46 (1978).

preclude the application of foreign antimonopoly laws.[25] This means that China has given its Anti-Monopoly Law extraterritorial validity mainly for the purpose of having "equal weapons." In practice, China will rely more on the reciprocity principle.

In performing comity analysis for extraterritorial application of antimonopoly laws, antimonopoly agencies typically regard foreign government-related anticompetitive conduct as exceptions like the principle of foreign sovereign immunity, the principle of foreign sovereign compulsion,[26] and the act of state doctrine. Although China's Anti-Monopoly Law makes no provision for these cases, China's international law theories do not reject incorporating these principles or doctrines as international customs into its own legal systems.[27] In other words, these principles and doctrines will be considered by antimonopoly agencies as part of the comprehensive comity analysis.

All in all, although China's Anti-Monopoly Law only makes very abstract and brief provisions for its extraterritorial validity, according to China's international law practice in the past, it is reasonable to foresee that competent bodies will still abide by established principles and rules in international laws in legal practice without drastic departures.

III. INTERNATIONAL COOPERATION WITH RESPECT TO COMPETITION LAW ENFORCEMENT

A. China's Position on International Competition Policy Cooperation and the Status Quo

With the growing economic globalization and the increase of transnational operations, China has realized that it is necessary to seek effective international cooperation in order to alleviate conflicts and controversies in extraterritorial application of antimonopoly laws. This will also benefit the effort to crack down upon international cartels. The legislative process of China's Antimonopoly Law is in itself a demonstration of international cooperation in competition policy. During the whole legislative process, foreign experts and antimonopoly officials from agencies of various countries have, on many occasions, provided legislative counseling and comments, and have exchanged opinions and views with their

25. During the course of enacting and implementing the Anti-Monopoly Law, there were never legislative proposals or working plans for enacting blocking statutes.

26. *See, e.g.*, the opinion in *Hartford Fire. See also* Trugman-Nash, Inc v. New Zealand Dairy Bd., 954 F. Supp. 733 (S.D.N.Y. 1997).

27. Chapter 5 of China's Anti-Monopoly Law provides for "Exclusion or Restriction of Competition by Abusing Administrative Power," which is different from antimonopoly laws of western countries; therefore, it is significant to stress that China's Anti-Monopoly Law does not apply to antimonopoly conduct concerning foreign governments.

Chinese counterparts. All of these activities have been taken to ensure that both the basic framework and content of China's Anti-Monopoly Law are not essentially different from those of major western countries. This legislative process has resulted in successful international cooperation.

In July 2003, China submitted its report of "Hardcore Cartels and Voluntary Cooperation" to WTO (the Report).[28] This Report highlights that international cooperation on competition policy consists of two aspects. One is cooperation with respect to competition law enforcement, and the other is capacity build-up relating to competition policy and the construction of a competitive culture. As a developing country, China's most urgent challenges at present are how to improve its capacity and acquire experience. Therefore, China hopes to prioritize cooperation on competition policy and the construction of a competitive culture in order to promote the exchange of information and the sharing of experiences among members, as well as to facilitate the formation of a consensus through capacity build-up, which will in turn pave a solid foundation for future cooperation. Capacity build-up is not only an important method, but also an integral part of the future framework. The Report also mentioned that international cooperation should take a progressive stance and that participating nations may exchange laws and regulations regarding antimonopoly policies as part of the cooperation while even closer international cooperation in specific cases may also be envisaged.

In November 2003, China and the EU entered into the "Memorandum of Understanding on Setting up a Dialog Mechanism on Competition Policy," which was the first step for China in creating international cooperation in the field of competition policy. For the EU, the purpose of dialogue with China is to establish a long-term mechanism for mutual counseling in the field of competition policy, and to expand the EU's technical aid and capacity aid with respect to competition legislation and enforcement in China. This agreement reflects China's stance to regard capacity build-up and information exchange as a priority in international cooperation of competition policy in the initial phase after establishing its competition law system, as well as its intention to gradually expand the scope of cooperation.

Currently, China's international cooperation efforts on competition policy are also reflected in the free trade agreements it has entered into with multiple countries. For example, China has already signed the Free Trade Agreement with the Association of Southeast Asian Nations (ASEAN), Chile, Pakistan, New Zealand, Singapore, Peru, and Costa Rica, while the FTAs with other countries and regions like Australia, the Gulf Cooperation Council (GCC), Iceland, Norway, and the Southern African Customs Union (SACU) are under negotiation.[29] These signed or to-be-signed agreements all contain clauses on competition

---

28. WT/WGTCP/W/241.

29. *See* http://fta.mofcom.gov.cn/english/index.shtml.

policy, some of which are quite detailed. A good example is Chapter 9 on Trade Services in the "Free Trade Agreement between China and New Zealand," which contains provisions specific to "monopoly and provider of monopoly services" that are similar to provisions specified by Article 8 of WTO's GATS. These clauses have undoubtedly created binding obligations under international laws. In terms of content, these clauses have concentrated on abuses of market dominance and administrative monopolies.

Generally speaking, while China believes it is necessary to conduct international cooperation on competition policy, it is still quite cautious. Although it hopes to gradually expand the extent and scope of cooperation, its main focus at present is on capacity build-up and information exchange, with active bilateral or regional cooperation on competition law enforcement and cooperation in specific cases. In addition, China attaches emphasis to multilateral platforms such as WTO, APEC, UNCTAD, and ICN by which it can exchange views on international cooperation with other countries.

International experience shows that a nation's international cooperation efforts generally are dominated by its competent agency. One of the prerequisites for international cooperation in competition policy is that the competent agencies in charge of competition are independent, unified, professional, authoritative, and have certain enforcement power. Currently, although China has empowered the Anti-Monopoly Bureau of MOFCOM to be in charge of international communication and cooperation on competition policies, due to the fact that the Bureau is only partially responsible for antimonopoly law enforcement, it lacks sufficient independence and authority. This inevitably will have an impact on the efforts to promote international cooperation.

B. Prospects for China to Conduct International Cooperation in Competition Policy

There are basically three forms of international cooperation. First, there is procedural cooperation, whereby antimonopoly agencies of different nations conduct procedural cooperation with respect to investigating and obtaining evidence, like exchange of information, regular consultation mechanisms, and so forth. Second, there is positive comity, which means according to bilateral or multilateral agreements, a country may require another country to give "sufficient and friendly consideration" to anticompetitive conducts that have happened in the latter country but have damage effects in the former. Third, there is convergence, which means unifying antimonopoly rules at an international level. All three of these cooperative methods have now developed to a certain degree in international antimonopoly cooperation, but to varying extents.[30]

---

30. Huang Yong & Li Zhiqiang, *Conflict of Laws and International Cooperation in the Implementation of Antimonopoly Laws*, *in* New Developments of Competition Law in the Economic Globalization Era 220 (Wang Xiaoye ed.).

Most international cooperation on competition law enforcement is still in the preliminary phase of procedural cooperation and coordination. In the foreseeable future, China will conduct procedural cooperation in the form of bilateral or regional cooperation to improve and develop its own legislation and enforcement through the exchange of information and access to technical aid.

An important institutional basis for conducting positive comity is that both sides of the cooperation have sound competition laws and effective law enforcement systems. However, relevant legislation and law enforcement systems in China have yet to be perfected. Differences and gaps still need to be closed between China and developed countries. Even where the positive comity principle has been put into practice, neither has it been implemented well, nor has it always had satisfactory results in international practices.[31] Therefore, China believes that at the current stage, it is still premature to conduct cooperation by means of positive comity.

As for international efforts in unifying antimonopoly laws, unlike some developing countries, China does not have a strongly contrary position. Rather, it believes that it is unwise to ignore the rapid progress of economic globalization and that more pragmatic methods may be used with respect to specific implementation.

First, China is of the opinion that it is better to discuss and establish unified competition law rules under the framework of the WTO. This is not only because competition law is highly interrelated with trade policies when dealing with transnational transactions, but also because the WTO has accumulated successful experience in dealing with other trade-related legal affairs, such as trade-related intellectual property rights and trade-related investment issues. Furthermore, among various existing international organizations, the WTO has been one of the most effective in dealing with trade-related competition issues. Now China has become the largest export country and the second largest import country worldwide[32] and is increasingly facing opposing views in trade. This is a practical reason for China to advocate promoting cooperation on competition policy and enforcement under the WTO framework.

Second, there are four specific options for reaching unified competition policy under the WTO framework: ministerial declaration or decisions of ministerial conference, multilateral agreement, nonbinding multilateral framework agreement, and partially binding multilateral agreement.[33] China advocates that at the current stage, voluntary cooperation is preferable. That is, it tends to embrace

---

31. *See* the report of China, *Hardcore Cartels and Voluntary Cooperation* to WTO, WT/WGTCP/W/241.

32. News from China's MOFCOM website, *available at* http://www.mofcom.gov.cn/aarticle/i/jyjl/k/201006/20100606950315.html.

33. (Japan) Mitsuo Matsushita, *WTO's Principles & the Role of Competition Policies*, Chinese version translated by Zhu Zhongliang, *in* GLOBAL L. REV. (Spring 2003).

the third option of nonbinding multilateral framework agreement. One important reason for China's position is that quite a number of countries have not yet had an antimonopoly law of their own. The main function this kind of multilateral agreement is to declare WTO competition policy in a centralized and explicit way, and to regulate competition policies and coordinate law enforcement of members on a nonmandatory basis. This option deals mainly with the fundamental content of members' competition policies and laws, including coordination among members in such aspects as mutual notification, information exchange, active comity, and provision of aid to developing country members. Since this agreement is nonbinding, the dispute resolution mechanism of the WTO does not apply, nor will a special international competition law enforcement body be set up. All that is necessary is to establish relevant coordination and cooperation mechanisms. This option does not preclude the option of a multilateral agreement open to all WTO members. On the basis of these agreements, a system of binding and unified competition standards may be established, even to the extent that one day, an international competition authority may be set up to safeguard fair competition in the world economy, which will be a conduit to maintaining competitiveness in the world market by lowering the threshold for less developed countries to access the market and keeping that threshold at that level.[34]

Third, as for a specific framework principle, WTO's Working Group on Interaction between Trade and Competition held its 19th formal meeting at Geneva in September 2002, during which the core principles were discussed. The core principles on competition, as listed in the Doha Declaration, include transparency, nondiscriminatory treatment, and procedural fairness. Since these principles are consistent with the WTO's fundamental principles, China does not oppose them but emphasizes that these core principles are merely a basis for further development and evolution of WTO competition laws, and that these principles should also be reasonably defined and allow explicit exceptions. For example, when a developing country supports mergers among domestic leading companies in order to better meet international competition, this practice should not be regarded as discriminatory enforcement of its domestic antimonopoly laws. Rather, this should be seen as a necessary method to confront the imbalance of economic development between developed and developing countries. Therefore, in their implementation, these principles should consider preferred and special treatment for developing countries.

Fourth, as for specific framework content, China is of the opinion that cooperation should currently be targeted at hardcore cartels. Generally speaking, competition policies implicate fundamental economic policies of a country, and

---

34. Huang Yong & Li Zhiqiang, *Conflict of Laws & International Cooperation in the Implementation of Antimonopoly Laws*, *in* New Developments of Competition Law in the Economic Globalization Era 222 (Wang Xiaoye ed.).

different countries are at different stages and thus may have different criteria for competition. Even in the United States, a country with ample antitrust enforcement experience, its antitrust policies have undergone many adjustments and are still evolving and developing. Since there are no definite criteria, it is improper to demand all countries to adopt unified criteria and norms in making fundamental policy adjustments. But hardcore cartels are different. They are especially damaging and are often operated by transnational enterprises, making developing countries most vulnerable to serious damage due to their relatively underdevelopment in law enforcement. Therefore, it is easier to reach consensus by focusing on framework agreements for combating hardcore cartels with less resistance in policy coordination among countries.

In summary, it is China's view that because of the large gap between developed and developing countries in economic and legal construction, future multilateral competition framework should give priority consideration to the status quo of developing countries. For example, developed countries should take voluntary steps in restricting export cartels which impair international competition. And the majority of misuses of intellectual property rights through international cartels have mainly taken place in developed countries. Therefore, developed countries should not enforce competition laws differently either domestically or abroad. Meanwhile, China also stresses that it is unacceptable to impose international cooperation with other nations as a mandatory obligation, or to link international cooperation with trade issues like market access. Instead, cooperation on a voluntary basis should be the cornerstone of a multilateral competition framework in order to achieve gradual progress toward a comprehensive and unified competition policy.

CONCLUSION

With the establishment of China's market economy system and the continuance of its opening-up policy, China has become increasingly aware of the importance of antimonopoly laws and the importance of guaranteeing China's engagement in international economic activities by means of law. Through years of relentless efforts, China has promulgated its Anti-Monopoly Law and established the generally accepted principle of the effects doctrine in order to evade the negative impact of foreign monopolistic conduct on market competition in China. Although there are no express norms or sufficient experience yet, according to China's existing theories and practice of international law, it can be reasonably predicted that in line with the comity principle, China will conduct comprehensive legal analysis and balance interests in a way that fully respects the sovereignty of other nations, as well as international customs, when applying the effects doctrine. In international cooperation on antimonopoly laws, China will focus on information exchange and competence build-up and on conducting cooperation on competition law enforcement in individual cases on bilateral or regional levels, but will temporarily not proceed to positive comity. At the multilateral level, China supports the discussion and formulation of a unified competition policy under the WTO framework, but in a gradual manner. At present, China tends to prefer nonbinding voluntary cooperation or nonbinding multilateral framework agreements, with a focus on discussion of hardcore cartels that are generally thought to be most harmful.

8. COOPERATION, COMITY, AND COMPETITION POLICY IN SINGAPORE

BURTON ONG*

I. COMPETITION LAW AND POLICY IN SINGAPORE: AN OVERVIEW

Singapore's competition law regime was introduced relatively recently through the enactment of the *Competition Act*[1] on November 19, 2004. Prior to this date, there were no statutory prohibitions against anticompetitive conduct by undertakings either acting singly or in combination with each other, though competition-related provisions had been put into sector-specific regulatory regimes designed to facilitate the liberalization of key industries previously occupied by single state-owned monopolies.[2] Modelled after the United Kingdom's *Competition Act 1998*, which was in turn premised on the European competition law provisions found in Articles 81 and 82 of the Treaty of Rome, Singapore's competition law regime consists of three principal prohibitions. First, there is the section 34 prohibition against "agreements between undertakings, decisions by associations of undertakings or concerted practices which have as their object or effect the prevention, restriction or distortion of competition within Singapore." Second, there is the section 47 prohibition against "any conduct on the part of one or more undertakings which amounts to the abuse of a dominant position in any market in Singapore." Third, there is the section 54 prohibition against "mergers that have resulted, or may be expected to result, in a substantial lessening of competition within any market in Singapore."

These non-penal statutory prohibitions are administered by the Competition Commission of Singapore (CCS), a specialist statutory agency housed within the Ministry of Trade and Industry.[3] The CCS is responsible for issuing guidelines interpreting the scope of the statutory prohibitions and investigating and

---

* Associate Professor, Faculty of Law, National University of Singapore. The author would like to thank Professor M. Sornarajah for his helpful comments on an earlier draft of this work. The usual disclaimers apply, of course.

1. Chapter 50B, Act No. 46 of 2004, *available at* http://statutes.agc.gov.sg.

2. For a more detailed analysis of the origins of competition law in Singapore, see Burton Ong, *The Competition Act 2004: A Legislative Landmark on Singapore's Legal Landscape*, SINGAPORE J. LEGAL STUD. 172 (2006).

3. Further details about the structure of the CCS can be found on their Web site: http://www.ccs.gov.sg.

prosecuting alleged instances of anticompetitive conduct, as well as making determinations of liability as the tribunal of first instance for matters related to the *Competition Act.* Appeals can be made from the decisions of the CCS to the Competition Appeal Board, the members of whom are statutorily appointed by the relevant Minister, and further appeals may be brought before the Singapore High Court and Court of Appeal on points of law or decisions relating to the quantum of a financial penalty.[4] Rights of private action are conferred on parties injured by anticompetitive conduct prohibited under the Act and may be exercised after the CCS has reached a decision that an infringement of one of the relevant statutory prohibitions has occurred, and only after no further appeals may be brought regarding that decision.[5]

With a resident population of just over 5 million people housed on a small island just over 700 square kilometres in size, Singapore's economy is primarily fueled by tertiary level high-technology, manufacturing, and service industries. Heavily dependent on foreign imports to meet the needs of domestic consumers, with all major segments of the economy export-oriented in nature, Singapore is often described as an archetypical small open economy.[6] The island nation is situated in Southeast Asia, a region comprising a diverse range of developing economies, most of which were formerly under colonial rule. The ten countries located within this region—Singapore, Malaysia, Indonesia, Thailand, Brunei, the Philippines, Vietnam, Cambodia, Laos, and Myanmar—are members of a loose political alliance known as the Association of Southeast Asian Nations (ASEAN). The goals of ASEAN include the establishment of an ASEAN Economic Community by 2020 by creating a regional free trade area with economic integration as an end goal.[7] Part of this process of regional integration, which is very much in its infancy, involves the development of a "regional guideline on competition policy by 2010," even though only about half the members of ASEAN currently have enacted domestic competition laws of their own.[8]

---

4. Section 69(4) provides that the CCS may impose a financial penalties on an errant undertaking up to a sum not exceeding 10 percent "of such turnover of the business of the undertaking in Singapore for each year of infringement" for up to a maximum of three years.

5. Section 86 *Competition Act, supra* note 1.

6. Singapore was ranked second in The Global Enabling Trade Report 2008, published by the World Economic Forum, in a global survey of the openness of 118 economies worldwide to international trade and investment. More recently, in The Global Competitiveness Report 2010-2011, which was published by the same organization, Singapore was ranked third in an international survey of 139 countries.

7. Further details about ASEAN can be obtained from the alliance's Web site at http://www.aseansec.org.

8. See paragraph 41 of the *ASEAN Economic Community Blueprint 2007,* available from the alliance's Web site, under which all member countries "endeavour to introduce competition policy . . . by 2015."

II. THE EXTRATERRITORIAL REACH OF SINGAPORE'S COMPETITION LAW REGIME

While there have been no reported decisions or investigations involving issues arising from the extraterritorial application of Singapore's competition laws thus far, it is nevertheless very clear from the statutory provisions in the *Competition Act* that the legislature clearly contemplated the possibility of anticompetitive harm arising from acts carried out beyond Singapore's territorial limits. Explicit statutory language can be found within the Act to extend the scope of the statutory prohibitions to include such conduct. Section 33(1) provides that the section 34, section 47, and section 54 prohibitions are applicable to any case:

> Notwithstanding that—
>
> (a) an agreement referred to in section 34 has been entered into outside Singapore;
> (b) any party to such agreement is outside Singapore;
> (c) any undertaking abusing the dominant position referred to in section 47 is outside Singapore;
> (d) an anticipated merger will be carried into effect outside Singapore;
> (e) a merger referred to in section 54 has taken place outside Singapore;
> (f) any party to an anticipated merger or any party involved in a merger is outside Singapore; or
> (g) any other matter, practice or action arising out of such agreement, such dominant position, an anticipated merger or a merger is outside Singapore.[9]

This makes it abundantly clear that an infringement of Singapore's *Competition Act* can occur even if the relevant actors are outside of Singapore, or if the anticompetitive conduct alleged originates from or has taken place entirely outside of Singapore, so long as the impugned conduct has as its "object or effect the prevention, restriction or distortion of competition *within Singapore*" (the section 34 prohibition), "amounts to the abuse of a dominant position *in any market in Singapore*" (the section 47 prohibition), or may result in "a substantial lessening of competition within any market *in Singapore*" (the section 54 prohibition). It would therefore appear that an "effects"-based approach has been statutorily adopted in Singapore such that it would probably be unlawful—to take the facts of *Hartford Fire*[10] as an example—if foreign undertakings conspired to force domestic parties normally in competition with each other to collectively and uniformly alter their commercial terms and conditions. However, in the absence of any case law or precedents from CCS involving investigations into conduct with

---

9. This provision was modeled after section 32 of the *India Competition Act 2002*.
10. Hartford Fire Ins. Co. v. California, 509 U.S. 764 (1993).

an extraterritorial dimension,[11] it remains to be seen whether Singapore's competition regulator will adopt a "pure" effects-based approach, or if it will require the presence of additional links between the parties and Singapore before it takes action.[12]

A. Abuse of Dominance, Within and Beyond Singapore's Territorial Borders

In the context of the section 47 prohibition against the abuse of a dominant position, the extraterritorial character of the scope of the statutory provision is even more striking. Subsections (1) and (3) of section 47 provide:

> (1) [A]ny conduct on the part of one or more undertakings which amounts to the abuse of a dominant position in any market in Singapore is prohibited.
>
> . . .
>
> (3) In this section, "dominant position" means a dominant position *within Singapore or elsewhere*.[13] (emphasis added).

This means that if a foreign-based undertaking has a limited market presence in Singapore, but nevertheless enjoys a position of market dominance in its

---

11. While the second infringement decision taken by the CCS against an association of express bus operators for price-fixing involved undertakings that operated transport services between Singapore and various locations in Peninsula Malaysia, all the parties to anti-competitive agreement were based in Singapore and the focus of analysis was on bus passengers who commenced and completed their journeys in Singapore. See Case No. CCS 500/003/08, [2009] SGCCS? Re: Price Fixing in Bus Services from Singapore to Malaysia and Southern Thailand (decided Nov. 3, 2009).

12. Legal commentators analyzing the landmark decisions of the U.S. courts involving extraterritorial applications of the Sherman Act—*U.S. v. Aluminum Co. of America*, 148 F.2d 416 (1945), *U.S. v. Imperial Chemical Industries* 100 F. Supp. 504 (S.D.N.Y. 1951), and *U.S. v. The Watchmakers of Switzerland Information Center, Inc.* 133 F. Supp. 40 (1955) and 134 F. Supp. 710 (1955)—have pointed out that these cases did not rest purely on the adverse economic effects that the foreign conduct in question may have had on the United States, but also involved other links, such as nationality, supplied by the fact that American corporations or their foreign subsidiaries were involved in the conspiracy. *See* M. Sornarajah, *The Extraterritorial Enforcement of U.S. Antitrust Laws: Conflict and Compromise*, 31 Int'l & Comp. L.Q. 127, 137–38 (1982).

13. While Singapore may have modeled its competition law regime after the Anglo-European competition law framework, it should be noted that the scope of section 47 prohibition is significantly broader in at least one respect: the alleged infringer need not occupy a dominant position within any market *in Singapore*. This is unlike the position taken under Anglo-European jurisprudence where non-EC-based undertakings have to possess a dominant market position *within* the Common Market before they can be considered to have violated Article 82 EC. For a further discussion of the differences between the Singapore and EC approaches toward the abuse of market dominance, see Burton Ong, *Exporting Article 82 EC to Singapore: Prospects and Challenges*, 2(2) Competition L. Rev. 99, 109–12 (2005).

home market, it will still be treated as a dominant undertaking capable of abusing its market dominance in Singapore so long as the impugned conduct has an adverse effect on competition "in any market in Singapore."[14] Given that the statutory prohibition does not require that the allegedly abusive conduct take place within Singapore, it is therefore entirely possible for a foreign undertaking to abuse its dominant position in a foreign market by engaging in exclusionary commercial conduct outside of Singapore—foreclosing access to foreign suppliers or distributors, for example—and still run afoul of the section 47 provision so long as the end result of its behavior is an appreciably adverse impact upon competition in any market within Singapore.

These deliberately crafted statutory provisions reflect the legislature's awareness of the necessity of enacting a competition law in Singapore that is broad enough to deal with competition case scenarios that may include a variety of extraterritorial features. Many suppliers of goods and services in Singapore are multinational corporations controlled from beyond Singapore's territorial limits. These undertakings may enter into restrictive agreements or engage in exclusionary practices anywhere in the world, but the anticompetitive effects generated by such conduct may eventually be transmitted to domestic markets within Singapore. Such legislative foresight has been translated into a competition law framework which very clearly empowers the CCS to investigate allegations of anticompetitive conduct notwithstanding the extraterritorial dimensions to these scenarios.

B. Intramarket Extraterritoriality: Conduct Taking Place Within a Transnational Geographical Market but Beyond Singapore's Territorial Borders

Apart from situations where the relevant undertakings are based outside of Singapore, or whose allegedly anticompetitive conduct has taken place outside of Singapore, issues of extraterritoriality are likely to emerge in a significant way in at least one other category of cases. These are scenarios where, although the parties involved are domestic undertakings and the impugned conduct has taken place entirely within Singapore, the relevant markets in question extend beyond Singapore's territorial borders. As a regional trading, manufacturing, and financial services center, Singapore-based undertakings are very likely to do business with traders and customers from neighboring countries, particularly within the ASEAN region. This means that when defining the relevant geographical market, the CCS may very well have to look beyond Singapore's national borders and analyze transnational markets straddling two or more neighboring states. Market investigations in these cases would require an analysis of market conditions in

14. Paragraph 3.1 of the CCS Guidelines to the Section 47 Prohibition sets out a two-step test to assess whether the prohibition applies: first, "whether an undertaking is dominant in a relevant market, either in Singapore or elsewhere"; and second, "if it is, whether it is abusing that dominant position in a market in Singapore."

these other countries—the degree of competition offered by foreign traders, the bargaining power of foreign buyers, the local regulatory environment, and so forth. This category of cases can be said to involve instances of "intramarket extraterritoriality," as opposed to the cases contemplated earlier, which involved instances of extraterritorial conduct emanating from outside Singapore that negatively affects competition within Singapore as a properly defined relevant market.

Given the factual complexities which arise from cases involving extraterritorial dimensions, the CCS will face a number of practical constraints if and when it encounters such scenarios. First, given its limited resources and relative inexperience as a national cross-sectoral competition regulator, these sorts of cases may not rank very high on their list of investigation and prosecution priorities. Second, the statutory investigatory and punitive powers conferred upon the CCS can only be exercised and enforced within Singapore's territorial limits, creating evidentiary difficulties for the competition regulator if the case required it to establish that anticompetitive conduct had taken place abroad or to evaluate the impact of foreign market conditions on competition in a transnational geographical market that encompassed Singapore. Third, to the extent that these cases involve transnational geographical markets that encroach into foreign jurisdictions with their own competition law regimes, there is a possibility that the regulatory agencies in these under jurisdictions may subscribe to views that are not consistent with the positions taken by the CCS, giving rise to potential interstate diplomatic minefields that the competition regulator might want to avoid. Such scenarios are most likely to arise in cases involving state-owned enterprises or government-linked undertakings where other broader national interests and policy objectives, ranging from national wealth investment diversification strategies to the protection of foreign relations with neighboring states, may come into conflict with the efficiency-promoting competition policies of the relevant competition regulators.

C. International Law Issues Arising from the Extraterritorial Application of Singapore's Competition Laws

International law places limits on a state's jurisdictional competence to apply its laws extraterritorially in relation to acts by parties that take place beyond the state's territorial boundaries. Whether a state has jurisdiction over extraterritorial conduct can be analyzed from two perspectives. First, the state must have "prescriptive" (or "substantive" or "legislative") jurisdiction over the matter—which means that it must have competence under international law to make laws that cover conduct occurring abroad. Second, the state must have "enforcement" jurisdiction, which includes having "adjudicatory" or "judicial" jurisdiction to try a case, enabling it to issue orders and apply sanctions against the relevant parties.

There are two principal bases for a state's applying its laws to situations involving instances of extraterritorial conduct. First, a state has jurisdictional competence to regulate the behavior of its citizens abroad, including business entities and commercial undertakings incorporated under its law (the "nationality principle"). Second, a state has jurisdictional competence to regulate conduct within its own territory (the "territoriality principle"), which includes the power to regulate conduct that originates from outside the state but is completed within the territorial limits of the state ("objective territoriality").[15] The classical example involves crimes being committed across state boundaries, such as a gunman who commits a homicide by shooting his weapon from just across the territorial limits of the forum. The nationality and territoriality principles define the scope of a state's competence to legitimately extend the coverage of its criminal laws extraterritorially. But to what extent do these international law principles operate upon the extraterritorial scope of Singapore's competition law?

The competition law prohibitions such as those found in Singapore's *Competition Act* are premised on the particular market-oriented economic policies of a state. While these prohibitions are not defined as criminal wrongs, unlike the specific crimes defined in other criminal law statutes in Singapore which have an extraterritorial scope of application,[16] the sanctions that may be imposed upon infringers by the CCS include fines, which are clearly penal in character.[17] In addition, as the national competition regulator, the CCS is a public body exercising the sovereign powers of a state, powers that are not shared by private litigants, and that seek to vindicate public rights and prevent public injury. Given these characteristics, public international lawyers generally agree that the limits of a state's prescriptive jurisdiction with respect to its competition laws, when they are applied extraterritorially, are very similar to the limits governing a state's jurisdiction in criminal law matters.[18]

Looking at statutory prohibitions against anticompetitive behavior found in Singapore's competition laws in light of the objective territoriality principle

---

15. As one leading commentator has noted, "generally accepted and often applied is the objective territoriality principle, according to which jurisdiction is founded when any essential constituent element of a crime is consummated on state territory." *See* IAN BROWNLIE, PRINCIPLES OF PUBLIC INTERNATIONAL LAW 299 (Oxford Univ. Press 6th ed.). However, adopting a "constituent elements" approach to competition law infringements, which are not proper crimes, is problematic because competition law prohibitions are typically not defined in terms of specific acts, but rather in terms of their adverse economic effects. *See* Michael Akehurst, *Jurisdiction in International Law*, 46 BRIT. Y.B. INT'L LAW 145, 195–96 (1972–73).

16. *See, e.g.*, § 37 of the Prevention of Corruption Act (Chapter 241) ("Liability of citizens of Singapore for offences committed outside of Singapore"), and § 8A of the Misuse of Drugs Act (Chapter 185) ("Consumption of drug outside Singapore by citizen or permanent resident").

17. As Brownlie, n.15 above at p.298, puts it "anti-trust legislation often involves a process which, though formally 'civil', is in substance coercive and penal."

18. *See* Akehurst, *supra* note15, at 191–92.

derived from international law, one can only speculate at this stage how far the CCS will adopt an "effects"-based theory of jurisdiction when investigating and prosecuting cases involving extraterritorial dimensions.[19] Given the high degree of dependency Singapore has on foreign trade to sustain its domestic economy, it would not be difficult to imagine situations arising in which foreign parties engage in anticompetitive behavior that takes place *entirely* outside of Singapore, but the adverse effects of such behavior are felt within Singapore.

Other international law jurisdictional issues that arise from having competition laws with an extraterritorial reach relate to the state's enforcement jurisdiction, or its competence to implement or execute its laws against the offending party, and its adjudicatory jurisdiction, which is concerned with its competence to make judicial determinations in legal proceedings against an offending party. The basic principle behind a state's enforcement jurisdiction is that, without any proper justification, a state cannot take measures to enforce its own national laws on the territory of another state without the consent of the latter.[20] These enforcement measures may range from compelling the production of documents located abroad or obtaining evidence from foreign witnesses, to collecting fines imposed as a result of noncompliance with the orders issued by the tribunal. In the absence of any competition law, bilateral cooperation, or enforcement treaties[21] between Singapore and other countries, the CCS may find itself

---

19. It is not clear if Singapore would follow, for example, the "intended effects" approach articulated in *U.S. v. Aluminum Co. of America*, 148 F.2d 416 (1945), where Justice Hand concluded that U.S. jurisdiction existed whenever the foreign parties intended to affect U.S. commerce and their conduct had an actual effect within the United States, or if it will adopt something along the lines of the "primary effects" approach advocated by one writer. *See* Akehurst, *supra* note15, at 198, where the author argues that a state's extraterritorial jurisdiction over an antitrust matter should be limited to the cases where the primary effect of the act is felt in that state, an approach which requires consideration of two factors: "(1) are the effects felt in one State more direct than the effects felt in other States? (2) Are the effects felt in one State more substantial than the effects felt in other States?"

20. The same issues arising from an overly expansive application of the "effects"-based theory of objective territoriality, discussed earlier in the context of a state's prescriptive jurisdiction, also arise when such arguments are made to justify a state's enforcement jurisdiction where, for example, the forum tries to enforce its orders against undertakings outside its territorial limits by taking action against related persons or property actually within its territorial jurisdiction. Brownlie has argued that "there is no essential distinction between the legal bases for and limits upon substantive (or legislative) jurisdiction, on the one hand, and on the other, enforcement (or personal, or prerogative) jurisdiction. The one is a function of the other. If the substantive jurisdiction is beyond lawful limits, then any consequent enforcement jurisdiction is unlawful." *See* Brownlie, *supra* note 15, at 308.

21. These would include, most notably, the agreements between the EC and the United States on September 23, 1991 and June 4, 1998. *See European Communities-United*

practically constrained when it seeks to investigate allegations of anticompetitive conduct that has taken place outside of Singapore as it may encounter difficulties in persuading the legal institutions of another state to assist in the exercise of its enforcement powers against uncooperative foreign undertakings beyond Singapore's territorial limits.

Similarly, even if the CCS were able to conduct its investigations against these foreign undertakings and concluded that an infringement of Singapore's competition laws had occurred, it may not be able to execute judicial orders[22] against them unless the infringers had assets within Singapore. It is unlikely that the CCS would succeed in enforcing its infringement decisions via the national courts of the foreign territories in which these undertakings are located. This is because, in addition to the difficulties the CCS may have in persuading a foreign court that it has the requisite enforcement jurisdiction over the foreign parties, at least under the conflicts of law rules adopted by states that have common law legal systems, the courts are generally unwilling to enforce foreign judgments that are premised on the violation of penal or quasi-penal statutes that reflect the particular public policy concerns of a specific state.[23] The section below will address the matter of how issues of adjudicatory jurisdiction might be addressed by the CCS by drawing analogies from the framework of private international law principles used by the Singapore courts to determine when a tribunal ought to consider itself a competent forum to deal with a particular case and when it should decline to hear a case on the grounds that the proper forum for the case lies in the tribunals of another state.

States: Agreement on the Application of Their Competition Laws 30 I.L.M. 1487 (1991) and *European Communities-United States: Agreement between the European Communities and the Government of the United States of America on the application of positive comity principles in the enforcement of their Competition Laws* 37 I.L.M. 1070 (1998).

22. While standing outside of the Singapore judicial hierarchy, the *Competition Act* provides that the directives of the CCS may be enforced by the Singapore District Court with "the same force and effect . . . as if it had been an order originally obtained in the District Court." *See* §85(2) *Competition Act, supra* note 1.

23. *See United States of America v Inkley* [1989] QB 255, where the Court of Appeal held that it had no jurisdiction to enforce an action by a foreign state to enforce in the English courts the execution of its own penal laws, based on the authority of earlier decisions of the House of Lords in *Huntington v. Attrill* [1893] A.C. 150 at 157 ("The rule that the courts of no country execute the law of another applies not only to prosecutions and sentences for crimes and misdemeanors, *but to all suits in favour of the state* for the recovery of pecuniary penalties for any violation of statutes for the protection of its revenue or other municipal laws, and to all judgments for such penalties") and *Government of India v. Taylor* [1955] A.C. 491 at 511 ("One explanation of the rule thus illustrated may be thought to be that enforcement of a claim for taxes is but an extension of the sovereign power which imposed the taxes, and that an assertion of sovereign authority by one state within the territory of another, as distinct from a patrimonial claim by a foreign sovereign, is (treaty or convention apart) contrary to all concepts of independent sovereignties".).

III. COMITY AND THE EXERCISE OF JURISDICTION BY TRIBUNALS IN SINGAPORE

This section is concerned with how the CCS will decide when it should assume jurisdiction over an extraterritorial competition law matter and when it should, as a matter of comity or courtesy under international law norms, let some other foreign tribunal or competition authority investigate and prosecute the case. Without any domestic precedents directly addressing this issue, the discussion below is premised on first principles derived from the legal status of the competition regulator as a quasi-judicial tribunal that ought to adopt an approach similar to the one taken by the Singapore courts when determining its own competence to adjudicate a particular case involving allegations of foreign anticompetitive conduct. This will be followed by an examination of the first two cases handled by the CCS, involving foreign undertakings seeking its approval to enter into cooperative agreements containing restrictive arrangements that had negative effects on competition in Singapore, to illustrate how the principles of *forum non conveniens* ("natural forum") developed by the courts in the context of private international law might be usefully applied in the context of Singapore's competition laws. Finally, a hypothetical case scenario based on the factual matrix of the *Hartford Fire* case will be evaluated under Singapore's competition law framework.

A. The Competition Regulator as a Quasi-Judicial Tribunal and "Natural Forum" Considerations

As Singapore's national competition regulator, the CCS performs a mix of quasi-legislative, prosecutorial, and judicial functions. It is responsible for issuing detailed guidelines to complement the provisions in the *Competition Act*, conducting investigations into allegations of anticompetitive conduct, and prosecuting cases, as well as determining the appropriate financial penalties and remedial orders to be imposed upon those who have been found liable for infringing the statutory prohibitions against anticompetitive conduct. As the sole regulatory agency responsible for enforcing Singapore's general competition laws, the CCS operates as a quasi-judicial tribunal, even though its legal status is, strictly speaking, that of a "body corporate with perpetual succession"[24] that has been set up as a statutory board under the Singapore Ministry of Trade and Industry.

Unlike the specialist industry regulators responsible for enforcing sector-specific competition laws in the telecommunications, media, and energy markets, the CCS does not have a well-defined constituency of statutorily licensed operators to supervise. The CCS's jurisdiction extends to all undertakings in all sectors of the Singapore economy not exempted under the Third Schedule of the

24. Section 3 *Competition Act*, *supra* note 1.

Competition Act. Given its functional status as a quasi-judicial[25] tribunal, and the fact that competition law exhibits characteristics of both criminal and civil law, it is submitted that the CCS's approach toward deciding if it should exercise jurisdiction over a case involving elements of extraterritoriality ought to be consistent with the principles adopted by the Singapore courts when addressing the same question, albeit in the context of adjudicating private law disputes between parties. Such jurisdictional issues arise in regular judicial proceedings primarily in two contexts—first, when the courts are asked to grant leave to serve proceedings[26] on parties outside of Singapore and second, when the courts are asked to grant a stay of proceedings which have been commenced in Singapore on the ground that there is another forum which is the more appropriate forum for the trial of the action ("*forum non conveniens*"). In both contexts, the Singapore courts apply the same "natural forum" principles to determine if the case ought to be heard in Singapore. This means that if Singapore is the natural forum for the case, then the courts will assume jurisdiction; but if the natural forum lies with the courts of another country, then jurisdiction will be declined by the forum. The Singapore courts have explicitly recognized the doctrine of *forum non conveniens* as one that is based on the principle of comity between nations, and that it is of fundamental importance that a forum is satisfied that it is competent to adjudicate over a particular case before jurisdiction is assumed.[27]

When deciding if they should accept jurisdiction over a particular case brought before it, the Singapore courts adopt the two-stage approach devised by the English House of Lords in *Spiliada Maritime Corporation v Cansulex Ltd.*[28] The first stage involves determining if there is another available forum with which the legal action has the most "real and substantial connection." This would involve assessing and balancing a wide variety of relevant connecting factors, including the domiciles of the parties, the locations in which their businesses operated, the jurisdiction in which the acts complained of occurred, the law governing the relevant transaction (if any), and other factors that may influence the convenience or expense of hearing the case (such as the location of witnesses) in

25. One might take the view that the CCS is a judicial, rather than simply a quasi-judicial, institution on the basis that its decisions are subject to appellate review by the Singapore courts rather than through judicial review processes governed by administrative law principles. If this characterization of the CCS is correct, then there is a an even stronger case for the CCS to adopt the "natural forum" principles embraced by the Singapore courts.

26. Order 11, rule 1of the *Rules of the Supreme Court of Singapore* ("Cases in which service out of Singapore is permissible").

27. *The "Rainbow Joy"* [2005] 3 Singapore Law Reports 719 at [18]–[19].

28. *"The Spiliada"* [1987] AC 460, followed by the Singapore Court of Appeal in *Brinkerhoff Maritime Drilling Corp v PT Airfast Services Indonesia* [1992] 2 Singapore Law Reports 776 and *Rickshaw Investments v Nicolai Baron von Uexkull* [2007] 1 Singapore Law Reports 377.

a particular jurisdiction. If at the end of this stage the court concludes that there is no other available forum which is clearly more appropriate, then it will normally accept jurisdiction over the case. If there is another forum that is clearly more appropriate to hear the case, then the court will not exercise jurisdiction over it—by refusing to grant leave for service overseas or by granting a stay of proceedings that have commenced in Singapore—unless there are circumstances by reason of which justice requires that it should assert jurisdiction and allow the case to be heard in Singapore. This involves a second stage of analysis into the interests of all the parties to the case and the ends of justice, and the mere fact that the plaintiff has a legitimate personal or juridical advantage if the proceedings were conducted in Singapore is not regarded as decisive.

Private international law principles such as those described above do not traditionally apply to criminal and public law cases and quasi-criminal regulatory areas such as securities regulation, primarily because these are branches of the law involving a state's attempt to exercise its sovereign powers in furtherance of its public policy and regulatory objectives. Unlike purely private law disputes, which are focused on achieving justice as between the private parties themselves, these "public interest" branches of the law raise public international law jurisdictional issues concerned with circumscribing their scope of application. However, the natural forum principles developed by the courts, and their evaluation of the various connecting factors between the facts of a case and the potential forums in which it could be tried, are still relevant towards determining *any* tribunal's competence to adjudicate matters involving extraterritorial elements and may provide the competition regulator with useful analytical tools to determine if it should take on a particular case. If the CCS adopts the principles of comity espoused by the Singapore courts, then it will have to recognize that it should not take the initiative in those extraterritorial cases that can be more competently pursued and evaluated by competition regulators in other countries.[29]

---

29. The effect of the Singapore competition regulator applying such "natural forum" principles when deciding if it should assume jurisdiction over a particular case would bear some resemblance to the "jurisdictional rule of reason" approach proposed by Kingman Brewster in the context of American antitrust law. *See* Kingman Brewster, Jr., Antitrust and American Business Abroad 446–48 (1958). As one commentator has explained it, Brewster's approach is essentially allocational in nature, with the antitrust court assigning a case to one court system or another from the outset of the case. Applying a "jurisdictional rule of reason" approach to cases involving extraterritorial dimensions would require a court, when deciding if it should apply American antitrust law to extraterritorial conduct, to balance a range of factors, such as the relative significance of the conduct within each country, the extent to which there is an explicit purpose to harm or affect the forum nation's consumers, the relative seriousness of the effects in the forum nation compared with those abroad, the nationality or corporate locations of each of the parties, the fairness of applying forum laws to the litigants, and the degree of conflict between the laws and policies of the forum and the other state(s). *See* Diane P. Wood, *Conflicts of*

B. Competition Law Cases with Extraterritorial Dimensions: the CCS's Experience with Price-Fixing and Conduct-Alignment Arrangements in International Airline Alliance Agreements

The facts of the first two reported decisions of the CCS—both involving negative clearances of agreements between foreign airlines flying into and out of Singapore—are illustrative of how the regulator did have the requisite adjudicatory competence to evaluate cases involving foreign parties and extraterritorial conduct. In *Re Qantas Airways and British Airways*,[30] the parties had entered into a long-term joint services agreement along the "kangaroo route" from Australia to Europe, and vice versa, via Singapore. The agreement contained severe restrictions on competition, including price-fixing provisions and other arrangements to coordinate their seating capacity and eliminate overlapping flights, which was notified under the *Competition Act* for the CCS's examination. The agreement was eventually cleared as one that did not infringe the section 34 prohibition against anticompetitive agreements on the grounds that it fell within the scope of the "net economic benefit" exemption found in the Third Schedule of the Competition Act—that it was an "agreement which contributes to (a) improving production or distribution; or (b) promoting technical or economic progress, but which does not (i) impose on the undertakings concerned restrictions which are not indispensable to the attainment of those objectives; or (ii) afford the undertakings concerned the possibility of eliminating competition in respect of a substantial part of the goods or services in question."[31] The parties to the agreement were respectively based in the UK and Australia, and the agreement in question was, presumably, made in one of these jurisdictions. Singapore was, however, the natural forum for obtaining a competition regulator's approval for the agreement because the agreement was to be implemented with respect to flights arriving in and departing from Singapore. While the consumers who benefited most from improved flight connectivity as a result of the agreement were at either end of the "kangaroo route," rather than passengers originating from Singapore, the productive efficiencies arising from the cost-savings generated by the cooperation between the airlines were enjoyed in Singapore. These connecting factors made the CCS the most appropriate competition regulator to evaluate the pro- and anti-competitive effects of the agreement within the framework established around the section 34 prohibition.

Similarly, in another case involving another airline joint services agreement, the CCS was clearly an appropriate forum to evaluate whether the pro-competitive

---

Jurisdiction in Antitrust Law: A Comment on Ordover and Atwood, 50 LAW AND CONTEMP. PROBS. 179, 182 (1987).

30. Case No. CCS 400/002/06, [2007] SGCCS 1 (decided Feb. 13, 2007). For a more detailed discussion of the case, see Burton Ong, *Competition Law Takes Off in Singapore: An Analysis of Two Recent Decisions*, 3(2) COMPETITION POL'Y INT'L 101 (2007).

31. Paragraph 9, Third Schedule, *Competition Act*, *supra* note 1.

justifications for an agreement outweighed their appreciably adverse effects on competition. In *Re Qantas Airways and Orangestar Investment Holdings*,[32] the agreement was between airlines based in Singapore and Australia that served routes between Singapore and various Australian cities, as well as between Singapore and various destinations within Southeast Asia. The agreement was conditioned upon the parties obtaining regulatory approval from the competition regulators in both Singapore and Australia, which it did, and it was cleared by the CCS as not infringing the section 34 prohibition on the basis that it satisfied the requirements of the net economic benefit exemption. Once again, the CCS was an entirely "natural forum" to evaluate the pro-competitive claims made by the parties under the agreement, namely the improvements to Singapore's air connectivity, cost-savings from operating out of Singapore, and other ancillary benefits to Singapore's economy from increased passenger traffic through Singapore. While the CCS reached essentially the same conclusions about the overall legality of the agreement as the Australian Competition and Consumer Commission (ACCC), which had unconditionally authorized the agreement for a period of five years on the basis that it was "likely to result in a benefit to the Australian public . . . [that] would outweigh the detriment to the public constituted by any lessening of competition that is likely to result from the Agreement in markets in Australia,"[33] it was a conclusion reached after an independent analysis and evaluation of the anti- and pro-competitive features of the agreement. In addition, it should also be noted that the CCS made it a point to emphasize that its decision was based on the state of the aviation market at the time of the assessment and that its decision was subject to review if there was a material change of circumstance—arising from the "volatile and dynamic" global aviation market—which prevented the anticipated effects of the agreement from being actualized in Singapore. The more nuanced and qualified approach by the Singapore competition regulator, as compared to the one taken by the Australian regulator, reflects the different domestic economic perspectives of each national competition agency.

C. Applying Singapore's Competition Laws to a Hypothetical *Hartford Fire* Scenario

If the facts of the *Hartford Fire*[34] case were to arise, hypothetically, in a case brought to the attention of the CCS, where a group of foreign reinsurance undertakings conspired to force insurance companies in Singapore to uniformly alter their commercial arrangements with customers in Singapore, under an agreement made and executed entirely in a foreign country that is legal under the laws of that country, it is likely that the case would be analyzed along the following lines.

---

32. Case No. CCS 400/003/06, [2007] SGCCS 2 (decided Mar. 5, 2007).

33. *See supra* note 31, at paragraph 14.

34. *See supra* note 10.

This would most likely qualify as an agreement that infringes the section 34 prohibition against "agreements between undertakings . . . which have as their object or effect the prevention, restriction or distortion of competition within Singapore." Such an agreement is likely to have appreciably adverse effects on competition on the entire domestic insurance market given the oligopolistic character of the insurance industry in Singapore. That the agreement was made outside Singapore and by parties who are outside Singapore are not obstacles to the application of this statutory prohibition in light of the express statutory allowances for such extraterritorial elements in sections 33(1)(a) and (b) of the *Competition Act*. Furthermore, there are no defenses or exemptions available to such anticompetitive agreements on the basis that they are legal under the laws of some other state. It remains unclear, however, whether the CCS will interpret the "effects"-based limb of the section 34 prohibition narrowly to require that parties to the conspiracy must have acted with the intention of preventing, restricting, or distorting competition within Singapore, whether they must have specifically targeted the insurance market in Singapore, or if these anticompetitive effects on the market in Singapore were simply the foreseeable consequences of their actions.

However, even if an infringement of the section 34 prohibition is established, the CCS is likely to face practical constraints on its ability to investigate and prosecute the foreign parties in this case, particularly when they do not have any presence or assets within Singapore. Furthermore, the limitations on its enforcement jurisdiction abroad and the absence of international agreements between Singapore and other states in the arena of competition law enforcement would make it difficult for the CCS to initiate proceedings against these foreign parties unless it had an extraordinarily helpful complainant with access to critical evidence of the conspiracy. If the conspiracy was not targeted specifically at insurers in Singapore, but also extended to insurers in larger markets in other countries, it would probably let the more experienced competition regulators in those countries take the lead in such a case and play a supporting role in the process instead. The next section will outline the relevant statutory provisions empowering the CCS to cooperate with foreign competition regulators in such circumstances, as well as the ongoing and future efforts by the CCS to engage in cooperative arrangements with competition regulators from other jurisdictions.

IV. INTERNATIONAL COOPERATION

Section 88 of the *Competition Act* provides that the CCS may, with the approval of the Minister for Trade and Industry, enter into cooperative arrangements with any "foreign competition body" under which the parties agree to share information with and provide assistance to each other so as to facilitate the performance of their respective functions as competition regulators. "Foreign competition body" is defined under the section to mean any person or agency in whom "there are vested functions under the law of another country or territory with respect to the enforcement or the administration of provisions of law . . . concerning competition between undertakings." The CCS is therefore statutorily empowered to enter into cooperation agreements with other competition agencies in other countries that would enable it better discharge its duties in cases that involve parties or conduct originating from these countries. However, no such formal arrangements have been entered into thus far.

A. Informal Channels of Cooperation with Foreign Competition Regulators

The approach the CCS appears to have adopted thus far is to engage other competition authorities through informal channels that provide it with the opportunity to learn from the regulatory practices and experiences of these authorities. Such channels include its participation in the activities of the intergovernmental agency groupings like the ICN (International Competition Network), the UNCTAD IGE (United Nations Conference on Trade and Development Intergovernmental Group of Experts on Competition Law and Policy), and the OECD (Organisation for Economic Co-operation and Development) Global Forum on Competition.

Other cooperative initiatives between the CCS and its foreign counterpart agencies have included government-sponsored staff attachment programs with foreign competition regulators such as the ACCC (Australian Competition and Consumer Commission), the UKCC (United Kingdom Competition Commission) and UK OFT (Office of Fair Trading), the Irish Competition Authority, and the NZCC (New Zealand Competition Commission), as well as staff training workshops conducted by speakers from the USFTC (United States Federal Trade Commission) and the Antitrust Division of the U.S. Department of Justice and the ACCC.

B. Treaty Obligations in Singapore's Free Trade Agreements Concerning Interstate Cooperation on Competition Policy Matters

Singapore has entered into a number of Free Trade Agreements (FTAs)[35] with its trading partners since 2000, and many of them contain specific provisions about interstate cooperation in areas concerning competition policy and enforcement. Most of these treaty obligations are broadly worded provisions that require the competition authorities in each signatory state to cooperate and coordinate with each other on matters of competition law and policy,[36] and require each state to

35. The full text of all the FTAs to which Singapore is a party to can be found at www.fta.gov.sg.

36. *See* Article 14.3 ("Cooperation") of the Peru-Singapore Free Trade Agreement (PeSFTA, signed on May 29, 2008, expected to enter into force in early 2009); Article 7.3 ("Cooperation") of the Panama-Singapore Free Trade Agreement (PSFTA, signed on

notify the other of enforcement activity that "may affect important interests of the other Party,"[37] to provide publicly available information concerning their respective competition law enforcement activities at the request of the other,[38] to enter into consultations with the other on specific competition law matters affecting trade and investment between the parties at the request of the other, and to "accord full and sympathetic consideration to the concerns of the other Party."[39]

Some of these FTA provisions explicitly recognize the potential cross-border scenarios that may arise where anticompetitive behavior occurs in one state, but the adverse effects on competition are felt in another state. For example, Article 9.4 of the 2005 Trans-Pacific Strategic Economic Partnership Agreement between Singapore, Chile, Brunei, and New Zealand requires that:

> Each party shall notify the other Parties of an enforcement activity regarding an anti-competitive business conduct if it:
>
> (a) considers that the enforcement activity is liable to substantially affect another Party's important interests;
> (b) relates to restrictions on competition which are liable to have a direct and substantial effect in the territory of another Party; or
> (c) concerns anti-competition acts taking place principally in the territory of another Party.[40]

Mar. 1, 2006, entered into force on July 24, 2006); Article 9.3 ("Cooperation") of the Trans-Pacific Strategic Economic Partnership Agreement (Trans-Pacific SEP between Singapore, Chile, Brunei, and New Zealand, entered into force on Nov. 8, 2006); Article 15.6 ("Cooperation") of the Korea-Singapore Free Trade Agreement (KSFTA, entered into force on Mar. 2, 2006); Article 12.4 ("Cooperation") of the United States-Singapore Free Trade Agreement (USSFTA, entered into force on Jan. 1, 2004); Article 104 ("Cooperation on Controlling Anti-competitive Activities") of the Japan-Singapore Economic Agreement for a New Age Partnership (JSEPA, entered into force on Nov. 20, 2002); and Article 3(3) ("Competition") of the Agreement between New Zealand and Singapore on a Closer Economic Partnership (ANZSCEP, signed on Nov. 14, 2000).

37. *See* Article 14.4 ('Notifications') of the PeSFTA, Article 9.4 ('Notifications') of the Trans-Pacific SEP.

38. *See* Article 14.5 ('Transparency and Information Requests') of the PeSFTA, Article 7.4 ('Transparency and Information Requests') of the PSFTA, and Article 12.5 ('Transparency and Information Requests') of the USSFTA.

39. *See* Article 14.6 ('Consultations') of the PeSFTA and Article 7.5 ('Consultations') of the PSFTA. Similar consultation provisions can be found in Article 9.5 ('Consultations and Exchange of Information') of the Trans-Pacific SEP, Article 15.5 ('Consultations') of the KSFTA, Article 12.6 ('Consultations') of the USSFTA, Article 6 ('Consultation and Review') of the Singapore-Australia Free Trade Agreement (SAFTA, entered into force on July 28, 2003), and Article 50(2) ('Competition') of the European Free Trade Area (EFTA)-Singapore Free Trade Agreement (ESFTA, entered into force on January 1, 2003).

40. A similar concern with cross-border anticompetitive conduct is found in Article 3(3)(c) of the ANZSCEP, which requires Singapore and New Zealand to "endeavour to

Several of these FTAs also contain provisions requiring Singapore to eventually consider committing itself to formal bilateral cooperation agreements in the area of competition law and policy. In the Singapore-Australia FTA, for example, which was entered into force before Singapore enacted its competition laws, the parties agreed to consult each other and review the scope of the FTA's competition policy chapter "within six months of a generic competition law coming into effect in Singapore . . . with a view to negotiating amendments . . . that may be necessary to ensure the comprehensive protection in their respective territories of the legitimate commercial interests of businesses of the other Party," including the possibility of a separate competition law and policy cooperation bilateral agreement.[41] In a similar vein, in the Korea-Singapore FTA, Article 15.6 provides that:

> Within six (6) months from the coming into effect of a generic competition law in Singapore, the Parties shall consult with a view to making a separate arrangement between their competition authorities regarding the scope and content of co-operation and co-ordination.[42]

As such, while the CCS has not announced any formal cooperation treaties with any other foreign competition regulator at present, it would not be unexpected if such bilateral treaties were to emerge down the road from the FTAs that Singapore has signed with Australia, Korea, Chile, Brunei, and New Zealand.

C. Regional Cooperation Toward Developing a Competition Policy for ASEAN (the Association of Southeast Asian Nations)

One significant arena for international cooperation between the CCS and foreign competition regulators lies much closer to home—within the ASEAN community of which Singapore is a member—in light of the economic integration objectives of this regional grouping. The 2007 ASEAN Economic Community Blueprint articulates the need for greater cooperation between competition regulators from member countries:

> B1. Competition Policy

---

exchange information and explore the scope for further cooperation between them, with particular emphasis on *transactions or conduct in one that has competition effects in the other's market, or in both Parties' markets.*" (emphasis added).

41. *See* Article 6(2) ("Consultation and Review") of the SAFTA, as well as Article 6(3) which goes further to explain that "the Parties shall also discuss the desirability of concluding a *rrangements for cooperation and mutual assistance in competition policy* and enforcement, *either as amendments* to this Chapter *or as separate arrangements* between their respective competition authorities." (emphasis added).

42. Likewise, under Article 9.3(2) of the Trans-Pacific SEP, Singapore has agreed with Chile, Brunei, and New Zealand that "the Parties through their respective competition authorities will seek a cooperation agreement after the date of the entry into force of this Agreement."

41. The main objective of the competition policy is to foster a culture of fair competition. Institutions and laws related to competition policy have recently been established in some (but not all) ASEAN Member countries (AMCs). There is currently no official ASEAN body for cooperative work on CPL to serve as a network for competition agencies or relevant bodies to exchange policy experiences and institutionalise norms on CPL.

Actions:

(i) Endeavour to introduce competition policy in all ASEAN Member Countries by 2015;
(ii) Establish a network of authorities or agencies responsible for competition policy to serve as a forum for discussing and coordinating competition policies;
(iii) Encourage capacity building programmes/activities for ASEAN Member Countries in developing national competition policy; and
(iv) Develop a regional guideline on competition policy by 2010, based on country experiences and international best practices with a view to creating a fair competition environment.[43]

The substantive process of devising a regional guideline on competition policy is likely to be fraught with challenges ahead—both legal and political in character—given the vast socio-economic disparities between the various member states that comprise the ASEAN grouping. Furthermore, the inherent ambiguity of the phrase "fair competition environment," used to describe the overall objectives of the regional competition policy, is a potential source of tension given the different approaches that may be taken when interpreting "fairness" as a policy objective, against other efficiency-related or integration-promoting objectives, when each state develops its own competition law regime. The nature and extent of the cooperation arrangements contemplated under the Blueprint have not yet been made publicly known, and any progress on this front will depend very much on the prevailing political climate in each of these member states.

43. Paragraph 41, ASEAN Economic Community Blueprint, released at the Thirteenth ASEAN Summit, Singapore, Nov. 18–22, 2007. The Strategic Schedule accompanying the Blueprint suggests that the implementation of these goals is expected to take place between 2010 and 2015.

9. COOPERATION, COMITY, AND COMPETITION POLICY IN AUSTRALIA

PROFESSOR ALLAN FELS* AND ZAVEN MARDIROSSIAN **

I. INTRODUCTION

The internationalization of trade and commerce has had a significant effect on competition law policy and enforcement worldwide. The proliferation of competition regimes in developed and developing countries has increased the potential for cooperation and conflict between overlapping jurisdictions.[1] There are a number of measures, and others have been proposed, to address the enforcement challenges presented by global competition. These include the extraterritorial application of domestic competition laws, positive and negative comity procedures, bilateral and multilateral cooperation agreements, and convergence of procedural and substantive competition policies. This chapter examines Australian competition law and policy with respect to foreign conduct and the state of international cooperation in Australia.

Part One of the chapter outlines the circumstances in which Australia applies its substantive competition laws extraterritorially, as compared with the "effects" test applied in the United States. To highlight these contrasting approaches, the chapter also details the controversy surrounding the "*Westinghouse* litigation" in the 1970s and 1980s. At first sight, the amount of Australian blocking legislation enacted in response to the United States' extraterritorial application of its competition laws is surprising. However, despite the history of conflict between the two nations, a unique feature of Australia's cooperative arrangements regarding competition policy is that Australia was the first to sign a cooperation treaty with the United States pursuant to its International Antitrust Enforcement Assistance Act of 1994 (IAEAA) (discussed in Part Three).[2]

Part Two of the chapter discusses Australia's approach to comity. It demonstrates that while comity considerations do not usually arise in the extraterritorial application of Australian competition laws, comity is nevertheless an important

---

* Dean, the Australia and New Zealand School of Government, Victoria, Australia.

** Partner, Arnold Bloch Leibler, Victoria, Australia.

1. *See* James F. Rill & Mark C. Schechter, *Challenges Presented by Globalization to Competition Policy* 1 (Paper presented at the Canadian Competition Policy: Preparing for the Future, Toronto, Ontario, June 19, 2001).

2. Japan and Brazil followed Australia in signing the IAEAA.

consideration for Australian courts in deciding whether to grant an anti-suit injunction or, to a lesser extent, in declining to exercise jurisdiction on the grounds that another jurisdiction is more appropriate. The relevant principles are applied to a hypothetical scenario based on the facts in *Hartford Fire Insurance Co. v. California*[3] in the United States, which illustrates the contrasting approaches of Australian and United States' courts. In this context, it also considers the impact of prior review by foreign authorities on domestic actions.

Part Three of the chapter considers the cooperative arrangements regarding competition policy in which Australia participates, explaining their role and content. It focuses particularly on the unique aspects of cooperation between Australia and the United States, and also the extraordinarily high level of cooperation with New Zealand—a distinctive feature of Australian competition law. This cooperative arrangement goes beyond mere agreement-making and has incorporated unprecedented concepts such as multi-jurisdictional statutes, the ability of Australian and New Zealand courts to sit in each other's country, and expansive powers of enforcement bodies to facilitate cross-jurisdictional investigation, exchange of evidence, and commencement of proceedings. This unique level of cooperation can be attributed to the nations' shared background of legal influence with respect to competition law policy and a long history of shared legal, cultural, and economic heritage. Part Three of the chapter also discusses Australia's participation in international bodies and the important role played by government networks in achieving convergence, compliance, and cooperation between competition regimes.

II. PART ONE: EXTRATERRITORIALITY

A. Introduction

"Extraterritoriality" generally refers to the exercise of jurisdiction by a state over activities occurring outside its borders.[4] The traditional international legal use of the term "extraterritorial legislation" covers two different types of laws: legislation that regulates the conduct of nationals abroad,[5] and legislation that applies to conduct by non-nationals outside the territory of the legislating country.[6] There is a strong common law presumption against extraterritorial jurisdiction.

---

3. 509 U.S. 764 (1993) ("*Hartford Fire*").

4. Deborah Senz & Hilary Charlesworth, *Building Blocks: Australia's Response to Extraterritorial Legislation*, 2 Melbourne J. Int'l L. 69, 70 (2001).

5. *Id.* at 72 (citing as an example Part IIIA of the Crimes Act 1914 (Cth), which makes it an offense for an Australian citizen or resident to, while outside of Australia, engage in various indecent sexual acts that involve children under the age of 16.

6. *Id.*

In Australia, its exercise is usually statute-based,[7] and the legislature must clearly show the necessary intention for the statute to have extraterritorial effect.[8]

B. Australia's Substantive Competition Laws

Australia's substantive competition laws are predominantly contained in Part IV of the *Trade Practices Act 1974* (Cth) (the Act). Part IV of the Act contains prohibitions against:

- anticompetitive contracts, arrangements, and understandings;
- price-fixing and other cartels;
- monopolization and misuse of market power;
- anticompetitive mergers and acquisitions;
- resale price maintenance; and
- secondary boycotts that affect competition.

1. The General Extraterritorial Operation of the Act The definition of "market" in section 4E of the Act[9] clarifies that the Act is primarily concerned with conduct affecting competition in Australia. However, section 5 of the Act recognizes that conduct outside Australia may affect competition in Australian markets. As Judge Merkel commented in *Bray v Hoffman-La Roche Ltd,*[10] the Act "has been framed on the assumption that when conduct is made a contravention of the Act it is only conduct in Australia that is meant unless the conditions set out in section 5 apply."[11]

2. Section 5 of the Act Section 5 of the Act provides for the extended application of Parts IV, IVA, V, VB, and VC of the Act.

Section 5(1) provides that various parts of the Act, including Part IV, extend to conduct outside Australia, provided the party engaging in the conduct is an

---

7. Butterworths, *Halsbury's Laws of Australia*, vol. 14 (at Oct. 13, 2009) 215 Foreign Relations, 3 Territory and Jurisdiction [215–380] (citing as an example *In the Marriage of Ibbotson and Wincen* (1994) 122 Fam. L.R. 385, where the court considered that it had jurisdiction to convict and punish for an act of contempt of court committed by a foreign national outside the territorial limits of Australia, although in the case it found the contempt to have been committed within Australia). For the source of extraterritorial legislation, note that the *Statute of Westminster 1931* (UK) "declares and enacts" that the Commonwealth Parliament has full power to make laws having extraterritorial operation.

8. *Jumbunna Coal Mine, NL v. Victorian Coal Miners' Ass'n* (1908) 6 C.L.R. 309, 363 (O'Connor, J.).

9. Section 4E of the Act states: "For the purposes of this Act, unless the contrary intention appears, market means a market in Australia and, when used in relation to any goods or services, includes a market for those goods or services and other goods or services that are substitutable for, or otherwise competitive with, the first-mentioned goods or services."

10. (2002) 118 F.C.R. 1 ("*Hoffman-La Roche*").

11. (2002) 118 F.C.R. 1, 16.

Australian citizen, a person ordinarily resident in Australia, an Australian incorporated entity, or a body corporate carrying on business in Australia.

Section 5(1A) extends section 46A (misuse of trans-Tasman market power) to conduct outside Australia engaged in by New Zealand residents, New Zealand corporations, and bodies corporate carrying on business in New Zealand.

Section 5(2) extends section 47 (exclusive dealing) and section 48 (resale price maintenance) to conduct outside Australia in relation to the supply of goods or services in Australia.

Section 5(3) limits the extraterritorial reach of the Act, requiring persons seeking damages in private actions to obtain ministerial consent before relying on the extraterritoriality provisions of the Act. The Minister is obliged to give consent unless, in the Minister's opinion, it is not in the national interest, and the conduct concerned was required or specifically authorized by the law of the country in which it was engaged in.[12]

(a) Carrying on Business in Australia Whether a corporation is incorporated in Australia is uncontroversial. However, whether a corporation is "carrying on business in Australia" is less straightforward. The expression is not defined in the Act, although section 4(1) defines "business" as including a business not carried on for profit. In *Luckins v. Highway Motel (Carnarvon) Pty. Ltd*,[13] Judge Gibbs said that the expression may have different meanings in different contexts. It is a question of fact[14] and will usually entail a "series or repetition of acts."[15] The relevant date is the point at which the conduct occurred, rather than the time of prosecution.[16]

(i) Place of Business Although having a place of business within Australia is not a requirement of carrying on business in Australia,[17] foreign corporations do not carry on business in Australia simply because they use agents as distributors of their products in Australia or advertise their foreign business in Australia.[18]

(ii) Subsidiary Companies In *Hoffman-La Roche*, foreign entities conspired to fix the price of vitamins and implemented their agreement regionally through their subsidiaries. The key question was not whether a business was carried on within the jurisdiction, but whether that business was carried on by the Australian subsidiaries on their own account, or on behalf of the foreign parent. As Judge Merkel stated, the mere fact that a subsidiary is part of an integrated global enterprise is insufficient to attribute the acts of the subsidiary to the foreign parent

---

12. *Trade Practices Act 1974* (Cth) § 5(5).
13. (1975) 133 C.L.R. 164, 178.
14. (1975) 133 C.L.R. 164, 178.
15. *Hoffman-La Roche* (2002) 118 F.C.R. 1, 18 (citing *Thiel v. Comm'r of Taxation* (Cth) (1990) 171 C.L.R. 338, 350 (Dawson J.)).
16. *Hoffman-La Roche* (2002) 118 F.C.R. 1, 17.
17. *Hoffman-La Roche* (2002) 118 F.C.R. 1, 19.
18. *See Tycoon Holdings Ltd. v. Trencor Jetco Inc.* (1992) 34 F.C.R. 31, 38.

and pierce the corporate veil.[19] The court must examine in detail the functions of the subsidiary and the relationship between the corporations.[20]

(b) Natural Persons In the case of natural persons, Australian citizenship is uncontroversial. However, whether a person is "ordinarily resident" in Australia is a question of fact and degree.[21] In each case, it is necessary to isolate the factors that give rise to some connection with Australia, such as the frequency, duration, and purpose of visits to Australia; family or business ties; and the ownership and use of property in Australia. The fact that a person is a resident of another country does not preclude a finding of ordinary residence within Australia.[22]

3. Specific Provisions that Operate Extraterritorially In addition to section 5, which extends the application of various parts of the Act, the following provisions of the Act are specifically intended to apply extraterritorially.

(a) Section 46A Section 46A prohibits misuse of market power in any market in Australia or New Zealand, or Australia *and* New Zealand. The nature of the prohibition is the same as in section 46,[23] and applies to New Zealand and New Zealand Crown corporations in the same way as it does to Commonwealth and Commonwealth authorities under section 2A.[24] The extraterritorial impact of section 46A has triggered amendments to the *Federal Court of Australia Act 1976* (Cth). Part IIIA was inserted to deal with trans-Tasman proceedings and, for example, empowers the Federal Court to make an order or grant an injunction restraining a person from engaging in conduct, or requiring a person to do an act, in New Zealand.

(b) Section 50A—Acquisitions that Occur Outside Australia Section 50A was drafted to deal with acquisitions occurring outside Australia that affect Australian markets. When a controlling interest is acquired in a body corporate outside Australia that is likely to substantially lessen competition in an Australian market, the Treasurer, the Australian Competition and Consumer Commission (ACCC), or any other person may apply to the Australian Competition Tribunal (the Tribunal) within 12 months of the acquisition. If the Tribunal is satisfied that the acquisition would have that effect, and that in all the circumstances it is

---

19. *Hoffman-La Roche* (2002) 118 F.C.R. 1, 21.

20. *Hoffman-La Roche* (2002) 118 F.C.R. 1, 20. In undertaking this exercise, His Honour outlined a number of relevant considerations that had been canvassed in previous cases, including, for example, whether the profits are treated as profits of the parent company and whether the persons conducting the business were appointed by the parent company.

21. *Re Vassis; Ex parte Leung* (1986) 9 F.C.R. 518, 525.

22. *See Levene v. Comm'rs of Inland Revenue* [1928] A.C. 217; *Comm'rs of Inland Revenue v. Lysaght* [1928] A.C. 234; *Inland Revenue v. Cawalader* (1904) 7 F(CtofSess) 146.

23. Russell V. Miller, Miller's Annotated Trade Practices Act: Australian Competition and Consumer Law 379 (30th ed. 2009).

24. *Trade Practices Act 1974* (Cth) § 46A(8).

not outweighed by other public benefits, the Tribunal may make a declaration accordingly. If such a declaration is made, the parties have six months (unless the Tribunal permits longer) to remedy the situation. While the declaration is in force, the parties cannot continue to carry on the business in Australia.[25]

(c) Trade Practices Amendment (Cartel Conduct and Other Measures) Act 2009 The recent introduction of the *Trade Practices Amendment (Cartel Conduct and Other Measures) Act 2009* (Cth) has broadened the extraterritorial reach of the Act in several significant ways with respect to cartel conduct.[26]

First, parties to a contract, arrangement, or understanding are no longer required to be in competition "in a market."[27] This is significant because under the Act, "market" is defined as a "market in Australia." Removing the concept of "market" from "in competition" therefore removes the requirement for a territorial nexus to Australia, and the courts and the ACCC may look beyond Australia to determine whether parties are in competition.[28]

Second, the definition of "party" has been extended. If a body corporate is party to a contract, arrangement, or understanding, its related bodies corporate are now also considered to be parties.[29] This definition will extend to overseas related bodies corporate, and the courts and the ACCC will be able to consider these overseas entities when determining whether parties are in competition.[30]

These amendments to the Act have important implications for overseas companies carrying on business in Australia, for Australian companies with overseas offices and subsidiaries and for associated individuals.[31]

C. The United States' Position

How, then, do the conditions under which Australia applies its substantive competition laws extraterritorially compare with the position in the United States? Historically, the United States has purported to regulate the conduct of multinational corporations on a number of bases, including the "extended personality"

---

25. Trade Practices Act 1974 (Cth) § 50. *See* Russell V. Miller, Miller's Annotated Trade Practices Act: Australian Competition and Consumer Law 427 (30th ed. 2009).

26. *See* Jackie Mortensen, *Extending the Extraterritorial Reach of the Trade Practice Act*, 614 Australian Trade Practices News 1, 1 (2009).

27. *Trade Practices Act 1974* (Cth) § 44ZZRD.

28. *Trade Practices Act 1974* (Cth) § 44ZZRD.

29. *Trade Practices Act 1974* (Cth) § 44ZZRC.

30. Jackie Mortensen, *Extending the Extraterritorial Reach of the Trade Practice Act*, 614 Australian Trade Practices News 1, 2 (2009).

31. *Id.* (also discussing the effect of the amendments on extradition and information-sharing with foreign governments).

theory,[32] the "contractual submission" theory,[33] and the controversial "effects" test.

The "effects" test was introduced in *United States v. Aluminium Co. of America*.[34] The United States Government alleged that a Swiss company, Alliance, and its shareholders (French, German, Swiss, British, and Canadian companies) had breached U.S. antitrust legislation by agreeing to set a quota for the production of aluminium exported to the United States.[35] The main issue was whether the United States antitrust legislation extended to foreign nationals outside the United States.

Judge Learned Hand, on behalf of the other members of the court, stated that:

> any state may impose liabilities, even upon persons not within its allegiance, for conduct outside its borders that has consequences within its borders which the state reprehends; and these liabilities other states will ordinarily recognize.[36]

On this basis, the court found that the legislation was intended to extend to conduct engaged in overseas, provided the intended effect of the conduct was prohibited by the legislation.[37] *Alcoa* therefore "shifted the focus in jurisdictional disputes from the location of the conduct to the location of the effect of the conduct—a significant move away from the traditional rule of territorial sovereignty.[38]

In 1993, the application of the effects doctrine was approved by the United States Supreme Court in *Hartford Fire*. The majority held that antitrust law

---

32. Under this theory, either the parent of a U.S. incorporated subsidiary or the subsidiary of a U.S. incorporated parent can, pursuant to a variety of American laws and judicial interpretation, be regarded as subject to U.S. laws. *See* Warren Pengilley, *U.S. Trade and Antitrust Laws: A Study of International Legal Imperialism from Sherman to Helms Burton*, 6 COMPETITION & CONSUMER L.J. 187, 189 (1998).

33. The U.S. Export Administration Act of 1979 requires a "Submission Clause" to be agreed to by foreign companies purchasing U.S. technology. The clause requires that U.S.-based technology not be used in violation of U.S. laws. According to Pengilley, this seems reasonable in a sense, but problems arise where changes in U.S. policies, usually expressed retrospectively, were not foreseeable at the time the relevant foreign companies acquired the U.S. technology and contracted on the basis that they were free to use it as they wished. *Id.* at 191.

34. 148 F.2d 416 (2d Cir. 1945) ("*Alcoa*").

35. *See* Senz & Charlesworth, *supra* note 4, at 81 n.58; .Eugene Khoo, *The Reach of U.S. Antitrust Law and Its Effect on Australia*, 14 QUEENSLAND LAWYER 134, 136 (1994).

36. *Alcoa*, 148 F 2d 416, 423 (2d Cir. 1945).

37. *Alcoa*, 148 F 2d 416, 444 (2d Cir. 1945) (Learned Hand, J.); AUSTRALIAN INTERNATIONAL LAW: CASES AND MATERIALS 292 (Harry Reicher ed., 1995).

38. Senz & Charlesworth, *supra* note 4, at 81; Khoo, *supra* note 35, at 137.

applied where foreign conduct "was meant to produce and did in fact produce some substantial effect in the United States."[39]

D. Comparison—United States and Australia

The position of the United States is therefore quite different from that of Australia. Section 5 of the Act does not involve an "effects" test, but rather an evaluation of whether the entity involved is incorporated in Australia or carries on business in Australia, or the person involved is a citizen of Australia or ordinarily resident in Australia. Judge Merkel noted in *Hoffman-La Roche* that conduct outside Australia by an entity not carrying on business in Australia or not incorporated in Australia was not covered by section 45 of the Act at all, even though it may have anticompetitive effects in Australia.[40]

His Honour also suggested that there was much to be said for applying the U.S. "effects" test in Australia.[41] However, as Pengilley notes, the Australian government deliberately decided not to adopt this test as a jurisdictional base, following the "*Westinghouse* litigation" in the 1970s and 1980s.[42]

1. Westinghouse Litigation The *Westinghouse* litigation arose after uranium producers in the United States successfully lobbied the U.S. government to ban uranium imports, and to order that all future uranium had to be purchased domestically. The U.S. market at the time was approximately 70 percent of the world market, and these actions caused uranium producers in Great Britain, Australia, Canada, and South Africa to form a cartel in order to stabilize world prices.

Westinghouse had previously contracted to supply its customers with uranium at fixed prices subject only to inflation. After uranium prices increased by over 800 percent in three years, Westinghouse became unable to supply uranium under its contractual obligations. It was sued for an estimated US$2 billion in damages.

Westinghouse's survival depended upon its offsetting these claims. It commenced proceedings against 29 domestic and foreign uranium companies, including several Australian companies, alleging that because the conduct impacted the U.S. economy, the United States had jurisdiction.[43]

Companies headquartered or doing business in Australia, Canada, the United Kingdom, and South Africa did not enter appearances, believing that this would be a submission to the jurisdiction of the United States, which they opposed.

---

39. *Hartford Fire*, 509 U.S. 764, 796 (1993).

40. (2002) 118 F.C.R. 1, 17 (Merkel, J.).

41. *Id.* at 15 (Merkel, J.).

42. *See* Warren Pengilley, *When are Foreign Corporations Subject to the Trade Practices Act?*, 18(6) AUSTRALIAN & NEW ZEALAND TRADE PRACS. L. BULL. 83, 87 (2002).

43. *See* Pengilley, *supra* note 32, at 198.

Instead, the governments of these countries submitted amicus curiae briefs, arguing that the U.S. courts had no jurisdiction over the entities involved.[44]

On appeal, the Court of Appeals dismissed the briefs, stating: "shockingly to us, the governments of the defaulters have subserviently presented for them their case against the exercise of jurisdiction."[45] The court subsequently found that it had jurisdiction, entered default judgments against the non-appearing foreign companies, and permitted Westinghouse to calculate its financial loss.[46]

The various Westinghouse claims against the foreign companies were eventually settled. The commercial reality of the situation meant that once the court found that it had jurisdiction, judgment against the defendants could be executed against their U.S. assets, thus denying access to the U.S. market.[47]

2. Australian Response to Westinghouse Litigation The Australian government objected to the United States' exercise of extraterritorial jurisdiction in the *Westinghouse* litigation on political, economic, and legal grounds.[48] Along with many other countries, Australia took a number of legislative steps in response, including enacting impediments to obtaining evidence, blocking legislation, and "clawback" legislation.

(a) Impediments to Obtaining Evidence The Australian *Foreign Proceedings (Prohibition of Certain Evidence) Act 1976* (Cth) (FPA) was immediately enacted in response to the *Westinghouse* litigation.[49] The FPA authorized the Australian Attorney General to prohibit giving evidence to a foreign tribunal if it found that the tribunal was likely to exercise jurisdiction or powers inconsistent with international law or comity, or to protect the national interest.[50]

(b) Blocking Legislation The Australian *Foreign Antitrust Judgments (Restriction of Enforcement) Act 1979* (Cth) (FJA) was also enacted in response to the *Westinghouse* litigation. The FJA provided that a judgment of a foreign court under antitrust law should not be recognized if the Attorney General was satisfied that it was inconsistent with international law or comity, or that its non-recognition was in the national interest. Under the FJA the Attorney General could also make a

44. *Id.* at 198 *In re* Uranium Antitrust Litig., Westinghouse v. Rio Algom Ltd., 480 F. Supp. 1138 (N.D. Ill. 1979).

45. *In re* Uranium Antitrust Litig., 617 F.2d 1248, 1255 (7th Cir. 1980).

46. Pengilley, *supra* note 22, at 199.

47. *Id at 199.*

48. Senz & Charlesworth, *supra* note 4, 91–94.

49. The legislation was introduced into, and passed by, both Houses of Parliament on the same day. This was, as Pengilley surmises, "perhaps a Parliamentary record for brevity of debate and agreement by Parliamentary members as to the appropriate desired outcome." *See* Pengilley, *supra* note 32, at 210–211.

50. *Foreign Proceedings (Prohibition of Certain Evidence) Act 1976* (Cth) § 4(1). Similar legislation was passed in New Zealand, Canada, and South Africa, and then subsequently in Belgium, Denmark, Finland, France, Germany, Italy, the Netherlands, the Philippines, and Sweden: *See* Pengilley, *supra* note 32, at 211–12.

"reduction order" if he believed that a foreign judgment for damages for loss was unobjectionable, but that an automatic increase in damages (such as automatic treble damages under U.S. antitrust law) should not be enforced in Australia.[51]

On June 6, 1979, the Attorney General entered an order under the FJA declaring that the judgment on issues of liability given in favor of Westinghouse against the nine foreign defendants, and the preliminary injunctions in favor of Westinghouse, would not be recognized or enforceable in Australia.[52]

(c) "Clawback" Legislation After the Antitrust Cooperation Agreement was signed by Australia and the United States in 1982, the FPA and the FJA were repealed and replaced by the *Foreign Proceedings (Excess of Jurisdiction) Act 1984* (Cth) (FPEJA).[53] The FPEJA contains "clawback" provisions, which permit an Australian company that has suffered a loss under a judgment of a United States court executed against its U.S. assets, to recover the loss against the Australian assets of the United States' judgment creditor. Obviously, the U.S. judgment must be regarded in Australia as having been obtained in excess of jurisdiction. The use of defensive clawback provisions was pioneered by the United Kingdom.[54] However, Khoo believes the Australian provisions are more comprehensive than their United Kingdom counterparts.[55]

3. Current Australian Attitude Toward the U.S. Position According to Sweeney, over the past 15 years, the level of hostility generally towards the U.S. extraterritorial enforcement of competition laws has reduced considerably[56] for the following reasons:

- A growing number of states now recognize that anticompetitive activities are bad for their own economies. This has produced a rush of new competition regimes and has fostered a spirit of cooperation, resulting in a number of collaborative initiatives.[57]

---

51. *Australian Foreign Antitrust Judgments (Restriction of Enforcement) Act 1979 (Cth)* § 3 See generally Pengilley, *supra* note 32, at 211.

52. Senz & Charlesworth, *supra* note 4, at 91 (citing *Foreign Antitrust Judgments (Restriction of Enforcement) Act 1979*—Order by the Attorney General, *Commonwealth of Australia, Government Gazette*, Special Gazette S 105 (June 8, 1979)).

53. For a discussion of the relevant provisions of the FPEJA see Senz & Charlesworth, *supra* note 4, at 94–97.

54. *See* Senz & Charlesworth, *supra* note 4, at 96 (citing the *Protection of Trading Interests Act 1980* (UK) ch. 11). For a discussion of the background to the Act and an analysis of its provisions, see Vaughan Lowe, *Blocking Extraterritorial Jurisdiction: The British Protection of Trading Interests Act, 1980*, 75 AM. J. INT'L L. 257 (1981).

55. Senz & Charlesworth, *supra* note 4, at 96 (citing Khoo, *supra* note 35, at 146).

56. Brendan Sweeney, *Combating Foreign Anti-Competitive Conduct: What Role for Extraterritorialism*, 8(1) MELBOURNE J. INT'L L. 35, 86 (2007).

57. *Id.* at 87.

- A number of states have indicated that they are prepared to apply their competition laws extraterritorially, which has tended to mute complaints by those states against U.S. extraterritorialism.[58]
- U.S. antitrust authorities and, more recently but to a lesser degree, U.S. courts, have become more sensitive to the legitimate concerns of other states. Consequently, competition law extraterritorialism is no longer just an aggressive, unilateral U.S. phenomenon—it can operate in a cooperative environment.[59]

Sweeney notes, however, that notwithstanding the easing of international tension, extraterritorialism remains contentious because:[60]

- Although more countries now have their own competition laws, the laws lack uniformity, increasing the likelihood of policy conflict and incompatibility across jurisdictions.
- Notwithstanding that extraterritorialism is now accepted by more states, the extraterritorial reach of U.S. antitrust law remains broader than many are willing to accept.
- Uniformity in procedural rules is more difficult to achieve across jurisdictions than in substantive competition rules, as they are not specific to competition law, but form part of a state's general legal system.[61]

III. PART TWO—DECLINING THE EXERCISE OF JURISDICTION (*HARTFORD FIRE* SCENARIO)

A. Introduction

Having examined the circumstances in which Australian courts may assert jurisdiction to apply Australian competition laws to extraterritorial conduct, and comparing this with the position in the United States, this section looks at Australia's approach to comity. In the context of extraterritorial jurisdiction, comity has been described as a "pragmatic principle of reciprocal expectation," which counsels judicial or governmental restraint when enforcing extraterritorial legislation.[62] The relevant principles are discussed in relation to the following scenario, which is based on the facts in *Hartford Fire*. There is also a brief discussion of the impact of prior review by foreign authorities.

---

58. *Id.*

59. *Id.*

60. *Id* at 86–87.

61. *Id.*

62. Senz & Charlesworth, *supra* note 4, at 83 (citing Harold Maier, *Jurisdictional Rules in Customary International Law*, *in* Extraterritorial Jurisdiction in Theory and Practice 70–71 (Karl Meessen ed., (1996)).

The defendants are a group of foreign private reinsurers (which sell reinsurance to primary insurers). Local competition authorities seek to prosecute the defendants on charges of conspiring to restrict the terms of coverage of commercial insurance available in the local market. The conspiracy was intended to force primary insurers (which sell insurance to consumers) to change the terms of coverage in certain specified ways. The agreement among the defendants was made and executed entirely in a foreign country and is legal under the laws thereof. Furthermore, that country has a comprehensive and legitimate competition policy system.

B. U.S. Approach to *Hartford Fire*

In *Hartford Fire*, the majority conducted a two-stage inquiry. At the first stage, they determined whether the Court had jurisdiction under the Sherman Act[63] in relation to the conduct. At the second stage, they determined whether, if jurisdiction existed, the Court could (or should) decline to exercise jurisdiction on grounds of comity.

In relation to the first stage, the Court found "that the London reinsurers engaged in unlawful conspiracies to affect the market for insurance in the United States and that their conduct in fact produced substantial effect."[64] Accordingly, applying the "effects" test, the Court determined that it had jurisdiction under the Sherman Act. The majority also found that comity considerations were not relevant at this stage of the inquiry.[65] Justice Scalia dissented on this point, contending that comity concerns figure into the prior analysis of whether jurisdiction exists:

> Though it clearly has constitutional authority to do so, Congress is generally presumed not to have exceeded . . . customary international-law limits on jurisdiction to prescribe.
>
> Consistent with that presumption, this and other courts have frequently recognised that, even where the presumption against extraterritoriality does not apply, statutes should not be interpreted to regulate foreign persons or conduct if that regulation would conflict with principles of international law.[66]

As to whether a court with Sherman Act jurisdiction should ever decline to exercise jurisdiction on grounds of international comity, the majority considered that it did not need to decide the question:

> [E]ven assuming that in a proper case a court may decline to exercise Sherman Act jurisdiction over foreign conduct . . ., international comity would

63. Sherman Antitrust Act, 15 U.S.C. §§ 1–7 (1890).
64. *Hartford Fire*, 509 U.S. 764, 796 (1993).
65. *Hartford Fire*, 509 U.S. 764, 797 (1993).
66. *Hartford Fire*, 509 U.S. 764, 815 (1993).

> not counsel against exercising jurisdiction in the circumstances alleged here.[67]

Accordingly, the substantial question was found to be whether there was "in fact a true conflict between domestic and foreign law."[68] While the London reinsurers' conduct was consistent with British law and policy, this was not enough for the court to consider such a conflict to exist:

> "[T]he fact that conduct is lawful in the state in which it took place will not, of itself, bar application of the United States antitrust laws," even where the foreign state has a strong policy to permit or encourage such conduct. . . . Since the London reinsurers do not argue that British law requires them to act in some fashion prohibited by the United States, or claim that their compliance with the laws of both countries is otherwise impossible, we see no conflict with British law.[69]

C. Australian Approach to *Hartford Fire*

How then would an Australian court deal with the *Hartford Fire* scenario? As outlined above, Australian competition laws do not have a wide-sweeping jurisdictional base such as the "effects" test in the United States. This means that at the jurisdictional stage of inquiry, far less extraterritorial conduct is covered by the Act than the position in the United States under the Sherman Act. The *Hartford Fire* scenario illustrates this point. The defendants are neither incorporated in Australia nor carrying on business in Australia, meaning that their conduct is not covered by the Act, and comity considerations do not arise. Justice Scalia's dissenting judgment in *Hartford Fire*, in which he believed that comity considerations should be factored into the prior analysis of whether jurisdiction exists, provides a useful analogy to the Australian position. It is the same prior analysis, or consideration of comity, that was undertaken by the legislature in drafting section 5 of the Act and in choosing not to adopt the "effects" test as a jurisdictional base. It is the legislature, rather than the judiciary, that has the prerogative to make political judgments about the manner in which Australian competition laws should be applied.

1. Stays and Anti-Suit Injunctions Comity considerations do arise in Australian courts, however, when a court is considering whether to stay its own proceedings in favor of proceedings in another jurisdiction, or to grant an anti-suit injunction restraining a person amenable to its jurisdiction from

---

67. *Hartford Fire*, 509 U.S. 764, 798 (1993).

68. *Hartford Fire*, 509 U.S. 764, 798 (1993) (quoting Societe Nationale Industrielle Aerospatiale v. U.S. Dist, Ct. for S. Dist. of Iowa, 482 U.S. 522, 555 (1987) (Blackmun, J., concurring in part and dissenting in part)).

69. *Hartford Fire*, 509 U.S. 764, 799 (1993) (citations omitted).

commencing or continuing proceedings in another country. Although on the facts of the *Hartford Fire* scenario the issue does not arise (the conduct is legal under the laws of the foreign country and there is therefore no alternative forum to be considered), the Australian approach is briefly considered below.

(a) Stay of Local Proceedings—Forum Non Conveniens Australian courts may stay their proceedings in favor of another jurisdiction only if the Australian court is a "clearly inappropriate" forum.[70] In *CSR Ltd. v. Cigna Insurance Australia Ltd.*,[71] the Court said that the power is to be exercised in accordance with the general principle empowering a court to dismiss or stay proceedings which are oppressive, vexatious, or an abuse of process, and that the rationale for the exercise of the power is the avoidance of injustice.[72] The Court also said it was clear from this rationale that the power is an aspect of the inherent or implied power every court has to prevent its processes being used to bring about injustice.[73]

(b) Anti-Suit Injunctions The counterpart of a court's power to *prevent* its processes from being abused is its power to *protect* the integrity of those processes once set in motion.[74] In *Cigna*, the Court said that it is this power of protection that authorizes the grant of anti-suit injunctions in certain cases.[75] The power is not restricted to defined and closed categories, but can be exercised when necessary for the administration of justice or to protect the court's own proceedings or processes.[76]

The majority in *Cigna* said that comity considerations are especially relevant in this context:

> The cases concerned with injunctions in restraint of proceedings in foreign courts recognise that, although an injunction of that kind operates *in personam*, it nevertheless interferes with the processes of the foreign court and

---

70. *Voth v. Manildra Flour Mills Pty. Ltd.* (1990) 171 CLR 538. In this case, the Court declined to adopt the "more appropriate forum" test laid down by the House of Lords in *Spiliada Maritime Corp v. Cansulex Ltd.* [1987] AC 460 and accepted, instead, the test propounded by Judge Deane in *Oceanic Sun Line Special Shipping Co. Inc. v. Fay* (1988) 165 C.L.R. 197.

71. (1997) 189 C.L.R. 345 ("*Cigna*").

72. *Cigna* (1997) 189 C.L.R. 345, 391.

73. *Cigna* (1997) 189 C.L.R. 345, 391 (citing, *e.g.*, Jackson v. Sterling Industries Ltd. (1987) 162 C.L.R. 612, 617, 639–40; Hamilton v. Oades (1989) 166 C.L.R. 486, 502).

74. An example is the power to grant a Mareva injunction. A'Mareva injunction'is an interlocutory remedy which is incidental to the exercise by a court of its jurisdiction to enter judgment for a debt or damages and is designed to prevent a defendant from divesting itself of assets whereby enforcement of such judgment might be frustrated: *See* Jackson v. Sterling Industries Ltd. (1987) 162 C.L.R. 612, at 621 per Judge Brennan. The term is derived from the case Mareva Compania Naviera SA v International Bulk Carriers SA [1975] 2 Lloyd's Rep 509; [1980] 1 All ER 213.

75. *Cigna* (1997) 189 C.L.R. 345, 391.

76. *Cigna* (1997) 189 C.L.R. 345, 392.

may well be perceived as a breach of comity by that court. . . . For this reason, the cases also emphasise that the power to grant injunctions in restraint of foreign proceedings should be exercised with caution.[77]

2. Impact of Prior Review by Foreign Authorities In Australia, the impact of prior review by foreign authorities is legally irrelevant, in the sense that an Australian court is not compelled to follow the decisions of courts in other jurisdictions. However, a foreign authority's reasoning in relation to, for instance, an international cartel or anticompetitive conduct arising from similar facts may be persuasive. Further, an enforcement agency such as the ACCC is likely to take into account the views or decisions expressed by foreign authorities, although it is not compelled to adopt them and would not do so if it was against Australia's interests.

(a) Penalties Prior review may be a relevant consideration in the court's assessment of an appropriate penalty. In *ACCC v. Roche Vitamins Australia Pty. Ltd., BASF Australia Ltd., and Aventis Animal Nutrition Pty. Ltd.,*[78] collusive conduct by the respondents affected the supply of animal vitamins in Australia. The conduct derived from arrangements entered into overseas by affiliates and related corporations of the respondents. The Court considered that the joint penalty proposed was supported by the quantum of penalties imposed by the Federal Court of Canada and one of the U.S. district courts in relation to similar conduct by the related corporations.

(b) Reduced Penalties While an Australian court may be persuaded by a foreign court's reasoning in assessing an appropriate penalty, it would be unusual for an Australian court to reduce a respondent's penalty because of the quantum of penalty imposed in a foreign jurisdiction.[79] In assessing an appropriate penalty, Australian courts consider the effect of the impugned conduct on Australian markets, and a penalty imposed in another jurisdiction is unlikely to be relevant in this context.

77.*Cigna* (1997) 189 C.L.R. 345, 395–96. *See, e.g., British Airways Board v. Laker Airways Ltd.* [1985] A.C. 5,8 95; *Compagnie des Bauxites de Guinea v. Ins. Co. of N. Am.*, 651 F.2d 877, 887 (3d Cir. 1981), *aff'd on other grounds sub nom. Ins. Corp. of Ireland, Ltd. v. Compagnie des Bauxites de Guinee*, 456 US 694 (1982); *Société Nationale Industrielle Aerospatiale v Lee Kui Jak* [1987] A.C. 871, 892; *Re Maxwell Communications Corporation plc (No 2)* [1992] B.C.C. 757, 773. *See also* Hartley, *Comity and the Use of Antisuit Injunctions in International Litigation*, 35 Am. J. Comp. L. 487 (1987).

78. (2001) A.T.P.R. 41-809.

79. There has not been a case in Australia in which this has occurred, although it may be a relevant consideration in assessing a respondent's financial capacity to meet a proposed penalty.

IV. PART THREE—COOPERATIVE ARRANGEMENTS REGARDING COMPETITION POLICY

A. Introduction

The difficulties in concluding effective multilateral agreements on competition law enforcement and policy have long been recognised by the ACCC. Spier observed in 1997 that apart from the European Union, which he considered to have an effective harmonized competition policy regime, national sovereignty considerations have often severely confined the scope and content of regional agreements regulating competition law.[80] Spier also recognized that countries were increasingly establishing bilateral arrangements between competition agencies in order to formalize cooperation. He said these arrangements were helpful not only in reducing the disagreements between parties in the application of their competition laws, but also in providing a catalyst for further cooperation.[81]

Today, the ACCC is party to many cooperation agreements, free trade agreements and treaties with counterpart competition and consumer protection agencies around the world.[82] This section focuses on Australia's relationship with the United States and New Zealand, and considers Australia's participation in international bodies such as the International Competition Network (ICN) and the Organisation for Economic Co-operation and Development (OECD). It also examines the role of government networks in the development of competition regimes.

B. Australia and the United States

Broadly speaking, the attitudes of U.S. courts and antitrust bodies have been highly influential in the development of competition law policy and enforcement in Australia. Although the attempt in 1962 to establish a Trade Practices Act in Australia rejected the United States and Canadian models,[83] the 1974 Act currently in force was modelled on U.S. antitrust legislation.[84] The two jurisdictions

---

80. Hank Spier, *The Interaction Between Trade and Competition Policy: The Perspective of the ACCC* (Paper presented at the Seminar on International Trade Policies after the WTO Singapore Ministerial Conference, Taipei, May 2, 1997), *available at* http://www.accc.gov.au/content/index.phtml/itemId/95970.

81. *Id.*

82. A comprehensive record of these agreements and treaties is available on the ACCC Web site, http://www.accc.gov.au/content/index.phtml/itemId/255435/fromItemId/255432.

83. The late Sir Garfield Barwick examined and rejected U.S. trade practices legislation when he foreshadowed a model for the Australian Trade Practices Act in the Federal Parliament on December 6, 1962.

84. The then Commonwealth Attorney General, Senator Lionel Murphy, introduced the *Trade Practices Act 1974* (Cth) using U.S. antitrust legislation as its model.

have fundamentally similar objectives with respect to competition matters. The development of similar laws, analytical frameworks, and fact-finding methods has enabled them to make significant progress with their cooperative arrangements.

1. Cooperative Arrangements with the United States In April 1999, the Australian and U.S. governments signed a treaty providing for the exchange of evidence on a reciprocal basis for use in competition law enforcement.[85] The treaty contains positive and negative comity procedures and is one of the few international cooperation agreements the United States has entered into pursuant to its International Antitrust Enforcement Assistance Act of 1994.

In July 2000, the ACCC signed agreements with the U.S. Federal Trade Commission (FTC) to facilitate law enforcement cooperation with respect to consumer protection. The agreements relate to notification of enforcement activities, cooperation, coordination, and exchange of information, and enable the ACCC and FTC to better combat fraudulent, misleading, and unfair commercial conduct.

The Australia-United States Free Trade Agreement[86] came into force on January 1, 2005, and has been described as "represent[ing] a landmark in improving Australia's trade and investment relationship with the world's most dynamic and richest economy and largest merchandise and services exporter and importer."."[87] Chapter 14, entitled "Competition Related Matters," states that:

> The Parties recognize the importance of cooperation and coordination between their respective authorities to further effective competition law enforcement in the free trade area. The Parties shall cooperate in relation to the enforcement of competition laws and policy, including through mutual assistance, notification, consultation, and exchange of information.[88]

2. Immunity Policy U.S. antitrust authorities have also been highly influential in the ACCC's detection and prosecution of cartels, an issue which has gained increasing prominence in the international competition law arena. The ACCC's immunity policy, a key feature of the current enforcement regime for the anti-cartel provisions of the Act, was derived predominantly from the 1993 U.S. Department of Justice Corporate Leniency Policy. The amendments made

---

85. *Agreement with the Government of the United States of America Mutual Antitrust Enforcement Assistance*, Apr. 27, 1999, [1999] ATS 22 (entered into force Nov. 5, 1999).

86. *Australia-U.S. Free Trade Agreement*, May 18, 2005, [2005] ATS 1 (entered into force Jan. 1, 2005). *See also U.S.-Australia Talks to Start*, FINANCIAL TIMES 5 (London), Nov. 4, 2002.

87. Overview of the Australia-United States Free Trade Agreement (AUSFTA), *available at* http://www.dfat.gov.au/trade/negotiations/us_fta/outcomes/01_overview.html.

88. *Australia-US Free Trade Agreement*, May 18, 2005, [2005] ATS 1, art 14.2(3) (entered into force January 1, 2005).

to the policy in 2005 were strongly influenced by the views of the U.S. Department of Justice as to the key components of an effective immunity policy—namely, transparency and predictability.[89]

C. Australia and New Zealand

In the context of international cooperation, Australia's relationship with New Zealand deserves particular attention. The economies of the two countries are becoming increasingly integrated as a result of shared legal and political heritage, their geographical proximity, and the similarity of policy measures adopted by both governments.[90] Competition laws are significantly in harmony, as competition law provisions of the *New Zealand Commerce Act 1986* (NZ) were closely modeled on Part IV of the Act.[91] Convergence of consumer protection and competition regimes between the two countries is particularly high by international standards.

1. Cooperative Arrangements with New Zealand The Australia-New Zealand Closer Economic Relations Trade Agreement[92] (ANZCER) was entered into in 1983 to develop closer economic relations between Australia and New Zealand by removing all impediments to trade and to develop trade under conditions of fair competition.[93] From 1990, a single trans-Tasman market had been achieved, and the emphasis then moved towards harmonising business law between the two countries.[94]

The ACCC entered into a further agreement with the New Zealand Commerce Commission in 2007.[95] The agreement acknowledges previous arrangements between the two enforcement agencies and recognizes, among other things, that it is in the interest of both countries to share information, evidence, and

---

89. *See* Scott D. Hammond, *Cornerstones of an Effective Leniency Program* (Paper presented at the ICN Workshop on Leniency Programs, Cracking Cartels Conference, Sydney, Nov. 22–23, 2004) 2, *available at* http://www.usdoj.gov/atr/public/speeches/206611.htm.

90. Productivity Commission 2004, *Australian and New Zealand Competition and Consumer Protection Regimes*, Research Report, Canberra.

91. 1990 CER Steering Committee Report (1990 Report), 14–15 (cited in Ross Patterson, *Harmonisation of Australia and New Zealand Competition Law: Never the Twain Shall Meet?*, 8 TRADE PRACS. L.J, 17, 18 (2000).

92. *Australia New Zealand Closer Economic Relations Trade Agreement*, Mar. 28, 1983, [1983] ATS 2 (entered into force Jan. 1, 1983).

93. Ross Patterson, *Harmonisation of Australia and New Zealand Competition Law: Never the Twain Shall Meet?*, 8 TRADE PRACS. L.J. 17, 17 (2000).

94. To this end, in 1988, both governments signed a Memorandum of Understanding on the harmonization of business law.

95. *Agreement Between the Australian Competition and Consumer Commission and the New Zealand Commerce Commission*, July 31, 2007, *available at* http://www.accc.gov.au/content/index.phtml/itemId/564911.

documentation to facilitate effective enforcement and promotion of their respective competition, consumer, and regulatory functions.

2. Legislative Reform Significant legislative reform has been undertaken in both countries over the past few decades. New provisions were introduced into the Act and the *New Zealand Commerce Act 1986* (NZ) to cover misuse of market power in trans-Tasman trade, marking the replacement of antidumping laws between the two countries.

The *Federal Court of Australia Act 1976* (Cth) has also been amended to add to the Federal Court's powers with respect to sections 46A and 155A (and 155B) matters. For example, if the Federal Court considers that a proceeding would be more conveniently or fairly held in New Zealand, then it can direct that the proceeding be conducted or continued in New Zealand. The Federal Court can also administer an oath or affirmation while sitting in New Zealand, and may hand down the judgment for an Australian proceeding while sitting in New Zealand.

3. Enforcement Mechanisms The ACCC's enforcement mechanisms have also been expanded to permit access to documents or other information located in New Zealand. Section 155 of the Act generally empowers the ACCC to require persons to furnish information, produce documents, or give evidence in relation to possible breaches of the Act. The introduction of section 155A extended those powers, allowing the ACCC to require persons in New Zealand to provide documents or information in relation to a possible breach of section 46A. It is an offense in New Zealand not to comply with a reasonable request for information from the ACCC.

4. Differences Notwithstanding these unique legislative arrangements, Australian and New Zealand competition laws are not harmonized in every respect. For example, New Zealand competition law uses the concept of market dominance, while Australia uses concepts of market power and substantial lessening of competition. New Zealand also uses different market concentration ratios than Australia in assessing proposed mergers and acquisitions.

D. Australia's Participation in International Bodies

1. International Competition Network (ICN) The ACCC is an active participant in the ICN and was a founding member. The ICN is a network of competition agencies whose objectives are to:

- provide competition authorities with a venue for maintaining regular contacts;
- address practical competition concerns; and
- facilitate dynamic dialogue in order to promote global consensus and convergence towards sound competition policy principles.[96]

---

96. *See* International Competition Network, *About the International Competition Network*, *available at* http://www.internationalcompetitionnetwork.org/index.php/en/about-icn (accessed on May 22, 2010).

Currently, the ICN members represent 102 national and multinational competition agencies from 91 jurisdictions. It is the only international body devoted exclusively to competition law enforcement. Members undertake projects through a variety of working groups, and annual conferences and workshops give members an opportunity to discuss the projects and their implications for enforcement. The ICN is not a rule-making body:

> Where the ICN reaches consensus on recommendations, or "best practices", arising from the projects, individual competition authorities decide whether and how to implement the recommendations, through unilateral, bilateral or multilateral arrangements, as appropriate.[97]

2. Organisation for Economic Co-operation and Development (OECD) "The OECD is part of the system of Western international institutions developed after World War II and is the main forum for monitoring and evaluating economic trends and developments in its 30 member countries."[98] Australia signed the Convention founding the OECD on June 7, 1971, thereby pledging its commitment to achieving the OECD's fundamental aims, which are to:

- achieve the highest sustainable economic growth and employment and a rising standard of living in member countries, while maintaining financial stability, and thus to contribute to the development of the world economy;
- contribute to sound economic expansion in member as well as non-member countries in the process of economic development; and
- contribute to the expansion of world trade on a multilateral, nondiscriminatory basis in accordance with international obligations.[99]

3. OECD Competition Committee The OECD Competition Committee is described as the world's premier source of policy analysis and advice to governments on how best to harness market forces in the interests of greater global economic efficiency and prosperity.[100] The Committee has said:

> Well-designed competition law, effective law enforcement and competition-based economic reform promote efficiency, economic growth and employment for the benefit of all. OECD work on competition law and policy actively encourages decision-makers in government to tackle anti-competitive

---

97. *Id.*

98. *See* Australian Government, Department of Foreign Affairs and Trade, Australia and the OECD, *available at* http://www.dfat.gov.au/oecd/ (accessed on May 22, 2010).

99. *See generally* the OECD Web site, http://www.oecd.org.

100. *See* OECD, About Competition, http://www.oecd.org/about/0,3347,en_2649_37463_1_1_1_1_37463,00.html (accessed on Oct. 15, 2009). www.oecd.org/competition.

practices and regulations and promote market-oriented reform throughout the world.[101]

4. Government Networks and the Way Forward It is clear that competition law and policy is being more widely adopted and applied throughout the world, and convergence and cooperation between jurisdictions is becoming increasingly widespread. However, despite the recognition of global competition problems brought about by globally organized business, there is not yet a global agreement, convention, or treaty on competition law, nor a world competition authority.

Anne-Marie Slaughter, in her important study *A New World Order*, encourages us to abandon the traditional concept of the international system as a system of states subject to rules created by international institutions. Slaughter suggests that a world order based on government networks, working alongside and even in place of more traditional international institutions, holds great potential in the development of domestic regulatory behavior, including competition regulation.[102]

Drawing on Slaughter's work, Sweeney observes that domestic competition authorities have engaged with each other and with other relevant state and non-state actors in a variety of formal and informal networks to produce the outline of a global competition system.[103] According to Sweeney, these networks have operated at three levels—first, to produce a more thorough understanding of competition principles and norms with the object of building international convergence; second, to provide technical assistance to enable states to build domestic capacity; and third, to develop modalities for greater international cooperation and coordination. He contends that by constructing a governance system that produces acceptable solutions to international problems while remaining within the paradigm of domestic rule-making, competition authorities have arguably avoided the dilemma of illegitimacy inherent in global government.[104]

On the flip side, however, Sweeney argues that the horizontal networks (e.g., links between counterpart officials across borders) that presently dominate the field may need to be supplemented by some binding vertical arrangements (e.g., links between government officials and their supranational counterparts). As an example, he states that the incentives for protectionism built into the system may require supranational oversight to ensure that commitments to nondiscrimination are honored. He states further that in a world beset by severe economic crisis, domestic politics may place an unbearable strain on an international

101. *Id.*

102. Anne-Marie Slaughter, A New World Order 10 (2004).

103. Brendan Sweeney, *International Competition Law and Policy: a Work in Progress*, 10 Melbourne J. Int'l L, 58, 68 (2009).

104. *Id.* at 68–69.

merger system that relies on notions of comity and rational discourse. Ultimately, Sweeney concludes that despite remarkable advances over the last two decades, international competition law is still very much a "work in progress."[105]

V. CONCLUSION

As this chapter demonstrates, the extraterritorial application of Australia's substantive competition laws is generally based upon the form and nature of the parties' specific connection to Australia. This can be contrasted with the U.S. approach, which focuses on the substance of the parties' conduct and the anticompetitive effects it may have. This fundamental difference has been reflected in Australia's responses to the U.S. exercise of extraterritorial jurisdiction, including the various legislative attempts that Australia has made to curb its ambit over the years.

Australian courts, like their United States counterparts, may decline to exercise extraterritorial jurisdiction on the grounds of comity where another jurisdiction provides a more appropriate forum for resolution of the dispute. However, as Australian courts take a more conservative approach in exercising extraterritorial jurisdiction, circumstances are less likely to arise in which it is appropriate for Australian courts to decline to exercise jurisdiction in order to preserve international comity. Where this issue does arise, Australian courts focus primarily on the potential injustice that may be caused to the parties in determining whether to dismiss or stay proceedings. This Australian approach is distinct from the U.S. focus on the extent of conflict between domestic and foreign law. The fact that a foreign institution has previously reviewed the circumstances of a dispute will generally be regarded by Australian courts as of little relevance in determining whether to decline to exercise jurisdiction.

Australia's participation in bilateral and multilateral arrangements reflects increasing international cooperation in forming and implementing competition policy. Similar competition law objectives have enabled Australia and the United States to make significant progress with cooperative arrangements relating to the exchange of evidence and competition law enforcement, with Australia drawing on the immunity policy experience of the United States. The close relationship between Australia and New Zealand, and the increasing integration of the two nation's economies, has facilitated what is perhaps one of the highest degrees of convergence between international competition regimes in the world.

Such bilateral arrangements are particularly important given the difficulties in establishing a truly global consensus with regard to competition policy. It remains important to focus on promoting formal bilateral cooperation

105. *Id.* at 69.

arrangements and extending those that exist, as well as promoting a multilateral policy dialogue. It is also clear that government networks have an important role to play in achieving convergence, compliance, and cooperation between competition regimes. As Slaughter has observed, such networks have addressed problems that are more amenable to regulation by information, dialogue persuasion, and collective learning than by traditional command and control techniques.[106]

106. Anne-Marie Slaughter, A New World Order 57 (2004).

10. INTERNATIONAL ANTITRUST INSTITUTIONS

D. DANIEL SOKOL*

I. INTRODUCTION

Until relatively recently, antitrust law was something of a novelty. Few countries had such laws on the books, and fewer countries took antitrust enforcement seriously. A series of events, including the fall of Communism, a global movement toward greater economic liberalization, and the spread of international trade through reductions in trade barriers, all have contributed to the rapid proliferation of antitrust laws and agencies around the world in both developed and developing countries. Though formal international antitrust institutions have been proposed since the League of Nations, the increasing number of antitrust agencies has pushed the creation and further development of international antitrust institutions more in the past 10 to 15 years than in the entire earlier history of antitrust.

This chapter examines various formal international antitrust institutions. It begins by exploring the different types of international conduct that suggest the need for an international institutional response. The chapter then provides a discussion of the different existing supranational antitrust institutions. These institutions vary in terms of size (global vs. regional), design (hard vs. soft law), and effectiveness. Next, the chapter explores the strengths and weaknesses and the effectiveness of each of these international antitrust institutions. This chapter concludes that soft law international antitrust organizations are the best institutional choices to reduce the problems of international antitrust. Particularly noteworthy has been the rapid development and effectiveness of the International Competition Network (ICN). The ICN has, in its short history, made significant strides in increased harmonization in procedural issues and some substantive issues. How much convergence is optimal and how best to effectuate it remain open questions not merely for the ICN, but for all existing (and potentially new) international antitrust institutions.

International antitrust institutions exist because domestic antitrust systems are inadequate to address certain forms of anticompetitive behavior. International anticompetitive behavior takes two forms. The first is a spillover effect of anticompetitive effects from one jurisdiction to another (e.g., mergers, cartels). The second is a market access problem. Government may restrict access of foreign entrants to the market through ineffective enforcement or discriminatory laws

* Assistant Professor, University of Florida Levin College of Law.

and regulations. Both spillover and market access concerns impact antitrust. Often the solution to differing regulatory regimes is to allow for competition across jurisdictions—a type of regulatory federalism. Purely domestic institutional responses, such as courts and antitrust agencies, seem incapable of adequately addressing these concerns.

Countries can experiment with the appropriate level of antitrust enforcement based on their own preferences via international federalism of a purely domestic-based antitrust enforcement regime.[1] However, because of the scope and negative consequences of antitrust market access and spillover problems, a global federalism-style solution may be inappropriate. These problems may require some level of global governance. Regulatory competition at the domestic level may lead to conflicting rules. These conflicting rules may in turn reduce global welfare. Different substantive approaches regarding innovation and dominant firms create compliance difficulties. Microsoft remedies between the United States and the European Union illustrate this type of tension. Indeed, opportunities may arise in a system of conflicting domestic rules for firms to arbitrage these rules for anticompetitive purposes. The impact of suboptimal domestic disagreement strengthens the case for greater international coordination and convergence even as such convergence may risk a single global suboptimal standard. There is a diversity of institutional approaches to global governance and a number of different issues involving international antitrust harm across borders that require some sort of international response. This set of problems has led to the creation of a number of different international antitrust institutions. By institutions, I mean both formal (laws and regulations) and informal rules (customs and norms) of the game, as defined by North.[2]

As other chapters in this book suggest, one way antitrust agencies address the spillover effect is through comity (positive and negative). As these chapters illustrate, formal comity has its limitations. A problem with the use of formal comity is that because there are an ever-increasing number of jurisdictions with antitrust agencies, a patchwork of cooperation agreements in conjunction with comity may be ill-suited to address issues that have become truly global. Though the United States has only made one formal comity request to the EU, in fact, informal comity between the United States and the EU (and indeed between the United States and many other jurisdictions) happens all the time. This reality raises the question in international antitrust: what is the appropriate institutional structure that creates and builds trust so that agencies can use informal comity and cooperation on a regular basis to solve global antitrust problems (assuming that informal mechanisms are preferred over formal ones)? The answer is in the institutional design for existing international antitrust

1. Charles M. Tiebout, *A Pure Theory of Local Expenditures*, 64 J. Pol. Econ. 416 (1956).

2. Douglass North, Institutions, Institutional Change and Economic Performance (1990).

institutions or through the creation of new ones to meet the needs of global antitrust problems if no existing institutional alternative can be modified. Creating better institutions requires choosing among the various formalized international antitrust institutions that can address this key international issue. To create effective institutions, one must first analyze the nature of the existing problems that face international antitrust.

II. PROBLEMS OF INTERNATIONAL ANTITRUST

What, then, are these problems of international antitrust that require an international institutional response? The problems can be broken down into two cross-jurisdictional themes: procedural and substantive. The procedural problems are problems of coordination, such as how laws across jurisdictions allow sharing of information or how agencies can coordinate issues such as leniency requests. Harmonization across jurisdictions can remove unnecessary costs of doing business by eliminating or reducing multiple procedures and approaches. Therefore, the best institutional solution for this problem is the one that best creates a set of harmonized global practices that reduce transaction costs.

Substantive concerns involve differences in both legal and economic approaches to the types of conduct that agencies find to be anticompetitive and the burdens of proof that firms must show. On an international level, a key concern is that when one of the major powers in antitrust (the European Union and the United States) has a standard with too low a threshold for a finding on wrongdoing, this lower standard effectively operates as the global standard because remedies often have global implications.[3] Even if the United States and the EU have a similar substantive approach, if other jurisdictions have vastly different analytical approaches, some of these approaches may still create increased costs for doing business in a given jurisdiction in addition to potentially reducing consumer welfare.

Problems can be broken down into four types of situations, each of which has procedural and substantive concerns. There is an additional problem with each situation, which is how to address capacity constraints of agencies both established and new (though particularly the new ones) to undertake certain types of work. There are now over one hundred antitrust agencies around the world, including some in jurisdictions such as Jersey, Greenland, Zambia, and Vietnam. Most antitrust agencies are relatively young with high employee turnover rates, making the creation of a well-trained staff with institutional memory difficult. These younger agencies often lack the capacity to take on the cases that may be

3. William E. Kovacic, *Competition Policy in the European Union and the United States: Convergence orDivergence?* Bates White Fifth Annual Antitrust Conference, Washington, D.C., June 2, 2008, available at http://www.ftc.gov/speeches/kovacic/080602bateswhite.pdf.

the most injurious to their economies, such as international cartels. Moreover, young agencies sometimes take various substantive analytical shortcuts in areas such as merger control or abuse of dominance. Such shortcuts may make foreign firms bear the brunt of bad agency decision-making where a more than cursory analysis would suggest that efficiency would not be harmed by the behavior in question.

International institutions can assist in providing technical assistance and capacity building for these younger antitrust agencies. As this chapter will explore later in its discussion of particular international antitrust institutions, capacity building has become an increasing priority for international organizations. Capacity building will remain a priority in the near-to-medium term as China and India become more active in antitrust. Even in smaller jurisdictions, there is a sense that antitrust can be used as a development tool to police against malfunctions in the market and government-created economic distortions.

A. Mergers

An increasing number of "national" firms have operations across the globe. As a result, firms face both procedural and substantive concerns in merger control as many jurisdictions may have a nexus to the transaction. The procedure-related concerns that affect the international system can increase transaction costs. There are over seventy antitrust regimes with merger control. Lack of transparency, significant (sometimes contradictory) variation, and unnecessary delay can create substantial problems. For example, a large merger may require filings in forty different jurisdictions. For the merging parties, there are three procedural questions that must be answered in each jurisdiction, all of which may have their own jurisdictional rules: whether to file, when to file, and how long parties must wait until the antitrust agency reviews a filing. Different rules add to the cost of doing business and increase the amount of resources that firms must allocate to the merger process and away from firm management. Moreover, the cost of delay creates uncertainty for merging parties. Add together the additional costs, delay, and uncertainty, and in a worst-case scenario, the deal may unravel altogether.[4]

There also may be substantive differences in standards that can affect a deal. The two best-known examples are *GE/Honeywell* and *Boeing/McDonnell-Douglas*, which created significant transatlantic tensions based on different substantive approaches to mergers. Merger review is resource-intensive on the part of an antitrust agency. Knowing when to intervene because of the potential anticompetitive effects is not easy and may require sophisticated economic analysis.

4. D. Daniel Sokol, *Monopolists Without Borders: The Institutional Challenge of International Antitrust in a Global Gilded Age*, 4 BERKELEY BUS. L.J. 37 (2007).

Younger agencies may not have the human capacity to know when to intervene or how best to craft a remedy that provides the necessary intervention.

B. Cartels

For many years, there were substantive differences in view across jurisdictions about the harmfulness of cartels. International consensus is that cartels create significant international harm. Increasing scholarship has begun to quantify the damages of cartels that operate across countries.[5] Distinct from domestic cartels are international cartels—those that operate across countries and across continents. International cartels have spillover effects across the world and create overcharges in every country that exceed penalties. Because of their international nature, it is harder to detect and effectively deter these cartels vis-à-vis purely domestic cartels. The key procedural difficulty across jurisdictions in cartel enforcement is how to enable various entities to cooperate in investigations. A second issue (neither substantive nor procedural) is how to create better practices to build up the capacity of agencies so that they can make more effective use of agency resources to combat international cartels. It also requires changes in laws to allow the newest techniques to be used—these include prison sentences, leniency, and increased financial penalties. On substantive issues, cartel soft law is about creating the appropriate incentives to create deterrence through the global costs of cartel participation exceeding the benefits.

C. Unilateral Conduct

Unilateral conduct by firms, such as refusals to deal with competitors or vertical relationships, is the area of the biggest differences in analytical approach across jurisdictions. Such substantive differences matter because of the potential effect of remedies. A remedy that is structural in nature or involves conduct may affect not merely that jurisdiction but potentially all other jurisdictions. This may be particularly important in sectors where innovation is a key part of the sector. Compare, for example, the U.S. approach in *Microsoft* to that of Europe, as well as other potential cases in the EU along similar lines, such as *Apple* and *Intel*. In the context of capacity building, younger agencies may rely more on analytical shortcuts, such as market shares, to determine if there has been an abuse of dominance. Such shortcuts may tend to lead to erroneous prosecutions and may increase business uncertainty, thereby reducing efficiency.

5. John Connor, Global Price Fixing: Studies in Industrial Organization (2d ed. 2007); John Connor, *Price-Fixing Overcharges: Legal and Economic Evidence, in* Vol. 22 of Research in Law and Economics (John B. Kirkwood ed., 2007); John Connor, *Optimal Deterrence and Private International Cartels* (in journal review).

D. Government and Mixed Restraints

Antitrust intersects with international trade in a number of ways. The two are complimentary, as antitrust focuses on the competitive situation within a country whereas trade focuses on the various governmental barriers that affect international competition. In some situations, government-created trade barriers or barriers that have both private and government components may be used to promote anticompetitive behavior. This behavior may have either market access or spillover effects. How best to address these types of behavior is a challenge to antitrust. In some situations, a domestic antitrust agency may not be able to act because it lacks jurisdiction through an immunity to antitrust oversight. In other situations, the task of antitrust is to use competition advocacy to reduce these government-created or condoned barriers. Younger agencies may lack the capacity to create competition advocacy programs to study, identify, and advocate the removal of such anticompetitive barriers.

III. GLOBAL INSTITUTIONS

A. Hard Law—WTO

There have been a number of attempts to create global antitrust institutions. Many of these have focused on "hard law" institutions. Hard law is a formalized governance model that relies upon formal rules to bind countries and their sub-units. Although there were attempts made to create a binding set of hard law antitrust commitments upon the founding of the modern international trade system after World War II, these efforts to attack anticompetitive practices foundered, and the issue was not revisited until the 1990s, under the guise of the WTO.

The origin of the WTO antitrust institutional approach dates back to the foundations of the current international trading system. The International Trade Organization charter had a section on restrictive trading practices. Though the ITO itself never materialized, there were elements within the GATT and then the WTO that affected the intersection of international trade with antitrust. With the creation of the WTO and with the understanding that non-tariff barriers could be just as trade restrictive as tariff barriers, policymakers began to draw explicit linkages between the two areas. Lord Brittan in 1992 at the World Economic Forum expressed a key connection between trade and antitrust when he suggested that, on their own, each area of law was insufficient to address international competition problems. In 1996, the WTO Singapore Ministerial put the intersection of trade and competition on the negotiating table for the Doha round of WTO negotiations. Discussions began under a Trade and Competition Working Group the following year. At first, all issues of the intersection were on the table for discussion.

Over time, politics removed a number of the more contentious issues in the trade and antitrust interface from the discussion. A number of these are worth describing. Countries discussed how to best address market access issues given the political dynamics. There was a general reluctance of antitrust agencies to trust trade lawyers to understand the nature of competition. One fundamental distinction between antitrust and trade is that each has its own mode of analysis. Antitrust looks at anticompetitive conduct, and trade looks to whether there has been discriminatory behavior. There are a number of instances in which the two are not the same. In fact, the WTO has explicitly rejected an antitrust analysis in its case law.[6]

By 2001, under the Doha Declaration, the WTO Trade and Competition Working Group focused on what the Working Group deemed to be core principles of interface: transparency, nondiscrimination, procedural fairness, voluntary cooperation, capacity building, and limitations on hard-core cartels. The irony is that the "core" issues the WTO sought to address were exactly those issues that soft law antitrust institutions were already in the process of addressing. Indeed, soft law international antitrust institutional alternatives, as will be explained below, were already in the process of making significant progress in these areas. Because of the success of soft law institutions on these very issues, a WTO focus in these areas became redundant, at best, because of the superiority in the institutional design of soft law to create credible commitments and changes in law and policy where needed on these issues. But by 2003, the WTO had dropped competition policy from the Doha round of trade negotiations, and the issue became moot from a practical perspective.

One reason the WTO hard law approach was not embraced involved the fear of the global lock-in of a suboptimal set of standards. Creating binding commitments locks countries into a global standard, which, given the difficulty of WTO trade negotiations, is difficult to alter over time. Lock-in into the WTO system creates a lack of democratic accountability as the decisions of all member countries are tied together based on the policy preferences of the economically dominant countries. A number of developing countries expressed this concern in the Trade and Competition Working Group discussions. Because of the relative strength of the United States and the EU, these entities are able to coerce less powerful countries into accepting their preferences as part of the international system. However, once the system is in place, the system also serves to limit the choices of the United States and European Union; they become locked into policy choices based on the WTO as well. Particularly, the United States antitrust agencies worried that the WTO would limit U.S. prosecutorial discretion.

As the WTO sets the floor for permissible regulation, it encourages convergence of legal regimes based on the commitments that countries undertake. Any commitment to reduce anticompetitive trade-related restraints that affect

---

6. *Canada—Measures Relating to Exports of Wheat and Treatment of Imported Grain*, WT/DS276/AB/R, adopted Sept. 27, 2004, at para. 145.

antitrust creates the potential for a democracy deficit because the trade regime is far removed from voter preferences and there has not been an affirmative ceding of supranational authority to the WTO akin what Member States have ceded to the EU. In certain ways, the nature of WTO convergence is without precedent. The claim can be made that this harmonization lacks the political basis and therefore the legitimacy of other harmonization projects. The best-known other multinational harmonization has been at the EU level. However, there are some significant differences between EU and WTO harmonization.[7] Because the WTO system does not have the role of integration of the EU, it must show greater deference to domestic regulation, which is a function of the domestic political process. Unlike the WTO, the EU had certain prerequisites for creating a constitutional system. This includes the explicit federal power to regulate member states in antitrust and the idea that country-level concerns cannot trump EU-wide antitrust.[8] WTO law in contrast only allows for indirect regulation of its members.

A second problem with the WTO is the nature of the WTO adjudicatory system. Adjudication is only between states; there are no private causes of action. Therefore the use of the WTO comes with certain adjudication costs. Because complaints are between states, a private party must convince its government to bring a claim on its behalf. For an industry to be able to convince its country to bring a claim, that country must be willing to expend the political and financial capital to bring a case. The country needs to have a sense that it has an above-average chance of winning, and that by bringing such a case it will not harm itself in the future with any precedent that the case sets. Finally, because of the power dynamics of the WTO, these costs of adjudication of potential claims often benefit developed world countries and developed world business interests.[9]

B. Soft Law

Soft law is an institutional choice for domestic-level agency implementation over hard law's international adjudication. This choice may involve information costs and decisions about which institutions are more likely to have better information. Soft law uses benchmarking of general practices. This allows for flexibility for countries to adhere to the benchmarked better practices based on the country's own unique legal, political, and economic background. Competition law,

---

7. Robert Howse & Kalypso Nicolaidis, *Legitimacy and Global Governance: Why Constitutionalizing the WTO is a Step Too Far?*, *in* THE ROLE OF THE JUDGE IN INTERNATIONAL TRADE REGULATION: EXPERIENCE AND LESSONS FOR THE WTO 325 (Thomas Cottier & Petros C. Mavroidis eds., 2003).

8. European Court of Justice, Inno/Atab, Nov. 16, 1977, case 13/77; European Court of Justice, Ahmed Saeed, Apr. 11, 1989, case 66/86.

9. GREG SHAFFER, DEFENDING INTERESTS: PUBLIC-PRIVATE PARTNERSHIPS IN WTO LITIGATION (2003).

even if based on the same general principles, may look different across countries. Sometimes soft law requires the legislature to play a role domestically by changing laws to conform to benchmarked norms.

When agencies increase the exchange of information, this reduces the information costs across jurisdictions. Some of this information exchange may occur informally through meetings of regulators and the establishment of personal relationships among counterparts in different jurisdictions. In other cases, information exchanges may be formalized through agreements across agencies or through soft law institutions. International antitrust institutions help to facilitate trust. Trust increases the ability of agencies to share information and to provide for informal comity. To draw from the larger contracts literature, informal contracting might make sense in lieu of formal rules in the context of repeat performers (such as antitrust agencies) who must trust each other to lead to efficient outcomes.[10] As I will illustrate below, trust-based repeat relationships through soft law international institutions have assisted in the creation of private ordering to address many of the most pressing international antitrust issues.

For most issues within antitrust, it may be optimal to allow for the sort of country-level tinkering in doctrine and economic approaches by which better practices can emerge. This requires an institutional preference that allows for a bottom-up version of norm creation rather than a WTO hard law solution. At the first level, one jurisdiction creates a superior practice. At the second level, the norm is made into a general norm at the level of international institutions. It then goes from bottom-up to top-down as the international institutions help to spread the norm to other jurisdictions.[11] Muris suggests that jurisdictions adopt these norms, and the implication is that they do so voluntarily. However, there is a level of soft coercion in this adoption. When the United States and the EU are behind such norms, there is a powerful snowballing effect; other countries want to join in to be seen as part of the "club" because this legitimizes their own agency's standing. They also rely on the EU and the United States for technical assistance and capacity building, and U.S. and EU experts will push this agenda. Aid may be contingent on implementing these norms. There also may be a

10. *See generally* AVNER GREIF, INSTITUTIONS AND THE PATH TO THE MODERN ECONOMY: LESSONS FROM MEDIEVAL TRADE (2006); Robert C. Ellickson, *Of Coase and Cattle: Dispute Resolution Among Neighbors in Shasta County*, 38 STAN. L. REV. 623 (1986). For an exposition of private ordering in an antitrust context, see D. Daniel Sokol, *Order Without (Enforceable) Law: Why Countries Enter Into Non-Enforceable Competition Policy Chapters in Free Trade Agreements*, 83 CHI.-KENT L. REV. 231 (2008).

11. Timothy J. Muris, Competition Agencies in a Market-Based Global Economy (Brussels, Belgium, July 23, 2002) (prepared remarks at the Annual Lecture of the European Foreign Affairs Review), *available at* http://www.ftc.gov/speeches/muris/020723brussels.shtm.

shaming effect through international institutions, which I will cover below in the discussion of the various soft law institutions.

Soft law works across three dimensions: obligation, precision, and delegation. Soft law lacks the formal binding of hard law: obligation serves to bind states to commitments. This allows for lower-stakes bargaining among soft law participants.[12] In soft law antitrust, there is little obligation. The nonbinding nature of recommended practices allows for each country to adopt (or not adopt) such practices as they see fit. Nevertheless, there is still some obligation as norm creation and diffusion pushes countries to adopt these practices as their own.

Precision allows for the definition of rules. International law can be less or more precise. The more precise, the harder the law. Soft law's lack of precision makes it more malleable than hard law. Precision can be restrictive, and sometimes ambiguity is a good thing, allowing for flexibility and compromise. Lack of precision allows states to achieve greater compromise over time as more states can read their own understandings into a commitment. It may encourage more cooperation among parties that have divergent interests and levels of power. Additionally, soft law may change as circumstances require it to do so. Under soft law, there is no need for countries to renegotiate international commitments and seek domestic approval for these changes, as would be required under a formal treaty. Instead, the lack of precision allows for certain benefits—the creation and implementation of general norms at the country level that take into account the particular political and economic realities of that country. In soft law antitrust, broad principles in antitrust allow for each country to adopt the language and theoretical underpinnings behind it in a manner that can be more easily incorporated within the existing legal and political traditions. This flexibility allows for "fit" within an existing tradition and is not a pure transplant across legal systems that might not apply in the new setting similar to the way it does it its original setting.

Delegation is a mechanism by which states grant power to international organizations in order to overcome information costs and increase commitments.[13] Delegation can elucidate and elaborate legal norms, implement rules, and facilitate the enforcement of such rules.[14] Under delegation, third parties may be authorized to interpret and apply rules and resolve disputes. In principle,

12. Kenneth W. Abbott & Duncan Snidal, *Hard and Soft Law in International Governance*, 54 Int'l Org. 421, 434 (2000).

13. Mark A. Pollack, *Delegation and Discretion in the European Union*, *in* Delegation and Agency in International Organizations (Darren G. Hawkins, David A. Lake, Daniel L. Nielson & Michael J. Tierney eds., 2006).

14. Kenneth W. Abbott, Robert O. Keohane, Andrew Moravcsik, Anne-Marie Slaughter, & Duncan Snidal, *The Concept of Legalization*, 54 Int'l Org. 401, 406 (2000).

delegation of decision-making allows for potential efficiencies.[15] In this regard, imprecise rules that have high levels of delegation can become more precise over time as judicial rulings fill in the gaps to create greater precision.[16] However, delegation removes an element of sovereignty.

Soft law delegation allows the agents of delegation to have more control without the direct democratic check of elected officials. Yet soft law may preserve elements of sovereignty better than hard law. In its delegation, soft law removes less discretion of domestic actors. Accountability of soft law transgovernmental and transnational organizations occurs as soft law institutions operate through persuasion of officials by their counterparts in other countries. Cooperation increases in such forums, and this serves to empower domestic politicians rather than to reduce their accountability.[17] Soft law also has the advantage of providing a method of integration when political controversies over sovereignty might otherwise stymie such integration.[18] Because nothing in soft law antitrust has been delegated to international adjudicators, antitrust agencies do not worry about the loss of their prosecutorial discretion, particularly to international institutions that lack the capacity and institutional competence to undertake such rigorous antitrust analysis.

Having distinguished between hard and soft law in antitrust, it is now important to distinguish between types of soft law antitrust. Soft law includes both transgovernmental and transnational approaches. The transgovernmental approach, which includes the Organisation for Economic Co-operation and Development (OECD) and United Nations Conference on Trade and Development (UNCTAD), involves an institutional structure based upon discussions among government sub-units. In the case of antitrust, this means antitrust agencies. In contrast, the transnational approach has a broader set of participants, which includes nongovernmental actors. The ICN utilizes this approach and includes law firms, economic consulting firms, academics, and civil society groups in its various working groups. There are also purely nongovernmental organizations such as bar associations and academic groups that meet regularly. However, these groups do not play a major role in norm creation and the development of

---

15. On the various costs and benefits of delegation, see Cass R. Sunstein, *Factions, Self-Interest, and the APA: Four Lessons Since 1946*, 72 Va. L. Rev. 271 (1986).

16. Kenneth W. Abbott, Robert O. Keohane, Andrew Moravcsik, Anne-Marie Slaughter, & Duncan Snidal, *The Concept of Legalization*, 54 Int'l Org. 401, 406 (2000).

17. Joseph S. Nye, Jr. & Robert O. Keohane, *Between Centralization and Fragmentation: The Club Model of Multilateral Cooperation and Problems of Democratic Legitimacy*, KSG Faculty Research Working Papers Series RWP01-004, Feb. 13–16, 2001.

18. Fritz Scharpf, *Legitimate Diversity: The New Challenge of European Integration*, *in* The State of the European Union, 6: Law, Politics, and Society (Tanja Börzel & Rachel A. Chichowski eds., 2003).

agency better practices. Therefore, a discussion of these groups is beyond the scope of this chapter.

1. **OECD** The OECD discusses competition policy through its Competition Committee. Competition Committee members include OECD member countries along with a number of agencies that have been given membership status even though their countries themselves are not OECD members (e.g., Brazil). The Competition Committee has been in existence since the 1960s. However, during its early years, few OECD members had competition laws, and enforcement in most countries was spotty. Things began to change in the 1980s and 1990s. It was in the 1990s that the Competition Committee began to increase its productivity and expand the types of issues it addressed. In part, this was a reaction to the inclusion of competition policy as a possible topic for negotiation at the WTO and in part recognition of the need to reduce a significant divide between U.S. and European approaches to competition policy.

The OECD's role and the types of activities it undertakes have changed over time. Traditionally, Competition Committee meetings have been an opportunity for senior agency officials to meet and discuss substantive issues and areas of potential cooperation. A number of OECD resolutions have been passed to address greater cooperation. One key function of the Competition Committee has been to provide peer reviews of member countries' antitrust systems. Peer reviews serve as outside diagnostics of the strengths and weaknesses of such systems. The reviews describe the country's current system and analyze how well it works. The peer review process serves to better assess the current situation and future direction of a country's antitrust system, and also creates a series of takeaways on how that country's own agency can improve the system. A given peer review, written by the OECD staff or by a consultant, focuses on the cases brought and institutional issues within the domestic legal and political systems. Other antitrust agencies ask questions about the peer review during the presentation, and the country under review has an opportunity to respond to the questions. Because of the deliberate process in a review session, a number of peer review comments might also be applicable to other countries confronting similar issues and might provide some hints as to methods to structure enforcement priorities or particular approaches to take. Even though nonbinding, the peer reviews may help to facilitate change in a domestic legal system by providing support that the change is necessary by, for example, stressing that the creation of higher penalties is crucial for effective deterrence. Because the Competition Committee conducts this exercise among sister agencies, there is a potential shaming effect among peer agencies that promotes compliance with the recommendations. Moreover, these recommendations may serve as a tool for legitimate domestic legislative change.

In more recent years, through the Competition Committee's Global Forum on Competition and Latin American Competition Forum, OECD peer reviews have expanded to include a number of nonmember and non-observer OECD countries.

Both of these forums are noteworthy for how the OECD has expanded its reach to include agencies from around the world at different levels of economic development. This has increased the number and spectrum of voices at the OECD.

In addition to peer reviews, the OECD staff prepares discussion documents to facilitate roundtable dialogue on specific issues in competition policy. Recent discussions have included dynamic efficiencies in merger analysis, how antitrust agencies provide the private sector with more effective guidance on monopolization issues, and plea bargaining settlement of cartel cases. Senior agency representatives (often agency heads) present their views on these issues. The OECD often facilitates the conversation by inviting an outside presenter to explore the issue. The roundtable discussion helps participants take stock of existing understandings and approaches to a given issue. When consensus has been reached on an issue, the OECD prepares recommended practices. It is the identification and implementation of best practices in which OECD efforts have begun to show great promise in addressing these problems. The OECD has not yet reached a point where it can create norms in the area of monopolization in large part because there is no consensus among OECD member agencies. Moreover, with the dissolution of its trade and competition discussion group (at the behest of the United States), the OECD lacks the ability to create norms in trade and antitrust intersection problems.

In many ways, the OECD has transformed itself in recent years as a result of competition with other international antitrust institutions and has found new niches through which to offer unique but complimentary outputs relative to other antitrust institutions. It has undertaken its own technical assistance programs since the early 1990s. However, these efforts have increased significantly in recent years and now include OECD competition centers in Asia and Central Europe that provide training and conferences for antitrust agency officials in those regions. The OECD has extended its work into the broader area of law and regulation and promotes a pro-competitive regulatory toolkit to increase competition in OECD countries through less restrictive regulation. It is now in the process of rolling out the competition toolkit to mid-income countries such as Mexico. In the area of competition advocacy, OECD efforts are increasingly effective, thereby perhaps indirectly attacking government anticompetitive practices—something the WTO, using a trade-based hard law solution, has not been able to do for political reasons.

2. UNCTAD UNCTAD is the second of the transgovernmental antitrust organizations. As a UN organization, it has its origins in the dependency theory movement of the 1960s and 1970s.[19] It created a model code for competition policy in 1980 that demonstrated some hostility to multinational firms. Because the United States has been unreceptive (as has the European Union, to

19. Raúl Prebisch, *Commercial Policy in the Underdeveloped Countries*, 49 Amer. Econ. Rev. 251 (1959).

a lesser extent) to the UNCTAD message, UNCTAD's code and its other outputs have lacked the norm-creating value of OECD outputs. In many ways, the UNCTAD day-to-day operations are similar to those of the OECD. UNCTAD conducts peer reviews, holds annual meetings to discuss various topics, and undertakes technical assistance. Because UNCTAD participation focuses on developing-world membership, UNCTAD meetings focus more on capacity constraints of developing-world antitrust agencies than the OECD's do. As a consequence of the lack of significant involvement of the major powers (United States and EU), UNCTAD does not set the worldwide antitrust agenda. UNCTAD has value in building up relations across very young agencies and in focusing on issues that have a specific developing-world context. However, because the ICN and the OECD have undertaken more outreach to the developing world, and developing world agencies have spent more time and resources on these competing institutions that have greater general norm-creating ability, UNCTAD's role among international antitrust institutes will remain secondary.

3. ICN The ICN, established in 2001, is a relatively new international antitrust institution. Its members include all of the world's antitrust agencies regardless of size or level of economic development. The ICN has its origins in two key developments. First, it is the intellectual brainchild of the important International Competition Policy Advisory Committee (ICPAC) report of 2000. ICPAC was a Department of Justice response to developments in the WTO. The hearings and submissions that occurred during the tenure of ICPAC and the final report were an attempt to take stock of the current situation of international issues in antitrust, to identify what requirements and institutional design issues were critical to thinking about the future of international antitrust, and to propose specific recommendations. In the course of the ICPAC discussions, it became clear that the Department of Justice was quite concerned about the potential negative impact of a hard law antitrust solution at the WTO. In place of such a solution, ICPAC promoted the creation of a soft law Global Competition Initiative to discuss antitrust issues among the world's antitrust agencies.

Since the European Union was the chief promoter of a WTO-based approach, somehow the United States needed to co-opt the Europeans to join in support of the soft law alternative that the United States had proposed. What brought the Europeans to the soft law approach was a crisis. This crisis occurred in the merger area, centering around the proposed merger of GE and Honeywell. The Department of Justice approved the merger of the two U.S.-based firms while the European Commission opposed the merger based on an alternative analysis. Merger disagreements were not new between the EU and the United States. However, in *Boeing/McDonnell Douglas* and a number of late 1990s pharmaceutical merger cases, the EU and the United States eventually were able to come up with a set of mutually agreeable conditions for merger approval. But then *GE/Honeywell* exposed what was, at the time, a fundamental disagreement across the Atlantic about merger control. In the wake of transatlantic discord, the business community on both sides of the Atlantic pushed for resolution of a number of issues that *GE/Honeywell* had exposed, both substantive and procedural, that portended the prospect of significantly greater costs of getting a deal through a myriad of potentially conflicting merger control systems.

Initially, ICN work was in mergers. It quickly expanded into cartels, regulated areas, capacity building, and unilateral conduct. The ICN has had an important impact on creating change (both perceived and directly measurable) in the implementation of benchmarked better practices across a number of different areas both procedural and substantive. Two qualities explain the success of the ICN: (1) institutional design and (2) a modest agenda that began with issues in which it would be possible to measure success relatively easily and quickly.

The ICN is unlike other international antitrust institutions. It is different because it is transnational rather than transgovernmental. It has active involvement from academics, private sector attorneys from in-house and law firm backgrounds, economists from consulting firms, and civil society groups. This participation spans both developing and developed world nongovernmental actors. These nongovernmental actors bring input that comes from their own experiences. Having additional resources to scrutinize ideas and discuss the analytical approaches and specific language of various work products allows those most affected by government enforcement of antitrust laws to provide their perspectives and input into the potential effects of such enforcement that agencies themselves might not readily foresee. Moreover, stakeholder involvement in the deliberative process provides a sense of ownership of the various outcomes to a larger group. This allows for buy-in domestically to the larger set of constituent groups that are not involved in the deliberative process, because the process may be seen as more legitimate from a participatory perspective. Also, the increased number of contact points in the creation of norms in both procedural and substantive areas of antitrust law and policy through ICN participation allows for more rapid diffusion of these norms. The ICN's membership includes lesser-developed and younger agencies. Many of these agencies can develop a common sense of understanding about better practices in competition policy and a how to create a better context to affect change.

It is not merely the increased participation that makes the difference in ICN work products. Another factor that aids in norm diffusion is the lack of an ICN bureaucracy. Bureaucracies can create opportunities for free-riding by antitrust agency leadership and staff. The ICN is a virtual institution, without any headquarters or permanent staff. Therefore, opportunities for free-riding at the ICN are limited. Agency participants include the European Commission, agencies from EU member states, and U.S. antitrust enforcers; all play an active role in supporting the work of the ICN. Without such active support from the major powers of antitrust, the ICN would not be able to accomplish much in terms of output and even less in terms of norm creation and diffusion. Success breeds additional success and creates momentum for the ICN.

The breadth of ICN outputs is considerable. The first stage of work in many groups is to undertake surveys in which the agencies describe their experiences in a certain area of law. The cartel working group provides a good example. In this group, the mandate is to improve cartel enforcement for both domestic and international cartels, regardless of the size of the country or the age and experience of a given antitrust agency. Work in this group has included creating a working paper that defines what is meant by a "hard-core" cartel, how ICN members define such conduct, what institutions within a given antitrust system address this conduct, and what makes penalties effective. Additional work includes the creation of templates for legislation, rules, regulations, guidelines, and information about cartel cases. With a centralized location of knowledge, member countries can better adapt successes in one country to their own within the appropriate legal, political, and economic contexts. Another tool to aid in the adoption of better practices has been the creation of a manual that includes techniques to improve cartel enforcement. To reinforce a number of the norms being adopted by antitrust agencies on cartel matters, the ICN has sponsored a yearly workshop on cartel enforcement. These outputs have helped to increase the capacity of younger agencies to effectively address international cartels and to improve their domestic cartel capacity. It also allows for better sharing of non-confidential information through the creation of personal relations at the agency leadership and staff levels. Similar work outputs and processes are underway in the merger group and in other groups such as capacity building, where there is a yearly ongoing set of activities.

The various ICN reports have been cited as outside authority to justify increased competition advocacy and changes to existing laws. ICN work products are an outside force for policy change, and its better practices have the stamp of international legitimacy. The use of these work products may allow agencies to more easily push for domestic change. The creation of such better practices and increased capacity building overall has made the occurrence of another *GE/Honeywell* less likely and has generally improved the capacity of agencies.

The ICN has succeeded because of its modest agenda. It began with work in procedural mergers issues, such as merger notification and substantive issues of cartels where agreement was likely and where, over time, countries could easily implement better practices. However, the ICN's continued success is somewhat questionable, given the fact that much of the low-hanging fruit of easy accomplishments is no longer available. The ICN has begun to address issues of monopolization, where there is significant disagreement around the world. If the ICN finds itself unable to create better practices after taking stock of existing approaches in unilateral conduct, and if the ICN is unable or unwilling to address other key international antitrust issues such as the intersection of antitrust with international trade, it will lose momentum. Should the interest of ICN members (and in particular the major powers) wane as a result, the ICN will not remain effective.

IV. REGIONAL INSTITUTIONS

Developments in international institutions do not occur exclusively at the global level. Regional organizations play an increasingly prominent role in international antitrust matters. Regional antitrust organizations take both hard law and soft law forms. For purposes of length, this chapter overlooks the EU itself as well as the European Competition Network; the European situation is a unique and well-developed blend of political and economic integration. Instead, the remainder of this chapter explores other forms of regional antitrust institutions. Though these institutions are different, some common themes emerge. First, regional institutions have significant political constraints that reduce their effectiveness. Capacity constraints that limit effectiveness also are common. However, there has been progress in recent years, particularly in the soft law institutions. In part, this may be due to the reduced cost in the creation of soft law organizations.

A. Mercosur

The Mercado Común del Cono Sur (Mercosur) is a preferential trade agreement among Brazil, Argentina, Paraguay, and Uruguay. Like the EU, its original purpose was political in nature—to create an integrated southern hemisphere with the eventual goal of a common external tariff.[20] The roots of competition policy in Mercosur trace back to Decision N° 21/94. The key competition policy provision in Mercosur is Decision N° 18/96, the Protocol for the Defense of Competition ("Fortaleza Protocol"). The Fortaleza Protocol addresses issues of institutional design, substantive standards, and increased cooperation. The Fortaleza Protocol adopted a rule of reason standard, and created a common timetable for merger control across the Mercosur countries. As a regional common market, Mercosur has some important similarities with the EU. Mercosur (in theory) provides for coordination across agencies to address trans-border anticompetitive behavior. The Protocol calls for increased harmonization across domestic competition laws for conduct and merger control. Moreover, it created cooperation mechanisms across antitrust agencies. However, many of these provisions remain undeveloped due to lackluster implementation.

Mercosur countries have been resistant to the creation of a sub-regional competition authority.[21] Questions exist as to why Mercosur's competition policy remains unfulfilled. Part of the answer is that, because of functional issues, Mercosur does not work. In Argentina and Brazil, the goals, agency structures, and enforcement mechanisms of competition policy differ greatly.[22]

---

20. El Desafío de Integrarse Para Crecer: Balance y Perspectivas del MERCOSUR en su Primera Década (Daniel Chudnovsky & José María Fanelli eds., 2001).

21. OECD, Competition Law and Policy in Brazil: A Peer Review 72 (2005).

22. Jose Tavares de Araujo, Jr. & Luis Tineo, *Competition Policy and Regional Trade Agreements*, *in* Trade Rules in the Making Challenges in Regional and Multilateral

Another part of the explanation involves the political process. By creating too demanding a schedule for competition policy implementation, Mercosur lost momentum in competition policy issues and made it more difficult to meet goals; member countries continuously postponed them.[23] A lack of political will to move Mercosur forward more generally has infected the competition policy elements of the agreement. If there were a stronger political will toward greater potential economic integration, countries would push for greater coordination and harmonization in competition policy. A further explanation may be that the lack of supranational institutions existing at the beginning of Mercosur delayed the development of a common competition culture. This problem is not unique to Mercosur; creation and harmonization of competition laws also took time in the EU context.

There are significant structural limits in Mercosur to top-down regional competition harmonization and to mechanisms for addressing trans-border conduct. The Fortaleza Protocol does not contemplate a supranational authority along the lines of the EU to adjudicate disputes that have region-wide impact. Nor does it allow for binding review of decisions made by domestic competition agencies.[24] Mercosur also remains weak in those areas specific to government restraints on competition. There are no explicit disciplines regarding state aids. Another regulatory gap is in antidumping. Unlike other agreements that create a common external tariff, Mercosur allows for antidumping remedies against other Mercosur members. Though antidumping was to have been phased out by the end of 2000, it remains in force. Argentina is a significant user of antidumping against other Mercosur members. For example, fully one third of Argentine's antidumping actions initiated have been against other Mercosur members, usually against Brazilian companies.[25] The significant use of antidumping within Mercosur has considerable implications on competition within the countries; it erects entry barriers for foreign goods and services, where in many cases allowing entry would reduce monopoly power of incumbent (domestic) firms.

More general development of common competition rules for Mercosur mergers remains unfulfilled. Uruguay has a basic competition law in place, but the Fortaleza Protocol has not been incorporated into Uruguayan domestic legislation.

NEGOTIATIONS (Miguel Rodriguez Mendoza, Patrick Low, & Barbara Kotschwar eds., 1999).

23. André Filipe Zago de Azevedo, *Mercosur: Ambitious Policies, Poor Practices*, 24 REVISTA DE ECONOMÍA POLÍTICA 4 (2004).

24. André Filipe Zago de Azevedo, *Mercosur Agreement on Competition Policy—How Effective Has It Been and How to Promote Further Cooperation?*, Working Paper, Competition Policy Foundations for Trade Reform, Regulatory Reform, and Sustainable Development, CEPR 7 (2005).

25. José Tavares de Araujo Jr., *Política de Concorrência no Mercosul: Uma Agenda Mínima*, *in* EL DESAFÍO DE INTEGRARSE PARA CRECER: BALANCE Y PERSPECTIVAS DEL MERCOSUR EN SU PRIMERA DÉCADA 154 (Daniel Chudnovsky & José María Fanelli eds., 2001).

To date, Paraguay lacks a competition law. Yet Paraguay and Argentina have incorporated the Fortaleza Protocol into their domestic legislation as international legal obligations have become part of domestic law under a monist theory.

To enforce the Fortaleza Protocol, two institutions were to be created—the Mercosur Trade Commission ("TC") for adjudicatory purposes and the Committee for the Defense of Competition ("CDC") for enforcement. Though the TC has functioned since the Ouro Protocol of 1994, the CDC has not yet been set up. To compensate for the lack of progress based on the Fortaleza Protocol, Mercosur's Technical Committee on Competition approved a Memorandum of Understanding ("MOU") in 2003 to increase cooperation. MOU provisions include notification procedures, information exchange, and technical assistance. All Mercosur countries have incorporated the MOU into national law.[26] Additionally, Mercosur members took interim measures in 2002, signing the Regulation for the Application of the Competition Protocol in Mercosur. This regulation created a Competition Committee to enforce the Fortaleza Protocol.[27] In 2004, the TC asked that the Fortaleza Protocol be revised to make the CDC effective (or for that matter, to finally create it), strengthen cooperation among agencies in cross-border cases and mergers, eliminate the focus on interagency cooperation on trade-distorting conduct, and provide technical assistance by Argentina and Brazil for Uruguay and Paraguay.[28]

B. Andean Community

Members of the Andean Community include Bolivia, Colombia, Ecuador, Peru, and (until recently) Venezuela. The Andean Community emerged as a result of the Cartagena Agreement of 1969. The Andean Community competition policy structure was the first attempt to address competition policy in South America at the regional level. Decision 285 of 1991 established common rules to address distortions of competition. At the time the agreement entered into effect, only Colombia had a competition law.

---

26. Frédéric Jenny & Pierre Horna, *Modernization of the European Legal System of Competition. Law Enforcement: Lessons from other Regional Groupings*, *in* COMPETITION PROVISIONS IN REGIONAL TRADE AGREEMENTS: HOW TO ASSURE DEVELOPMENT GAINS 314 (Lucian Cernat, Philippe Brusick, & Ana Maria Alvarez eds., 2005).

27. Maria Celia Andrade, *Competition Law in Mercosur: Recent Developments*, 6 GLOBAL COMP. REV. 1, 2 (2003).

28. Barbara Rosenberg & Mariana Tavares de Araújo, *Implementation Costs and Burden of International Competition Law and Policy Agreements*, *in* COMPETITION PROVISIONS IN REGIONAL TRADE AGREEMENTS: HOW TO ASSURE DEVELOPMENT GAINS 209 (Lucian Cernat, Philippe Brusick, & Ana Maria Alvarez eds., 2005). OECD, COMPETITION LAW AND POLICY IN BRAZIL: A PEER REVIEW 211 (2005).

The Andean Community competition framework is modeled on the EU, in both substance and enforcement mechanisms.[29] Decision 285 of the Andean Community established regulation of antitrust applicable to trans-border practices within the region and to practices originating in third countries that affect more than one Andean country.[30] Under Decision 285, where there was no spillover effect of anticompetitive conduct across jurisdictions, only national law applied. Where there was a spillover effect, Decision 285 charged the Secretariat of the Andean Community with investigating the anticompetitive conduct. The Decision applied a rule of reason standard. However, the weakness of Decision 285 was that its standard for a determination of harm was similar to that of antidumping rather than an antitrust harm. That is, harm was measured by harm to competitors rather than by harm to competition.[31] Decision 285's use of an antidumping framework created conceptual confusion in its implementation. Additional elements that limited its effectiveness included the lack of a binding effect of judgments to force firms to implement decisions, and the lack of political will to enforce competition policy among Andean Community member states. This explains why litigants rarely invoked Decision 285 in its 13 years of existence.

Recognizing the weakness of Decision 285, the Andean Community approved Decision 608 of 2005, which revoked and superseded Decision 285. The principles of Decision 608 are based on nondiscrimination, transparency, and due process.[32] The normative framework for Decision 608 contrasts with Decision 285 in that the basis for Decision 608 is efficiency. The Decision allows for sanctions to be imposed, including cease-and-desist orders for anticompetitive practices, imposition of conditions or obligations, and fines. It departs from Decision 285 in a number of respects. It provides in detail the mandate of the General Secretariat of the Andean Community to conduct investigations and adjudicatory proceedings against anticompetitive behavior. This includes the ability to mandate an end to conduct while still in the investigative phase of a proceeding. Participation in proceedings has also been broadened. The Decision allows for private rights of action, whereas under Decision 285, only national competition agencies could bring cases.

---

29. Jose Tavares de Araujo, Jr. & Luis Tineo, *Competition Policy and Regional Trade Agreements*, *in* TRADE RULES IN THE MAKING CHALLENGES IN REGIONAL AND MULTILATERAL NEGOTIATIONS (Miguel Rodriguez Mendoza, Patrick Low, & Barbara Kotschwar eds., 1999).

30. Decisión 608, Normas para la protección y promoción de la libre competencia en la Comunidad Andina (Mar. 29, 2005).

31. Jose Tavares de Araujo, Jr. & Luis Tineo, *Competition Policy and Regional Trade Agreements*, *in* TRADE RULES IN THE MAKING CHALLENGES IN REGIONAL AND MULTILATERAL NEGOTIATIONS 450–51 (Miguel Rodriguez Mendoza, Patrick Low, & Barbara Kotschwar eds., 1999).

32. Article 3.

A second area of additional coverage under Decision 608 is in substantive anticompetitive offenses which are actionable. The Decision includes bid-rigging in its coverage of public tenders. Under abuse of dominance provisions, the Decision now includes a cause of action for predatory pricing. Another provision now makes the erection of entry barriers an abuse of a dominant position. The Decision also creates the Andean Committee for the Defense of Free Competition. The role of the Committee, which consists of a member of each of the national agencies, is to coordinate and provide advice to the General Secretariat.

Even with the advances of Decision 608, a number of anticompetitive practices remain outside the reach of regional competition policy. The Decision does not include merger control within its purview; that is left to national authorities. Where the effects of the merger are based on a regional relevant market, or where the most effective remedy might be divestment in a third country, the lack of coverage may be problematic. Another area in which there may be inadequate coverage is with antitrust immunities. Decision 608 allows each country an allowance for antitrust immunities. These exclusions and exceptions include cases where there would be significant benefits for the development of production, processing, distribution, or commercialization of goods and services, or where economic or technological progress could be developed. Exceptions for coverage also include instances where member countries provide preferential terms in depressed areas, do not eliminate competition in a substantial part of production, or are in accordance with the Andean legal system.[33] Because of the recent vintage of Decision 608, it remains unclear if it will be more effective than Decision 285. No noticeable increase in the number of cases has occurred since the implementation of Decision 608.

C. CARICOM

The Caribbean Community (CARICOM) is the regional economic integration organization of the Caribbean, through the CARICOM Single Market and Economy ("CSME"). The nations of the Caribbean basin established CARICOM in 1973 under the Treaty of Chaguaramas. The Treaty was revised in 2001 to allow for a common market via the CSME. The CSME will provide for the removal of all external tariffs and will increase regulatory harmonization, although full implementation is behind schedule.

CARICOM's current governance structure has only limited effectiveness. CARICOM has been an economic agreement first and a political agreement second. This lack of emphasis on political issues has generated implementation problems, and issues of sovereignty have continually impeded increased economic

33. Article 6. This bears similarity to Article 86 of the Treaty of Rome. It remains unclear if the law in practice will be enforced similarly to the current enforcement of Article 86 or if it will be more permissive of state aid.

liberalization of the trade bloc. The CARICOM economic environment is particularly fragmented.[34]

Under the original Treaty of Chaguaramas, Article 30's restrictive practices included competition policy provisions. In the revised Treaty of Chaguaramas, Chapter 8 addresses these practices and creates a supranational body to take on both administrative and adjudicative functions. The Commission is to apply the rules of competition to anticompetitive cross-border business practices, to promote and protect competition, and coordinate the implementation of the CARICOM competition policy.[35] Competition policy is part of a larger vision of liberalized trade in goods and services within the CSME.

CARICOM has greater capacity constraints than other regional frameworks. The countries within CARICOM are small economies. Many of these economies will never have the funding to establish their own domestic antitrust agencies, even though their economies are fragile.[36] For some countries, funding is scarce even for police, tax, and finance agencies, and these needs supersede the need to create a national antitrust agency. Of all CARICOM members, only Jamaica, Guyana, St. Vincent, Trinidad and Barbados have competition legislation. A regional competition authority would be able to overcome this type of capacity constraint. It could also have advantages in addressing conduct where there is cross-border effect within CARICOM.[37]

The revised treaty provides for a CARICOM Competition Commission, which CARICOM recently established. For countries that will be unable to set up their own agencies, the Competition Court and CARICOM competition legislation will operate in lieu of a domestic agency and domestic law. In addition to serving in a domestic function for some CARICOM members, the Commission will serve a supranational purpose to address trans-border issues within CARICOM. These dual functions will allow the Commission to remedy both domestic and trans-border anticompetitive behavior. One limitation is that when national authorities differ from the Commission as to who will conduct an investigation, the Commission must cease its investigation and refer the issue to the CARICOM Council for Trade and Economic Development for a decision. Because the Council is a political body, this may create opportunities for politically based decision-making that might prevent prosecution of politically sensitive cases.[38]

---

34. Vindelyn Smith-Hillman, *First a Glimmer, Now a ...? The Prospect of a Caribbean Competition Policy*, 40 J. WORLD TRADE 405, 412 (2006).

35. Articles 173–74.

36. Taimoon Stewart, *Is Flexibility Needed When Designing Competition Law for Small Open Economies? A View from the Caribbean*, J. WORLD TRADE 725 (2004).

37. Vindelyn Smith-Hillman, *First a Glimmer, Now a ...? The Prospect of a Caribbean Competition Policy*, 40 J. WORLD TRADE 405, 407 (2006).

38. Frédéric Jenny & Pierre Horna, *Modernization of the European Legal System of Competition Law Enforcement: Lessons from Other Regional Groupings*, in COMPETITION

Under the revised Treaty, the Commission will provide for transparency and nondiscrimination for CARICOM member states in competition matters. The revised treaty will require increased cooperation among national competition regulators and with the regional Commission. Under Article 169, the objectives of CARICOM competition policy are to promote economic welfare and consumer efficiency. Article 171 establishes the Competition Commission and allows the Commission to penalize anticompetitive conduct. The competition rules allow for certain exclusions of behavior under Article 183. Because so many of the CARICOM countries are least developed nations, special and differential ("S&D") treatment plays an important role in a larger competition policy.

The revised treaty also allows for dispute settlement for competition issues. Because the treaty allows for state-to-state dispute settlement, one issue that remains is to decide who will use the dispute settlement mechanisms. The CARICOM system may empower both individuals and countries with possible redress against anticompetitive conduct. The CARICOM Commission can investigate claims of such conduct. If this alone does not remedy the situation, the Commission may ask for an order from the CARICOM Court to force a conduct-based remedy. This order can be appealed by the company involved.[39] A CARICOM competition framework allows for a region-wide competition agency when there is no domestic ability to provide for such an agency.

D. ASEAN

The Association of Southeast Asian Nations (ASEAN) includes countries of southeast Asia. Though a regional competition policy has been proposed for ASEAN,[40] the creation of a formal competition policy structure for ASEAN is not foreseeable in the near term. Not all ASEAN members have fully functioning competition laws or agencies—at present the only countries with such laws are Indonesia, Singapore, Thailand, and Vietnam. While there have been increasing efforts at economic integration across ASEAN countries, these have generally resulted in nonbinding discussions across agencies. The first ASEAN meeting on competition policy took place in 2003. In recent years, there has been somewhat of a breakthrough in both ASEAN generally and in competition policy specifically. ASEAN is endeavoring to achieve an ASEAN Economic Community by 2015. As such, this integration would reduce significant barriers to entry of goods and services across countries in the region. As a result, competition policy

---

Provisions in Regional Trade Agreements: How to Assure Development Gains 311 (Lucian Cernat, Philippe Brusick, & Ana Maria Alvarez eds., 2005).

39. Sheldon A. McDonald, *The Caribbean Court of Justice: Enhancing the Law of International Organizations*, 27 Fordham Int'l L.J. 930, 938 (2004).

40. Lawan Thanadsillapakul, *The Harmonisation of ASEAN: Competition Laws and Policy from an Economic Integration Perspective*, *in* Competitiveness of ASEAN Countries: Corporate and Regulatory Drivers (P. Gugler & J. Chaisse eds., 2010).

has taken on greater importance. This is a recent change; as recently as 2004, the ASEAN members did not have competition policy as part of their agenda for regional integration. However, countries with and without competition laws have come to understand the importance of competition policy to economic growth.

Interest in competition policy first took form in the ASEAN Consultative Forum for Competition, in which agency leadership would meet to discuss issues. The Forum's conferences have begun the process of discussing substantive approaches and views. There is a mix of formalized methods and informal discussions. In ASEAN, informal discussions through a soft law transgovernmental organization led to the creation of a more formalized ASEAN institution (see *infra*) to follow up on regional integration and competition policy. This was a bottom-up approach.

ASEAN's efforts have led to increased interaction and the building of trust across agencies in the region. In just a few years, this program has had a number of successes. Competition agencies (and their equivalents in those ASEAN members that lack such agencies) organize a number of events, use the Forum as a way to train member country staff, and invite participants from developed world donors and enforcement agencies. The success of the Forum, and its impact more generally on ASEAN, has resulted in an additional important development. Competition policy has been linked to the larger economic integration of ASEAN. In 2007, ASEAN leaders agreed on the establishment of a network of competition agencies to discuss and coordinate common competition policies and develop a regional policy framework.[41] To undertake this work, ASEAN set up an ASEAN Experts Group on Competition (AEGC), with the support of the ASEAN Secretariat. The purpose of the Experts Group is to study and make recommendations on competition policy and law enforcement on a regional basis. It has focused on capacity building in ASEAN agencies in the areas of competition policy, advocacy, creating new competition agencies, and setting up the priorities of such agencies.

E. Africa

Africa has seen increased regional cooperation in competition law and policy. Capacity constraints are particularly acute in Africa, given the paucity of financial resources, which in turn leads to high turnover across agencies. This makes the development of strong institutional ties to address transnational problems difficult. There are three regional antitrust institutions—one for each of the major trading areas—COMESA, SADC, and EAC, each of which faces similar capacity constraints. Consequently, regional antitrust remains at a rather early stage across each of these institutions.

---

41. ASEAN Economic Community Blueprint, 2007.

V. CONCLUSION

The problems of international antitrust will not go away. Indeed, a number of the international problems would exist regardless of the institutional choices made as to how to address them. Nevertheless, over time, particularly since the establishment of the ICN, international antitrust institutions are playing a more important role in reducing cross-border anticompetitive practices and distortions across legal systems that increase transaction costs. The failure of the WTO to address international antitrust issues was a direct cause for experimentation across both international and regional soft law institutions. The early prognosis of soft law global institutions since 2001 has been moderately positive. With a modest agenda, these institutions have accomplished a great deal in reducing transaction costs, through creating increased harmonization across multiple jurisdictions. Moreover, they have served to foster increased trust and cooperation across agencies. Over time, these institutions also have helped to shape and implement norms based on better practices. Norm implementation has helped to improve the effectiveness of antitrust institutions in both the developed and developing world to improve consumer welfare.

Effective international antitrust soft law institutions work in large part because of the commitment of the EU, its Member States, and the United States to support these institutions, and a general acceptance by agencies around the world of the various work outputs of the OECD and the ICN. The United States and the EU have the most to gain from a system that works, particularly with each other but also with the rest of the world. On the one hand, the two powers compete for dominance in the intellectual debate on antitrust in terms of system design and analytical presumptions. On the other hand, they want to increase the capacity of developing world antitrust agencies to deter practices that both the United States and the EU find abhorrent, particularly on procedure but also on basic substance. In recent years, the United States and the EU have moved closer in substance on horizontal mergers and cartels, to where there are now more similarities than differences. In dominance, there is still a wide divide in a number of areas that can be internationalized, such as in assessing dominance. The EU is much more suspicious, based on institutional design (administrative and very limited private rights of action), political and economic history, and case law. Because of the lower cost of reaching agreement in soft law institutions and their ability to constantly tweak the outputs and norms, soft law institutions have provided an opportunity to make progress on what the ICN had addressed as "core" issues of international antitrust as well as other issues of high importance, which the WTO never attempted to address in a significant way.

One lesson from the recent history of international antitrust institutions is that where countries can coordinate solutions to their spillover problems through the ICN or OECD and take effective measures, there is no need for binding rules. Benchmarking and bottom-up harmonization can cure spillover effects over time. This holds true particularly in cases where the goal is coordination itself, rather than substantive convergence on approaches to enforcement. Even substantive differences can be overcome eventually if based on solid economic theory through a stock-taking and analysis process and through the creation of better practices to minimize the distortions across domestic antitrust regimes.

All of the problems of international antitrust cannot be solved immediately through soft law. Even if they could be, it might be unwise to push for convergence upon a single standard—some experimentation is good. There should be some level of federalism to allow for these experiments, the better to see new practices based on economic thinking to emerge and spread to other jurisdictions—soft law does this better than hard law. The ICN does particularly well, though the OECD is carving out a new niche with its technical assistance programs and with more inclusion of developing world viewpoints in its programming. This makes UNCTAD less necessary, and therefore it is in search of a new mission—it is not at the forefront of efforts and lacks the institutional backing of both the EU and the United States.

As the OECD, ICN, and UNCTAD play more prominent roles, the participatory and accountability elements of these institutions must be addressed. Even in soft law, there is a reduction in domestic sovereignty. By being effective, soft law institutions cut into decision-making at the national level, as soft law institutions push countries to adopt better practices.[42] This is a form of soft coercion, pushing domestic practices in a new direction. Because of decisions made in international organizations "the decisions of domestic administrators are increasingly constrained by substantive and procedural norms established at the global level."[43] Legislatures remain uninvolved in this process. Strong results and positive outcomes facilitated by the institutional choice of soft law antitrust organizations may outweigh concerns about a democracy deficit.[44]

Yet these concerns of democratic accountability exist in every institution. Some institutions are better than others at addressing these concerns. The concern of democratic accountability in the case of transgovernmental actors may be lessened along two fronts—efficiency and accountability. To overcome the democracy deficit, soft law institutions must create transparency and encourage broad participation of stakeholders.[45] Greater accountability requires occasional

---

42. Joshua Cohen & Charles F. Sabel, *Global Democracy?*, 37 N.Y.U. J. Int'l L. & Pol. 736 (2005).

43. Benedict Kingsbury, Nico Krisch, & Richard B. Stewart, *The Emergence of Global Administrative Law*, 68 Law & Contemp. Probs. 15, 25 (2005).

44. Increased harmonization may be likely over time when the social benefits outweigh the costs. Julie Roin, *Taxation Without Coordination*, 31 J. Legal Stud. 61 (2002).

45. Jonathan Zeitlin, *Social Europe and Experimentalist Governance: Towards a New Constitutional Compromise?*, *in* EU Law and the Welfare State: In Search of Solidarity (Gráinne de Búrca ed., 2006).

peer review, the better to benchmark the effectiveness of the antitrust authority against its peers.[46] Increased information through transparency allows domestic actors to hold their antitrust authorities accountable. Some soft law institutions have increased transparency directly by making their work products available online (particularly the ICN) and have influenced member agencies to do the same.

The limits of the effectiveness of soft law generally suggest that the current wave of successes might become more modest in the future. However, as antitrust constantly evolves based on refinements in economic thinking, perhaps new challenges will sustain the momentum for soft law international institutions.

46. Phedon Nicolaides, Arjan Geveke, & Anne-Mieke den Teuling, *Improving Policy Implementation in an Enlarged European Union: The Case of National Regulatory Authorities*, European Institute of Public Administration 46 (2003). *See also* Damien Geradin & Nicolas Petit, *The Development of Agencies at EU and National Levels: Conceptual Analysis and Proposals for Reform*, Jean Monnet Working Paper 01/04 (2004).

PART TWO

POLICY PROPOSALS

11. THE PROBLEM WITH COOPERATION

PAUL B. STEPHAN*

In a book devoted to international regulatory cooperation, my role is that of the skunk at the picnic. Moreover, I am not here to take up the easy cases, where international cooperation functions rather clearly as a means of erecting barriers to entry in industries where incumbents have the capacity to procure government support.[1] Instead, I will focus on the one area of economic regulation that seems to complement, rather than thwart, markets. My brief is to make the case against international cooperation regarding competition policy. The case rests on three propositions: A large portion of international economic transactions involve innovative, knowledge-based industries; no international consensus exists about the optimal structure of such industries; and in the absence of consensus about optimal industry structure, cooperation that purports to promote competition policy may instead protect incumbents and stifle innovation.

The task is daunting. Even among skeptics of economic regulation, competition policy enjoys a special exemption.[2] Rather than distorting market outcomes in pursuit of particular policy goals, competition policy seeks to make markets work better. It identifies and suppresses private efforts to interfere with the free interaction of supply and demand, particularly by punishing producers that deter

---

* John C. Jeffries, Jr. Distinguished Professor of Law and Elizabeth D. and Richard A. Merrill Research Professor, University of Virginia. The views expressed herein are an extension of arguments made in Paul B. Stephan, *Global Governance, Antitrust, and the Limits of International Cooperation*, 38 Cornell Int'l L.J. 173 (2005), *reprinted in* Economics of European Union Law 419 (Edgar Elgar: Cheltenham, Paul B. Stephan ed. 2007), an earlier and abridged version of which appeared as *Against International Cooperation*, in Competition Laws in Conflict: Antitrust Jurisdiction in the Global Economy 66 (The AEI Press: Washington, D.C., Richard A. Epstein & Michael S. Greve eds. 2004). A reader interested in fuller citation to the relevant supporting research or a more extensive development of my position may consult those sources. I am grateful to Bert Lazerow for his comments and criticism.

1. *E.g.*, Enrico Colombatto & Jonathan R. Macey, *A Public Choice Model of International Economic Cooperation and the Decline of the Nation State*, 18 Card. L. Rev. 925 (1996); John O. McGinnis & Mark L. Movsesian, *The World Trade Constitution*, 114 Harv. L. Rev. 511 (2000); Paul B. Stephan, *Accountability and International Lawmaking: Rules, Rents and Legitimacy*, 17 Nw. J. Int'l L. & Bus. 681 (1996-97).

2. Fred S. McChesney, *Talking 'Bout My Antitrust Generation: Competition for and in the Field of Competition Law*, 52 Emory L.J. 1401 (2003) (noting tendency and expressing skepticism).

willing sellers from dealing with willing buyers. Unique among regulatory schemes, competition policy uses a free market as its touchstone for normative outcomes.

And if domestic competition policy is good, then international implementation of competition policy should be even better. Democratically accountable governments face incentives to prefer domestic producers over foreign consumers, as well as domestic consumers over foreign producers. The natural course of democratic politics thus should lead states to support industrial structures that, from the perspective of global consumer welfare, are suboptimal. The widespread support of export cartels by advanced industrial states provides an obvious example.[3] Competition policy produced by negotiation and compromise should, in theory, punish producers that seek to thwart willing sellers from dealing with willing buyers even when producers act with their home country's blessing. Cooperation enables states to trade concessions that sacrifice domestic interest groups in pursuit of global welfare.[4]

On first blush, then, the case for cooperation seems compelling. This type of regulation complements rather than substitutes for market mechanisms. The gains from greater market efficiency and enhanced consumer welfare overwhelm local losses suffered by producers. The puzzle, if there is one, is why we don't see extensive and robust international competition policy in the real world, given the apparently attainable gains.

Three reasons occur to me why, in the contemporary world, international implementation of competition policy is limited and weak: The present international system lacks the institutional capacity to implement real cooperation; cooperation requires difficult political choices, not merely technical competence; and there is no consensus about the object of cooperation across a broad range of economic sectors.

First, robust international cooperation requires strong international institutions, which take decades to develop. One implication of this explanation is that, because much good can be achieved through cooperation, we should expect to see a progressive development of cooperation as the institutions that undergird international economic relations mature.[5] The debatable assumption in this argument is that international relations tend toward progressive development. But by assuming that real benefits will flow once the necessary institutional

3. *Symposium in Honor of Professor James A. Rahl: An International Antitrust Challenge*, 10 Nw. J. Int'l L. & Bus. 98 (1989).

4. *See, e.g.*, Andrew T. Guzman, *The Case for International Antitrust*, 22 Berk. J. Int'l L. 355 (2004).

5. For an expression of this faith in progressive development in international institutions, see Andrew T. Guzman, *Global Governance and the WTO*, 45 Harv. J. Int'l L. 303 (2004).

development has taken place, this position presumes that the barriers are essentially technical rather that political.

There are good reasons to believe, however, that more is at work than the slow pace of progressive development of international institutions. Cooperation is not just technically difficult, but fraught with risks and hard political choices. Changes in economic regulation produce losers as well as winners, and potential losers often have political clout. States do not easily give up national champions or open up protected markets to robust competition by foreigners. One cannot consider the benefits of cooperation without also assessing the potential costs, which can be political as well as technical.

Moreover, even if the political as well as technical hurdles could be overcome, it is not clear exactly what international cooperation over competition policy would do. This point rests on two different but interrelated economic theories. First, the theory of industrial organization, which undergirds competition policy, seeks to identify when regulatory intervention can increase efficiency by optimizing the market structure of a particular industry. This theory, however, admits to limits. As a field of economic research, it is rich and suggestive, but it is not hard science. Important debates exist about optimal industrial structure, especially regarding industries that draw heavily on knowledge and innovation as inputs. In the absence of consensus, cooperation may be chimerical.

Second, public choice theory, a positive economic theory of public decision-making, provides an explanation for the failure of states to implement optimal competition policy at the international level. This theory, like the theory of industrial organization, also is rich and significant, and addresses directly the question of why democratically accountable governments systematically pursue goals other than welfare maximization. It provides the robust prediction that, at the national level, states will systematically sacrifice efficiency to favor producers over consumers. Extended to international negotiations, this theory also indicates that governments will cooperate to favor some producers at the expense of general welfare.

These reasons complement each other because uncertainty about optimal industrial structure can mask rent-seeking and political choices that facilitate the interests of discrete groups at the expense of general welfare. Genuine disagreements about the requirements of good competition policy will allow governments to resolve their doubts in a way that advantages certain groups and reduces efficiency. International cooperation can entrench these tendencies. And this combination of risk and fear about outcomes may explain why do not observe greater investments in international cooperation.

Put broadly, the argument in favor of greater international cooperation over competition policy rests on normative claims rather than positive analysis. It does not sufficiently address predictions drawn from positive theory about the thwarting of normative goals. Cooperation, rather than bolstering markets, may end up stifling competition and deterring innovation.

I. OPTIMAL INDUSTRY STRUCTURE

It is possible to state the conditions that define an optimal industry structure, but it not so easy to specify how to meet those conditions in a given market under stated technological conditions. For a structure to maximize consumer welfare, it should minimize costs of production, permit the maximum number of market entrants consistent with a profitability constraint, and deter barriers to innovation. In mature industries with stable technology, determining what such a structure would look like may be easy. But in industries characterized by potential economies of scale (typically due to heavy dependence on knowledge-based inputs such as research and development), it becomes much harder for experts to agree on the most efficient industry structure.

Yet, international transactions, the domain over which international competition policy must operate, is dominated exactly by those industries for which optimal structure is hard to specify. Stated in pure dollar volume, the lion's share of international sales takes place within the rich world and does not involve basic commodities or low-technology manufactured goods (textiles, for example). Moreover, again by dollar volume, much of the trade in basic commodities involves goods produced either by state-owned companies or industries subject to extensive government control, such as petroleum products. The scope of international transactions that take place in an industry where it would be possible both to reach consensus about the dimensions of an optimal structure and where insurmountable political obstacles to reform do not exist, then, is very small.[6]

Consider first the scale of trade among rich countries as well as of trade involving state-controlled industries. According to the WTO, world merchandise trade for 2006 came to $11.8 trillion, on which $3.7 trillion took place within Europe, $905 billion within North America, $710 billion between Europe and North America, $248 billion between Japan and North America, and $168 billion between Japan and Europe (49% of the total). Moreover, 30% of the overall value of merchandise trade in that year involved fuels, the producers of which, for the most part, are insulated by government regulation from competition policy, whether imposed domestically or externally.[7]

---

6. The insight that much international trade involves goods with increasing returns to scale, rather than commodities to which classical analysis applies, can be found in Paul R. Krugman, *Increasing Returns, Monopolistic Competition, and International Trade*, 9 J. Int'l Econ. 469 (1979). For elaboration, see Paul R. Krugman, *Is Free Trade Passé?* 1 J. Econ. Persp. 137 (1987).

7. World Trade Organization, International Trade Statistics 2007 (World Trade Organization: Geneva, 2007). I recognize that these figures reflect the pre-financial crisis world. I am skeptical about the prospects of the crisis leading to a fundamental change in international economic relations or the structure of the world economy. Still, the reader may wish to regard this data with caution.

The EU's trade in services for 2005 amounted to $2.2 trillion, of which over 80% involved rich countries; the comparable figures for the U.S. are $635 billion and 64%; for Japan $241 billion and 67%; for Canada $118 billion and 86%; and for Hong Kong $ 98 billion and 58%. These five traders together account for 87% of global trade in services. The majority of crossborder commercial transactions, in other words, involve only rich countries, not states that rely heavily on primary products for international trade.[8]

I do not mean to ignore the absolute size of global transactions in goods produced by mature industries with stable technology. Even a small fraction of $17 trillion, the best available estimate of the size of global crossborder transactions, could be a big number. If any substantial portion of these industries suffer from a suboptimal structure due to private agreements rather than government policy, the resolute enforcement of competition policy could generate significant welfare gains. The point is relative rather than absolute: The low-hanging fruit for international competition policy are sparse, even if their overall value may be large.

This would not be a problem if states concentrated their competition policy enforcement on cases where a strong consensus exists about optimal market structure. But those states that take competition policy seriously do not respect such a limitation. To the contrary, the United States and the European Community, the two principal proponents of an aggressive competition policy, have sought, either alone or jointly, sanctions against Microsoft, the world's largest software company; Intel, the principal producer of microprocessors; and the proposed mergers of GE and Honeywell in the aerospace industry, and Boeing and McDonnell-Douglas in the aircraft industry. These are exactly the industrial sectors where serious disagreements about optimal industry structure exist.

Of course, competition authorities do a lot more than regulate high-tech industries. Still, each of the industries involved in the above cases depends on research and technological change, which means both that any combination might produce economies of scale and that the existing industrial structure is inherently unstable. These attributes do not make the case for calling off government enforcement of competition policy. But they do mean that reasonable regulators can come to diametrically opposed conclusions about the desirability and nature of government regulation in pursuit of optimal industrial structure.

II. STRUCTURAL ASPECTS OF PUBLIC DECISION-MAKING

The absence of a consensus about optimal industrial structure in those industries that are most important to international commerce does not mean only that

8. *Id.*

we should expect something other than uniformity. National regulators face strong incentives to favor local producers that harm mostly foreign consumers, and to sanction foreign producers even if they operate efficiently. The regulatory concern, then, is not random disagreements among regulators, but rather systematic skewing of competition policy to pursue ends other than optimal market structure.

What makes international cooperation over this sphere of competition policy so problematic is the absence of clear standards within the discipline to distinguish reasonable efforts to impose an optimal industry structure from the more conventional forms of economic protection. Consider, for example, the European Community's case against Microsoft in comparison with that brought by the U.S. Justice Department. The European Community has imposed more stringent measures, including a fine that exceeds the annual contribution of some member states to the community. Does this indicate that the European Community has disregarded scale economies to cut down a foreign giant, even if no European company stands ready immediately to take up the market slack, or that the Justice Department relaxed normal rules to allow a national champion to collect monopoly superprofits abroad? In the absence of a consensus about the optimal industrial structure in such a rapidly evolving commercial environment, these questions remain unanswerable.

If the issue of optimal industrial structure is opaque for a large portion of the international economy, then intergovernmental cooperation presents a problem. Governments represent a wide range of constituencies wielding varying degrees of influence. It seems unrealistic to assume that, when bargaining with each other, governments pursue the "national interest," conceived as an unweighted aggregation of all interests of their subjects. To the contrary, most observers would expect some interests to wield greater weight, mostly due to lower organizational costs relative to their adversaries. Public choice theory rests on this positive claim, for which abundant empirical evidence exists.

Opacity adds to the problem by raising the cost of monitoring. As a general matter, one would expect that the more unsettled are the standards for evaluating the policy objectives of an international bargain, the more likely that the bargainers would reach results favored by groups with lower organizational costs at the expense of outcomes with a broader and more favorable welfare effect. Areas that lack clear standards for assessing regulation thus provide the greatest opportunities for private rent-seeking.

In general, competition policy presumes that incumbents seek to protect their market position from new entrants so as to cartelize an industry. Theories of regulation consider the possibility that incumbents procure exactly this result not through private agreements (the subject of competition policy) but rather by persuading regulators to embrace their desired outcome. The industry's incumbents might capture the regulators outright, or simply make it too costly for the regulators to deviate too far from the incumbents' desired outcomes.

One check on such regulatory tendencies is public pressure informed by effective advocacy. In industries where the barrier to entry is government regulation rather than technological and knowledge gaps, critics easily can make the case that government actions sacrifice the interests of consumers in favor of incumbent producers and thus run counter to good competition policy. But in new and innovative industries, monitors will find it hard to challenge rules that favor incumbents. Mastery of the relevant technology may have general safety and environmental consequences, and incumbents with greater experience in the industry will find it easier to claim that mastery. Government regulation can reinforce an incumbent's inherent advantage and strengthen existing barriers to entry. Skeptics may suspect that the regulation protects incumbents more than it pursues general welfare, but making the case will be exceedingly difficult.

III. THE HISTORICAL RECORD

The evidence that governments will employ international cooperation to promote cartelization on behalf of incumbents in a new-technology industry is substantial. A classic instance involves the then-cutting edge civil aviation industry at the end of World War II. Innovation during the war, including the development of jet engines and radar, plus the experience acquired from conducting massive airborne operations, put the industry on the cusp of enormous expansion. Widespread economic devastation and political aftershocks from the war, however, meant that the industry faced significant risks as well as opportunities. The solution was to cartelize the international market through government management of air routes. There was, of course, no formal allocation of market shares among states, but governments (in particular the United States) used their authority to license carriers (and in most countries to own and subsidize a national champion) effectively to limit the supply of services and to maintain high prices.[9] This system remained in place for over thirty years.

Deregulation by the United States in the late 1970s challenged and, to some extent, weakened the cartel. But even today barriers to entry in the civil aviation field are hard to reconcile with good competition policy and largely reflect government, rather than industry, decisions. The lesson to be learned from this episode, then, is that international competition focused on an emerging, new-technology industry – exactly the industries that matter the most in terms of international trade – can be inimical to optimal industry structure.

While international air transport might represent the most egregious example of state-sponsored cartelization in an emerging, new-technology industry, it

9. U.S. implementation of this system is at the heart of the dispute in *Chicago & Southern Air Lines, Inc. v. Waterman Steamship Corp.*, 333 U.S. 103 (1948).

is not unique. The rise of the semiconductor market in the 1980s produced an international effort to manage the industry so as to limit competition. And the growth in value of information industries in the 1990s led to an international effort to suppress low cost information dissemination culminating in the WIPO Treaty. This instrument obligates states to reduce competition in reproducible work through a mix of heightened penalties and stringent anticircumvention requirements to thwart copying of digitalized works.[10] In each case, one might make the argument that peculiarities of the industry, in particular the lag time between investments and subsequent payoffs and the uncertainty of future demand, justify some limits on competition. The point, again, is that when governments congregate to determine how to cooperate in the regulation of emerging industries, the outcome is often hard to reconcile with optimal industry structure.

IV. COOPERATION AS A FORM OF REINFORCEMENT

One might respond to the above account of government-sponsored international cartelization by asserting that none of these episodes involved cooperation among competition authorities. A proponent of international cooperation might argue that intergovernmental negotiations dominated by particular industrial groups, whether the international air carriers or the entertainment industry, will reach incumbent-friendly outcomes, but that unleashing competition policy enforcers will not produce similar results. Because competition policy enforcers maximize consumer welfare rather than producer welfare, they will not fall prey to the kinds of pressures that distort the outcome of other kinds of economic negotiations.

At first blush, this argument might seem hopelessly naive. Whatever the technical expertise of a government official, the normal pressures generated by democratic politics will continue to exert their influence. Unless an international institution could isolate competition policymakers from the mechanisms of political accountability, the outcome of their deliberations should not differ significantly from those of other kinds of economic experts. At most, specialists in competition policy might have a more highly developed, and perhaps somewhat tragic, sense of the likely economic consequences of the choices that their political masters force on them.

A proponent of international cooperation among competition officials might make two complementary arguments in response. First, in political terms international collaboration among these officials might provide mutual reinforcement

---

10. *See* Pamela Samuelson, *The U.S. Digital Agenda at WIPO*, 37 VA. J. INT'L L. 369 (1997).

and strengthen their position in struggles with domestic adversaries whose interests run counter to better competition policy. Second, in economic terms collaboration might lower the cost of generating information about the benefits of good competition policy and thus offset the advantage that well organized interest groups enjoy in pressing the case for their positions. Neither of these responses, however, is persuasive.

A number of political scientists and their supporters in the legal academy have asserted that international collaboration (as they call it, networking) among government specialists results in information-sharing, alliance building, and other group-reinforcing mechanisms. Networking not only enables these specialists to better perform their tasks but also strengthens their hand in domestic policy debates. International collaboration thus induces a virtuous cycle enabling good policy to triumph over obstructing interests.[11]

The theory of public choice also identifies conditions under which the natural tendency toward suboptimal public decisions can be ameliorated. Groups with low organizational costs enjoy an advantage over their political adversaries in terms of generating and disseminating information about their favored outcomes. *Ceteris paribus*, lowering the cost of acquiring and distributing information about the deficiencies of those outcomes will make it more difficult to embrace them. International collaboration is one mechanism for lowering those costs.

These theories undoubtedly identify potential benefits from greater collaboration. But they also have shortcomings. The political theory assumes, but does not demonstrate, that competition regulators as a group share a set of normatively desirable preferences. Based on other examples of international regulatory competition, however, this assumption seems overly strong. Competition regulators as a group may share a preference in favor of domestic protection, especially with regard to incumbents, and be overly skeptical of potential gains from economies of scale or scope. Unless we can verify empirically that the group's preferences favor outcomes that will generate greater benefits than costs, we cannot assume that empowering the group will further global welfare.

For essentially the same reasons, we cannot assume that enhanced cooperation among competition regulators will lower the cost of information about good policy. If the regulators as a group favor suboptimal outcomes such as incumbent protection or undervalue economies of scale or scope, we cannot expect that the collaboration will lead to better and cheaper information about good policy.

My emphasis on the need to validate the core assumptions of these arguments is not whimsical. For roughly the last decade and a half, competition

11. *See, e.g.*, MARGARET E. KECK & KATHRYN SIKKINK, ACTIVISTS BEYOND BORDERS: ADVOCACY NETWORKS IN INTERNATIONAL POLITICS (1998); ANNE-MARIE SLAUGHTER, A NEW WORLD ORDER (2004); Paul Schiff Berman, *Global Legal Pluralism*, 80 S. CAL. L. REV. 1155 (2007). For a recent critical review of these claims, see Pierre-Hughes Verdier, *Transnational Regulatory Networks and Their Limits*, 34 YALE J. INT'L L. 113 (2009).

regulators have conducted a natural experiment in regulatory collaboration. Perhaps not enough time has lapsed to test the validity of the theories, and perhaps the degree of collaboration that exists is insufficient to generate the benefits that the theories predict. But, for whatever reason, the results of this experiment do not support the claim that competition policy specialists have greater sway domestically as a result of their increased international networking.

For more than a decade now, the International Competition Network (ICN) has coordinated outreach efforts by the U.S. Justice Department to encourage the development of competition policy in the developing world. Networking among more developed states, conducted by the Competition Committee of the Organization for Economic Cooperation and Development, has gone on for even longer. These structures, along with the ongoing contacts memorialized in the U.S.-E.C. executive agreement on antitrust enforcement, may have made it easier to prosecute several core price-fixing cartels. But one must look long and hard for signs of more robust competition policy enforcement.

In the United States, it is impossible to detect any appreciable increase in the influence of the Department of Justice's Antitrust Division since the creation of the ICN. The E.C.'s Commission has flexed its muscles over the last decade, but it remains unclear whether its enforcement initiatives represent sound competition policy or instead disguised protection. Moreover, the European Court of Justice has manifested some skepticism about the Commission's enforcement efforts even as they have increased.[12] And Japan seems no closer to developing a serious competition policy than it was before all this networking started.

Two explanations occur to me for the unimpressive performance to date of international competition policy networks. First, competition policy does not have the public salience of other issue areas, such as corruption, human trafficking, slavery, or subjugation of women. Attacks on large business enterprises *per se* may have some general populist appeal, but modern competition policy has gone beyond such primal attitudes. Especially in the United States, its focus has evolved to the promotion of consumer welfare through increasing industry efficiency.[13] This commitment entails a recognition that some industries can exploit economies of scale and scope, and that a regulatory approach that categorically rules out such exploitation would detract from, rather than promote, consumer welfare. The resulting policy analysis is supple and important, but not reducible to the kinds of pithy phrases that make for a good op-ed column, much less sound bites on network news. These limitations seriously constrain the ability of competition policy experts to rally popular attention in opposition to special interests.

---

12. *Microsoft Corp. v. Commission*, [2007] E.C.R. II-3601; Atlantic Container Line AB v. Commission, [2003] E.C.R. II-3275; *Airtours PLC v. Commission*, [2002] E.C.R. II-2585.

13. *See* Frank H. Easterbrook, *The Supreme Court, 1983 Term – Foreword: The Court and the Economic System*, 98 HARV. L. REV. 4 (1984).

Second, as discussed above, competition policy experts have not reached a consensus on the questions most relevant to international commerce. Capital-intensive industries where knowledge constitutes an important input and rapid innovation a necessary condition of survival do not lend themselves to classical monopoly analysis. And once cut adrift from classical analysis, competition policy experts have to hedge their arguments and defer more to the claims of others, even if those other claims may have dubious competition effects.

This point also serves as a response to those who believe that, even if comprehensive international cooperation on competition policy is unattainable, it remains possible to cooperate on core areas such as price fixing and cartels for commodities and simple manufactured goods. In an ideal world it might be possible to limit cooperation to easy cases (as perhaps the U.S. Department of Justice and the E.C. Commission do under their cooperation agreement), where neither political interests nor conceptual disagreements interfere with enforcement. But specifying a credible *ex ante* definition of easy cases seems impossible. And without a clear boundary on the range of issues open to cooperation, the possibility of international collusion to protect incumbents in high-technology industries cannot be excluded.

V. CONCLUSION

On balance, the case for international cooperation over competition policy turns on dubious premises and unrealistic hopes. It might just be possible that someone can design an institution that both insulates competition policy specialists from the conventional pressure to provide rents to special interests and confines the range of cooperation to subjects on which competition policy has reached a solid and general consensus. But specifying either of these features seems challenging, and imposing both, highly unlikely.

What seems much more likely is a continuation of the status quo. Competition regulators meet regularly and cooperate some. These endeavors enjoy only the slightest institutional structure and a very modest budget. The interaction accomplishes little but also does little harm. Officials from the richest countries get to spend a little more time in the Sixteenth Arrondissement in Paris, perhaps bad for their waistlines but probably good for their overall sense of joy.[14] They do not do much to capture the gains that a truly global competition policy might realize. But they also do not collaborate much to stall economic progress and gouge consumers for the benefit of industry incumbents. For this we should be grateful. One can hope, then, that the future of international cooperation will look much like the present.

14. The OECD's headquarters rests in the Sixteenth.

12. COORDINATION OF INTERNATIONAL COMPETITION POLICIES

An Anatomy Based on Chinese Reality

YONG HUANG*

INTRODUCTION

With the gradual perfection of a trade policy integration mechanism as represented by the WTO, the tangible frontier barrier is fading, and the focus is now on the intangible domestic barrier. Coordination of competition policies, a topic that has been discussed for almost a century, is emerging on the forum of economic policy agendas. Developed countries, developing countries, international organizations, regional organizations, and international networks have all been involved in the global regulation structure of competition policies. This article strives to analyze the shaping of competition policy and, using China as an example, discusses the possibility of the international coordination of competition policy based on an analysis of the international coordination framework.

I. ANALYSIS OF THE COMPETITION POLICY INTERNATIONAL COORDINATION FRAMEWORK

A. Basic Aspects of Competition Policy International Coordination

Competition policy coordination arises when competition laws and underlying policies conflict with individual countries' competition regulation and policy objectives. Traditionally, competition policy coordination falls into three categories: global, regional, and bilateral. First, bilateral cooperation of competition policy has become increasingly common and includes:[1] (i) agreements regarding mutual providing of technical support pursuant to competition laws; (ii) agreements regarding the resolution of cooperation problems as a result of the implementation of competition laws; (iii) agreements regarding bilateral jurisdiction assistance, which provides antitrust assistance stipulations; and (iv) antitrust assistance stipulations contained in bilateral free trade compacts. Second, in the

---

* Yong Huang is a law professor in the Law School of the Beijing-based University of International Business & Economics (UIBE), and he is also the Director of the UIBE Competition Law Center.

1. Wang Zhongmei: *International Coordination of Competition Rules*, Renmin Press, 139–53 (2005).

regional cooperation field, of the more than two hundred member states of FTA, many have competition policy stipulations. Except for the European Union (EU), the Australia New Zealand Closer Economic Relations Trade Agreement (ANZCERTA) provides that antidumping measures no longer apply to the trade between two countries. Stipulations regarding marketplace abuse apply to the entire Australian-New Zealand market, and the two countries mutually recognize the extraterritorial application of respective domestic competition regulation based on the "doctrine of effect."[2] Chapter 15 of the North American Free Trade Agreement (NAFTA), "Competition Policy, Monopolies and State Enterprises" makes general stipulations about competition rules and stresses the importance of cooperation among member states.[3] As a tariff union, the Southern Common Market or Mercado Común del Sur (MERCOSUR), comprised of member states Argentina, Brazil, Paraguay, and Uruguay, sets forth in detail 17 kinds of forbidden competition restrictive acts in "Protocol Guaranteeing the Competition in South American Common Market."[4] The Asian-Pacific Cooperation (APEC), as an economic forum, stipulated three competition policy goals in its "Osaka Action Agenda," and relying on its "Principles of Reform on Promoting Competition and Loosening Regulation," endorsed various principles such as nondiscrimination, transparency, and accountability at the ministerial meeting in 1999.[5] Third, global coordination of competition policy is carried out mainly by four organizations.[6] The UN's "Multilateral Agreement of Fair Principle and Rules regarding the Regulation over Restrictive Business Acts" has no legal effect since it was not approved by underdeveloped countries.[7] The OECD's "Common Suggestions on Restrictive Business Acts Impacting International Trade among Member States" has no substantial binding effect,

---

2. *See* The Australia-New Zealand Closer Economic Relations Trade Agreement, and Exchange of Letters, Australian Treaty Series 1983 No. 2, Jan. 1, 1983, *available at* http://www.austlii.edu.au/au/other/dfat/treaties/1983/2.html (last visited Apr. 18, 2010).

3. North American Free Trade Agreement, U.S.-Can.-Mex., Dec. 17, 1992, 32 I.L.M 289 (1993), *available at* http://www.nafta-sec-alena.org/en/view.aspx?x=343&mtpiID=146 (last visited Apr. 18, 2010).

4. *Protocol of the Defence of Competition in MERCOSUR*, Decision 17/96, December 17, 1996.

5. *See* Report from Eleventh APEC Ministerial Meeting, Aukland, New Zealand, Sept. 9–10, 1999, *APEC Principles to Enhance Competition and Regulatory Reform: Open and Competitive Markets are the Key Drivers of Economic Efficiency and Consumer Welfare, available at* http://www.oecd.org/dataoecd/48/52/2371601.doc (last visited Apr. 18, 2010).

6. These organizations are the United Nations (UN), the Organisation for Economic Co-operation and Development (OECD), the World Trade Organization (WTO), and the International Competition Network (ICN).

7. *See* the United Nations Set of Principles and Rules on Competition, http://www.unctad.org/en/docs/tdrbpconf10r2.en.pdf (last visited Apr. 18, 2010).

and only applies to member states.[8] At the time of the drafting of an "International Antitrust Law Code,"[9] during which time it was established that the WTO was not able to form legal documents, the United States clearly opposed the competition policy negotiation started by the Singapore Meeting under the WTO. Instead, the United States suggested establishing the International Competition Network (ICN), which is an informal network composed of the recognized antitrust authorities from developed and developing countries.[10]

B. Substantial Effect Analysis of Competition Policy International Coordination

In the framework of competition policy international coordination, the carrying out of bilateral coordination appears to be most dynamic. In the execution of the different types of bilateral coordination agreements mentioned above, there are still issues to be resolved. Technical support agreements are easier to implement than bilateral support agreements since they do not concern substantial coordination. Likewise, each of the other three kinds of coordination has its own limitation. Meanwhile, in the implementation of competition policy's regional coordination, various substantial norms and procedural norms have been established, which are already embedded into the regional trade agreements according to different models, and which are gradually displaying the scale effect.

Compared with the relatively widespread bilateral communication and coordination and regional coordination practices, there is great divergence in the global coordination of competition policy. The EU has been actively promoting negotiation on competition policies under the World Trade Organization (WTO) framework, but that effort has not produced much outcome. On the other hand, the United States is focusing on the establishment and operation of the International Competition Network (ICN), a network similar to G-7. This kind of situation may continue to exist for a long time.

If we interpret the basic competition policy international coordination framework from another perspective, we find that there are various similarities between very extreme coordination models, such as unilateral antitrust enforcement and international competition law code. If we categorize them as agreement-type

---

8. *See Revised Recommendation of the Council Concerning Co-Operation between Member Countries on Anticompetitive Practices Affecting International Trade*, dated Sept. 21, 1995, *available at* http://www.oecd.org/dataoecd/60/42/21570317.pdf (last visited Apr. 18, 2010).

9. *See* Draft International Antitrust Code as a GATT-MTO Plurilateral Trade Agreement, 64 Antitrust & Trade Reg. Rep. (BNA) 1628 (Special Supp. Aug. 19, 1993).

10. *See* International Competition Network, Memorandum on the Establishment and Operation of the International Competition Network.

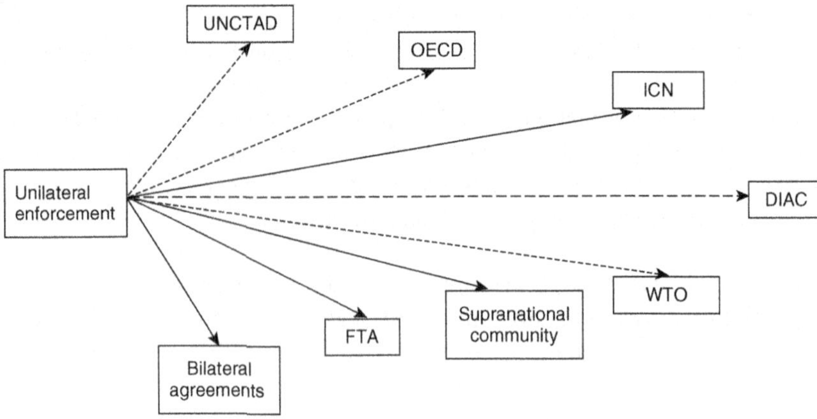

coordination models and nonagreement-type coordination models,[11] we can draw preliminary conclusions. On one hand, agreement-type coordination models can be implemented more easily if they are subject to unilateral enforcement and are separate from the international competition law code. A case in point is the emergence of bilateral agreements and free trade agreements; yet these instruments could not be turned into an international competition code, because consensus could not be reached at this level. On the other hand, nonagreement-type coordination can be implemented more easily if it is subject to the international competition law code and does not fall under unilateral enforcement, such as by the ICN. Also, the nonagreement-type coordination model that is bound by unilateral enforcement will not likely have any substantial effect.

We will analyze the implementation premises and institutional binding of a country's competition policy, using China as an example. We will then examine competition policy international coordination in a comparative perspective, and then discuss the future of competition policy international coordination.

II. IMPLEMENTATION PREMISES OF CHINA'S COMPETITION POLICY: STATE OBJECTIVE AND LEGAL FRAMEWORK

According to China's present official definition:

> Competition policy refers to the economic policy implemented by market economy countries to include and promote market competition. By enacting and implementing competition policy, the state can protect and promote

11. Agreement-type coordination models refer to a coordination pattern characterized by a formal agreement. Nonagreement-type coordination models refer to a coordination pattern characterized by initiative oriented mechanisms.

> market competition, make sure that competition mechanism can play the vital role in the market, in order to elevate production efficiency and optimize the resources allocation. Competition policy is the basis on which the anti-monopoly law is enacted, and the anti-monopoly law is the expression of competition policy.[12]

In order to discuss the implementation of competition policy, we should first look at the state objective and regime structure behind China's competition policy framework.

A. State Objective of China's Competition Policy

Competition policy is legislated in the form of anti-monopoly law. Examining the legislative history of anti-monopoly law, we find that there are various internal influences, and that the leading influences in enacting China's competition policy are the state objectives. Competition policy is legislated in the form of anti-monopoly law. Examining the legislative history of anti-monopoly law, we find that there are various internal influences, and that the leading influences in enacting China's competition policy are the state objectives. There are four main influences/state objectives. The first objective is to establish and perfect the market economy. Since it opened its markets, China's economic structure has undergone a transformation from planned economy to market economy. The revision of the Constitution of the People's Republic of China in 1993 requires that "the state practice socialist market economy." The internal logic of "market economy" requires China to abolish the old legal framework, which is adaptable to planned economy, and to establish a new framework that encourages competition. Establishing and maintaining a competition mechanism is an indispensable factor in sustaining the new framework.

The second objective is to regulate excessive government power. Administrative monopoly is a widespread and difficult problem in China's economic system, and the ultimate resolution to this problem depends on economic and political reform. However, the time needed to accomplish reform exceeds the amount of time the competition mechanism can endure. The realistic and applicable method is to restrain government power by adopting a number of technical restrictions within the framework of the anti-monopoly law.

A third objective is to protect the country's security. With China's rapid integration into the global economy, many people believe that China may lose its present advantages. These people regard the anti-monopoly law as a useful tool to protect the country's interests and the Chinese enterprises concerned.

Finally, the fourth objective in enacting China's competition policy is to reduce the gap between social incomes. China's economy is growing quickly,

12. NPC Standing Committee Legal Affairs Commission Economic Law Office: *Anti-Monopoly Law of PRC: Article Interpretation, Legislation Reasons and the Related Regulations*, Peking University Press, 2007, page 44.

and the gap between incomes has already become a serious problem. Since fairness is a deeply rooted tradition in traditional Chinese thinking, many people seek their share of the benefits being produced by economic growth. The requirement has already been reflected by the Chinese Communist Party's (CCP's) ideal in constructing a "harmonious society." In order to build a harmonious society, the government needs to reduce the gap between incomes; the Chinese people, in supporting the enactment of the anti-monopoly law, believe that in order to reduce the income gap, monopolies should be eliminated.[13]

B. Legal Framework of China's Competition Policy

China's competition policy is legalized for the first time by the anti-monopoly law, which also designates the manner of enforcement.

Article 4 of the anti-monopoly law provides that "the state shall make and implement competition rules appropriate for the socialist market economy and improve macroeconomic measures for a united, open, competitive, and well-ordered market system." Competition rules are the necessary requirement of marketization, as well as the mechanism for the implementation of competition policy. This article is no doubt a revelation of the legislation of China's competition policy. In light of this article's objective, it is worth mentioning macroeconomic measures. It is well known that anti-monopoly law, as a means of government interference with economy, actually helps market regulation, while the aim of macroeconomic measures is to achieve economic effects within a short period of time by more aggressive means. To integrate this kind of aggressive model into anti-monopoly law likely will have negative results. In the course of legislation, macroeconomic measures was, for a time, an intense topic, which required taking into consideration political factors. But legislators eventually adopted the opinions of scholarly advisors and changed the expression from "intensify and perfect macroeconomic measures" to "perfect macroeconomic measures."[14]

---

13. For a more complete discussion, *see* Huang Yong, *Pursuing The Second Best: The History, Momentum, And Remaining Issues Of China's Anti-Monopoly Law*, 75 Anti-monopoly Law Journal No.1 (2008), pages 118–124.

14. The Standing Committee of the National People's Congress (NPC) points out in explaining the articles and legislation the reasons for the anti-monopoly law:We should take our country's real situation into consideration in promulgating the anti-monopoly law: on the one hand, we should further perfect our extant competition rules, take a resolute attitude in restraining the concluding of monopolistic agreements, abusing dominant market position, and excluding and restricting competition by way of unreasonable concentration, so as to maintain the market competition; at the same time, the system design should be place under the direction of national macroeconomic regulation, considering the coordination of relationship between anti-monopoly law and the implementation of national industrial policy and various economic policy as a whole, scientifically handling the relationship between realizing competition objective and other social public objectives, including and promoting the orderly market competition, so as to build up a united,

However, misinterpretation of Article 4 in putting the anti-monopoly law into practice will greatly influence competition policy.[15]

Article 9 of the anti-monopoly law provides, "the Anti-monopoly Committee under the State Council is responsible for organizing, coordinating and guiding the anti-monopoly work" The first duty it shall perform is "(i) making competition policies."[16] According to this Article, the Anti-monopoly Committee, under the State Council, will be responsible for studying and drafting competition policies. Legislators further note that, as the central authority which organizes, coordinates, and guides the nationwide anti-monopoly work, the Anti-monopoly Committee should start out from a macro perspective, give a comprehensive analysis of China's economic development situation and market structure, draft the competition policy taking into consideration China's actual situation, and make it the basis for anti-monopoly law enforcement.[17] The Article clearly emphasizes the expression "competition policies" and stipulates that the drafting agency of competition policies is the Anti-monopoly Committee under the State Council.

The organizational rules of the Anti-Monopoly Committee further outline the way that China's competition policy would be forged. In the Main Functions and Members of the Anti-monopoly Commission of the State Council, it is provided that the Committee is charged to "study and form relevant competition policies; investigate and evaluate the general competition situation and publish reports; draft and publish anti-monopoly guidelines; coordinate anti-monopoly enforcement, and carry out other responsibilities designated by the State Council."[18] The Director of the Committee is a Vice Premier of the State Council, and the Vice Directors include the ministers from the Ministry of Commerce (MOFCOM), the National Development and Reform Commission (NDRC), and the State Administration of Industry and Commerce (SAIC), plus the Deputy

---

open, competitive, orderly market system in China. *See* NPC Standing Committee Legal Affairs Commission Economic Law Office: *Anti-Monopoly Law of PRC: Article Interpretation, Legislation Reasons and the Related Regulations*, Peking University Press, 2007, page 15.

15. Taking into consideration the political influence during the legislation process and the vagueness of the language of this Article, misinterpretation can occur by reemphasizing macroeconomic measures, in particular industrial policy measures, that exclude competition policy concerns in competitive markets.

16. Art 9, Anti-Monopoly Law, adopted at the 29th Session of the Standing Committee of the 10th National People's Congress and promulgated on August 30, 2007, effective from August 1, 2008.

17. NPC Standing Committee Legal Affairs Commission Economic Law Office, *Anti-Monopoly Law of PRC: Article Interpretation, Legislation Reasons and the Related Regulations* 44 (Peking Univ. Press 2007).

18. Notice of the General Office of the State Council on the Main Functions and Members of the Anti-monopoly Commission of the State Council, http://www.lawinfochina.com/law/displayModeTwo.asp?id=7190&keyword= (Translation available by subscription at http://www.chinalawinfo.com) (last visited Jun. 18, 2010).

Secretariat-General of the State Council. Members of the Committee include officials from the MOFCOM, NDRC, SAIC, Ministry of Industrialization and Information, Ministry of Supervision, Ministry of Finance, Ministry of Transportation, State Administration of State-owned Assets, State Intellectual Property Office, State Council Legislative Affairs Office, China Banking Regulatory Commission, China Securities Regulatory Commission, China Insurance Regulatory Commission, and China Electricity Regulatory Commission. The daily responsibilities of the Committee are carried out by the Ministry of Commerce, with Madame Ma Xiuhong, Vice Minister of Commerce, being the Secretariat-General of the Committee. That means all of the ministries mentioned will play a role in the formation of China's competition policy.

Article 8 provides that "the plenary meeting of the Anti-monopoly Committee under the State Council is attended by all the members," and its initial duty is "to make studies on competition policies concerned, and to make suggestions to the State Council."[19] In addition, "the plenary meeting is held according to the necessity, usually once in a half year. Principals of relative work units and departments can attend the plenary meeting as nonvoting delegates with regard to different situations."[20] Article 6 provides that the "Ministry of Commerce undertakes the specific work of the Anti-monopoly Committee under the State Council," and its initial duty is to "organize the anti-monopoly law enforcement department to draft the overall market situation assessment report, the relative competition policies and the anti-monopoly guide."[21] Articles 11 and 12 provide that "market competition assessment report, anti-monopoly guide and relative competition policies are suggested or drafted by member units concerned in line with their respective work obligations under the organization of the Ministry of Commerce."[22] Articles 11 and 12 further stipulate an approximate division of work for drafting the competition policies. One thing should be noted, however. The "member units concerned" include all the members that attend the anti-monopoly committee's plenary meeting. The makeup of the anti-monopoly committee and the makeup of the plenary meeting of the anti-monopoly committee clearly define the scope of related departments that can take part in enacting competition policy. Meanwhile, the scope of other related policies and the interests, strategy, and system restrictions inherent in those policies, that can influence the competition policies may also be defined. Under this legal framework, the decision-making process of China's Competition Policies can be further outlined.

---

19. Art 8, Anti-Monopoly Law, *supra* note 16.
20. Art 8, *Id.*
21. Art 6, *Id.*
22. Art 11-12, *Id.*

C. Decision-Making Process of China's Competition Policies

The decision-making process of government economic policy is a complicated structure-function system. The basic framework is similar among various countries, but different domestic political systems and the restriction of international political and economic systems make the decision-making process appear greatly different.[23] The current decision-making process of China's competition policies has not been institutionalized, but according to state objectives and the legal framework, we believe that China's competition policy decision-making process should mainly take the following two factors into consideration. First, one should consider the strategy and system restrictions of China's competition policies, including the restriction of relative policies (e.g., trade policies, industry policies, national security strategy, and intellectual property strategy) and the restriction of the domestic system (e.g., the Party and the Central Government, the Central Government, and the local governments). Second, one should consider the interest influences and international factors of Chinese competition policies. The major interest groups that can impose influence include state-owned enterprises, transnational companies, consumers, nongovernmental enterprises, and nongovernmental organizations. Related international factors include the restriction of foreign governments and international mechanism.

Generally speaking, the state objective has played a long and definitive guiding role in shaping China's competition policies. With the restriction of the strategy pattern on China's competition policies and the system structure shaping China's competition policies, and the influence and correlation of interest groups and international factors, the decision-making surrounding specific competition policies can be formed within the extant legal framework. At the same time, the sequential formation of specific competition policies influences the state's strategy and ultimately influences the adjustment and progress of the state's long-term objectives.

III. SYSTEM RESTRICTION IN FORMING CHINA'S COMPETITION POLICIES: STRATEGY PATTERN AND REGIME STRUCTURE

We believe that the state competition policies are under the direct guidance of the competition policies' state objectives. However, there are many state objectives which not only relate to acts on competition policies but also relate to many other strategic areas. Therefore, the strategy pattern in which China's competition policies are positioned must have an influence on the transformation of state objectives regarding competition policies, as well as on the expected outcomes.

---

23. Sheng Bin: *Political & Economical Analysis of China's Foreign Trade Policy*, Shanhai Sanlian Bookstore, 2002, page 138.

Moreover, the current regime structure will further complicate the influences on competition policies generated by the strategy pattern. Due to path dependence, conflicting policies and strategies of the current political system have been embedded into the competition regime, hence internalizing the clashes within the regime. However, because no empirical evidence is available, we could only provide a preliminary analysis of the identifiable systematic constraints that restrict China's competition policy.

A. Strategy Pattern Restraining China's Competition Policies

1. Trade Policy Trade policy encompasses the various measures taken by a government to interfere with foreign trade activities in order to realize its specific trade interest. Generally speaking, the conflict between trade policy and competition policy is reflected in trade relief measures, taking into consideration factors like the protection of competitors and trade protection. Trade relief measures are in great conflict with the value and objectives of anti-monopoly law. The starting point for the Chinese government in adopting its trade policies includes realizing the gross balance, structure adjustment, and macro-regulative trade development plan and the corresponding trade control; adopting non-neutral encouragement and stimulation to realize trade development strategy; implementing industrial policy to promote the development of strategic industries; maintaining the state economic security; and keeping international income and expenses balanced.[24]

Facing complicated economic globalization and competition among countries, trade policy is of vital importance to China, which has just joined the WTO. Now, the influences of trade policy toward competition policy are also gradually showing up in China. China's response to United States accusations regarding its vitamin production factories reflected the influences that non-neutral trade policy may have on competition policy. If this kind of influence is not reconciled, uncontrollable negative effects may result.[25] The case highlighted the possible disputes and controversies raised by the stipulations on foreign trade in Article 15 (about exemption) of China's anti-monopoly law. For the time being, with the spreading of the economic crisis, the influences of policies that are generated by Article 15 of the anti-monopoly law may have to undergo a greater test.[26]

---

24. *See* Sheng Bin, at page 138, *Id.*

25. On November 6, 2008, after three years of judicial procedure, the U.S. court rejected the four Chinese Vitamin C producers' pleading for suspension. The case was scheduled to go to trial the case. *See* http://www.caijing.com.cn/2008-11-20/110030477.html (January 18, 2009).

26. Article 15 provides: "Monopoly agreements between undertakings that can be proven to fall under any of the following cases shall be exempt from the application of article 13 and 14: ...(v) for the purpose of mitigating the severe decrease of sales volume or

2. Industrial Policy Industrial policies are measures taken by the government to interfere with the allocation of resources among industries. Apparently, such interference will result in the allocation of resources being quite different from the resources allocation established by the market mechanism.[27] Especially with respect to government-leading development countries, the importance of industrial policies is not negligible. In China, "industrial policy" is interpreted by the government as "a series of economic policies such as prior development of key industries, propping up the infant industries, restricting excessive industries, correcting market failure and making up market deficiency, instituted to quicken the development."[28] Since the term "industrial policy" was first mentioned in "the Seventh Five-Year Plan of the National Economy and Social Development" issued in 1986, due to the overall transformation nature of the market economy, industrial policy has always taken the leading position in the national economic policy. In 1989, the state promulgated "Outline of China's Industrial Policy" and "Decision on the Key Point of Present Industrial Policy." Since the 1990s, the government has promulgated "Program of the National Industrial Policy in the 1990s," "Program of Chinese Agricultural Development in the 1990s," and other specialized industrial policies concerning automobiles and so on. Although the marketization is constantly deepening today, the influence of industrial policy toward competition policy is still very great. For example, in *InBev/Anheuser Busch Merger*, the conditional approval decision made by the anti-monopoly law enforcement authority was clearly influenced by industrial policy.[29] It also reflects the controversial industrial policy consideration that is written into the Chinese

---

excessive overstock during economic recessions. (vi) for the purpose of protecting the legitimate interests of international trade and foreign economic cooperation . . . ."

27. *See* Jiang Xiaojuan: *Industrial Policy During the Economic Transformation Period—Empirical Analysis of China's Experiences and the Prospect,* Shanghai Sanlian Bookstore, Shanghai People's Press, 1996, page 16.

28. Lan Shiliang, *The Direction of Chinese Industrial Policy, in* Economic Workers' Studying Materials, State Council Development and Research Center, 6th issue of 1998, page 12.

29. The conditions included the following: First, the new company after the merger should neither increase the original AB company's 27 percent shareholding proportion in Qingdao Beer Co. Ltd., nor increase Yingbo Group's 28.56 percent shareholding proportion in Guangzhou Zhujiang Beer Co. Ltd. Second, the new company is not allowed to hold the shares of Beijing Yanjing Beer Co. Ltd. and Huarun Snowflake Beer (China) Co. Ltd. Also, if the controlling shareholders or the shareholders of the controlling shareholders of the Yingbo Beer Group change, the Ministry of Commerce must be informed immediately. If any condition is to be violated, Yingbo Beer Group should notify the Ministry of Commerce beforehand, and nothing should be carried out before obtaining approval from the Ministry of Commerce. http://www.legaldaily.com.cn/0705/2008-11/23/content_986311.htm (Jan. 18, 2009).

competition code which requires the merger review agency to consider factors that would "affect the development of national economy."[30]

3. National Security Strategy National security strategy is an extensive strategic system. State economic security is generally regarded as one of the core objectives of national security strategy.[31] At present, it is mainly the state economic security that correlates with the anti-monopoly law. The anti-monopoly law fundamentally maintains the entire country's market competition order, bringing into full play the action of competition mechanism and promoting the healthy development of the social economy. National security is not only an economic problem, it is also a political problem, which requires that the state economic matters be controlled by the government and by businesses that deal with the national economy. It also forbids interference and control of resources, finance, and industries by foreign governments and enterprises. In the course of enacting China's anti-monopoly law, there have been debates over security problems resulting from the merging of foreign-funded enterprises. Some people suggested maintaining national security objectives by carrying out anti-monopoly investigations of merging foreign-funded enterprises, however, others opposed the suggestion.[32] Legislators reached a consensus at last and provided a reply and clarification over the relationships between the two opinions of Article 31[33] of the anti-monopoly law, namely, that national economic security investigations and anti-monopoly investigations are based on different laws, undertake different functions, and realize different objectives. But in present practice, due to the strong ideological opposition against foreign investment, the problem of national security still influences the anti-monopoly law. While the general public confuses National Security Review with Anti-monopoly review, the popular reaction to the acquisition of Huiyuan by Coca Cola reflects the reality that there is still a reason to use national security as an excuse to influence the normal operation of the anti-monopoly law.[34]

---

30. Art 27, Anti-Monopoly Law, *supra* note 16.

31. *See* Cao Rongxiang: *Economic Security—The Open and Risks of the Developing Countries*, Social Science Literature Publishing House, 2006, pages 44–47.

32. Actually, the objective of national security is entirely different from the objective of the anti-monopoly investigation of merging businesses; national security should not be realized through the anti-monopoly investigation of merging businesses. Huang Yong, *Approval or Forbidden: A study on Anti-monopoly Law Regarding the China Mainland Undertakings Merging, in* the 17th issue of YUEDAN CIVIL & COMMERCIAL LAW LEGAL REVIEW.

33. Article 31 provides, "In the case that national security is concerned besides the examination on concentration in accordance with this law, the examination on national security according to the relevant regulations of the State shall be conducted as well as on the acquisition off domestic undertakings by foreign capital or other circumstances involving the concentration of foreign capital."

34. In this case, the ideal of "national brands failure" is widely accepted. According to statistics, "82.95% netizens oppose the acquisition of Huiyuan by Coca Cola."

4. Intellectual Property Strategy Intellectual property (IP) is gradually becoming a strategic resource for national development and the core element of international competitiveness. The in-depth objectives of both IP and anti-monopoly are the same, and that is to promote social welfare and protect public interest. However, excessive interference with the exercise of IP may restrain people's positivity in innovation, and over-protection of the exercise of IP will lead to the infringement of free and open competition. Therefore, it is very important to maintain a balance between them. Since the introduction of reform and policy, China has been paying more attention to IP. In 1992, the "Understanding Memo on the Protection of IP," concluded during the Sino-U.S. IP negotiations generated a direct influence on the protection of trade secrets by "Countering Unfair Competition Law." The "State Intellectual Property Strategy Program," instituted by the state in 2008, pointed out that it is necessary to "promulgate relative laws and regulations, reasonably define the limit of intellectual property, prevent IP abuses, and maintain a fair and competitive market order and the public's legal rights."[35] At present, the influence of IP policy on competition policy is mainly seen in the anti-monopolistic regulation of IP abuses. Taking the "DVD patent united licensing" case as an example,[36] Chinese DVD undertakings have paid to the "6C" and "3C" patent pool unions more than 3 billion RMB, and they may have to pay as much as several tens of billions RMB.[37] In practice, determining to how to apply article 55 properly and balance competition policy and IP strategy are urgent problems[38] for anti-monopoly law.

Famous national brands like Dabao, Robust, Zhonghua, Wahaha, and Huiyuan were acquired one by one, and the netizens wonder why most national brands cannot escape the fate of being acquired after they have become famous? *See* http://news.xinhuanet.com/forum/2008-09/07/content_9805264.htm (2009-1-18).

35. The Program also points out that "developed countries mainly promote the economic development by innovation, bring into full play the intellectual property to maintain their competitive advantages; the developing countries take great initiative adopting intellectual property policy measures which are adaptable to the countries' situation." *See* http://www.sipo.gov.cn/sipo2008/yw/2008/200806/t20080610_406106.html (2009-1-18).

36. In this case, Philips, Sony, and Pioneer formed a "3C" patent pool. Similarly, Hitachi, Panasonic, JVC, Mitsubishi, Toshiba, and Time Warner formed a "6C" patent pool and abused their dominant position to extract profits from DVD player manufacturers. They also allegedly violated the antitrust law by including invalid patent, as well as refusing to deal and margin-squeezing. At that time, China do not have its own antitrust law, so the case was settled according to Patent Law, although some firms did obtain antitrust remedy abroad.

37. Wang Xianliln, Shou Bu & Wang Liping, *Intellectual Abusing of Transnational Companies in China, in* INTERNATIONAL BUSINESS, the 21st issue of 2005.

38. Article 55 provides, "This law is not applicable to conducts by undertakings to protect their legitimate intellectual property rights in accordance with the IP law and relevant administrative regulations; however, this law is applicable to the conduct of undertakings

B. Shaping the Regime Structure of China's Competition Policy

Under China's administrative system, administrative decision-making is an organizational structure in which multiple administrative departments are combined. This kind of situation is also seen in the policy decision-making of competition policy.

1. The Party and the Central Government The Party and the Central Government need to consider the overall economic policy as a whole; competition policy is only one of the factors to be considered. Their job is to coordinate and integrate the information, suggestions, and applications provided by various departments, and then come up with central decisions.

According to the anti-monopoly law, the Anti-monopoly Committee under the State Council is responsible for promulgating competition policy. It is therefore the highest legal decision-making institution for making competition policy. At the same time, it should be noted that there are also trans-department institutions and meeting mechanisms at the Central Government level, which are potential influences on competition policy. Of these institutions, the most important is the finance and economy leaders group of the Central Committee of Communist Party of China (CCCPC), which was founded in March of 1980. On March 17, 1980, the standing committee of the Political Bureau of the Central Committee of the CPC decided to establish the "finance and economy leaders group" to replace the "finance and economy committee under the State Council," which had been established on March 14, 1979. As a united institution of the Political Bureau of the Central Committee of the CPC and the State Council, the finance and economy leaders group is the highest decision-making department in the area of economic policy. There is no doubt that important competition policy problems, as part of the integrated economic decision-making, will also be brought before the decision-making system of the central finance and economy leaders group in the future. However, under the macroeconomic control policy led by the central finance and economy leaders group, the importance of competition policies in integrated economic decision-making is still a question.

2. The Central Administrative Departments At the central administrative departments level, since each department's function, responsibility, and the pressures it has to face are different—for example, considering job assessment and the incentives of promotion, as well as the economic motives to obtain the largest share from the limited resources—the starting points and points of reference for each department to make decisions are also different. This sometimes leads to conflicts in the objectives and means adopted.[39]

---

to eliminate or restrict market competition by abusing intellectual property rights stipulated in the IP law and administrative regulations."

39. *See* Sheng Bin, *supra* note 23, at page 113.

According to the anti-monopoly law and the working rules of the Anti-monopoly Committee under the State Council, enforcement of anti-monopoly law is jointly undertaken by MOFCOM, NDRC and SAIC. As suggested in the operating rules of China's Anti-Monopoly Committee,[40] under the present system pattern, since there is no independent anti-monopoly law enforcement authority, the influence mechanism of competition policy is both complicated and vague.

First, of the three anti-monopoly law enforcement departments, the NDRC[41] and the MOFCOM[42] are both comprehensive administrative departments whose responsibilities are directly influenced by the orientation of traditional policies like macro-economic measures, industrial policy, and trade policy. Competition policy ranks relatively low in their policy-making priority rating, so it is unknown how much influence competition policy will have. Second, the State Administration for Industry and Commerce, as part of the anti-monopoly law enforcement authority, is also charged with law enforcement and countering unfair competition and food safety in the consumer market. Competition policy does not take the prior status among its policy portfolio.[43] Last, according to the working rules of the Anti-monopoly Committee under the State Council, the member units of the Anti-monopoly Committee also include 11 other departments.[44] It means that each of the above-mentioned departments at the central government level can influence the making of competition policy to some extent.

---

40. Notice of the General Office of the State Council on the Main Functions and Members of the Anti-monopoly Commission of the State Council, *supra* note 21.

41. Whether regarded from a traditional perspective or on the basis of the present obligations of the Development and Reform Commission, industrial policy should always be the major policy objective of this department. *Regulations on the National Development and Reform Commission's Main Obligation, Internal Organs and Manning Quotas. see* http://www.ndrc.gov.cn/gzdt/t20080821_231802.htm (2009-1-18).

42. Whether regarded from a traditional perspective or on the basis of the present obligations of the Ministry of Commerce, trade policy should always be the major policy objective of this department. *Regulations on the National Development and Reform Commission's Main Obligation, Internal Organs and Manning Quotas,* see, http://www.mofcom.gov.cn/aarticle/ae/ai/200808/20080805739577.html (2009-1-18).

43. As a specialized economic management department, the State Administration for Industry and Commerce is more focused on competition policy requirements, but the difference between anti-monopoly law and countering unfair competition law puts this department in a mixed competition policy position. *See* http://www.saic.gov.cn/zzjg/zyzz/ (2010-6-27).

44. The other 11 departments are, namely, the Supervision Department, the Finance Department, the Communication and Transportation Department, State-owned Assets Supervision and Administration Commission, the Ministry of Industry and Information Technology, the State Intellectual Property Office, Affairs Office of the State Council, China Banking Regulatory Commission, China Securities Regulatory Commission, China Insurance Regulatory Commission, and China Electricity Regulatory Commission,

However, competition policy has not been clearly defined as a responsibility of the 11 members of the plenary meeting of the Anti-monopoly Committee. These departments will no doubt try to influence competition policy based on their respective interests within the scope of their duties.

3. Local Governments Under the regulation framework of the anti-monopoly law, local governments have no right to take part in competition policy-making, which is done at the central government level. Instead, local governments are often the regulated objects of competition policy in many fields. This kind of situation is closely related to the current Chinese government structure and economic structure, and will influence the shaping of competition policy.

The Chinese government's structure and economic structure can be represented as the "M-Type."[45] Essentially, it is a multiple layer and multiple area structure organized according to the principle of territory. To understand the reasons for both the Chinese economic success and emerging problems, one must understand the power separation reform within the M-Type framework.[46] During the power separation between 1979 and 1993, many enterprises originally subject to the Central Government were turned over to the local governments. The fundamental responsibility of local economic development has now been transferred to the local authorities, which now enjoy more rights. The power separation reform is being carried out in an environment where marketization is continually growing, and the circulation of commodities and factors between different regions is not very smooth. Separation of power renders more areas and means to local governments, turning them into local protectionists. In the new phase of reform, since 1994, reformers have switched their focus from implementing power separation to seeking a balance between power separation and power concentration based on the market. The increase of local governments

---

45. When analyzing American Industry, Williamson used the "U-Type" and "M-Type" to describe different industrial structures, with the former referring to the unitary structure of firms that were established according to function in the late nineteenth and early twentieth century, and the latter referring to the multilayered structure of firms that were established according to product or geography in the 1820s. We use the concept of U-type and M-type in a way similar to Williamson's analysis. However, in this article, M-Type refers to multilayer, multiregional hierarchy, but not multidepartment hierarchy. *See* Qian Yingyi & Xu Chenggang, *Why China's Economic Reform Unique: M-Type Hierarchy and the Entry and Expansion of Non-Stated Owned Sectors, in Competition for Growth: Political Economics of China's Growth,* compiled by Zhang Jun, Zhou Li'an, Gezhi Publishing House & Shanghai People's Press, 2008, page 9.

46. The 15 years of economic reform since 1979 also accompanied the power separation process. Power separation, marketization, and opening–up to the outside world constitute three major themes of the economic reform. Qian Yingyi, Weingast, *The Chinese Characteristic Economic Federalism Maintaining the Market, in* COMPETITION FOR GROWTH: POLITICAL ECONOMICS OF CHINA'S GROWTH, compiled by Zhang Jun, Zhou Li'an, Gezhi Publishing House & Shanghai People's Press, 2008, page 25.

during the reform is a result of power separation, and a functional united market economy is not equal to China's "feudal princes economy."[47] This effort can still be seen in official documents, even in the twenty-first century.[48] Therefore, under the present economic power separation pattern in China, although local governments have no direct access to competition policy-making, relevant information, suggestions, and applications can still reach the highest economic decision mechanism at the Party and the Central Government level. The influence of the local governments in shaping competition policy will continue to exist for a long time.

IV. EXTERNAL INFLUENCES ON THE SHAPING OF CHINA'S COMPETITION POLICY: INTEREST GROUPS AND INTERNATIONAL FACTORS

In the process of shaping China's competition policy, besides constraints within the system, there exist external influences from interest groups and other international factors. Moreover, the internal influences are substantively linked with the external ones. On the one hand, interest groups such as state-owned enterprises (SOEs) may transform their interest appeals into trade policy, industrial policy, or other strategic policy objectives through the so-called "centralized administrative" government authorities they are under. On the other hand, multinational corporations (MNCs) may obtain preferential trade and investment policy treatment by using foreign governments, international mechanisms, or the systematic structure of the Chinese government, so as to get an easy competition policy. Undoubtedly, the composition of those forces will have a significant impact on the realization of China's national competition policy objectives, which further demonstrates the uniqueness of the shaping of China's competition policy against the backdrop of its transformation.

---

47. For more information, please refer to Qian Yingyi, Weingast, *The Chinese Characteristic Economic Federalism Maintaining the Market, in* COMPETITION FOR GROWTH: POLITICAL ECONOMICS OF CHINA'S GROWTH, compiled by Zhang Jun, Zhou Li'an, Gezhi Publishing House & Shanghai People's Press, 2008, pages 28–35.

48. In 2001, the State Council issued "Regulations on Forbidding Regional Blocks in Market Economic Activities" and "Decision on Consolidating and Standardize Market Economic Order." In 2003, the third plenary meeting of the sixteenth session of the CCP passed "Decisions on Several Problems in Perfecting Socialist Market Economic System by the CCCPC." In 2007, the seventeenth nationwide delegations conference of the CCP issued "Raise the Great Banner of the Socialism with Chinese Characteristic and Fight for New Victories in Constructing Well-to-do Society." The documents mentioned above all include specialized discussion about this problem. *See* Yong Huang & Shan Jiang, *Thirty Years of PRC Anti-monopoly Law under "State-Market" Yardstick: From Retrospective and Prospective Viewpoints*, ASCOLA (forthcoming).

A. Interest Groups that Influence China's Competition Policy

An interest group is an organization that has been established on the basis of sharing one or more common views and putting forward certain requests to other groups or organizations of the society.[49] Interest group as a term has not been formally recognized by the Chinese political lexicon. However, like it or not, with the tendency of welfare-redistribution becoming increasingly apparent, and people grouping themselves into different bodies together based upon their own interests, interest groups will inevitably emerge. Nevertheless, it is worthwhile to note that interest groups in Chinese society are apparently different from their counterparts in western countries. Chinese interest groups have to state their interests cautiously and must seek support from the government by "legitimate" means and for a "reasonable" reason. They have to make sure their interests conform to the overall goals of the Communist Party and the government and constitute no threat to national stability. Therefore, their influence is still marginal.[50] Yet, in the context of current systematic structure, the relevant interest groups may well influence the formation of competition policy by combining their interests with government authorities.

1. State-Owned Enterprises For some time, socialist countries that are in the process of planning their economies have regarded SOEs as "a realistic foundation of realizing planning economy" and "[i]n order to implement planning economy, all (or at least most) enterprises of the whole society are to be transformed to SOEs."[51] In China, implementing a strategy of nationalization is not only requested and strongly recommended by socialist ideology, but it is also decided on an economic basis that exists under certain circumstances.[52] After the adoption of the reform and opening-up to the outside world policy, SOEs still act as the foundation of the development of the entire Chinese economy, and the industrial sectors in which they are playing a role are more and more concentrated. At present, regulated industries (banking, electricity, telecommunications, etc.) and industries where SOEs are established by law by policy (petroleum and tobacco, for example) are in a legal or de facto dominant position and have "monopolized" China's key sectors related to national interest and people's livelihood. They are natural targets of anti-monopoly law. That is why the relationship

---

49. David Truman, The Governmental Process 33 (New York: Knopf 1971).

50. *See* Sheng Bin, *supra* note 23, at page 116.

51. Jin Bei, *The Fundamentals of the Reform of State-Owned Enterprises*, Beijing Publishing House, 2002. The state-owned enterprise (SOE) itself is a combination of politics and economy, as well as a tool for governmental, political, and economic policies. Jin Bei as Editor in Chief, *Competition Order and Competition Policy*, Social Science Literature Publishing House, 2005, Page 340.

52. Lu Junrong, *Industrial Features of State-Owned Enterprises: International Experience and Governance Observations*, Economics and Science Publishing House, 2008, page 160.

between anti-monopoly law and those industries has become one of the biggest conflicts in the process of legislation. Combined with the assistance of sectoral regulatory authorities, the dominant SOEs strongly pressed for complete antitrust exemption. Though the exemption was not granted, they finally forced the lawmakers to rewrite the bill several times, and eventually left a highly ambiguous provision in the law which in essence does not clarify whether regulated industries and state-owned firms are under the purview of the Anti-Monopoly Law.[53] From this, we can see how radical it was to compare the strengths of various parties. Our point of view is that the Anti-Monopoly Law has provided a substantive framework for addressing the issue of its implementation as it relates to SOEs. But in the current and continuing "centralized" administrative regime, the group of SOEs that is approaching oligopoly may be a subtle but substantial influence on competition policy.

2. Multinational Corporations By nature, the relationship between the host country government and MNCs is a complicated bargaining relationship. There will inevitably be a strong clash in the interests of the two parties. Such a clash requires adjusting interests on the basis of cooperation, the degree of which depends on the ability of both parties to cooperate and negotiate.[54] The MNCs have in-depth influence on the developing economy in terms of fundamental structure, competition mechanism, and interest allocation. When it comes to specific competition mechanism issues, there are two questions: first, are domestic enterprises capable of competing with MNCs, and second, will MNCs adopt monopoly and other improper means to compete with domestic enterprises?[55] In China, there were no MNCs during the period of planning economy, and since the adoption of reform and opening-up to the outside world policy, investment and operation of MNCs has become one of the key factors for forging ahead with the development of the Chinese economy. At the same time, because of the authority-decentralization process in the Chinese reform as mentioned above, local governments compete with each other for MNC resources. This results in many MNCs actually enjoying Super-National Treatment in many

---

53. Article VII of Anti-Monopoly Law provides, "For the undertaking in the state-owned economy controlled industries to which are related to national economic lifeline and state security, and in the industries to which the state grants special or exclusive rights, the state protect their lawful operation. The state also lawfully regulates and controls their operation and the price of their commodities and services, safeguards interests of consumers, promotes technical progresses." Paragraph 2 of the same Article provides, "Undertakings mentioned above shall lawfully operate, be honest and faithful, be strict self-discipline, accept social supervision, shall not damage interests of consumers using their dominant or exclusive positions."

54. For a detailed analysis, see Huang He, *Multinational Corporations and Contemporary International Relations*, Shanghai People Publishing house, 2008, pages 302–09.

55. *See* Huang He, at page 249, *Id.*

places and industries. In practice, several unfair and restrictive competition measures were found in the operation of some MNCs but were not punished because of a desire for foreign investment and incompleteness of laws and regulations at the beginning of reform and opening-up to the outside world. Only at the stage of consummating a socialist market economy do people begin to pay attention to quality of foreign investment, and competent authorities start to assess competition behaviors of foreign investors.[56] We believe that although the foreign investment policy in China is in the midst of transformation, the MNCs will continue to influence competition policy through their infiltrative network.

3. Private Enterprise In China, the impact of competition policy on private enterprises is substantial. In the period of constructing a socialist economy in China, "the SOE, as a reliable economic foundation for planning economy, should become a widely-adopted format of enterprise system."[57] During the process of transforming to a market economy, the SOEs phased out from occupying almost all industries. But because of the inertia that accompanied the planning regime and the interests of industrial regulatory authorities and already-in-place factories and merchants, this process has never existed on a voluntary basis. Accordingly, efforts made by private enterprises to enter into relevant industries are usually tremendous. Some policy incentives are given at the national level. To address those restrictive factors and the external environment that might confront nonpublic-owned enterprises, in 2005, the State Council promulgated *the Opinions on Encouraging, Supporting and Guiding the Development of Individually-Run Businesses and Other Forms of Non-Public Owned Economy* (referred to as "36 Articles of Non-public Economy"), which in principle, asks that things be done in seven framework aspects for a nonpublic-owned economy, including opening up market access, enlarging financial and taxation support, consummating social services, safeguarding the legitimate interests of entities and their staffs, guiding the upgrade of quality, improving government's regulation, and strengthening guidance and policy harmonization. However, up to now, tremendous obstacles have prevented private enterprises from entering those regulated industries. But taking private enterprises as a whole group and combining the

---

56. In 2005, the State Administration of Industry and Commerce (SAIC) released a report entitled *Competition Restrictive Behaviors of MNCs in China and Their Countermeasures*. Around the same time, the Economic Law Research Centre of Peking University released another report entitled *Keep Our Eyes on the Competition Restrictive Behaviors of MNCs in China*. These reports inspired discussions in various public forums about how to regulate MNC's competition restrictive behaviors in China, which also gave an impetus to the legislation of Anti-Monopoly Law.

57. *See* Lu Junrong, *supra* note 52, at page 33.

support from industrial associations, they have more and more channels to claim their interests, and some of the efforts have been effective.[58]

4. Consumer As provided in Article 1 of the Anti-Monopoly Law, "this Law is enacted for the purpose of preventing and restraining monopolistic conducts, protecting fair competition in the market, enhancing economic efficiency, safeguarding the interests of consumers and social public interest, promoting the healthy development of the socialist market economy." During the process of legislation, lawmakers understand that protection of consumer interests is the ultimate objective of Anti-Monopoly Law. However, in theory, since the community of consumers itself is bulky in size, dispersive in interest, and limited in organization and channels, the effectiveness of its reflection of opinions and appeals cannot always match the expectations of lawmakers, which means "the bigger the group is, the lower quantity of articles it could supply than the optimal quantity."[59]

In practice, we are not optimistic about consumers being able to assert their interests either. First, in most cases, consumers do not suffer the consequences or damages caused by competition restrictive behaviors. Second, in the current Anti-Monopoly Law in China, the system of private litigation has not been soundly established. The Supreme Court has already made it clear on this issue that lawsuits may be raised independently, apart from the implementation of antitrust law by administrative authorities.[60] But a series of additional issues, such as qualification of plaintiff, evaluation of compensation for damages, and collective litigation, have not been further clarified in the current system. Therefore, time is still needed to determine whether consumer interests could be realized, and to what degree the expected objectives could be achieved.[61]

---

58. In March 2008, the National Development of Reform and Development Committee(NDRC) and the Ministry of Commerce jointly issued the Notice on Relevant Issues Concerning the Operation of Private Product Oil Enterprises, which provides clear regulations on the qualification requirements of nonpublic-owned enterprises for entry into the oil product market in an orderly way as well as operating legally. *See* http://www.ndrc.gov.cn/zcfb/zcfbtz/2008tongzhi/t20080304_195947.htm (2009-1-18). However, in reality, serious problems still exist for nonpublic-owned capital to flow into oil product market in terms of both feasibility and operation stability. For this reason, corresponding industrial associations and organizations have conducted numerous seminars and lobbying activities.

59. Mancur Olson, *The Logic of Collective Actions: Public Goods and The Theory of Groups*, SJPC·Century Publishing House (2006), page 29.

60. Liu Lan, *Strengthening Judicial Review of Anti-Monopoly and Protecting Fair Competition by Law: Interview with the Principal of Administrative Tribunal of Supreme Court on the Implementation of Anti-Monopoly Law*. *See* http://rmfyb.chinacourt.org/public/detail.php?id=123368 (2009-1-18).

61. Nowadays, the problem of lack of supplementary regulations may be a major obstacle for consumers in claiming their interests. This was demonstrated in the case of a Beijing lawyer named Li Fangping, who sued CNC Beijing for discriminating against

5. Nongovernment Organizations The nongovernment Organization (NGO) is a neither-government-nor-enterprise institution or social organization that deals with general welfare services or production, or mutually beneficial and reciprocal services or production. According to the political theory of a pluralist group, the political process of pluralism is dynamic and will change according to the response of interest groups to reality, government activities, and behavior of other interest groups.[62] A specific alliance of interest groups will be formed for a specific issue.[63] Coupled with the development of overseas NGOs in the 1980s, a large number of foreign international NGOs came to China together with foreign capital and investment in large-scaled MNCs, stimulating the emergence of local NGOs. In recent years, the number of types of NGOs has increased to a six-digit figure, and the number is rapidly growing.[64]

The impact of these NGOs on competition policy cannot be ignored. For instance, in the legislation process of Anti-Monopoly Law, the American Bar Association submitted article-by-article comments on most of the publicized draft legislation and aired opinions and suggestions at special seminars. This sort of influence has continued to play a role since the adoption of the Anti-Monopoly law, when legislators drafted additional guidelines and concrete rules. Compared to the formal procedure of legislation, the formulation of competition policy is a relatively closed political process, but the potential channel for NGOs to pose influence has not been totally shut down. Some professional communities, particularly interest groups or group alliances, formed because certain issues will play an invisible and marginal role in the area of competition policy in the predictable future.

B. International Factors Linked to China's Competition Policy

1. Foreign Governments In the context of the global market, corresponding policies and laws of foreign governments are two of the important linking factors to formulating competition policy and executing its influence. The United States provides an example of popularizing competition policy in a unilateral way. Since the case of *Alcoa*, the extraterritorial application of antitrust law by the United States has been met with more resistance. After the case of *Harford Fire*, due to

---

"new citizens" by using its dominant position. *See* http://www.competitionlaw.cn/show.aspx?id=4135&cid=5 (2009-1-18).

62. Xie Xialing, *Prospects of NGOs in China*, published in *Social Changes and NGOs in the Context of Globalization*, with Fan Lizhu as Editor in Chief, Shanghai People Publishing House, 2003, page 252.

63. Tan Rong, *Political Research of American Interest Groups*, China Social Science Publishing House, 2002, page 39.

64. *See* Xie Xialing, at page 254, *Id.*

the difficult issue of jurisdiction in the American federal courts, the international community adopted a firm attitude of resisting the extraterritorial application of American federal courts. Foreign governments adopted different strategies to oppose the United States' antitrust measures, including discovery-blocking provisions, judgment-blocking statutes, claw-back provisions, and diplomatic protests.

As for China, since its competition law and competition policy are still in the early stage, and its overall foreign policy has set the tone to be mutually beneficial, the possibility of unilaterally pushing its antitrust implementation in a dynamic way is not so apparent. However, due to strategic patterns, regime structure, and the existence of interest groups, it is very possible for the execution of competition policy, which contains a mixture of factors for consideration, to have an extraterritorial impact. The intent of extraterritorial enforcement is not to respond to the American policy in particular, but rather to use it as a weapon to react and even to initiate antitrust enforcement to conduct with extraterritorial impact. The resulting impact might be inconsistent with foreign antitrust policy in general. But we are not sure if detailed theories are appropriate here.

However, because of possible resistance from other countries, the Chinese government should take into account the potential consequences when drafting and pursuing its competition policy. And in that sense, foreign governments have become the international factor which is linked to China's competition policy.

2. International Mechanism International mechanism is "a series of connotative or explicit principles, norms, rules and decision-making procedures surrounding the expectation of actors and converged to a certain domain of international relations."[65] Since World War II, international mechanism has played an increasingly important role in international affairs. It affects the information and opportunities that a government can obtain. The government's reputation can be damaged by failing to honor its commitment to support such an international mechanism. The way that international mechanism operates has constantly influenced a particular nation's calculation of its own interest and its position.[66] The success of UN, OECD, WTO, ICN and other regional organizations has been a good illustration.

China has gradually started to merge into the process of globalization since its adoption of reform and opening-up to the outside world policy. Between 1948

65. Robert Keohane, *After Hegemony: Cooperation and Discord in The World Political Economy*, Shanghai People's Publishing House · Century Publishing House (2006), translated by Su Changhe et al., page 57.

66. *See* Robert Keohane, at page 24, *Id.*

and 1979, China joined or signed on to 48 international treaties. Between 1980 and 1998, that number climbed to 177.[67] Thereafter, especially when it entered the twenty-first century, this tendency has continued and intensified with China's accession to the WTO. China is active in joining various kinds of international organizations, participating in, or even leading regional organizations, and carrying out different forms of multilateral diplomatic activities. In the process, China has already been involved in the system of international mechanism and thus been influenced by it, therefore playing a bigger and bigger role. China has been integrated with the world community, benefitting from and contributing to the operation of international mechanism. China's cooperation with OECD and UNCTAD has been conducted mainly in capacity-building. Its involvement in other international organizations and regional organizations also covers relevant competition policy issues. There is no doubt that international mechanism has been an important factor relating to China's competition policy.[68]

V. EXPRESSION OF INTERNATIONAL COORDINATION OF COMPETITION POLICY: BASIC POSITIONS AND ROUTE OF COOPERATION

After analyzing the complicated process of the shaping of competition policy against the backdrop of transformation by using China as an example, it is not difficult for us to reach a conclusion. As far as the shaping of competition policies of countries with different types of system and at different developmental stages, it is unlikely that the process will be similar. The size or degree of constraints and impact caused by regimes, systems, and other factors are also different. Additionally, with the differences in terms of national interest, it is natural that the formulated competition policies could possibly conflict with each other,

67. *See The Yearbook of the People's Republic of China*, the P.R.C Yearbook Society 1999, since quoted from Cai Tuo, *China's Selection and Countermeasures in Globalization*, published in *Globalization, the Chinese Path*, Social Science Literature Publishing House, 2003, page 292.

68. For example, according to our observation, the direct reason for the *acceleration* of enacting of the Anti-monopoly Law was the dispute about China's market economy status in 2004. According to Article 15 of the *Protocol on the Accession of the People's Republic of China*, China was defined as a nonmarket economy country with conditions for as long as 15 years. The influences of the "nonmarket economy position" were manifold. And, there was a series of indicators that determined whether the "market economy position" would be admitted; these indicators themselves are also in dispute. However, it was generally agreed that as the fundamental legal framework of market economy, the anti-monopoly law was indispensable to the market economy. As a result, we finally saw the draft of the anti-monopoly law being submitted by the Ministry of Commerce to the State Council in 2004. In 2005, the State Council organized the first expert discussions, and the legislation of the Anti-monopoly Law was driven to the fast lane.

and it is rather difficult to find a unified path to try to temper the conflict. Based on this understanding, we may go further to discuss the issues of when competition policies shaped under different mechanisms express themselves in international coordination; first, the basic positions of each party in international coordination of competition policy and second, possible routes of cooperation for international coordination of competition policy.

A. Basic Positions of Each Party in International Coordination of Competition Policy

1. Basic Position of Developed Countries in Their Competition Policy Deeply influenced by the belief of "termination of history" after the Cold War, the mainstream view of developed countries is that freedom and democracy might be the "end point of the development of ideology of the mankind" and "the last form of governance of the mankind."[69] Within the system of freedom and democracy, the free market may "accommodate the desire of driving the wheel of history" in the economic domain.[70] The background in which developed countries adopt their competition policies is the so-called "world economic system," which views world politics and economy as a single global market in the hands of a minority of countries. After World War II, OECD of the United Nations, G8, and multilateral organizations like the IMF, the World Bank, and GATT/WTO were controlled by the developed countries and became platforms for their decisions about the world market.[71] At the end of the Cold War, the developed countries raised the so-called "Washington Consensus" in 1989 in order to assess to what degree the old concept of development economics, which had dominated Latin America's economic policy since the 1950s, had been replaced by the concept labeled by OECD as appropriate.[72] And this so-called common understanding

---

69. Francis Fukuyama, *The End of History and the Last Man*, China Social Science Publishing House (1999), translated by Huang Shengqiang & Xu Mingyuan, page 1.

70. Georg Wilhelm Friedrich Hegel asserted from the democratic revolution happening in the United States and France that history came to its end, and the reason was "the desire of driving the wheel of history," which was striving to be recognized, and had already been met in a society where universality and mutual recognition had been realized. No other social system of mankind may accommodate this desire in a better way. Therefore, history cannot make further progress. *See* Francis Fukuyama, *The End of History and the Last Man*, China Social Science Publishing House (1999), translated by Huang Shengqiang and Xu Mingyuan, page 9.

71. Frederic Pearson & Simon Payaslian, *International Political Economy: Conflict and Cooperation in the Global System*, Peking University Press (2006), translated by Yang Yi et al., page 466.

72. On the initial list, there were items such as budget discipline, reprioritization of public expenditures, taxation reform, liberalization of interest rates, competitive exchange rate of foreign currencies, trade liberalization, foreign investment liberalization, privatization, deregulation, and title ownership. *See* John Williamson, *Simplified History of the*

reflects the combination of major elements that developed countries have advocated in the global economic system. The implementation of competition policy was done on the same basis.

Moreover, most of the developed countries have a general blueprint or strategy for international coordination of competition policy, and their basic position is to extend their ideas, principles, and rules of competition law to other countries, so as to provide an integrated framework for domestic enterprises to get access to and operate in the markets of other countries. Naturally, developed countries adopt different methods of addressing this concern. Taking the European Union and the United States as examples, we can see that starting from their individual experience of developing competition law and competition policy, they advocated different paths of international coordination. The European Union leads the world in the area of cooperation, harmonization, and unification of competition law with ample theories and experience in practice, while the United States hopes that by adopting the modality of "extraterritorial application plus voluntary bilateral cooperation," it can avoid downgrading its level of antitrust implementation and handing over its jurisdiction to an international organization, which is caused by joining an international competition law treaty.[73]

2. Basic Position of Developing Countries in Their Competition Policy
Developing countries have different concerns than developed countries regarding whether and how to develop competition policy. From the perspective of the development stage in developing countries—compared with the relatively mature economic system of developed countries—the economic system of developing countries is still at the stage of further development and consummation. That is why developed and developing countries hold different concerns in economic policies. Therefore, when the developing countries work out their economic policies, they are making choices more for the purpose of meeting the pressure of globalization and maintaining domestic economic stability and development. Furthermore, developed countries regard economic integration as an important objective of economic development, because by doing this, they can spread their products, systems, and culture; the priority for developing countries, however, is to confront the arduous task of how to consummate an economic system and develop a national economy. The focal point of economic development, however, is domestic issues, which means economic integration is in a subordinate position in the process of economic development.[74]

Washington Consensus, published at Cui Zhiyan ed., *China and Globalization: Washington or Beijing Consensus*, China Social Science Publishing House (2005), pages 63–67.

73. Sheng Jiemin & Wu Tao, *Debates and Differences: Analysis and Projection of WTO Negotiation of Competition Policy*, published at Wang Yanlin ed., Competition Law Review, Vol. 1, China Political Science and Law University Press (2005).

74. It was for these reasons that developing countries stress topics like agriculture as the condition precedent to the negotiation of competition policy; what they did not realize,

When it comes to competition policy, many developing countries are reluctant about the theory. First, some small countries believe relaxation of regulation and openness of trade measures is sufficient to promote domestic competition, and that there is no need to adopt the rules of competition. Second, free competition, advocated by European countries and the United States, might result in developing countries being impaired by large multinational companies from developed countries. Third, it is difficult to transplant the existing competition law adopted by developed countries in developing countries. Fourth, developing countries lack the necessary infrastructure for the implementation of competition law, such as the appropriate systematic guarantees and technical support. Nevertheless, the foundation for competition policy and its international coordination is solid in reality, because most developing countries have been invaded by international cartels. In particular, countries not equipped by competition law have become a haven for multinational companies to carry out competition restrictive activities. In such circumstances, developing countries are more concerned with their economic policy. Against this backdrop, most developing countries respond to the challenges of competition policy against their national economy with a case-by-case approach and do not have an overall strategy.

3. Basic Position of China in Its International Coordination of Competition Policy China has its own unique development path. According to the conclusion by Joshua Cooper Ramo in his *The Beijing Consensus*, China's new guideline for development is pushed by its desire to obtain equal and peaceful quality growth. The guideline has adequate flexibility and can hardly become a theory. It has no goal of settling every issue with a unified solution. The definition of it is continuous innovation and experiment and active safeguard of the national borderline and interest; it stresses the reality as well as ideology, which reflects the ancient Chinese philosophic conception of not distinguishing between the theory and the practice.[75] Of the three theorems raised in *The Beijing Consensus*, the second one involves "efforts to create an environment in favor of sustainable and fair development."[76] It is our view that, although further deliberation is needed for

---

however, is that there is a lot to be done if the negotiation does begin. *See* Wang Zhongmei, *supra* note 1, at page 298.

75. *The Beijing Consensus* is undoubtedly a thought after Deng Xiaoping in terms of its structure, but it is closely linked with Deng's pragmatic opinion, which was illustrated by saying the best way to realize modernization is to "cross the river by touching the stone" rather than trying to take a "shock therapy" to achieve a big leap. *See* Shua Copper Ramo, *The Beijing Consensus*, published on *China and Globalization: The Washington Consensus or The Beijing Consensus*, with Huang Ping & Cui Zhiyuan as Editors in Chief, Social Science Literature Publishing House, 2005, page 5.

76. The first proposition is to reposition the value of innovation. The second theorem is that since chaos can't be controlled from the top, you need a whole set of new tools. The third theorem including a self-helping theory, emphasizes the use of leverage to push the hegomonist powers that might want to irritate you. Please refer to, Shua Copper Ramo,

the specific conclusions of the so-called *Beijing Consensus*, the unique Chinese development direction and path show themselves well in China's economic policy, including competition policy. Combined with the above-mentioned views, it is enough to say there is a gap between China and developed countries or the other developing countries in the area of competition policy.

Compared with developed countries, China's competition policy was generated in an imperfect and undeveloped market economy. This discrepancy in background requires China to pursue many untraditional competition policy objectives, including the above-mentioned establishing and consummating market economy, controlling excessive government power, safeguarding national security, and even shortening income gaps. Besides, when formulating competition policy, due to the stage the Chinese market economy is in and the constraints thereof, there are many completely different factors affecting the formation of competition policy in China and in western countries or other developing market economies. These factors include in particular the above-mentioned macro-control, export cartel, concentration of undertakings, and other factors that have influenced the development of the national economy. Although from the perspective of pure technical issues, the framework and contents of the Anti-Monopoly Law of China are not so different from those in Europe and the United States. Many factors in the Chinese market economy affect or even determine the implementation of its competition policy, which inevitably increases the difficulty of conducting future international cooperation and causes conflicts in the process.

Compared with other developing countries, China is in a transformation from a planning economy to a market economy. The systematic inertia brought by transformation has substantial impact on the shaping of competition policy. The system requires extreme government control and influence on a market economy. Currently, the primary objective of the Chinese government is to develop its economy, while competition policy will restrict and limit the government's approach to a certain extent. For example, when the economic growth overheats, the government might issue administrative orders to restrict the development of steel and other industries in the name of macro-control, while in times of economic deflation, the government might use its power to encourage business mergers or restructurings.

The implementation of competition policy will severely limit the ability of the government to adopt these policy measures. In the first sense, it might cause administrative monopoly problems if the administrative orders provide for measures in Section 5 of the Anti-monopoly Law. In the latter case, regulation on mergers and acquisitions in Anti-monopoly Law will act as a screen to a wave of

---

The Beijing Consensu, published on *China and Globalization: The Washington Consensus or The Beijing Consensus*, with Huang Ping and Cui Zhiyuan as Editors in Chief, Social Science Literature Publishing House, 2005, Page 12–21.

mergers pushed by the government. Therefore, under such a regime, it is hard for competition policy to be a priority of the Chinese government. Because its internal uniqueness leads to internal contradictions and conflicts, China exhibits various features from other countries, bringing more external conflicts with other countries when they implement their relevant policies. It can be predicted that the core and nature of these conflicts is not only between competition policies, but also between the overall economic policy and industrial policy of China versus the competition policy of the West in its traditional sense.

Facing so many potential conflicts, what could be the reason for China to take on the issue of international coordination of competition policy? We believe, in an outward-oriented economy, the strategy of diplomacy has significant influence on economic policy, including competition policy, because competition policy is an integral part of the general economic policy under the framework of diplomacy and economic cooperation. We would next evaluate the impact of China's foreign policy against its stance on competition policy.

Generally speaking, the primary economic objective of China's foreign policy and strategy is strongly associated with participating and integrating into the world system. In such a process, the recognition of China's international identity has changed from an "out-of-system country" to a country that is generally recognized and is determined to maintain the current international pattern in many aspects.[77] On this basis, we may know by reviewing China's foreign policy that since the Third Plenary Conference of the Eleventh Session of the Party's Assembly, China has always considered its opening-up to the outside world policy as a key strategic status of economic development, and has regarded "equal and mutually beneficial" to be an important guideline for its adoption of opening-up policy and processing of foreign economic and trade relations.[78]

---

77. Shi Yinhong, *International Politics and State Strategy*, Beijing University Press (2006), pages 194–95.

78. In 1982, The Report of The Twelfth Congress of Chinese Communist Party pointed out that: "it is a fundamental strategy of our nation to carry out reform and opening up to the outside world policy on the basis of equality and reciprocity, so as to enlarge foreign economic and technological cooperation." In 1987, The Report of The Thirteenth Congress of Chinese Communist Party pointed out that: "we need to further economic and technological cooperation with both developed and developing countries." In 1992, The Report of The Thirteenth Congress of Chinese Communist Party pointed out that: "we firmly carry out reform and opening up to the outside world policy, and will continue to strengthen economic and technological cooperation with countries around the world on the basis of equality and reciprocity . . . ." In 1997, The Report of The Fifteenth Congress of Chinese Communist Party stated that: "we need to work hard to open our economy . . . to develop an open economy and strengthen our international competitiveness . . . to lay down a political environment for fair competition so as to actively participate regional economic cooperation and global multilateral trade system." In 2002, The Report of The Sixteenth Congress of Chinese Communist Party pointed out that: "we will stick to the

In the twenty-first century, the Eleventh Five-Year Plan endorsed by the Fifth Plenary Conference of the Sixteenth Session of the Party's Assembly clearly stated an intention to "implement an opening-up strategy which is mutually beneficial and win-win."[79] In 2005, in the keynote speech, *Striving for Constructing a Continuously Peaceful and Universally Prosperous Harmonious World*, by President Hu Jingtao, the concept of Harmonious World was declared.[80] It seems a new foreign strategy is now taking shape in the mindset of Chinese leaders, and that is: in addition to the "traditional" school of ideology, [81] a new international perspective has now been added to their thinking, creating a limited, fast-growing belief upon multilateral cooperation, upon international organizations, and upon transnational non-political connection, believing that these efforts could promote China's national interests. One of the characteristics of this New Internationalism is that although limited, it has still rapidly (with some fluctuation) increased faith with the view that believing in multilateral cooperation, international organizations, and mechanism—as well as transnational nonpolitical intercourse—would strengthen of China's national interest and their own internal value.[82]

In making the above-mentioned analysis, we have come to two conclusions. First, the overall theme of China's foreign policy has a direction-leading impact on its path of international coordination of competition policy. Such an impact will be even more direct when the competition policy of China conflicts with policies of other countries, and diplomatic coordination might be needed.

---

combination of 'inbound' and 'outbound' investment, and increase the openness at all levels. In accordance with the new situations of globalization and accession to the WTO, we will participate international economic and technological cooperation and competition to a larger, wider and higher extend . . . and actively involve in regional economic communications and cooperations."

79. The Eleventh Five-Year Plan, endorsed by the Fifth Plenary Conference of the Sixteenth Session of the Party's Assembly. *See* http://news.xinhuanet.com/politics/2005-10/18/content_3640318.htm (2009-1-18).

80. Relevant views made in this report included: first, to implement multilateralism and realize common security; second, to stick with cooperation and realize common prosperity; and third, to build a tolerant and harmonious world. *See* Hu Jintao, *Work Hard to Achieve Permanent Peace and Mutual Prosperity in a Harmonious World, Speech on the 60th Anniversary of United Nations*, Sept. 19, 2005. *See* http://www.china.com.cn/chinese/news/971778.htm (2009-1-18).).

81. There are three dimensions within such a "tradition" ideology: first, the Chinese communism doctrines, in particular the notion and belief defined in the Marxism, Leninism and Maoism; secondly, the Chinese patriotism, or, more accurately the modern Chinese extreme nationalism; thirdly, the "pragmatic policies" school, or the reality-based thinking of international politics and foreign policy. See Shi Yinhong, *supra* note 77, at page 197.

82. Shi Yinhong, at pages 201–02, *Id.*

The implementation of China's competition policy will be carried out within the themes of its foreign policy as "harmonious world" together with "mutually beneficial and win-win," including comity and where multilateral cooperation could play a role, without the internal tendency of unilateral implementation. Second, with regard to the international coordination of competition policy, China should continue to pursue its pragmatic philosophy. Adopting reform and focusing on a problem-oriented way of responding to various challenges has meant taking the approach of "To cross the river by touching the stone" or "Be it a black cat or a white cat, a cat that can catch mice is a good cat"[83] to address the potential problems in the process of international coordination of competition policy.

B. Possible Cooperation Path for International Coordination of Competition Policy

Based on the above analysis of the basic positions of developed countries, developing countries, and China on the issue of international coordination of competition policy, we try to make a further analysis on the appropriate cooperation mode and area of competition policy from the standpoint of China and put forward a pragmatic path for such international coordination.

1. Mode of International Coordination From the above, we can see that in practice, each country or group has different approaches and beliefs. The current international coordination is still a formalism slogan rather than a concrete mechanism. Each country has its own distinct notion about the way that coordination should be conducted, and they have yet to agree upon any substantive measures. Given the imbalance of international economic development and the uniqueness of competition policy in individual countries, it is not possible to insist that all countries execute cooperation in a single manner. Instead, we think we should look for the greatest common denominator and use that as the vanguard for international coordination.

As to an analysis of the means of international coordination, Andrew T. Guzman came to two conclusions after his research. First, cooperation is more likely among countries which have similar trade patterns (e.g., countries within the OECD) than among countries with dissimilar trade patterns (e.g., developed and developing countries). When the trading partners of countries differ significantly, agreement will only be possible if the nations that gain from the agreement compensate the countries that lose. At the same time, regarding the pattern of international coordination, Guzman pointed out that agreement is more likely to occur in some forums than in others. Because antitrust agreements between developed and developing countries are unlikely without transfer payments, negotiations are least likely to yield agreement if they do not encompass any

83. The above are famous quotations by former Chinese leader, Deng Xiaoping. These quotation later became the wisdom behind and the metaphor for gradualism and pragmatism of China's reform and opening process.

other issues. Agreement might be possible within a WTO framework if payment is made from developing to developed countries. Bilateral negotiations provide the most promising forum for reaching agreement because they require only two countries to agree that cooperation will increase national welfare, and transfer payments through concessions in other areas of dispute are more likely.[84]

As mentioned above, when it comes to unilateral enforcement, the agreement-type coordination model is more effective; but in the terms of a possible international competition code, the nonagreement-type coordination model would have a bigger role to play. The conclusion reached by Guzman corresponds to our previous observations, the origin of which lies on the non-homogeneity of the economy of different countries. The existence of such non-homogeneity is, to a large extent, rooted in different trade modes. By making such an analysis, we conclude that currently, we should promote coordination on the basis of signing conventions among countries with higher homogeneity, including bilateral coordination and regional coordination.

The question then becomes: how can we define the region here? According to the Gravity Model of trade,[85] trade activity between two counties is in direct ratio to their GDPs, and in inverse ratio with their distance. Further, in bilateral trade activities between countries and regions, the factors of geography, economic scale of a trading partner, and natural incentives such as population are head-and-shoulders above the other factors. For instance, after testing the Gravity Model, we may illustrate that there is a connection between geography and the path for trading, and that the trade between two countries is in direct proportion to the countries' economic sizes (evaluated by output and population), while in inverse proportion to the geographic or cultural distance between the two countries.[86] Although robustness of this abstract model is limited by practical experience, it nevertheless provides a useful approach for us. The region should be defined as an organized state of formation in which participating members are highly interdependent and have a certain organizational cohesive force and recognition that is influenced by geographic, economic, and cultural factors.[87]

---

84. Andrew T. Guzman, *Is International Antitrust Possible?* 73 N.Y.U. L. Rev. 1501, 1505 (1998).

85. *See* Jeffrey A. Frankel, *Regional Trading Blocs in the World Economic System,* Inst. of Int'l Econ., 49–50. But Polak holds the opposite view. *Cf.* Jacques J. Polak, *Is APEC a Natural Regional Trading Bloc? A Critique of the 'Gravity Model' of International Trade,* 19 World Econ., 533, 534–37 (1996).

86. Liu Jun, *The Legal Approach to Regional Trade Agreements,* CITIC Publishing House (2004), page 58. For more complete exposition, see Paul Krugman, *The Move Toward Free Trade Zones, in* Policy Implications of Trade and Currency Zones 19–21 (1991), a symposium sponsored by the Federal Reserve Bank of Kansas City. Jeffrey A. Frankel & David Romer, *Does the Trade Cause Growth?* 89(3) The American Economic Review 379–399 (1999).

87. Liu Jun, at page 10, *Id.*

We believe that, as an intersection and common ground between Guzman's conclusion and the Gravity Model, regional coordination, is a viable and promising choice in the coordination of international antitrust laws, and is perhaps the prevailing choice.[88] Its advantages have been reflected in ANZCERTA, the most successful coordination case so far. As a result of the ANZCERTA, New Zealand promulgated its 1986 Competition Act, and eliminated anti-dumping measures between Australia and New Zealand in the 1988 supplemental agreement.

2. In the Area of Substantive Cooperation The likelihood of any substantive cooperation should be analyzed in the areas of cartel enforcement, merger control, and regulation of abuse of dominant position.

First, in the area of international cartels, although all countries strictly forbid cartel activities, the punishment posed by an individual country is not sufficient to make up for the cartel's influence in other affected countries. Additionally, without assistance from other countries, it is sometimes hard to judge the illegality. Therefore, it is essential to carry out international cooperation in this area. From the perspective of feasibility, on the basis of the illegality of horizontal (hard-core) cartel activities, we believe a generally unified core substantive standard should be reached with respect to collusive price fixing, market allocation, output limitation, joint boycott, and other similar activities. While in the area of vertical agreement, since some different understandings still exist—namely vertical price fixing, exclusive dealing, and bundle sale, which might fall under the scope of the rationality principle—it is not suitable to make a strict unification on these matters. Of course, the main limitation for international coordination in this area is the protection of business secrets. The implementation authorities of each country might have some reasonable considerations of national interest, so that a question mark has to be put on whether such cooperation is thorough.[89]

Second, in the area of international merger control, the substantive rules of review differ somewhat from country to country. Although each country uses similar standards in reviewing merger cases, including whether competition is substantially impaired or whether a dominant position is achieved or strengthened, the concrete methodology of economic analysis is not exactly the same and often generates different outcomes. At the same time, the parties of a transnational merger are usually enterprises with relatively larger domestic political and economic influences, so the relevant national interest is more substantive in this

---

88. We stress the mode of regional coordination because bilateral agreements between countries of similar background are motivated by self-interests, while the regional integration of competition policies has to be mobilized by conscious agenda, although these two different modes may coexist, like ANZCERTA. However, even bilateral agreements between countries of similar background can encounter substantial conflicts, which can be witnessed in the U.S.-EU case.

89. Wang Zhongmei, *supra* note 1, at page 209.

area, which further enlarges the discrepancy in efficiency assessment. In this area, we may consider convergence to a certain degree in terms of filing procedure and timetables, so as to reduce the risk of uncertainty undertaken by enterprises. To be more specific, we may reduce the differences on the timing requirements for filing, time requirements for early-stage registration, and the documents that are needed for registration.[90]

Third, in the area of regulating abuse of a dominant market position, since major countries have not reached a consensus, further consultation and exploration on this topic of a bilateral or multilateral competition coordination network are called for. At present, ICN is most active in this regard. Until 2008, the Unilateral Activities Working Group of ICN issued three related reports and two recommendations, according to its agenda.[91]

3. Possible Path After identifying the appropriate cooperation areas of competition policy, we may associate different modes of international coordination with these areas and draw up a potential path for international coordination of competition policy.

The first is global coordination. It is clear that theory and practice are far less than mature at the level of WTO negotiations. Based on this point, we should encourage developing countries to participate in cooperation in the ICN. As for those topics upon which it is easy to reach an agreement, such as regulation of international cartels, we may extend those common understandings with the precondition of participation by developing countries. As for the difficult topics, we may continue to draft text in the form of Best Practice, which could be provided to each party for discussion and revision.[92]

The second is bilateral coordination. Since bilateral coordination is carried out on a one-to-one negotiation basis, according to the degree of trust between different countries, we may choose from an agreement specially designed to tackle cooperation issues in implementation of competition law, an agreement

---

90. For example, OECD proposed the unification of merger filing in its Framework for a Notification and Report Form for Concentrations. *See* OECE, Notification ofTransnational Mergers Reports 1999. Similar advice was also suggested at the Recommended Framework for Best Practices in International Merger Control Procedures, jointly issued by the ICC and OECE in 2001.

91. 2007, Report on the Objectives of Unilateral Conduct Laws, Assessment of Dominance/Substantial Market Power, and State-Created Monopolies; 2008, Report on Predatory Pricing and Report on Single Branding/Exclusive Dealing; 2008, Dominance/Substantial Market Power Analysis Pursuant to Unilateral Conduct Laws—Recommended Practices, and State-Created Monopolies Analysis Pursuant To Unilateral Conduct Laws—Recommended Practices.

92. We should not ignore their influence over public opinion. Past experience proves again and again that changes in public opinion are always the indicator for policy adjustment. *See* Zhu Wenli, *International Political Economics*, Peking University Publishing House, 2004, page 248.

on mutual provision of technical support in competition law, a bilateral agreement of judicial assistance, or antitrust cooperation within a bilateral FTA to regulate international cartels, transnational mergers, and abuse of dominant market position individually.

The third is regional cooperation. Generally speaking, due to the relative homogeneity of countries in a region, and apart from cooperation in nonsubstantive standards with regard to hard-core cartels and international mergers, we may initiate the process of convergence and even integration in terms of substantive standards concerning vertical agreement regulation and international merger, so as to integrate the competition policy in the coordination mode of signing conventions. If such an agreement is reached on an adequately large level, we may then raise the already mature standard to a higher platform, such as the WTO. The establishment of regional cooperation will be unique too, so different degrees of integration can be accomplished according to specific compositions and features of each regional cooperation framework. This point has already been demonstrated within the different regional framework of the EU, NAFTA, MERCOSUR, and APEC. In the case of China, a possible path is to start from CEPA and CECA and take the lead in building up competition rules within the Greater China FTA, while at the same time participating and guiding the coordination under the framework of ASEAN so as to play an influential role thereof, pave the way for global coordination at a deeper level, and make a substantial advance in increasing the welfare of the world as a whole.

It is worth emphasizing that although we do not believe there exists a universal international coordination framework of competition policy, the most pragmatic path to take should be regional cooperation as its center, while gradually integrating other paths of coordination and promoting coordination between a regional organization and a country, as well as between regional organizations, which finally comes into the mode of regional cooperation being the mainstream with the coexistence of other coordination forms.

CONCLUSION: A UNIVERSAL PATH OF INTERNATIONAL COORDINATION OF COMPETITION POLICY?

Social science researchers ideally seek a universal method or path, so as to find a universal framework and the universal value it represents in order to integrate the solutions to questions from the world. However, when history entered the contemporary era, the world became more integrated in terms of economy, while being extremely fragmented in the political, legal, and cultural domains. As one of the policy types that is most closely related to market economy, the international coordination of competition policy seems to have a possibility of having a universal path. However, competition policy itself has also undertaken various historic and realistic influences in the process of shaping its national force and therefore is somewhat vague in expressing the national interest.

The multiplicity of the topic itself also makes the effort to pursue a universal path in this area almost hopeless. It is hard to say whether the effort will generate a desirable result. Then, what progress can a scholar make? We believe that it might be a valuable selection to describe an accurate picture of reality and trace out the advancing path in the jungle. As Martin Heidegger said, "There are roads in the jungle. Most of them suddenly disappear at untrodden places. These roads are called roads in the jungle. . . . Forestry workers and rangers know these roads and they also understand what is on the roads in the jungle."[93]

93. Martin Heidegger, HOLZWEGE, STPH Century Publishing House (2004), translated by Sun Zhouxing.

13. ANTITRUST WITHOUT BORDERS
From Roots to Codes to Networks

ELEANOR M. FOX*

INTRODUCTION

Antitrust law has moved from a national enterprise to an international enterprise. Markets transcend national boundaries, and many problems appear to require supranational or cooperative solutions. The 1990s were an era of visions of a multilateral framework, possibly under the aegis of the World Trade Organization. As the 1990s drew to a close, multilateral agreement seemed more remote, and networking solutions seemed more practical and attractive. International antitrust today is less "world antitrust" and more "antitrust without borders." This essay describes the intellectual journey from hierarchy to networking; although the journey is not over. Using the subsidiarity principle (what can be done as well or better at a lower level should be done at a lower level), it identifies the problems that can be tackled horizontally, and how and in what forum; it identifies the problems that still need a solution from the top; and it suggests that, at least in the short term, more targeted solutions will be sought for the truly global problems.

I. A PERSPECTIVE: WHERE WE HAVE COME FROM

Half a century ago, only a handful of nations had adopted antitrust law. Many preferred dirigisme or cooperation to competition. The biggest challenge to the American competition system was acceptance of cartels, not competition, as the rule of trade. When the United States sought to protect itself from offshore cartels, our trading partners invoked international law and comity, arguing that cartels, legal where formed, were insulated wherever their cinders landed.

Famously, in *Alcoa*,[1] the United States adopted the effects doctrine. Just as famously, in late 1989, there came a dramatic change. Most the rest of the world

---

* Eleanor Fox is Walter J. Derenberg Professor of Trade Regulation at New York University School of Law. The author is grateful for the support of the Filomen D'Agostino Research Fund. Earlier parts of this chapter are based on my testimony before the Antitrust Modernization Commission, Feb. 15, 2006, available at *http://govinfo.library.unt.edu/amc/commission_hearings/pdf/Statement_Fox_final.pdf.*

1. United States v. Aluminum Co. of America, 148 F.2d 416 (2d Cir. 1945).

embraced markets and antitrust, and many antitrust jurisdictions adopted some form of the effects test, validating jurisdiction over offshore actors and their acts that produced a significant effect in the regulating nation.[2] The nations adopted an effects test to protect themselves. If there were no effects jurisdiction, the world would surely need, and would already have, an international antitrust regime.

From the time of the fall of the Berlin Wall in late 1989, the U.S. antitrust agencies, the European competition authorities, and others extolled the importance of antitrust law in free market economies. Today, more than one hundred nations have antitrust (or "competition") laws. This is, by some measure, success.

There are some costs of success; small in the scheme of things, but palpable. In a globalizing world with national-level law, there would be differences in procedure and substance, overlaps and gaps of jurisdiction, lack of coherence, and conflicts. Some of the differences would be a matter of principle, related to capacity of antitrust authorities, stage of economic development of nations, and values or preferences of peoples. Some differences in outcomes would be related to different impacts of the same transaction or conduct in different markets; thus, different facts. Some differences would derive simply from lack of knowledge or perspective of less experienced agencies, or would stem from divergences on unimportant details, such as the earliest allowable date of premerger notification. Differences are a fact of life in a world in which scores of nations are reinventing and refining the antitrust wheel.

Antitrust agencies of the world have risen admirably to the challenges. Authorities, particularly of the United States and Europe, collaborate intensely when vetting the same mergers and pursuing the same cartels. Collaborations provide transparency and cross-fertilization. The U.S. and EU authorities have particularly close relations, backed up by a working group on mergers and documents detailing best practices.

Merger collaborations have had many successes. One well known example is the cooperation between the United States Department of Justice and the European Commission in the case of the merger of WorldCom and MCI. Enabled by confidentiality waivers, the agencies coordinated requests for information, jointly met with the parties, and concluded settlements that met the concerns on both sides.[3]

In this new era of cooperation, the Organization for Economic Co-Operation and Development (OECD) (especially for the developed countries), the United Nations Conference on Trade and Development (UNCTAD) (especially for

---

2. *See*, for the European Union, Ahlström Osakeyhtio v. Commission (Wood Pulp), [1988] ECR 5193.

3. Report of the International Competition Policy Advisory Committee to the Attorney General and Assistant Attorney General for Antitrust (ICPAC Report) (2000), p. 66.

developing countries), and the International Competition Network (ICN) play important roles. For many years, the OECD in particular has advanced the state of knowledge and cooperation. The ICN is a different construct— much younger and much less formal. Founded in 2001 as a network among the world's competition agencies to explore avenues for convergence and assistance,[4] the ICN is a ground-up network of all antitrust authorities of the world intended, at its inception, to discuss and solve practical problems and to pursue tasks capable of achievement. Initial efforts were devoted to harmonizing details of practice and process where divergent rules and practices imposed significant, unnecessary costs; for example, agreement on the earliest date on which pre-merger notification filings can be submitted and on the required nexus between merging parties and jurisdictions seeking to regulate the merger. Later projects approach more controversial issues, such as standards for identifying abuse of dominance.[5]

In terms of cooperation and the formation of shared norms, there is more to be done. I shall return to this subject. First, I reflect on substantive convergence and then comity; I comment on extraterritoriality and the bounds of jurisdiction; and I comment on notions for world antitrust. Finally, I ask: what problems remain, what is the lowest level at which they can be solved, and what is left for international antitrust?

II. SUBSTANTIVE CONVERGENCE

Substantive convergence of law is often extolled as a worthy and pressing goal in this world of national law and multitudinous jurisdictions. The value of convergence as a goal may be exaggerated. Convergence is good when it happens through the enlightened choices of the jurisdictions, for convergent law can produce more business certainty, save transactions costs, and increase trade. But nations in the antitrust family are at different stages of economic development and have different capabilities, perceptions, and priorities. Moreover, diversity has benefits, and openness of the channels for experimentation and adjustment has its own dynamic, pro-competitive rewards. Even within the United States, antitrust diversity thrives. The case law of the Third Circuit and the D.C. Circuit courts of appeals are not entirely congruent. The Clinton Administration's view of efficient and appropriate relief in the *Microsoft* monopoly case and the Bush II Administration's view of efficient and appropriate relief in the same case differed widely. The latter's perspective on the importance of dominant firms'

4. An international competition network (then named The Global Competition Initiative) was one of the principal recommendations of the ICPAC Report (2000). *See* ICPAC Report, Chapter 6, Preparing for the Future, 281–87, 300–01.

5. *See generally* Eleanor Fox, *Linked-In: Antitrust and the Virtues of a Virtual Network*, 43 INT'L LAW. 151 (2009).

freedom to act and the Obama Administration's appreciation of the importance of freedom from the clutches of abusive power put the two world views in relief. Acknowledgment of diversity is a concession to reality.

For transactions that are cross-border and especially global, there is a case to be made for a single rule of law or framework for the law—adopted multilaterally—all other things being equal. There is a credible argument that one substantive standard should govern global mergers. The United States has strongly opposed this idea when proposed in the context of multilateral agreement. Its officials have argued that nations have different standards and that there is not one standard fit for or accepted by all.[6] If there is not an appropriate single standard achievable through a multilateral regime, then can there be an appropriate single standard to be achieved through cajoled convergence?

Sunlight and engaged discussion are invaluable. They tend to produce convergence in some respects, but not in others. They are likely to lead to a better understanding of differences and more respect for them.

III. COMITY

Comity is a concept of discretionary reciprocal deference. It holds that one nation should defer to the law and rules (or dispute disposition) of another because, and where, the other has a greater interest; thus, a greater claim of right. Comity is a concept founded on process and relationship, not outcome. The outcome in the nation that is accorded the deference may not be the preferred outcome of the nation that defers.

Comity is an amorphous concept. Invoking the word does not reveal its practical meaning. Whether one nation has a greater claim of right than another is usually not obvious in the cases in which duties of deference are likely to be asserted.[7]

---

6. *See* Joel I. Klein, *No Monopoly on Antitrust*, FINANCIAL TIMES, Feb. 13, 1998, p. 20; Joel I. Klein, *Anticipating the Millennium: International Antitrust Enforcement at the End of the Twentieth Century*, *in* 1997 FORDHAM CORP. LAW INST. 9 (Barry Hawk ed., 1999).

7. *See* Laker Airways Ltd. v. Sabena, Belgian World Airlines, 731 F.2d 909 (D.C. Cir. 1984) (rejecting the claim that the U.S. courts should refuse to take jurisdiction over Laker's bankruptcy trustee's antitrust conspiracy suit against British and Belgian airlines).

Thus, invocation of "comity" does not answer the following questions: Should the United States have deferred to the European Community when it examined conduct by IBM-Europe that (the Europeans thought) was anticompetitive and harmed Europeans? Or should the European Commission have deferred to the United States when the United States withdrew its similar complaint against IBM-US at an advanced stage in the litigation? In *Microsoft*, should Europe and Korea have deferred to the United States even though they determined that conduct subsequent to the subject of the U.S. *Microsoft* case

Comity is a horizontal, nation-to-nation concept, seeking—by reciprocal deference—to maximize the joint interests of the affected nations by splitting their differences or otherwise dissipating conflict in view of repeated interactions expected to occur. It could play into the hands of nationalistic detente and the nurturing of national champions. A case in point is the *Hartford Fire*[8] case in which Lloyds of London underwriters agreed not to supply reinsurance and retrocessionaire coverage to U.S. primary insurers for sudden pollution claims and long tail policies.[9] The UK parliament had legislated the Lloyds' members' right of self-regulation,[10] and the Lloyds' members pled that what they had done was lawful where they did it and that the UK legislation filled the field. They and their government asked the U.S. court to refrain from exercising jurisdiction on grounds of comity. The court declined. Dismissal would have meant: go ahead and boycott our firms, and we will expect similar treatment from you when our ox is goring.[11]

"Comity" sounds good and does little work. Through all the years from the famous *Timberlane* case[12] to the present,[13] not one U.S. court has ever found that the interest of another nation outweighed the interest of the United States in cases in which the United States had an antitrust interest at stake.[14]

---

was anticompetitive and harmful to their citizens? Or should the United States defer to the decisions by other jurisdictions when they were the first to examine certain conduct?

8. Hartford Fire Ins. Co. v. California, 509 U.S. 764 (1993).

9. Long tail policies allow recovery whenever the harm occurs if the covered act occurs within the period of the policy.

10. The UK law affirmatively recognized the autonomy of the re-insurers by handing over the reins of (self) regulation to the industry. *See* Eleanor Fox, *National Law, Global Markets, and* Hartford*: Eyes Wide Shut*, 68 ANTITRUST L.J. 73 (2000).

11. There was a quite different articulation of the story by the defendants, but the case was decided on the face of the complaint.

12. Timberlane Lumber Co. v. Bank of America, 549 F.2d 597 (9th Cir. 1976). *Timberlane* was the parent of the U.S. antitrust comity "doctrine." In *Timberlane*, as it turned out after years of litigation on jurisdiction and comity, plaintiffs were at most deprived of a trickle of exports to the United States, and the conspiracy in Honduras could not have harmed U.S. competition. *See also Timberlane II*, 574 F. Supp. 1453 (N.D. Cal. 1983), *aff'd*, 749 F.2d 1378 (9th Cir. 1984), *cert. denied*, 472 U.S. 1032 (1985). This is one of the very few cases dismissed for lack of jurisdiction.

13. *Hartford Fire*, *supra* note 8, hinted at the unhelpfulness, if not irrelevance, of comity where offshore action is intended to affect and significantly does affect the regulating nation. *But see* Empagran S.A. v. F. Hoffmann-La Roche, Ltd. (*Empagran*), 542 U.S. 155 (2004) (using principles of comity in the construction of a statute).

14. *See* Eleanor Fox, *Extraterritoriality, Antitrust, and the New Restatement: Is Reasonableness the Answer?* 19 N.Y.U. J. INT'L L. & POL. 565 (1987).The antitrust agencies are better placed than courts to take account of (non-nationalistic) interests of other nations, as well as to take account of other agencies' or courts' analyses of the same issues,

In view of the enormous, naturally occurring convergence of the law and policy of nations towards common competition norms, the important question is not when should we defer to the (inconsistent) interests of other nations. The important question is how can the antitrust jurisdictions of the world work together to maximize their shared interest in competitive markets, to the benefit of consumers and robust business.[15]

In the absence of law that is as broad as the affected market, a wise regime would stretch its law, conceptually, to embrace the whole affected market, thus approximating world welfare.[16] Methodologies would allow authorities and courts to take account of antitrust harms beyond the nation's borders. Authorities would be empowered to share sufficient data so that less well-situated nations could effectively protect themselves from antitrust harms. The national law governing jurisdiction and remedies would be broadened so that, for example, national authorities in a jurisdiction with the largest consumer market would provide a forum in which smaller affected nations could be heard and their legitimate concerns satisfied, as proposed below.[17]

In sum, the comity concept is horizontal—nation-to-nation. The more fitting paradigm for the new century is overarching, global, and spiral. National antitrust would operate in the shadow of the true market.

IV. EXTRATERRITORIALITY AND THE BOUNDS OF JURISDICTION

Consistent with international law, nations have broad jurisdiction to prescribe regulatory rules. In essence, according to the Restatement (Third) of the Foreign Relations Law of the United States, nations may write rules that catch transactions and actors beyond their borders as long as the regulating nation is aiming to protect its own nonparochial interests, such as domestic consumer interests, and does so in a proportional way. Jurisdiction is then limited in two respects, according to the Restatement: (1) where a command of the actor's nation directly conflicts with the requirements of the regulating nation; and (2) where assertion of jurisdiction is unreasonable, in view of all of the interests, contacts, and regulations. In the realm of antitrust, these limits put very little constraint on a nation's permissible jurisdiction to prescribe, and properly so. The same transaction or conduct frequently

---

and they try to do so. *See* Eleanor Fox, *The European Court's Judgment in GE/Honeywell—Not a Poster Child for Comity or Convergence*, ANTITRUST (Spring 2006).

15. This effort includes protecting against overregulatory outcomes, while giving room to competing perspectives. Overregulation also harms efficiency and consumers.

16. *See* Eleanor Fox & Janusz Ordover, *The Harmonization of Competition and Trade Law: The Case for Modest Linkages of Law and Limits to Parochial State Action*, 19 WORLD COMPETITION L. & ECON. REV. 5 (Dec. 1995).

17. Text at note 4 *infra*.

has effects in many nations of a sort that antitrust law typically condemns. Indeed, in contrast to the 1940s at the time of the *Alcoa* case,[18] it is now well recognized among antitrust authorities worldwide that no nation "owns" a merger, and that it is fair game for any jurisdiction whose consumers are likely to be significantly adversely affected to examine an offshore merger and to enjoin or condition it.[19] *A fortiori*, antitrust authorities of the world recognize the legitimacy and even the imperative of pursuing offshore and world cartels that harm their citizens.[20]

Of course nations need not and do not exercise their prescriptive powers to the full. In the recent *Empagran* case,[21] the U.S. Supreme Court determined that Congress meant to exclude from the Sherman Act private damage suits by foreigners who bought from a world cartel abroad unless the foreign victims were harmed by the cartel's anticompetitive effect in the United States.[22] If nations choose to do so, they can require their nationals not to harm foreigners abroad by conduct that is illegal at home. They generally do not choose to do so.[23]

National legislators predictably limit their country's laws to what they see as good for them (in the short term).[24] Thus, national antitrust laws normally exclude export cartels from their laws' reach.

V. A WORLD REGIME?

Thus far we have spoken of contemporary times. Few fora are devoted to "world antitrust" in contemporary times. But not long ago, the subject held center stage in conversations about the future of antitrust.

---

18. *Supra* note 1.

19. *See* Gencor Ltd. v. Commission Case IV/M 619, Commission Decision of Apr. 24, 1996, O.J. L 11/30 (1997) and Institut Mérieux S.A., Docket No. C-3301, 1990 FTC LEXIS 291 (FTC consent order, Aug. 23, 1990).

20. For the principal European case, *see Åhlström Osakeyhtiö v. Commission (Wood pulp)*, Joined Cases C-89/85, 104/85, 114/85, 116-117/85 & 125-129/85, 1988 ECR 5193.

21. *Supra* note 13. *See* Eleanor Fox, *Extraterritoriality in the Age of Globalization; Conflict and Comity in the Age of Empagran ("Empagran")*, ANTITRUST REPORT 3 (Issue 4, 2005).

22. This is a tortured reading of legislative intent. The relevant part of the statute—the Foreign Trade Antitrust Improvements Act of 1982 (FTAIA)—is much more naturally read to mean that the required effect on commerce must constitute a Sherman Act violation by reference to a section of the Sherman Act other than the FTAIA. *See* Fox, *supra* note 20.

23. Ironically, freeing *American businesses* from legal constraints on their acts that hurt foreigners was the prime reason Congress enacted the FTAIA, which, as noted, was interpreted to limit *foreigners'* rights under U.S. law.

24. In the longer term, export cartels hurt the exporting country. *See* Fox & Ordover, *supra* note 16.

The 1990s were the decade of reflection and debate about a world competition regime. The idea was generated principally by the European Union, whose officials understand, probably more than others, the cosmopolitan virtues of "community," including the juncture of free movement and free competition. In 1995, a European committee of Wise Men proposed an international competition system, with a home in the WTO.[25] The system would have started with building blocks of transparency, nondiscrimination and due process, cooperation, and assistance to developing economies. It would eventually have included a framework for substantive rules—against cartels, abuse of dominance, and the other commonly condemned restraints, as applied to cross-borders effects. It would have offered dispute resolution. The committee's concept was adopted in substantial part by the European Union. After criticism—especially from the United States—the European Union watered down its recommendations and proposed a modest form of international competition law that would have encompassed the first-stage building blocks of nondiscrimination, due process, cooperation, and assistance. It would have incorporated only one substantive rule—a rule against hard core cartels. It would have eliminated dispute resolution except for failure to fulfill clear obligations, e.g., failure to adopt a law against cartels. This more modest proposal was provisionally placed on the agenda of the Doha Development trade round of the World Trade Organization. The antitrust program was, however, jettisoned from the trade agenda after failure of initial trade negotiations (on agricultural subsidies) at the Cancun meeting in 2003.[26] Developing countries were not convinced that international competition rules would be good for them; WTO antitrust might be another Trojan horse, as many regarded the agreement on Trade-Related Aspects of Intellectual Property Rights.[27] The United States was not convinced that international competition rules would hold any benefit for America that it could not achieve on its own, and feared that antitrust at the bargaining table would produce a watering down of good law and create an unaccountable bureaucracy.[28]

---

25. Group of Experts' Report ("Van Miert Report") (1995). *See* European Commission, XXVIth Report on Competition Policy (1996), p. 95.

26. *See* Joseph Stiglitz & Andrew Charlton, Fair Trade for All: How Trade Can Promote Development (2005), Chapter 1.

27. *See, e.g.,* Joel Trachtman, *Legal Aspects of a Poverty Agenda at the WTO: Trade Law and 'Global Apartheid,'* 6 JIEL 3 (2003); Jerome Reichman, *From Free Riders to Fair Followers: Global Competition Under the Trips Agreement,* 29 N.Y.U. J. Int'l L. & Pol. 11 (1997).

28. *See* Klein, *supra* note 6.For a different explanation of the failure of an antitrust regime in the WTO, see Andrew T. Guzman, *Global Governance and the WTO,* 45 Harv. Int'l L.J. 303 (2004), and Anu Bradford, *International Antitrust Negotiations and the False Hope of the WTO,* 48 Harv. Int'l L.J. 383 (2007) (arguing that agreement has been frustrated by lack of flexibility and vision in pursuing cross-issue regulatory bargains and by other collective action problems).

Meanwhile, international cooperation was steadily improving, in part through the new, grass-roots-up ICN; and the threat of serious case-specific conflicts was alleviated by the organically occurring soft convergence. If there was a movement for a comprehensive higher-up law of competition in the 1990s and early 2000s, it seemed to have receded in the face of the networking wave of the "new world order,"[29] informed as it has been by the spirit of the rule of subsidiarity: what can be done just as well or better at a lower level should be done at the lower level.[30]

VI. WHERE TO GO FROM HERE

It seems clear that cooperation has lessened tensions and produced more coherence, and it should be continued and deepened. Cooperation, along with intensive cross-fertilization, has alleviated conflicts and has helped to construct a more nearly seamless world. Merger enforcement has improved. Cartel enforcement has improved. For developing countries, cooperation has helped to transfer useful knowledge, and, by anchoring agencies in a culture of competition, it has helped agencies stave off protectionism, parochialism, and excessive regulation.[31]

Still, big tasks remain. Cooperation and soft convergence solve only some of the major antitrust problems of the world.

In contemplating problems and solutions, we have been much enlightened by the conversations of the last two decades: the contemplation of the need for international antitrust, the debate regarding models, the dropping of the antitrust measures from the Doha agenda, the birth and blossoming of the ICN, which itself has spurred heightened performance of the OECD and the UNCTAD, the surge and appreciation of networking, and the imprint of the subsidiarity principle.

I have listed below nine problems, some overlapping, and I ask in each case what can be solved on a horizontal (national or nation-to-nation) level, and what remains for solution through higher law.

---

29. *See* Anne-Marie Slaughter, A NEW WORLD ORDER (2004).

30. *See* The Treaty on European Union, Article 5.

31. The norm against protectionism and parochialism is deeply engrained in competition policy and advocacy by antitrust enforcers, even if not embraced by politicians. For the point of view of the European Competition Directorate, see Neelie Kroes, *Industrial Policy and Competition Law and Policy*, Chapter 10 *in* 2006 FORDHAM COMPETITION LAW INST. (B. Hawk ed., 2009).

A. The Problem of Gaps

The world has more than one hundred antitrust laws, which in some cases stop at a nation's shores and which are riddled with exemptions and non-coverage, often in response to vested interests. The biggest, most obvious gap involves export cartels and world cartels particularly impacting outsiders. In part, this gap persists because of the practical disenfranchisement of victim jurisdictions that lack resources and information and are vulnerable.[32] The second biggest, most obvious gap is anticompetitive state action or involvement, including state blessing of cartels and monopolistic abuses that predominantly or significantly hurt foreigners. This gap persists because of the still Westphalian deference to the state as sovereign.[33]

Solutions may need to be devised at a higher level, for political economy realities keep nations from mustering the constituencies necessary to eliminate nationalistic restraints without reciprocal agreements by trading partners. The agreement called for is a "flanking" agreement to perfect nations' promises, already in the WTO, not to sponsor or encourage import or export cartels.[34]

Other steps can be taken at a grass roots level. The OECD Hard Core Cartel recommendation[35] urges signatory nations to reexamine periodically their exemptions from a "no cartel" rule and to eliminate unnecessary exemptions. This process is vital to world competition in matters affecting trade and investment. The beginnings of a framework for a multinational agreement can be built ground-up, starting with guidelines, principles, or best practices, possibly in the OECD or the ICN if the ICN should expand its purview from "antitrust all the time."

B. The Problem of Overlaps

A number of jurisdictions' antitrust laws may apply to the same conduct or transactions, and treatment may be inconsistent, conflicting, or overregulatory; remedies may be pile-up remedies.

In addressing overlap problems, the antitrust authorities of the world have made much progress through informal cooperation, with and without bilateral agreements. A very high level of cooperation and coordination has been attained, within limits of (often over-claimed) confidentiality obligations that prevent the

---

32. Otherwise, effects jurisdiction tends to fill the gap.

33. The concept of the Westphalian state reverts to the Peace of Westphalia of 1648, signifying the tight and strong notion of the sovereignty of the state. This has sometimes been referred to as the "billiard ball" theory of the state. I use the concept here in contrast with the porous state, involving pooled and shared competences to solve problems that transcend borders.

34. Agreement on Safeguards, Apr. 15, 1994, Marrakesh Agreement Establishing the World Trade Organization, 1869 U.N.T.S. 154, 159.

35. OECD Document No. C(98) 35/FINAL.

sharing of information. The high levels are visible in vetting transnational mergers and investigating cartels. Still, occasionally, outcomes in jurisdictions differ, either because of differences in legal principles, different appreciation of the appropriate application of the same legal principles, or different factual contexts.

A higher-level solution is generally not needed. An intensified level of cross-border communications by officials engaging with the particular facts of the particular case is normally the best solution. Overregulatory pile-on remedies can be avoided by a second jurisdiction's seriously regarding the remedies ordered by a first jurisdiction and attempting to make its remedies consistent and not duplicative.[36] Such an obligation of sympathetic consideration could be written into cooperation agreements and could also be developed as an international best practice in the context of the ICN.

There remains to be developed a principle for bridging ad hoc conflicts, such as occurred in the merger cases of *Boeing/McDonnell Douglas*[37] and *GE/Honeywell*.[38] The ICN is an ideal forum for working out a recommended or best practice. For example, where a second jurisdiction anticipates taking a course of action that conflicts with a first jurisdiction, a consensus principle might require that the second jurisdiction sympathetically consider the analysis, reasoning, and remedies of the first jurisdiction and exercise restraint in condemning an approved transaction or unduly burdening a conditional transaction, with a view to enhancing the economic welfare in the world.[39]

C. The Problem of Myopic or Bounded Concern

Nations deal with *their* problems. They are normally indifferent to harms abroad launched by their firms. They feel free to ignore negative externalities abroad. This is the "not my problem" problem: Let the victim nation protect itself, and if it does not have the resources, expertise, information, or practical power to induce outsiders to obey the law (often a universal rule), so be it.

This problem is integral with the problem of gaps, discussed above. Indeed, it provides one explanation for gaps. The cartel externality problem has a natural home in the WTO, as discussed above. As for mergers and monopolies—whose effects usually occur at home as well as abroad—the problems are more likely to evidence themselves as overlaps, not gaps, and to this extent are amenable to a horizontal solution.

---

36. *See* ICPAC Report 76–78. See also Eleanor Fox, Modernization of Effects Jurisdiction: From Hands-Off to Hands-Linked, 42 J. Int'l Law & Politics 159 (2009) ("Hands-Linked").

37. Boeing/McDonnell Douglas, Case IV 877, 1997 O.J. (L336) 16 (Dec. 8, 1997).

38. General Electric Co. v. Commission, Case T-210/01, [2005] ECR II-5575.

39. See Eleanor Fox, Hands-Linked, supra note 36.

D. The Problem of Parochialism: "Happy to Hurt You and Aggrandize Me"

Parochialism and vested interest lobbies provide another reason for gaps and selfish concern. Parochialism, when it exists, adds invidiousness to the restraint and underscores the importance of a common solution. Parochialism can be identified and condemned by, for example, an ICN principle. Indeed, discrimination based on nationality is already condemned by ICN merger principles.[40]

E. The Problem of Lack of a "Vision from the Top"

In many cases, problems are truly global and integral. This is the case, for example, with transnational mergers where markets transcend borders. Productive efficiencies at home may not inure to consumers or the market at large.

A make-do solution could come at a horizontal level. The solution requires a flexibility of law and remedies beyond state bounds. For example, as suggested by ICPAC, the forum having the most contacts might take on the project of analyzing the whole merger, its benefits, and its harms, wherever they fall. It might host interventions by other complaining jurisdictions and grant relief copious enough to cure problems worldwide as if the world were in its nation.[41] Best or recommended practices could be worked out in the ICN. The necessary flexible extension of law and process would need to be legislated by national legislators—not an easy task under today's norms. But norms might change if one is forced to confront the fact that the alternative is either disarray or centralized international antitrust.

F. The Problem of "Antitrust as an Island," Isolated from the Mainland of Political Economy

Antitrust is not an island unto itself. It is deeply interrelated with trade, foreign investment, free movement of goods, services and capital, the law of intellectual property, sectoral regulation, and the wide variety of proposed and actual industrial policies.

This is a problem in search of articulation. Witness the coming of age of antitrust in China,[42] the pressures on antitrust in the wake of the financial crisis,[43]

---

40. *See* www.internationalcompetitionnetwork.org (<Working Groups, Merger, Recommended Practices>).

41. ICPAC Report, 76–78.

42. In China, early merger enforcement activity indicates the state's inclination to prohibit foreign takeovers that might lead to loss of a major Chinese brand name even if there is no loss of rivalrous competition. Thus, in 2009, China enjoined Coca-Cola's acquisition of Huiyuan Fruit Juice Group.

43. *See* David Lewis, *Chilling Competition*, in INTERNATIONAL ANTITRUST LAW & POLICY, 2008 FORDHAM COMPETITION L. INST. (B. Hawk ed., 2009).

and the voices of the developing countries in the negotiations at the Doha trade round: distribution and equity matter.[44]

There is room for constructive work and debate regarding appropriate and inappropriate industrial policy. Because the debate sits on charged territory, serious debate is often suppressed. Work should be done at the WTO to narrow the bounds of permissible antidumping laws and subsidies. Work should also be done at a horizontal networking level, perhaps at the ICN. To begin, a working group can ask, in the context of financial crisis: What general principles define protective measures that may be helpful to a nation? What national measures are likely to be helpful to world welfare, and how can they be coordinated to that end? Which are harmful to world welfare, and how could and should they be discouraged?

G. The Problem of Inventing 100 Wheels When One Will Do (Better)

This is the problem of unnecessary and costly duplication. An example is premerger notification. More than fifty jurisdictions require premerger notification, filing, and waiting to complete covered mergers. Large multinational mergers must normally comply with the rules and process of each.

The ICN has explored this problem. It has adopted recommended practices regarding, for example, the earliest date on which filing is permitted, so that firms can coordinate their filings and the required nexus with the jurisdiction, so that nations do not reach out unduly to grasp and tax mergers that threaten them no harm. More work needs to be done. There is a need for a common clearing house option for merger filings, so that one document filed in one place can provide all of the necessary preliminary information.[45] This can be done horizontally—by agreement among the jurisdictions. The ICN can be the forum for working out the details.

H. The Special Problems of Developing and Transitional Countries

The special problems are threefold. First, developing countries and emerging regimes are often unable to protect themselves from offshore acts and transactions that harm them. They do not have the resources, the information, and the commanding practical power. Therefore, they are especially vulnerable. Second, the substantive rules of law most suitable for them are often different from the rules of law most suitable for developed economies with well-functioning markets, little statism, qualitatively less corruption, mature antitrust systems, and large expert staffs. Yet, when international standards are formulated, they

44. *See* The Growth Report, Strategies for Sustained Growth and Inclusive Development, Michael Spence, chair (2008), *available at http://www.growthcommission.org*.

45. *See* ICPAC Report, page 97 n.24, for a proposal by Eleanor Fox, as well as an explanation of the hurdles to achieving such a system.

commonly replicate those of the developed countries.[46] Third, and related to both points above, the developing countries and emerging antitrust jurisdictions need help; they need a transfer of knowledge and know-how useful to their own contexts.

The third problem identified above is best handled on a horizontal level and is being addressed, although it still requires more thinking and action. Technical assistance is delivered generally by more developed countries to less developed ones. The European Union, Germany, South Africa, Italy, the United States and other nations, and groups working with donors such as International Development Research Centre, have been generous providers of technical assistance. Peer reviews by the OECD and the UNCTAD have been extremely helpful. A pilot project of the ICN established channels for informal exchange of advice, pairing givers and receivers, all of whom conducted their work through telephone and the Internet.[47] Technical assistance can be deepened. On-the-ground technical assistance can be better coordinated. The problem of home-country bias in advice-giving can be addressed through awareness and consciousness raising, but not, in any event, through higher law.

The first problem—vulnerability, has been treated in part above. If altruism will not move national policy, a better appreciation of the local good as a function of the common good might help.[48] The better-situated nations could use their national legislative powers to require their nationals to account for all harms they cause by consensus violations (e.g., cartels),[49] and at least to expand their rules of discovery so that violators within their borders and the evidentiary trails they leave can be explored at the scene of the wrongful acts.

The vulnerability problem means that developing countries with poor legal systems not only are unlikely to deter incoming cartels but also are unlikely to provide a system that will compensate their citizens, even while victims abroad get considerable recoveries. This is both unfair and inefficient. The United States

---

46. *See* Eleanor Fox, *Linked-In: Antitrust and the Virtues of a Virtual Network*, 43 INT'L LAW. 151 (2009); Daniel Sokol, *Monopolists Without Borders: The Institutional Challenge of International Antitrust in a Global Gilded Age*, 4 BERKELEY BUS. L.J. 37 (2007).

47. *See* www.internationalcompetitionnetwork.org/uploads/library/doc514.pdf.

48. In matters of world cartels, for example, the international good is the local good. Connor; Fox, & Ordover, *The Harmonization of Competition and Trade Law: The Case for Modest Linkages of Law and Limits to Parochial State Action*, 19 WORLD COMPETITION L. & ECON. REV. 5 (Dec. 1995).

49. Progress has been made in other fields. An example is the Basel Convention on the Control of Transboundary Movements of Hazardous Wastes and their Disposal. Mar. 22, 1989, 1673 U.N.T.S. 125. The Basel Convention provides that any state that is party to the convention may prohibit import of hazardous wastes. The other parties to the agreement are then required to prohibit the export of hazardous wastes to the prohibiting country. Export cartels are the hazardous wastes of exporting countries.

has stepped back from the plate, by its holding in *Empagran*.[50] Nor are other countries likely to come to the aid.[51] This means that either the developing countries must accelerate their economic and institutional progress and capability in some substantial way to help themselves—perhaps through regional free trade groupings, which can give them critical mass (but this is a slow and uncertain process)—or a world or transnational system or resource must be developed, or the problem will remain unattended. For example, a specialized group might be charged with analyzing data regarding proven cartels, such as the vitamins, lycine, or air fuel cartels, with identifying who was overcharged by how much, and with administering a fund for payouts.[52]

The remaining problem is the problem of differential law and the likelihood that developed countries' law will be the international standard, even when it is not the best standard for developing countries, both because developed countries have the expertise and power to "sell" their standard and because developing countries may not have the expert staffs and advisors to develop and successfully advocate the standards that are best for them, even as a dual-track alternative.[53] This problem can be partially cured by regional groupings, by more and more learning, and by consciousness. In any event, it is a problem for horizontal solution. It cannot be solved, and indeed may be undermined, by top-down antitrust.

CONCLUSION

The lack of traction thus far of world antitrust in the WTO, the rise of networking, and the common sense attraction of subsidiarity have focused our thinking on lower-level solutions to world problems. Today we are searching for horizontal solutions.[54] We are less hopeful and less trustful that comprehensive higher law will solve real problems. At the same time, our intellectual travels over the last two decades have helped us to identify the situations in which only higher-level solutions will do. The one problem that may be fully resistant to lower-level solutions is outward-oriented harm (export/world cartels) and the trade-restrictive

---

50. *See supra* note 13.

51. *But see* Case No. 3622 (C2227), *Fiatimpresit-Mannesmann Demag-Techint/Italimpianti, Bolletino della Autorita Garante della Concorrenza e del Mercado*, Mar. 4, 1996 (Italian Antitrust Auth. Feb. 15, 1996), granting relief likely to help the country (China) that would suffer the anticompetitive effect of the merger.

52. This idea was suggested to me by my student, Laura Collins, N.Y.U. J.D. class of 2010.

53. *See supra* note 5.

54. A number of horizontal solutions were proposed by the ICPAC Report. Some of these have been referred to herein. For a more complete account, see Appendix A.

state action that supports it. For this problem, we need flanking principles in the WTO. Other desirable multilateral solutions, such as a common clearing house option for merger filings, multilateralization of cooperation agreements, and a center for data analysis of identified world cartels, can be addressed at a networking level. At least, development of models can begin at grass roots. The idea of a Doha Dome over a roots-up garden[55] was a good idea in 2003 and is a good idea today; the roots and their offshoots could grow under one canopy of open and free competition not distorted by cronyism, parochialism, and artificial borders. The dome is sure to be no more than a virtual roof over our heads. It can guide us toward a coherent framework. It cannot protect us from the rain and sleet; but it probably never would have done so, even in the headier days of the vision of one-world antitrust in the WTO.

55. *See* Eleanor Fox, *International Antitrust and the Doha Dome*, 43 VA. J. INT'L L. 911 (2003). The "Doha Dome" was the skeletal framework suggested by the Doha trade agenda: nondiscrimination, due process, cooperation, assistance, and an obligation of nations to adopt and maintain a rule against cartels. *See* text *supra* at notes 25–26.

APPENDIX A

Selected recommendations of the International Competition Advisory Committee to the Attorney General and Assistant Attorney General for Antitrust (2000)

Excerpt from Testimony of ELEANOR M. FOX
before the Antitrust Modernization Commission Hearing on International Issues
Washington, D.C., February 15, 2006

The ICPAC Report makes many recommendations on methodologies to enhance cooperation and eliminate unnecessary conflict in the case of international mergers and international cartels. I refer the Commission in particular to Chapter 2 (Mergers: Facilitating substantive convergence and minimizing conflict), Chapter 4 (Cartels: Interagency cooperation), and Chapter 5, third subsection (Positive comity).

ICPAC took a cosmopolitan approach. It recommended, among other things, expanding bilateral cooperation, including cooperation with newer competition systems[1] and it recommended including on a discussion agenda multilateralization of inter-jurisdictional cooperation.[2]

ICPAC emphasized multi-jurisdictional work-sharing in merger review:

"The Advisory Committee views the creation of a nearly seamless multijurisdictional merger review system as the ultimate goal of all of these efforts toward expanded cooperation and coordination."[3]

Cooperation at the merger remedy stage was singled out for its importance. ICPAC suggested:

> In some cases it may be feasible to have only *one jurisdiction negotiate remedie with the merging parties that will address the concerns of both that jurisdiction and other interested jurisdictions*. In other words, the reviewing jurisdictions would identify the remedies necessary to address their competitive concerns, and the jurisdiction best positioned to negotiate and obtain the desired remedies would do so. An approach of this kind, for example, was successfully employed by the United States and the EU in the Halliburton/Dresser transaction. There, rather than negotiating separate undertakings with the merging parties, the EC relied on the provisions of a U.S. consent decree to satisfy its concerns regarding a perceived global problem in drilling fluids.[4]

---

1. ICPAC Report, p. 200.
2. *Id.*, p. 284.
3. *Id.*, p. 76.
4. *Id.*, p. 77, noting use of this approach also in Federal Mogul/T&N.

ICPAC also underlined the importance of work-sharing at the review state. It said:

In appropriate cases, it may be beneficial to limit the number of jurisdictions conducting independent second-stage reviews of a proposed transaction. Where the concerns of one country are likely to be the same as and subsumed by the concerns of a more distinctly affected investigating jurisdiction, it may be appropriate for the first country to refrain from independent investigation.

* * *

One way to safeguard against the possibility that the proceeding agency may reach a different result on the merits or a remedy different from the one the other jurisdictions might have reached, while at the same time gaining efficiency in the process and other potential benefits is to ensure sufficient participation in the process by the other jurisdictions. One jurisdiction could coordinate the investigation of a proposed transaction, take into account the views of each interested jurisdiction, and recommend remedies to address the concerns of all interested jurisdictions.[5]

ICPAC considered yet more advanced work-sharing as a vision for the future. It described this as follows:

The Advisory Committee also considered whether an even higher level of work sharing might be possible after more procedural and substantive convergence among merger review regimes has occurred. At this advanced level of work sharing, the coordinating agency would be required to accept the mantle of *parens patriae* for world competition. Accordingly, it would endeavor to evaluate procompetitive and anticompetitive effects of a proposed transaction on a global scale, taking into account all of the merger's costs and benefits to competition, not only the net effects within its borders. This approach arguably is superior to an approach in which each jurisdiction analyzes the effects of a proposed transaction within its own borders and ignores the

5. *Id.*, pp. 78, 80 (footnote omitted). The Report continues:

Under this advanced work-sharing arrangement, the coordinating agency would perform a centralized information gathering function following initial notification by the merging parties to all reviewing agencies. The coordinating agency would then assess the competitive effects of the proposed transaction in all relevant product and geographic markets. Each interested jurisdiction would be invited to submit comments to the coordinating jurisdiction regarding its particular concerns. The assessment of the coordinating agency would be binding on the coordinating agency but could either serve as a recommendation to other interested jurisdictions (with a presumption in favor of accepting the recommendation) or be binding on those jurisdictions as well.

harms or the benefits that the transaction may generate elsewhere. Multimarket assessment would position the coordinating jurisdiction to account for what had previously been viewed as externalities, thereby enabling it to assess the net effects of the proposed transaction (under a neutral welfare standard) on a global scale. The coordinating jurisdiction could then design remedies to address the concerns of all interested jurisdictions.[6]

For my own part, as a member of ICPAC, I suggested two further initiatives; one to put a check on overregulation, and one to provide a path to resolve system clashes. I quote below from the relevant portion of my Separate Statement.[7]

Overregulation: Globalization has put pressure on our system in which the laws of numerous nations apply to the same conduct or transaction. The pressure comes especially at the point at which competition law is regulatory rather than liberalizing; paradigmatically, premerger notification filing-and-waiting regimes. In this area, sound regulation requires coordination, and modes adopted by the European Union for its internal market are often instructive. I would go further than the Advisory Committee to propose an opportunity for mutual recognition of premerger notification filings when the market of a would-be regulating nation is subsumed by the broader global market.[8]

System clashes: We must find international solutions for systems clashes, probably with international dispute resolution. Actual cases provide helpful laboratories. Boeing's acquisition of McDonnell Douglas—which the U.S. cleared and the EU threatened to enjoin [and which nearly accelerated into a trade war]—is such a case. . . .

---

6. *Id.*, p. 81.

7. Separate Statement of Eleanor M. Fox, ICPAC Report, Annex 1-A.

8. I spelled out my proposal for an opt-in clearing house system as follows at ICPAC Report, p. 97, Chap. 3, footnote 24:

> Advisory Committee Member Eleanor M. Fox suggests another approach to facilitate efficient coordination of filings and reduce the burden on parties of multiple notifications. She proposes a common clearinghouse for premerger notification by firms that elect to opt into such a system. One way to achieve this would be to permit the merging parties to file with a disinterested clearinghouse center on the day of the first filing. Alternatively, if the first filing is in a mature antitrust jurisdiction and covers international markets where all or most of the impacts would occur, all interested nations would be bound to accept the first filing as their first and basic information about the merger. The notified center or jurisdiction would announce the filing to member nations (or to interested or potentially interested nations). The recipient agencies would be bound to use the information only for merger review. Any country receiving the announcement that believes its system requires notification of the transaction could request a copy of the notification. A copy of this request would go to the merging parties who could contest the jurisdiction of a requesting country before the filing is sent to that country.

There are various possible agreements that nations might consider that would keep an international merger on track as a competition case and prevent diversion into a trade war. The Advisory Committee has proposed several progressive measures, on the order of transparency.

I believe that we must move further, in view of the need for a world view and in view of the fact that conflict will otherwise always be resolved in favor of the nation that imposes the most aggressive remedies. In the absence of international rules and dispute resolution, we may eventually find it necessary to give the nation at the center of gravity a trumping right to enjoin or allow the merger (while other interested nations might retain the right to implement more modest, tightly tailored relief). But if any nation is, legitimately, to wear the mantle of *parens patriae* for the world, it would be obliged to count all costs of the merger, even those outside of its borders, as if they fell within its borders.[9] Indeed, we may reach the point—not just in merger law—at which counting all costs is an important obligation of all competition authorities vetting international transactions.

If national authorities do not broaden their perspectives to count all costs of conduct or transactions by their firms, we will probably move to international antitrust sooner rather than later, for these problems are world problems.[10]

Finally, as reflected above, many potential clashes can be diffused. The best way to diffuse them is not to decree comity or convergence but to solidify norms of talking, listening, reasoning and engaging. When authorities appear to be reaching different evaluations, e.g., of whether a multinational merger is anticompetitive, the authorities should explore and then pin-point for one another exactly where their differences lie, identifying inferences, presumptions, premises, and

---

9. My Separate Statement cross-references to the ICPAC Report, p. 64, Chap. 2, footnote 72, which reads as follows: Advisory Committee Member Eleanor M. Fox calls attention to the problem of clashes where one nation decides that a merger is anticompetitive and should be enjoined and another nation decides that a merger is procompetitive and should be allowed. In the absence of formal protocols for resolving the clash, the more restrictive nation always prevails. This member suggests that development of rules of priority in deciding to enjoin or not to enjoin and international merger may be needed. To be entitled to exercise such right of priority, however, the privileged jurisdiction would be required to accept the mantle of *parens patriae* for world competition. Accordingly, it would be obliged to count not only the net benefits within its borders, but all of the merger's costs and benefits to competition (under whatever neutral framework for analysis it applies). *See* Eleanor M. Fox, Extraterritoriality and Merger Law: Can All Nations Rule the World? Antitrust Report 2, Dec. 1999.

10. [Footnote 7 in Separate Statement of Eleanor M. Fox:] One appropriate "higher" solution would provide for international dispute resolution. The panel would begin to resolve the dispute by choice of law based on center of gravity. Thus, in Boeing/McDonnell Douglas, the panel would apply the U.S. rule to the true market.

critical evidence. By that means, they may be able to resolve differences. If not, they should be able to understand the basis of divergence.

I propose that the AMC consider recommending that the following three norms be adopted by competition authorities and, where appropriate, commissions and courts. The norms could be adopted in the context of ICN.

1. In matters involving cross-border spill-overs, competition authorities and courts should be sensitive to the perspectives of other enforcing nations that have ruled on or are addressing substantially the same problem. Where consistent with their law and goals, they should sympathetically consider integrating other nations' perspectives or relevant acts into their own thinking and analysis.
2. They should recognize existing relief decreed by another jurisdiction as contextual background, and strive to avoid unnecessary regulation.
3. In the event that a second nation takes jurisdiction over conduct or structure roughly within pronouncements of a jurisdiction that proceeds first, the decision-maker should write a reasoned opinion that engages with the first nation's perspective. By attentive and engaged process, some divergent outcomes may be avoided, and others legitimized.

14. FUTURE DIRECTIONS IN BILATERAL COOPERATION

A Policy Perspective

MAHER M. DABBAH*

I. INTRODUCTION

There is always a particular challenge to any discussion of bilateral cooperation in the field of competition law. This challenge is heightened when the aim is to consider the topic from a policy perspective. It can never escape one's attention that a great deal of ink has been poured on the topic, to the extent that one must wonder whether there is anything new to be added without necessarily repeating the account already offered in the literature. When considered carefully, however, the picture that seems to emerge in relation to the topic is that certain of its aspects—particularly the benefits that may arise from cooperating bilaterally—remain in need of further debate, especially for the purposes of exploring the possible future directions of bilateral cooperation in the field.

In offering a policy perspective, this chapter aims to tackle the question of how the mechanism of bilateral cooperation can fulfill its great potential. The chapter is structured as follows: Part II considers briefly the meaning of the term bilateral cooperation, especially how it is intended in the context of the present chapter. Part III highlights the different types of bilateral cooperation. Part IV offers a number of examples from practice on the bilateral cooperation between the European Union (EU) and U.S. competition authorities. Part V reflects on the status quo of bilateral cooperation. Finally, part VI looks to the future.

II. MEANING OF BILATERAL COOPERATION

For the avoidance of doubt, the term bilateral cooperation is used here in a considerably wider sense than that of bilateral cooperation agreements between two jurisdictions, whether those with negative comity[1] and/or positive

---

* Director, Interdisciplinary Centre for Competition Law and Policy (ICC), Queen Mary, University of London; Barrister of the Middle Temple. Special thanks are due to Sara Jameel for excellent research assistance.

1. Negative comity in this sense refers to mutual civility or courtesy shown by different sides: two parties showing mutual good manners, moderation, and self restraint.

comity[2] principle. It is true that these agreements—especially those with positive comity principle—have become the dominant form of bilateral cooperation in the field of competition law in recent years, and that they are united as situations of cooperation which are "competition-specific." Nevertheless, experience shows that bilateralism can be achieved in a variety of other ways, such as informal or *de facto* positive comity cooperation, free trade agreements, general economic cooperation agreements, association and partnership agreements, and even links established with entire regions (such as the Euro-Med and Neighborhood Agreements between the EU and Mediterranean countries). While these *means* of bilateral cooperation are not "competition-specific"—since in these cases the competition component is one element of a wider cooperation agreement or framework—they possess enormous importance in practice and have, among other things, contributed to advancing competition law globally.

I am aware that such interpretation of bilateralism goes well beyond the traditional, narrow meaning of the term.[3] However this wider interpretation is adopted here—specifically—because the term is not at all traditional. Nor is it, in fact, one to be narrowly understood. Bilateralism is an evolving concept that is

---

The incorporation of this particular concept into formal bilateral cooperation agreements in the field of competition law made them "first generation" agreements. *See, e.g.*, the USA-Germany Antitrust Accord (1976).

2. Bilateral agreements incorporating a positive comity principle represent a "second generation" of such agreements, which arguably came to emerge due to the inadequacy of negative comity agreements coupled with an increase in the complexity of competition law practice and enforcement, and an increase in parallel in the trust and confidence competition authorities developed between them. Positive comity agreements rest on a *positive* mechanism of actions, through which cooperation between competition authorities can be facilitated. The idea underlying this positive mechanism is quite simple to express: one party to the agreement (known as the requesting party) can ask the other party (known as the requested party) to address anticompetitive behavior within the latter's boundaries, which has effect on the interests of the former. The concept of positive comity therefore differs from that of negative comity in the context of bilateral cooperation in the sense that in the former situation, the parties do not pursue a minimum objective of preventing jurisdictional conflicts, which is the cornerstone of negative comity cooperation. The positive nature of comity here requires *positive* actions to be taken by the parties to achieve cooperation and offer reciprocal assistance within the framework of their agreement. These positive actions include—very crucially—a renunciation by one party of its right in favor of the other party, who would normally be in a better position to conduct an investigation in a given case. Examples of these agreements include the U.S.-EU agreements, U.S.-Brazil agreement, U.S.-Canada agreement, U.S.-Israel agreement, U.S.-Japan agreement, U.S.-Mexico agreement, EU-Japan agreement, and EU-Canada agreement.

3. The traditional meaning given to bilateral cooperation in the field of competition law has revolved around the existence of a bilateral cooperation agreement between *two* jurisdictions.

conditioned by different developments both from within and outside the field of competition law. The term bilateral cooperation should be understood in such a considerably wide sense in order to capture *all* situations in which the competition authorities of two jurisdictions are able to coordinate their activities, cooperate in various ways to enhance their respective enforcement efforts, and strive to eliminate any risk of conflict in their lines of work. This cooperation can be achieved with or without a formal mechanism for cooperation, meaning with or without a formal agreement between the jurisdictions concerned. The exact meaning of the concept very much depends on the context in which it is used and the aim or objective sought behind bilateral cooperation. To understand this particular last point, it is important to consider the aims of bilateral cooperation.

III. AIMS OF BILATERAL COOPERATION

Bilateral cooperation does not necessarily aim at one specific objective. Rather, a number of goals can be identified. Generally, these goals have been dressed up as the different benefits of bilateral cooperation, which the Organisation for Economic Co-operation and Development (OECD) has most famously attempted to advocate. These benefits have been identified as follows: improved effectiveness of the enforcement mechanism of the parties to the cooperation, improved efficiency in competition investigations, reduced need for sharing confidential and other information, avoidance of jurisdictional conflict, protection for the legitimate interests of the cooperating parties, and relief for firms from having to deal with more than one competition authority and from having to be faced with the risk of inconsistent decisions by two authorities.

This list of benefits, however, is not conclusive, and other benefits may be found. One crucial benefit flowing from bilateral cooperation is convergence. Convergence deserves particular emphasis because, among other things, it is a long-term benefit that goes beyond individual cases or isolated instances of cooperation toward developing a policy perspective on the whole exercise of understanding and applying competition law. To put things in the context of the present book, convergence here supports the role of bilateral cooperation as one of the strategies to internationalize competition law and policy.[4] The other notable strategies are multilateral cooperation, and, to a lesser extent, extraterritoriality.[5]

It is this aspect of bilateral cooperation that will be the main focus in this chapter since it is here that future directions are worth considering.

---

4. For a general discussion, see Maher M. Dabbah, The Internationalisation of Antitrust Policy (Cambridge Univ. Press 2003).

5. *See* Chapter 2_ for a discussion of extraterritoriality.

IV. EXAMPLES

It is generally agreed that the most obvious example of bilateralism in the field of competition law is furnished by the EU/U.S. cooperation. This is also the most important example because these two competition law regimes are the world's most advance and most influential. This latter point is of particular significance since, normally, one would expect little interest on the part of a powerful competition authority or the decision or policy makers in a strong competition law regime to move closer to another (rival) regime. Despite this seemingly natural conclusion, the EU and U.S. authorities have entered into two crucial bilateral cooperation agreements, namely the 1991[6] and 1998[7] agreements.

The EU/U.S. cooperation has had a number of positive outcomes in practice. Perhaps the most important of these has been the impressive degree of convergence achieved between the two regimes. This convergence has been made possible because the bilateral cooperation between the parties enabled them to better understand each other's competition law and policy and their respective approaches to various important issues of enforcement and analysis, and to strengthen their individual enforcement efforts and avoid many unnecessary divergences in their decisional practice that might lead to conflict.

The area of merger control especially features instances of convergence, with the European Commission's more economic-based approach in the appraisal of mergers under EU Regulation 139/2004 and the use—on occasion—by U.S. competition authorities of important EU-based concepts such as that of "dominance." For example, in the case of *Office Depot/Staples*,[8] the U.S. Federal Trade Commission utilized this concept in its opposition to the proposed merger between the parties: according to it, the merger would have created a dominant entity in the office supply market. This is highly notable given that the dominance test does not *stricto senso* feature in the substantive test contained in Section 7 of the U.S. Clayton Act of 1914 which refers to mergers leading to "substantial lessening of competition or tending to create a monopoly."[9]

Convergence between the EU and U.S. competition law regimes can be most notably seen in the *modus operandi* of EU and U.S. competition authorities. One of the major benefits of the U.S.-EU cooperation has been the creation of a *framework* for their competition officials to coordinate their enforcement efforts and to develop a common platform on which such coordination can grow. For example, the competition officials of one authority are able to attend proceedings within

---

6. EU/U.S. Competition Cooperation Agreement—Official Journal 95, 27.4.1995 pp. 47–52.

7. EU/U.S. Positive Comity Agreement—Official Journal L 173 of 18.06.1998, pp. 28–31.

8. FTC v. Staples, Inc., 977 F. Supp. 1066 (D.D.C. 1997).

9. Clayton Act, 15 U.S.C §§ 12–27.

the other under the 1999 Administrative Agreement on Attendance. Such attendance has happened in a number of important merger cases, including *Air Liquide/BOC,*[10] in which officials of the Federal Trade Commission attended an oral hearing within the European Commission, and *MCI WorldCom/Sprint,*[11] in which officials of the European Commission attended the "pitch" meeting between the Antitrust Division of the U.S. Department of Justice and the merging parties.[12]

The coordination of enforcement efforts between the EU and the United States, however, has not been limited to attendance and has extended to exchange of information discussing substantive issues in the relevant case and taking note of decisions adopted in the other regime. For example, in the case of *Exxon/Mobil,*[13] there was close coordination between the European Commission and the U.S. Federal Trade Commission on their appraisal of the transaction in question. Cooperation in this instance covered exchanging information, including confidential information, since the parties waived their right to confidentiality. Similar cooperation can be seen in cases such as *Allied Signal/Honeywell*[14] and *AstraZeneca/Novartis.*[15]

In the former case, *Allied Signal/Honeywell,* the coordination between the Antitrust Division of the U.S. Department of Justice and the European Commission ensured that they were able to discuss issues of market definition and the suitability of the divestiture remedies proposed by the merging parties. Discussing the latter was particularly important—especially for the European Commission—since the largest chunk of the assets in questions were located in the United States. In the latter case, *AstraZeneca/Novartis,* there were particularly helpful discussions between the U.S. Federal Trade Commission and the European Commission concerning the issue of remedies in the case: the authorities appreciated that commitments would have to be implemented worldwide, and, by conducting parallel negotiations with the merging parties and assessing the remedies together, they were able to avoid the risk of incompatible remedies.

---

10. Case No. COMP/M.1630 (January 20, 2000).

11. Case No. COMP/M.1741 (June 28, 2000).

12. Pitch meeting are meetings held by the Antitrust Division at the final stage of proceedings in merger cases.

13. File No. 991 0077; Docket No. C-3907 (U.S.) and Case No. IV/M.1383 (Sept. 29, 1999) (EU).

14. United States v. Allied Signal Inc. & Honeywell Inc., No. 99-2959, 2000 U.S. Dist. LEXIS 15099 (D.D.C. Mar. 22, 2000) and Allied Signal/Honeywell Case No. COMP/M.1601 (Dec. 1, 1999) (EU).

15. No. 001 0082; Docket No. C-3979 (U.S.) and Case No. COMP/M.1806 (July 26, 2000) (EU) Case No. COMP/M.1806 (July 26, 2000) (EU).

In another notable case, *Oracle/PeopleSoft*,[16] there was a highly important example of interaction between the two regimes with the European Commission taking into account developments in the case on the other side of the Atlantic. The Antitrust Division of the U.S. Department of Justice had decided to object to the merger in line with a view it shared with the European Commission that the merger was likely to give rise to competition problems in the relevant market, the market for software applications for automated financial management systems and human resources processes. This, however, was later rejected by the U.S. District Court (as far as the Department of Justice's position is concerned) because it found gaps in the definition of the relevant market. The European Commission embraced the views of the District Court and decided to clear the merger. The existence of the bilateral cooperation agreement between the United States and the EU meant that the European Commission was able to take into account evidence gathered as part of the proceedings before the District Court, something that doubtfully would have been possible in the absence of the agreement and the enforcement coordination it facilitated.

All of the above-mentioned cases show that the coordination has created many linkage points for the competition authorities on both sides of the Atlantic to make their bilateral cooperation as effective and meaningful as possible. This is of benefit not only to the authorities themselves but also to firms, who may have a number of concerns when their conduct, behavior, or transactions are investigated by more than one competition authority.

Clearly, the authorities have the interests of firms in mind. For example, in 2002, the EU and U.S. authorities published their Best Practices on Cooperation in Merger Investigations,[17] a highly important step that opened the door to *synchronization* of the merger review timetable on both sides of the Atlantic and *exchange of information* and analytical data on matters such as market definition, effects on competition, and merger efficiencies. The Best Practices also include directions for merging parties themselves, such as those aiming to encourage the parties to consider waiving their right to confidentiality in order to enable the authorities to exchange confidential information between them, which, in turn, can be very useful to the parties themselves.

The 1991 and 1998 EU/U.S. cooperation agreements have contributed significantly to bringing these two important competition law regimes closer to each other. Following the adoption of the agreements, the number of cases in which consultation and coordination of enforcement efforts have taken place grew phenomenally. The agreements also transformed contact between officials at the European Commission, the Antitrust Division of the U.S. Department of

16. Case No., C 04-0807 VRW (U.S.) and Case No. COMP/M.3216 (Oct. 26, 2004) (EU).

17. Oct. 30, 2002, *available at* http://www.ftc.gov/opa/2002/10/mergerbestpractices.shtm.

Justice, and the Federal Trade Commission from an infrequent occurrence to a daily routine in the work of the three authorities. These daily contacts have been prominent in the area of merger control. The advanced stage which the daily cooperation between the EU and the United States has reached in the area of merger control deserves special emphasis given the fact that both parties apply different procedural and substantive rules in the field of competition law in general and the area of merger control in particular.

V. REFLECTIONS: ASSESSING THE STATUS QUO

The comments made in the previous part on the EU/U.S. case show a positive outlook in relation to bilateral cooperation. However, a critical assessment is called for in order to verify whether this outlook is indeed positive.

The most remarkable aspect of the EU/U.S. cooperation is not how impressive this particular bilateral cooperation has been, nor the fact that it has brought two very different competition law regimes together. Rather, what is remarkable is that these examples, along with others, actually constitute the *exception* as opposed to the *rule*. The EU/U.S. example is a good one to inspire others to follow it, but it is far from being representative of the field.

Assessing whether the outlook of bilateral cooperation in general is positive requires widening the lenses to be able to look at a number of issues.

A. Has Bilateral Cooperation Fulfilled its Objectives?

To be frank, it is not clear there is full consensus that bilateral cooperation between competition authorities—wherever it exists in the form of an agreement—has achieved its objective. Even if we take the EU/U.S. example, many people have pointed to the shortcoming of the 1991 and 1998 agreements in completely fulfilling the aim of avoiding likely conflicting outcomes in competition cases, let alone offering a proper forum to deal with or solve disputes when these actually arise. Critics of this important example of bilateral cooperation often point to the always present, unavoidable possibility of conflict between the two regimes. Indeed, divergences do and can occur between the EU and the United States as seen from merger cases such as *GE/Honeywell International,*[18] *Boeing/McDonnell Douglas,*[19] and *Ciba-Geigy/Sandoz.*[20] In fairness, however, these cases of divergence have been extremely few indeed and, on the whole, can be explained with reference to the nature of the merger review process

18. Department of Justice Press Release, May 2, 2001 (U.S.) and Case No. COMP/M.2220 (July 3, 2001) (EU).

19. File No. 971 0051 (U.S.) and Case No. COMP/M.877 (July 30, 1997).

20. File No. 961 0055; Docket No. C-3725 (U.S.) and Case No. COMP/M.737 (July 17, 1996) (EU).

(prediction of future impact of operations from a present point when not all the facts may necessarily be complete or clear), the use of different theoretical models, and possible differences in outlook concerning the assessment of merger remedies.

For example, *GE/Honeywell* showed, among other things, the European Commission's concern over conglomerate effects, which were not taken into account by the U.S. Antitrust Division of the Department of Justice. In *Ciba-Geigy/Sandoz,* the U.S. Federal Trade Commission and the European Commission diverged not on the question of whether the merger was likely to create adverse effect in the market for crop protection and animal health (on which in fact they agreed), but rather on the extent of the remedies the parties needed to propose in order to eliminate all competition concerns. In the case, the U.S. Federal Trade Commission thought that the remedies proposed by the parties were not sufficient to address its concerns while the European Commission was satisfied with the remedy. Nonetheless, what must be recognized is that the possibility of divergence is always there and that this can be a serious issue.

B. How Much Cooperation?

In most cases of bilateral cooperation between competition authorities, the extent of cooperation appears to be ambiguous. Generally, there is an abundance of reporting that cooperation took place without, however, detailing how cooperation ensued and how extensive it was. For example, in the famous *Vitamins* cartel, following the announcement of an investigation by U.S. competition authorities for cartel practices in the vitamins market against Hoffmann La Roche, Basf Aktiengesellschaft, and Aventis (now Rhône-Poulenc), several competition authorities opened their own investigations. This included the Secretariat of Economic law (*Secretaria de Direito Econômico,* the "SDE") of Brazil. The SDE widely reported that cooperation took place with the U.S. competition authorities, but no detail has been given as to the extent of the cooperation. Another example is the *Lysine* cartel. The Brazilian SDE reported that a "great deal" of documents were obtained with the cooperation of the Antitrust Division of the U.S. Department of Justice without specifying what documents were obtained in the case.

C. What Is the Scope of Cooperation?

There is a clear lack of certainty as to whether cooperation—in the cases where this has extended to an exchange of information—covered *all* information in the possession of the relevant competition authorities. However, the position seems to be certain with respect to confidential information: the competition authorities engaged in bilateral cooperation have consistently maintained that the sharing of information, even if it involves the disclosure of documents, never includes confidential information where the relevant parties' consent has not been obtained.

This is not something, however, on which practitioners in the relevant regime can agree with confidence.[21]

Obviously, the issue of confidential information is a very difficult and sensitive one in practice. It has been said repeatedly that a major shortcoming or limitation from which bilateral cooperation seems to suffer relates to the exclusion of provisions allowing the exchange of confidential information. Competition authorities are unable to share confidential business information among themselves without the consent of the firms involved or a clear authorization under law. On the one hand, firms themselves may benefit from waiver of the right to confidentiality when their transactions are being reviewed by two authorities who have a bilateral cooperation agreement between them.[22] The lack of ability on the part of such authorities to exchange confidential information therefore might affect the interests of these firms because this may make it very difficult, if not impossible, for these authorities to conduct comprehensive investigations that are often in the best interests of merging parties. Indeed, even in the United States—arguably the country with the strongest tendency to opt for unilateral actions in the field of competition law—such a situation has been recognized.

In 1994, the U.S. Congress passed the International Antitrust Enforcement Assistance Act which permits the U.S. competition authorities to obtain and exchange with foreign competition authorities, where relevant, confidential information.[23] The Act also provides that U.S. authorities may open proceedings to obtain such information from U.S. nationals on behalf of foreign authorities, subject to their being satisfied that the latter will safeguard the confidentiality of the information and undertake to ensure reciprocity. A similar position exists in other competition law regimes. For example, under the Dutch competition law regime, the Netherlands competition authority can exchange confidential information obtained during the course of an investigation with foreign competition authorities. However the authority may do so only where the following are satisfied: the confidentiality of the information is sufficiently protected, adequate assurance is given that the information will not be used for purposes other than the enforcement of the foreign competition law, and disclosure of the information in question must be in the interest of the Dutch economy. Other examples

21. Japan may be used as an example here.

22. *See, e.g.*, the case of *Exxon/Mobil, supra* note 13.

23. 15 U.S.C §§ 6201–6212. U.S. authorities are permitted to disclose "antitrust evidence" to their foreign counterparts. In Section 6211, "antitrust evidence" is defined so as not to exclude confidential information as it covers any "information, testimony, statements, documents, or other things that are obtained in anticipation of, or during the course of, an investigation or proceeding under any of the Federal antitrust laws or any of the foreign antitrust laws."

can be found in Article 29 of the Malta Competition Act[24] and the Competition Ordinance of Pakistan.[25]

On the other hand, waiver of the right to confidentiality by firms may involve certain risks for them in cases where this information ends up in the hands of competitors or customers who might then abuse it or use it to launch their own actions against such firms. These are risks that are particularly high in competition law regimes that have a private enforcement strand.

D. Does the Existence of Formal Cooperation Agreements Actually Result in Formal Cooperation?

In practice, the formal cooperation agreements entered into by some competition authorities have resulted in virtually no instances of actual cooperation as stipulated under the relevant agreement. Indeed, in the case of certain competition authorities, despite an extensive web of bilateral agreements having been established, actual cooperation has not gone beyond being academic. For example the Ukraine has entered into agreements with Georgia, Azerbaijan, the Russian Federation, Lithuania, Poland, Hungary, Bulgaria, and the Czech Republic, among other countries, to no avail. On the other hand, there are instances in which—notwithstanding the absence of a formal agreement—competition authorities have opted for full and meaningful cooperation, which has included exchanging information in actual cases. A notable example here is the cooperation between Chile and the United States.

Obviously, the chances of meaningful cooperation, including exchange of information—notwithstanding the absence of an agreement—will be enhanced enormously by the existence of general laws in the country(ies) concerned,[26] bilateral agreements of general economic nature,[27] and international treaties.[28]

---

24. Act XXXI of 1994, as amended, *available at* http://www.unctad.org/sections/ditc_ccpb/docs/ditc_ccpb_ncl_Malta_en.pdf.

25. Competition Ordinance 2010, *available at* http://www.cc.gov.pk/.

26. *See, e.g.*, Act 24,767 in Argentina, which governs international cooperation in relation to criminal prosecution, adjudication, and application of penalties and makes it an obligation on Argentina to provide assistance to any country offering reciprocity or having ratified an international treaty to this effect.

27. See the Japan-Philippines Economic Partnership agreement which was entered into in September 2006. Although no specific cooperation agreement in the field of competition exists between the parties, the Agreement provides for cooperation between them in the field.

28. A few notable examples can be found here, including: the Inter-American Convention on Mutual Assistance in Criminal Matters, which makes it a binding obligation on parties to render to one another mutual assistance in relation to criminal investigations, proceedings, and prosecutions; the Civil, Commercial, Labour and Administrative Cooperation Protocol (Las Leñas Protocol) within which Argentina, Brazil, Uruguay, and Paraguay have undertaken to provide mutual assistance and wide cooperation in civil

Additionally, especially important here is whether compatibility exists between the laws of the countries concerned with regard to the nature of competition offenses, most importantly whether they are considered to be of civil or criminal nature under the competition law regimes of these countries.

VI. LOOKING AHEAD

The points made here serve to show that there are serious shortcomings, limitations, and ambiguities surrounding bilateral cooperation which, until now, have not been addressed properly. In the absence of specific measures or commitments aimed at tackling these problems, there is room, therefore, for one to consider how bilateral cooperation can be enhanced in the future.

The factors giving rise to the shortcomings, limitations, and ambiguities surrounding bilateral cooperation cannot be grouped together when thinking about possible solutions or suggestions for improvement. For example, the issue of confidential information cannot be coupled with that of conflicting outcomes and dispute resolution. The former may simply be addressed under national law or international treaty, whereas the latter would require a mechanism, such as a forum, to resolve the dispute For example, the OECD in its recommendations offers competition authorities the option of making use of its "good offices."[29]

In contemplating the future, I do not consider all of these aspects of bilateral cooperation. Rather, the interest here is to focus on the underlying theme of the discussion offered on bilateral cooperation in the use of bilateralism as an *international strategy* and its desirable outcome of convergence and advancing competition law. All of the shortcomings, limitations, and ambiguities notwithstanding, bilateral cooperation has been a highly important option through which competition law and policy have come to be considerably internationalized over the years. Bilateral cooperation has emerged in recent years as an important topic in the field of competition law generally, and in practice it has been playing a significant role in the application and enforcement of competition rules in different parts of the world.

However, looking ahead, it seems that bilateralism has a huge potential that remains unfulfilled as a strategy for internationalizing competition law. This is mainly so for two reasons. First, there is the lack of a *center of gravity* that could

enforcement matters; the Inter-American Convention on the Taking of Evidence Abroad, adopted under the auspices of the Organization of American States, which governs the execution of letters rogatory and establishes a framework for cooperation between the parties; and the Hague Convention on the Service Abroad of Judicial and Extrajudicial Documents in Civil or Commercial Matters 1965.

29. *See* Part IB paragraph 8 of the Recommendations on bilateral cooperation, *available at* http://www.oecd.org/dataoecd/60/42/21570317.pdf.

pull the different strands of bilateralism together and ensure that a coherent long-term vision is built with regard to how the vehicle of bilateralism can and should be driven along the internationalization of competition law route. Second, there is the *lack of sufficient knowledge* about the extent of bilateral cooperation at present and the prospects for developing it.

The discussion will now look at these two reasons in turn.

A. A Center of Gravity

Until now, bilateralism has been developed mostly in a piecemeal fashion: some competition authorities have taken the initiative to forge bilateral links with others, and occasionally, though notably, the OECD has been involved through publishing recommendations and offering a platform for *some* competition authorities to meet and collaborate in various respects. As such, bilateralism has ended up being a highly limited tool in scope, confined to certain competition authorities and used only in narrow cases.

This situation, however, can be improved dramatically if bilateralism was to play a more important, concrete role within the objectives of an international organization with a wide base. The International Competition Network (ICN) would be a suitable forum to do this because of its unique membership and the credibility it enjoys as an organization with sole emphasis on soft-law convergence. Building a bilateralism platform within the ICN would fit very well with the emphasis the Organization puts on convergence.

A number of ideas may be advanced here, and chief among these is building an initiative to develop bilateral cooperation's long-term benefit of convergence. For this to happen, the perceptions of bilateralism need to shift: rather than being seen as a tool to be created and used only when the parties realize they have many commonalities, created most obviously by overlap of jurisdiction—as has been the case with the EU/US cooperation—attention needs to be given to the contribution that bilateral cooperation could make toward advancing competition law, especially at a policy-making level, and achieving crucial convergence and harmonization among different rules and standards.

Essentially, therefore, what is being proposed here is a move toward a whole new generation of agreements. The idea of bilateral cooperation began in the 1960s and originally developed around negative comity—*first* generation agreements from the 1970s and 1980s that focused on good manners and courtesy. The 1990s brought the *second* generation of agreements, whose focus was on positive comity. The time is now ripe to advocate the developing of a *third* generation (3G) of agreements, which use a centralized international platform. These 3G agreements will not be limited to cooperation in actual cases. The focus will be on creating wide channels of cooperation through which all of the following can flow: hosting competition law events in the form of conferences and seminars, arranging training programs, and holding general and particular consultations aimed at advancing expertise and achieving convergence.

B. Lack of Knowledge

Bilateral cooperation has been unable to achieve its full potential simply because of lack of knowledge of the extent to which this form of cooperation is used in practice and lack of familiarity with the prospects it has for development. It is not entirely clear whether anyone in the field of competition law really knows exactly how many bilateral agreements (not to mention all informal bilateral links) actually exist, let alone how many of these are positive comity agreements, negative comity agreements, or mixed (positive and negative comity). This only shows lack of knowledge about the extent of bilateral cooperation as a *network* in practice. The other side of the coin is that many competition authorities themselves are uncertain about what prospects really exist for them to build a bilateral strategy. Indeed, many competition authorities are keen to enter into bilateral cooperation (not necessarily for the purposes of avoiding jurisdictional conflict, etc.), but their efforts are hindered because they simply do not know how to build the foundations for such cooperation, who would be interested in it, and who would be a suitable partner in their particular case.

The perceived inherently long-term nature and cost of entering into this type of agreement also makes the picture bleaker for the future of meaningful bilateral cooperation. At present, the number of bilateral agreements is fairly small, the sole focus has come to be given to positive comity, and they show clear exclusion of developing countries. There is also a lack of a proper role for firms to play within the framework of the agreements, which one may predict could be particularly helpful to the relevant competition authorities.

A centralized platform, such as a center of gravity as suggested earlier, would play an important role in dramatically changing this situation. Often these authorities need to be educated on how bilateral cooperation can help them build their expertise in the field of competition law and how to go about achieving it. By including bilateralism within the remit of a centralized platform, the focus on bilateralism can be shifted from that of a purely national affair to a strategy with an international component, and *it will be* much more realistic to achieve the objective of promoting competition law understanding and furthering those efforts seeking to realize meaningful convergence. In practical terms, a centralized platform would offer participating authorities a clear structure in which they can engage in dialogue with partners; and with the aid of an overseeing body, young and burgeoning authorities could more readily identify appropriate and willing partners. Furthermore, the platform could offer skeleton bilateral agreements, technical assistance programs, and perhaps even a physical setting in which discussions could take place. The availability of such resources can go a long way in reducing hesitancy toward engaging in bilateral cooperation by reducing the costs associated with it. It is perhaps this particular future direction—a change in policy perspective—in bilateral cooperation, therefore, to which some thought should probably be given.

15. THE CURIOUS INCIDENT OF POSITIVE COMITY—THE DOG THAT DIDN'T BARK (AND THE TRADE DOGS THAT JUST MIGHT BITE)

PHILIP MARSDEN*

Competition officials often expound on the value of international enforcement cooperation.[1] Such fervor seems to increase when there's been a bit of a storm. It's as if they want to pour oil on the waters.[2] So when we see a dispute or different approaches to a particular merger or practice, out come the figures describing the hundreds of cases where cooperation has gone smoothly.[3] Perhaps they feel a need to reassure us that despite a particularly noisy clash, "business as usual" means weekly and perhaps often daily cooperation.

Officials have also designed many tools to help them cooperate in enforcement. There are agreements and memoranda of understanding and even treaties.[4] These are all designed primarily to assist officials in their day-to-day

---

* Dr. Philip Marsden is Director of the Competition Law Forum and Senior Research Fellow at the British Institute of International and Comparative Law, London.

1. *Our Progress Towards International Convergence*, Christine A. Varney, Assistant Attorney General, Antitrust Division U.S. Department of Justice, Remarks as Prepared for the 36th Annual Fordham Competition Law Institute Annual Conference on International Antitrust Law and Policy, New York, Sept. 24, 2009, *available at* http://www.usdoj.gov/atr/public/speeches/250264.htm.

2. International Antitrust in The Bush Administration, Address by Charles A. James, Assistant Attorney, General Antitrust Division U.S. Department of Justice, Before the Canadian Bar Association Annual Fall Conference on Competition Law, Ottawa, Canada, Sept. 21, 2001, *available at* http://www.usdoj.gov/atr/public/speeches/9100.htm.

3. Convergence, Conflict, and Comity: The Search for Coherence in International Competition Policy,Remarks of Chairman Deborah Platt Majoras at the 34th Annual Conference on International Antitrust Law & Policy Fordham Competition Law Institute Fordham Law School, New York City, Sept. 27, 2007, *available at* http://www.ftc.gov/speeches/majoras/070927fordham.pdf.

4. *See, e.g.*, Agreement between the Government of the United States of America and the Government of the Federal Republic of Germany relating to Mutual Cooperation regarding Restrictive Business Practices (Bonn, June 23, 1976); Agreement between the Government of the United States of America and the Government of Australia relating to Cooperation on Antitrust Matters (Washington, D.C., June 29, 1982); Agreement between the Government of the United States of America and the Commission of the European Communities on the Application of their Competition Laws (Washington, D.C., Sept. 23, 1991, entry into force, Apr. 10, 1995); Cooperation and Coordination Agreement between the Australian Trade Practices Commission and the New Zealand Commerce Commission (July 1994); Agreement between the Government of the United States of America and the

notifications, or when authorities are of a like mind about a larger matter, but all that prevents them from coordinated enforcement is a national border. There is one instrument, however, that is particularly interesting and that does not share these traits. This is positive comity. Positive comity seems to be expressly designed to allow a very unique form of cooperation and operates when agencies have no direct common interest. It allows one agency to ask another to act to address a practice in the latter's jurisdiction that is not harming consumers in either agencies' market, and that does not violate the requesting agency's antitrust law. Instead, the practice in question is impeding a company in the requesting agency's market from entering the requested agency's market.

This instrument is unique, and since it was such a huge step-up from the previous, more usual forms of coordination, it took an incredible effort among authorites to agree to it. Since it has been introduced, however, demand for its use has not exactly risen to meet supply. This chapter examines this conundrum.

One of the aims of this book is to examine why there has been such limited use of enforcement cooperation and to recommend ways of ensuring that restrictive business practices do not evade prohibition by hiding behind national borders. When asked to contribute, I relished the opportunity to revisit this subject, having lost touch with developments in the area.

Government of Canada regarding the Application of their Competition and Deceptive Marketing Practices Laws (Washington, D.C., August 1, 1995 and Ottawa, Aug. 3, 1995); Agreement between the Government of the United States of America and the Commission of the European Communities on the Application of Positive Comity Principles in the Enforcement of their Competition Laws (Brussels and Washington D.C., June 4, 1998); Agreement between the Government of the United States of America and the State of Israel, regarding the Application of their Competition Laws (Washington, D.C., Mar. 15, 1999); Agreement between the Government of the United States of America and the Government of Australia on Mutual Antitrust Enforcement Assistance, (Washington, D.C., Apr. 27, 1999); Agreement Between the Government of Canada and the European Communities Regarding the Application of their Competition Laws (Apr. 29, 1999); Agreement between the Government of the United States of America and the Government of Japan regarding Cooperation on Anti-competitive Activities, (Washington, D.C., Oct. 7, 1999); Agreement between the Government of the United States of America and the Government of the Federative Republic of Brazil regarding Cooperation between their Competition Authorities in the Enforcement of their Competition Laws, (Washington, D.C., Oct. 26, 1999); Agreement between the Government of the United States of America and the Government of the United Mexican States regarding the application of their competition laws, (Mexico City, Oct. 2000); Cooperation Arrangement between the Commissioner of Competition (Canada), the Australian Competition and Consumer Commission and the New Zealand Commerce Commission regarding the Application of their Competition and Consumer Laws, (Wellington, Oct. 19, 2000, and Paris, Oct. 25, 2000); Memorandum of Understanding between the Commissioner of Competition (Canada) and the Fiscal Nacional Economico (Chile) regarding the application of their Competition Law (Santiago, Dec. 17, 2001).

Having been a competition official in the mid-1990s, at the height of international work on enforcement cooperation and positive comity in particular, I was keen to learn what was going on in the area and to see how the hard work we had all put in to negotiating positive comity commitments had played out in practice.

It had all started so well. The 1990s saw a flourishing and deepening of positive comity commitments. A new era of cooperation was heralded—beyond information exchange and coordination on cases; now an agency could actually deputize another to battle anticompetitive conduct on its behalf. In one fell swoop, this brought an end to the need for unilateral extraterritorial enforcement, at least between the contracting parties. Positive comity went beyond mere toleration, or taking note, of other trading partner's interests. It even went beyond working together. Now authorities would be required to act against conduct in their territory that was excluding foreign companies.

Then it all went rather quiet.

Perhaps most of the bilateral efforts had been subsumed, or taken over, by "network" cooperation—the more amorphous and less "measurable" cooperation that occurs at the International Competition Network, the European Competition Network, and their regional counterparts. Perhaps the bilateral case-by-case cooperation among actual case handlers was continuing, but this had been eclipsed somewhat by the network discussions and working groups among policy officials at these broader forums. I was still particularly interested in what had happened to positive comity though.

I had not heard much after the informal positive comity query in the 1996 *IRI/AC Nielsen* dispute[5] and the more formal request in 1997 in the

---

5. The EC described the informal interaction and its relationship to positive comity as follows:

> A . . . case regarding the investigation into the practices of AC Nielsen Company ("Nielsen"), a provider of retail tracking services, demonstrates how positive comity is expected to work in practice. Both the Commission and the Department of Justice received a complaint from IRI that Nielsen was abusing its dominant position in Europe and thus prevented IRI from establishing a competitive presence there. As the complaint was primarily addressed to contractual practices implemented in Europe and had its greatest impact within Europe, the Department of Justice let the Commission take the lead once it was confident that it had a firm intention to act. The Commission conducted negotiations wit h Nielsen to arrive at an acceptable solution ensuring that competition was not distorted. At every stage during negotiations the Department of Justice was informed of progress and given an opportunity to comment on the undertakings being sought from Nielsen. Once the Commission had secured the necessary undertakings from Nielsen, the Department of Justice was able to conclude that the practices it had been investigating would not continue, and thus it closed its investigation. Although the US did not formally request the Commission to take action in the IRI/Nielsen case, the approach taken by the US of standing back and awaiting the results of the Commission's investigation may provide an example of how positive comity may operate.

SABRE/AMADEUS matter[6] and was keen to know why. In the early 2000s, a colleague and I had reviewed cooperation and comity provisions in agency-agency and government-government agreements, and presented our findings to governments at the OECD Joint Working Party on Trade and Competition, but our research had been specific to particular country pairs (Costa Rica-Canada, EU-Mexico, and Chile-Canada) and did not produce all that many startling results.[7] Our research seemed to show that it was too early for any significant cooperation to develop, over and above what had been happening in the run-up to the agreements. This suggested that it was true, as some suspected, that such accords just provided a formal framework for *existing* cooperation.

But I was interested in more than that. I wanted to know what was going on with positive comity. It had been the sharp edge of international competition law enforcement cooperation when I was in government, the most unique innovation in that regard, and was also an important pressure point in the debate between the trade and competition worlds too.

The latter point was important because, by its very nature, positive comity was supposed to be triggered primarily for the benefit of some export interest. Some company was being kept out of a foreign market. It had trade and competition options, but they were all provocative. Bringing a Section 301 trade case,[8] or some action at the WTO, or even asking its government to extend its antitrust laws extraterritorially to solve the problem, were all semi-belligerant acts as they called into question the propriety of the foreign legal system. With positive comity, in contrast, the exporter could ask its government to ask the foreign competition agency to solve the problem using its own laws.

And, as I say, this was not just respectful of national sovereignty, but also of cooperation, but not as we knew it previously. Positive comity requests weren't about asking a foreign agency to stop some cartel from their country from exporting high prices and thus harming consumers in ours; that could be handled somewhat through domestic enforcement in our country, or ideally through bilateral cooperation.

EC submission to the WTO Working Group on the Interaction Between Trade and Competition Policy, WT/WGTCP/W/129, July 12, 1999.

6. Press Release, U.S. Department of Justice, Justice Department Asks European Communities to Investigate Possible Anticompetitive Conduct Affecting U.S. Airlines' Computer Reservation Systems (Apr. 28, 1997), *available at* http://www.justice.gov/atr/public/press_releases/1997/229081.htm.

7. *The Contribution of Bilateral Trade or Competition Agreements to Competition Law Enforcement Cooperation between the EU and Mexico; Canada and Chile; and Canada and Costa Rica* (London: CEPR 2005) (with P. Whelan).

8. Section 301 of the *Trade Act* of 1974 allows the United States Trade Representative to bring sanctions against a foreign government that tolerates anticompetitive business practices.

To me, what positive comity was all about was relieving some of the enormous trade friction that was arising through allegations of market access barriers created by business practices. Here, the problem would be some exporter in my country claiming that vertical arrangements, abuse of dominance, or cartels in a foreign jurisdiction were impeding its access *into* that market. My government had an interest in making the request because its exporter was being harmed. It couldn't use its competition laws because none of its consumers were being harmed, only the exporter. Thus pressure would build up on my government to do something under other laws, for example, its trade laws. The foreign authority receiving the positive comity request would have an interest in sorting out the problem, as it would increase entry into its market and improve competition, and thus benefit consumers there. It would also—one assumes—be pleased to avoid a trade war, which never seems to benefit anyone anyway, other than trade lawyers.

The late 1980s and 1990s had been a time of great trade tension, particularly concerning allegations that foreign governments were lax in enacting and enforcing competition laws and thus were tolerating business practices that were impeding access to their market.[9] Thus, when the first positive comity provisions went "live," so to speak, in the Canada-EU and U.S.-EU accords, it was perhaps natural to assume that that they would get rather a lot of use.[10] Instead, all seemed to go quiet on this front. The silence started around the same time that talks got more involved at the World Trade Organization's Working Group on Trade and Competition. I cannot point to a specific causal relationship, but I'd wager that the initiation of these frequent and quite detailed discussions in Geneva helped alleviate some tension. Here, for the first time, trade officials representing their export interests were brought together with officals from competition agencies who the former were bashing for supposedly tolerating exclusionary practices. It is possible that putting the two sides together in an open, formal, and diplomatic "working group" venue could have led to a degree of understanding, or appreciation of each other's viewpoints, and thus avoided some flashpoints. That is one way of looking at it. During those talks, I certainly noted a drop in trade complaints alleging anticompetitive practices.

There are other interpretations of course: most obviously, the first positive comity provisions were contained in agreements between jurisdictions like Canada, the EU, and the United States that weren't waging these sorts of battles

---

9. For a full history and discussion, see P. Marsden, A Competition Policy for the WTO (London: Cameron May 2003).

10. Agreement between the Government of the United States of America and the Commission of the European Communities on the Application of Positive Comity Principles in the Enforcement of their Competition Laws (Brussels and Washington, D.C., June 4, 1998); Agreement Between the Government of Canada and the European Communities Regarding the Application of their Competition Laws (Apr. 29, 1999).

against one another. The focus at the time was between the United States and Japan, which did not have a positive comity agreement.[11] This left these trading partners to pursue other means of resolving their disputes.

Their infamous Kodak-Fuji trade case at the WTO was central.[12] Here, the American trade representative, representing Kodak, brought suit against the Japanese government for allegedly creating a range of measures that impeded Kodak's access to the market, and for tolerating business practices by Fuji Film that essentially did the same thing through a network of vertical restraints. Before the WTO could opine on the business practices side of the claim, the United States narrowed its case to focus on the allegedly entry-impeding measures related to restrictions on large-scale retail stores and the like. The WTO found against the United States on every ground though. Kodak had dropped the business practices side of its claim for a number of reasons. First, the Japanese Fair Trade Commission had investigated Kodak's claims of a network of entry-impeding vertical restraints and found no violation of competition law. To claims that perhaps the JFTC was captured, and thus was part of the trade problem itself, some—including me—had opined that the practices in question would be legal under U.S. antitrust law too, so it was a bit rich for the United States to be complaining about what was going on in Japan. Equally, if we were wrong, and the practices violated both Japanese and American law, then the United States could expect a mirror claim to be made against it by Japan, on behalf of Fuji Film, since Kodak was doing precisely the same thing as Fuji in the United States. Such a counterclaim would benefit no one, and any finding of the WTO against toleration of the practices would threaten the coherent interpretation of competition law and alter the antitrust approach in both countries. It was a relief when neither party pressed this point.

In denying Kodak's claim on the public measures side, however, some observers and other companies may have assumed that the WTO had opined on the business practices themselves, got it wrong, and thus shown that the WTO was not a good forum in which to bring complaints about toleration of business practices. Alternatively, people who actually knew the facts could have agreed that the WTO panel got it right and could handle competition issues, but that without a firmer frame of reference, the WTO was still not adequately prepared to decide such cases. Detailed competition law provisions had not really come to the WTO yet, and so it was difficult to bring a claim that a government was expressly violating one of its commitments by tolerating business conduct that impeded entry. You could argue that your expectations of improved market access were being

11. They signed one positive comity agreement subsequent to this case: U.S.-Japan (1999) Agreement between the Government of the United States of America and the Government of Japan concerning Cooperation on Anticompetitive Activities.

12. Report of the Panel, *Japan—Measures Affecting Consumer Photographic Film and Paper* ("Fuji v. Kodak"), WT/DS44/R, pp. 370–476.

"nullified and impaired" by the foreign government, but this was a difficult case to run. The whole point of the discussions at the WTO Working Group on Trade and Competition was to see whether countries wanted to go down the route of more explicit provisions in this regard anyway.

As we know, they eventually failed to agree to do that, and the current WTO provisions related to business practices will have to suffice for now.[13] None of those relate to positive comity though, and so, with the withdrawal of the WTO from the scene and continued trade pressure, presumably, might we not have expected an uptick in the use of positive comity provisions? Perhaps, but that did not come about. Why not?

I. WHY NO INCIDENT OF POSITIVE COMITY?

I will offer a range of thoughts. First, there is the point above about trade representatives coming together with competition officials to hash things out at the WTO Working Group. That may have taken some heat out of the trade officials' usual allegations, as they learned about how competition laws were actually being enforced, and thus had a knock-on dampening effect on the new alternative to trade actions—positive comity requests.

Second, there has been a general increase in competition law enforcement capacity around the world, the introduction of competition laws, and, to a large extent, robust enforcement. So on that front too there may be less need for positive comity requests, or at least for formal requests as problems may be being sorted out domestically. On a related note, exporters may be getting more sophisticated and more trusting of foreign enforcement agency credibility, and thus may be more content to make complaints directly to the foreign agency rather than go through the convoluted process of convincing their government—and in particular their competition agency—to deputize the foreign agency to look into things.

Perhaps also there is the issue that the *AC Nielsen* and *SABRE* cases mentioned above were not exactly paragons of action. If so, the limited use of positive comity since then could be simply because it is perceived to have limited value.

There is another point though that I have written about elsewhere.[14] This relates to the substantive differences between competition laws themselves, rather than the limitations of coordination per se. These substantive differences may have made it unlikely for there to be many *westbound* positive comity

13. P. Marsden, *Competition after Cancun—a Personal View*, COMPETITION LAW INSIGHT (Oct. 2003); P. Marsden, *WTO Decides First Competition Case—With Disappointing Results*, COMPETITION LAW INSIGHT (May 2004).

14. P. Marsden, *The Divide on Verticals,in* ANTI-TRUST GOES GLOBAL (Brookings Institution Press, Royal Institute of International Affairs, Washington/London Oct. 2000).

requests—for example from the EU to Canada and the United States. There are significant differences across the Atlantic about whether the practices that would most likely become the subject of a positive comity request should be prohibited or not. This is a real divergence. It has already meant that what the EU thinks is anticompetitive—in terms of an abuse of a dominant position or a vertical restraint, at least—is not viewed that way in North America.[15] As a result, the EU might well not bother making any positive comity requests of Canada or the United States if it thought that they would likely be given short shrift. If so, then this dynamic takes away half of the transatlantic positive comity equation right from the start.

What about *eastbound* requests though? If it is true that the EU is less tolerant of some conduct than the United States, and if this conduct harms U.S. exporters' ability to enter the EU market, then one might expect that aggreived exporters would complain to the U.S. government and thereby trigger a west-to-east positive comity request to DG-Competition in Brussels. However, here a nice Catch-22 point arises. If the U.S. Department of Justice (DOJ) makes such a request, surely it would be an admission by them that there is a problem that could be remedied by EU law. The practices may indeed be keeping American exporters out of Europe, and they may indeed violate European law. But it is the U.S. DOJ that handles positive comity "asks," not U.S. Trade Representative. And if the practice would not have raised issues under U.S. law (if they were practiced in the United States), then the DOJ may be reluctant to make a positive comity request for fear that it would undermine its own enforcement approach. Of course, the DOJ could just make the request and say that it is purely a matter of the bilateral arrangement, and any action taken would only be under EU law and thus has no impact on its own approach. But it does seem a bit awkward at the very least. It may even be seen by those who criticize the U.S. approach to be a tacit admission that EU law is substantively more robust. That does not seem to be something that the U.S. authorities have been keen to admit; far from it, they seem quite ready to criticize the European approach.[16]

---

15. *See* ECJ, Case C-95/04 P, British Airways v. Commission [2007] I-2331, 86, and *compare with* Virgin Atlantic Airways Ltd. v. British Airways PLC, 69 F. Supp. 2d 571 (S.D.N.Y. 1999), *aff'd*, 257 F.3d 256 (2d Cir. 2001).

16. *See, e.g.*, former Assistant Attorney General for the DOJ Antitrust Division Thomas O. Barnett's statement following CFI judgment in Microsoft

> In the United States, the antitrust laws are enforced to protect consumers by protecting competition, not competitors. In the absence of demonstrable consumer harm, all companies, including dominant firms, are encouraged to compete vigorously. U.S. courts recognize the potential benefits to consumers when a company, including a dominant company, makes unilateral business decisions . . . .

See http://www.usdoj.gov/atr/public/press_releases/2007/226070.htm. European Commissioner for Competition Policy, Neelie Kroes, led the official response to this statement, reaffirming that the EC antitrust system is led by this same

More likely though, in such a scenario, a sophisticated U.S. exporter would not await the political niceties and delay of a positive comity request through its own government, but would just bring a complaint to Directorate General Competition itself, relying on EU law alone. Maybe that is all that is happening with western market access issues. The firms are doing it themselves. We certainly have seen very high profile U.S.-led complaints being brought in Europe under EU law, even against American companies.[17]

II. WEAKNESSES OF COOPERATION GENERALLY

There are broader systemic problems that might be at issue though, as well. The inherent weaknesses of bilateral cooperation itself, for example, may also apply to positive comity.

First, by its very nature, cooperation is discretionary. It operates on a case-by-case basis and cannot therefore be relied on as a matter of course or assumed to be available when new situations arise. This lack of reliability may cause agencies to be unwilling to make use of potential opportunities to cooperate.

Second, comity principles alone may not be a sufficient basis on which to ground effective cooperation. For example, such principles may not be able to resolve a conflict of jurisdiction where both countries believe that they have a predominant interest in a matter. The situations in which comity principles can be relied on may therefore, in practice, be more limited than would necessarily be assumed.

Third, successful cooperation on the basis of comity principles would require a jurisdiction to commit resources and effort to the action requested by a foreign government on behalf of a foreign company. This may be difficult for the requested agency to do politically and thus may result in a request being declined on the basis of "scarce resources" or not being an "enforcement priority," rather than on the merits.

In addition, comity may be less successful if the agencies involved are of unequal size and/or power. They may be less likely to interact frequently or to have a recurring need to rely on one another, in contrast, say, to the similarly placed U.S. and EU agencies who interact and assist one another regularly. In the absence of these factors, the larger agencies may have lower incentives to respond to the needs of the smaller authorities. Also, smaller jurisdictions simply

---

fundamental principle, although its resolution in this case was divergent from that of the United States. *See* http://ec.europa.eu/commission_barroso/kroes/antitrust_eu_us.pdf.

17. Microsoft Corp. v. Commission (T-201/04) [2007] 5 C.M.L.R. 11 (the primary case against Microsoft in the EU was brought by U.S. company Sun under European procedures alone).

may not have the resources to help foreign counterparts, or it may be politically unpalatable for them to rely on foreign agencies to remedy international conduct that is harming their consumers.

III. A CHANGING TIDE—A RETURN TO PROTECTIONIST CONCERNS

Perhaps these weaknesses do not matter since there has *been* so little call for positive comity. But they might also help explain why the provision has been used so infrequently. I am a little concerned, though, that in the current economic climate there might come to be more trade friction in this area. One thing that the recession seems guaranteed to continue to create is a rise in protectionism. There will be public barriers to entry—the usual protectionist measures—that competition law largely can do nothing about (other than attempt to limit their application, through interdepartmental advocacy—to the extent that competition officials are listened to at all). But also it seems likely that there will be an increase in the oft-feared privatized version of protection—practices that companies engage in to prevent their rivals from challenging their position. If this occurs, and I see no reason to expect that it will not, then the old mantras from Havana Charter days and the 1980s and 1990s will come back: private barriers to trade must not be allowed to hide behind national borders.

If the protectionist urge is as severe as the recession itself, then we might hear calls for equally strong measures to address exclusionary business practices. What form might these demands take? Actually, it is not hard to imagine. During the 1990s, there were quite vociferous demands from trade lawyers for special guarantees in international law to prevent just such protectionist private conduct. These voices were tired of talk of competition law cooperation. They sought much stronger medicine, which might help exporters, albeit at the expense of both the efficient operation of the market and international cooperation efforts too.

IV. A FRESH DEMAND FOR MARKET ACCESS WARRANTIES

The main proposal came from some Washington trade lawyers, in particular Richard Cunningham and Alan Wolff. They argued that competition policy would never provide a solution to the problem of private market access barriers. Cunningham and Wolff proposed that governments offer each other express "market access warranties" to ensure that when they say that they will open their markets, they actually do. Cunningham and Wolff also urged governments not to let antitrust's analytical "purity" get in the way of offering such warranties.

Pressure to think "out of the competition policy box" had been building for some time; the trade lawyers had lost faith in positive comity arguing that "few foreign antitrust authorities can be relied upon to attack conduct that affects U.S. producers because very few foreign competition agencies are as effective as the Department of Justice or the Federal Trade Commission."[18]

Wolff offered a forthright explanation of why governments should give up on ever hoping to find a competition policy "solution":

> What trade negotiators care about is not competition policy but market access—the ability to sell goods across a border. . . . Trade negotiators do not in fact care fundamentally if there are competition authorities in each WTO Member country or whether they are adequately staffed. They do not care what antitrust laws are on the books, whether prosecutorial discretion is exercised properly, or whether prosecution was effective. For the pragmatist trade policymaker, all that counts is the result—not the intent or the efficacy of the action.

The best answers to the present dilemma are arguably to be found wholly outside the realm of antitrust and competition law. *The guiding principle should be market access* with the focus confined to the following: (1) private behavior that impedes market access, (2) government behavior that reinforces private restraints, and (3) the combination of the two.[19]

Wolff argued that enforcement cooperation among competition authorities is not sufficient: either "for both practical and institutional reasons, positive comity is probably not the best answer. The better approach for WTO purposes may be to disregard issues surrounding the interaction of competition laws and competition authorities altogether and instead simply provide, among WTO Members, a more robust guarantee of market access."[20]

V. DISCUSSION SHOULD BE REPLACED WITH ACTION

As trade problems are identified and evidenced, Wolff argued that the appropriate trade solution will take form:

> With a trade solution, it would make no difference whether a local competition authority existed or how such an authority had decided to deploy its law enforcement resources. It would matter only that bargained-for sales opportunities were failing to materialise.

---

18. International Competition Policy Advisory Committee to the Attorney General and Assistant Attorney General for Antitrust, Final Report at 250–51 (Washington 2000) ("ICPAC Report") (http://www.usdoj.gov/atr/icpac/icpac.htm (citing A. Wolff & Dewey Ballantine, *Trade and Competition Policy: A Suggested U.S. Strategy*, at 4, ICPAC Hearings Nov, 4, 1999 ("Wolff, *A Suggested U.S. Strategy*")).

19. Wolff, *A Suggested U.S. Strategy*, at 7–8 (emphasis added).

20. Wolff, *A Suggested U.S. Strategy*, at 8.

> *The WTO membership can achieve this result by attaching to every trade concession an 'explicit warranty.' The warranty should clarify that each government commits to ensuring that its trade concessions will not be undermined by private restraints of trade, private collaboration with government bodies, and/or informal administrative guidance.*[21]

Though Wolff repeatedly stated that his solution did not depend on the existence or operation of a competition law, he limited the operation of the strict liability regime to the inappropriate toleration of the most severe violations of competition law:

> [T]o be effective, the scope of such a warranty would have to be well defined. Behaviour that could be held to impair a market access concession could come from a standard list of behaviours judged to be *per se* illegal. Examples could include price fixing, bid-rigging, monopolising essential port or distribution facilities, and actual or threatened refusals to deal.[22]

As some of these practices are not per se illegal under most, if any, competition laws at present, Wolff must have been contemplating some tightening up of existing competition laws, including those of the United States. Cunningham certainly did:

> [T]rade policy retains, as current US antitrust law does not, some aspects of the concept that a company deserves to be protected from the 'unfair' practices of a competitor. US antitrust law, by emphasizing disciplines on practices that reduce competition and lessen the efficiency of the marketplace, now focuses almost exclusively on promoting the interest of the consumer. Largely gone are concepts of protecting competitors from unfair practices or protecting weaker/smaller companies from the 'excessive' power of stronger/larger/dominant companies. As a result, once-important areas of US antitrust law, such as prohibitions on most vertical restraints and primary-line price discrimination cases, are now essentially non-existent.[23]

Cunningham explained the dilemma (which I also referred to above as a Catch-22):

> [V]ertical restraints are largely tolerated by the current . . . US competition policy. And that puts us in the position that essentially makes unilateral and bilateral action . . . impossible.

21. A. Wolff, *WTO Dispute Settlement and the Particular Problem of Trade and Competition Policy*, Remarks at a Dispute Resolution in the WTO, Washington, June 24, 1998 at 3, 4–5 (hereinafter "Wolff, *Dispute Settlement*") (emphasis added).

22. Wolff, *WTO Dispute Settlement*, at 5.

23. R. Cunningham, *Evaluating ICPAC and the ABA: An International Trade Lawyer's Perspective*, Remarks at 2000 Annual ABA Meeting at 7–8 ("Cunningham ABA") (citing the European approach with approval).

> It makes unilateral effort to address the issue impossible, even under Section 301, which has a provision which allows the United States Trade Representative to move against a foreign government that tolerates anti-competitive practices. And it makes unilateral action with regard to antitrust enforcement equally impracticable, *because in both cases, you are going to the mat with a foreign government on a practice which we ourselves say in our competition policy is not forbidden,* certainly absent rather unusual circumstances, nor a realistically challengeable anti-competitive practice.
>
> . . .
>
> It also makes bilateral negotiation of such issues as a trade matter unproductive not only because of the jurisdictional and evidentiary problems but also on a 'fairness' ground that *what we are asking them to ban—we don't ban.*[24]

Cunningham explained that this "leads you to a dead end because unless there is substantial government involvement in the market-access-denying practices, what you have to deal with is essentially what a competition policy lawyer would refer to as vertical restraints. And vertical restraints are largely tolerated by current, I'll underline the word *current,* and I hope somebody will ask me why I keep saying current, U.S. competition policy."[25]

Cunningham clearly wanted to change the U.S. position to a less tolerant antitrust approach to exclusive arrangements that impede foreign competitors. He had no problem with the prospect of creating a double standard within American antitrust, with one approach for purely domestic arrangements with no foreclosure effect beyond U.S. territory, and another for arrangements that do keep out foreign competitors:

> The issue is: does US competition policy in its current treatment of vertical restraints stand as a barrier to our finding a trade law approach to dealing with that? . . . . [T]here is ample room for US competition policy to coexist with the concept that vertical restraints as a market access barrier in international trade raise different issues and thus can be treated differently than . . . US policy would deal with them domestically in terms of our own law.[26]

The price of the market access express warranty was capitulation of American antitrust's current self-disciplined approach to the analysis of exclusive arrangements. Cunningham argued for such a sacrifice for the greater good of market access.

Cunningham noted that in practice, multinationals are already adhering to stricter foreign regimes, particularly those of the EU. Ultimately, global

---

24. Testimony of Richard Cunningham, Transcript of ICPAC Hearing at 26 (Nov. 4, 1998) (http://www.usdoj.gov/atr/icpac/icpac.htm ("Cunningham, Transcript") (emphasis added).

25. Cunningham, Transcript at 26.

26. Cunningham, Transcript at 27.

clearance of the *Boeing/McDonnell Douglas* merger depended on Boeing giving in to the European Commission's greater demands and sacrificing the exclusivity deals with the airlines that the U.S. FTC had allowed.[27] Cunningham argued that it does not serve U.S. trade interests for U.S. antitrust authorities to remain so rigid in defence of their regime.[28] To Cunningham, successful adoption of a "market access warranty" and greater international coherence in competition policy requires that U.S. antitrust return to the Old World. This approach was supported as a last resort measure by David Richardson who noted that:

> [I]f at the end of the day, Dick [Cunningham] and . . . the trade lawyers insist on a stronger identification of vertical arrangements as anticompetitive in themselves, I say then is the time perhaps for a bilateral [agreement] with the EU. *Let's see if we can move our treatment of vertical arrangements toward the EU's treatment of vertical arrangements, which is much more skeptical.*[29]

VI. ARE MARKET ACCESS WARRANTIES WELL-FOUNDED?

Of course, any concern about such proposals being resurrected may be rather alarmist. The current recession may not provoke such protectionist problems, and any such call for a market access warranty, and concomitant stiffening of competition law enforcement, may not be demanded. It is useful, analytically, to consider the warranty and its effects. This is particularly so since it expressly rejects both competition law and positive comity as a solution, yet oddly then calls for a change in competition law.

---

27. Cunningham, Transcript at 18–19:

> [C]orporations entering into mergers under conflicting standards may well decide it is in their best interest to comply with foreign restrictions, rather than rely on more lenient U.S. law.Consider one of the EU competition law principles applied to condition approval by the EU of the *Boeing/McDonnell Douglas* merger. The European Commission ('EC') viewed Boeing's exclusive supply relationships with certain U.S. airlines as a vertical restraint impermissible under EU competition law. The U.S., of course, no longer views most vertical restraints as a competition policy problem. This difference in the treatment of vertical restraints is a central element of the fundamental sea change in U.S. antitrust policy over the past quarter century. To consummate the merger and gain EU approval, however, Boeing made a commitment to the EU not to enter into exclusivity agreements with U.S., or any other, customers. . . .[A]n international company whose strategy contemplates future mergers must, in light of *Boeing/McDonnell Douglas*, consider seriously whether it should adhere to the more restrictive EU rules on vertical restraints.

28. Cunningham Transcript at 18.

29. Testimony of David Richardson, Transcript of ICPAC Hearing at 46 (Nov. 4, 1998) (emphasis added).

One initial problem with the proposal for a market access warranty arises from the fact that market access is much easier to demand than it is to define. When Members of the WTO Working Group asked the International Chamber of Commerce if "the business community [had] reached a consensus on a definition of 'market access'?," The response was a frank "No." However, after extensive discussion, the ICC Joint Working Party has found that "access to markets is a much broader concept that speaks to the notion of contestability, or, in other words the ability to compete effectively once you have gained entry to a market."[30] The ICC noted that "[c]ontestability theory offers no way of determining the relative propriety of barriers to entry or expansion, however."[31] In other words, such a theory could identify when a market might be difficult to enter, but not whether this was a problem that demanded a solution.

Moreover, others have found that "existing measures of market access identified in the economics literature cannot adequately differentiate between benign versus anti-competitive explanations for poor export performance."[32] Douglas Melamed had recognized similar problems; however, after setting out three possible explanations for why it might be difficult to access a market, he identified only one instance where real harm might be inferred:

> First, any particular access problem might have nothing to do with private, exclusionary conduct. It could reflect simply winners and losers in the marketplace.
>
> Second, access problems could be the result of private restraints that are used to insulate firms with market power from effective import competition. In those instances, the private restraints would seem both to violate sound antitrust principles and to undermine the trade communities' interest in increased market access.
>
> [Third] . . . exclusionary practices could cause access problems under different circumstances as well. Suppose, for example, that in an unconcentrated market a number of rivals of the would-be importer tie up, in aggregate, the lion's share of the most critical inputs by independent, parallel, and efficient restrictive vertical agreements that do not create market power.

30. ICC, *Replies formulated by the ICC Joint Working Party on Competition and International Trade to questions asked by Members of the WTO Working Group on The Interaction Between Trade And Competition Policy in Geneva in March 1998,* Doc. 225-103/68 (Oct. 6, 1998).

31. *Id.*

32. ICPAC Report at 254, n.185 (citing V. Suslow and S. Evenett, *Assessment of Empirical Literature on Cartels and Market Access: An Economic Analysis.* Paper prepared for the ICPAC (Sept. 23, 1999).

The urge for aggressive measures to increase market access is understandable in all these situations, but only the second is likely to be an occasion for the application of sound antitrust principles.[33]

The application of sound antitrust principles is, of course, what the proponents of the "market access warranty" seek to avoid. An antitrust review, after all, will be likely to reject the demands of their clients, unless they could supplement their perception of exclusion with evidence of harm to the competitive process.

Furthermore, such a new trade remedy would only increase international tension through the prospect of retaliatory trade actions. The market access warranties could also be used by foreign companies and governments to harm American commercial interests "back home": "holding foreign conduct to a stricter standard than even applied to U.S. companies would . . . reduce efficiency-enhancing vertical arrangements abroad, and ultimately in the United States, as our trade partners adopt mirror legislation."[34]

What would be preferable to trade wars, and even any false hopes that exporters will use positive comity itself, is something that I alluded to at the beginning of this chapter: a greater reliance on networks. Just as the trade sabre-rattling seemed to get less sharp when it was folded into international discussions at the WTO, so too might bringing the trade and competition communitiies together again offer some opportunities to work to each other's benefit. Equally, it is time that competition officials and international lawyers admit, as Eleanor Fox has, that "comity sounds good and does little work . . . . The comity concept is horizontal—nation-to-nation. The more fitting paradigm for the new century is overarching, global and spiral."[35]

VII. BACK TO THE FUTURE—THE RISE OF THE NETWORKS

This is where networks come in. As we know from Slaughter's path-breaking work in this area, transgovernmental networks are informal institutions that allow direct interaction between officials without much formal supervision by states and feature "loosely structured, peer-to-peer ties developed through frequent interaction rather than formal negotiation."[36]

Competition networks offer three key benefits in addressing the problems that arise with the current competition enforcement landscape.

---

33. D. Melamed, *International Antitrust in an Age of International Deregulation.* Address before the George Mason Law Review Symposium: Antitrust in the Global Economy at 8–9, Washington, D.C. (Oct. 10, 1997) (emphasis added).

34. Willkie ICPAC Submission at 29–30.

35. Eleanor Fox, *Antitrust Without Borders: From Roots to Codes to Networks,* Chapter 13 herein.

36. A.M. Slaughter, A New World Order (Princeton Univ. Press 2005)

- First, networks offer a forum for experimentation, sharing, and learning. They communicate information and also generate new meanings and interpretations of the information transmitted, thereby providing a context for learning by doing. It is important to note that they do this both formally and informally. This is vital to ensuring that agencies have the opportunities and support necessary to develop their effectiveness. Increased agency effectiveness is essential in order to promote appropriate and efficient competition enforcement, both domestic and international. International learning and peer pressure are important stimulants to improved agency performance.
- A key benefit of networks, where experience and best practice are shared, is the ability to engender "socialization" and thereby enhance trust and coordination between countries. This can be seen as a natural consequence of having people with common goals and interests working closely together and sharing ideas and practice. In the competition area, where international coordination of enforcement priorities and efforts is vital in addressing the opportunities for international anticompetitive behavior, the value of such "socialization" is clear. (However, it should be acknowledged that this is somewhat offset by the inability of competition networks generally to "bind" their members.)
- Second, networks can provide very efficient means to coordinate action. While this may be less directly relevant to the ICN than to other networks, the ICN may, by building trust and openness among its members, help facilitate coordinated action among sub-groups of its members.
- Third, networks offer a normatively attractive form of global governance in comparison to supranational bodies because they are composed of national officials who are subject to the same accountability mechanisms that control national governments. In other words, agencies participating in such a network are ultimately domestically accountable, which disarms allegations of a democratic deficit problem. Any fundamental changes in the domestic approach must come through domestic legislative action. While this means, for example, that changes to national procedures on mergers (to avoid duplication and inconsistency) may happen slowly, they happen in a domestically legitimate way that also ensures the necessary "buy-in" from business and consumers.

Networks are not perfect, by any means, and there are many who will have lingering concerns about deals hashed out in the green rooms of international jamborees, by officials with no mandate from an electorate. But the interaction of so many different officials from so many jurisdictions can be an important check in itself. Even if they all share one main interest, at least it is in effective and efficient competition law enforcement, a form of good governance in itself. ICN brings together only competition officials, and it works informally and through the promulgation of "best practices." The OECD involves governments and operates through Recommendations, which—while nonbinding—have considerable weight.

Both networks have meetings that involve nongovernmental advisors who will have their client interests close to their pocketbook. This can be both an important stimulus to overly bureaucratic torpor and a check on any over-reaching. So, in sum, increased reliance on networks, while a pretty amorphous solution to the very sharp problem that positive comity was designed to address, may really be the most appropriate way forward these days. Perhaps it is the kind of flexible solution that we need in these challenging times.

The cooperation required to negotiate the positive comity provisions was an important stepping-stone, and I do not mean to imply that they are a dead letter. Nevertheless, the kind of communication, cooperation, trust, and understanding that occurs within these networks has already resulted in best practice guidance, changes to domestic laws, and improvements in the effectiveness and efficiency of enforcement, and it is where the focus should be for the future.

16. INTERNATIONAL ANTITRUST COOPERATION AND THE PREFERENCE FOR NONBINDING REGIMES

ANU BRADFORD*

INTRODUCTION

Today, multinational corporations operate in increasingly international markets, yet antitrust laws regulating their competitive conduct remain national. Thus, corporations are subject to divergent antitrust regimes across the various jurisdictions in which they operate. This increases transaction costs, causes unnecessary delays, and raises the likelihood of conflicting decisions. The risks inherent in multi-jurisdictional regulatory review were prominently illustrated in the proposed *GE/Honeywell* acquisition, which failed following the European Union's ("EU") decision to prohibit the transaction despite its earlier approval in the United States.[1] Inconsistent remedies imposed on Microsoft following parallel investigations by both the U.S. and EU authorities serve as another example of the regulatory burdens companies face when dealing with multiple antitrust investigations.

Some commentators believe that inconsistent antitrust decisions reflect protectionism. The EU's negative *GE/Honeywell* decision, for instance, was alleged to be motivated by the EU's desire to protect GE/Honeywell's European rivals.[2] Others, including myself, have argued that protectionism motivates U.S. and EU antitrust enforcement only in the margins, and that the rare enforcement conflicts are better explained by the existing differences in the goals and analytical

---

* Assistant Professor, The University of Chicago Law School. I am grateful to Travis Bradford, Rachel Brewster, Rosalind Dixon, Einer Elhauge, Jack Goldsmith, Katerina Linos, Eric Posner, and Joel Trachtman for their helpful suggestions on the earlier drafts of this article.

1. *See* Press Release, U.S. Dep't of Justice, Justice Department Requires Divestitures in Merger Between General Electric and Honeywell (May 2, 2001), *available at* http://www.usdoj.gov/atr/public/press_releases/2001/8140.htm (last visited May 24, 2010); Commission Decision No. 2004/134/EEC, O.J. L 48/1 (2004).

2. William J. Kolasky, Deputy Assistant Attorney General, *Conglomerate Mergers and Range Effects: It's a Long Way from Chicago to Brussels,* Address at the George Mason University Symposium (Nov. 9, 2001), *available at* http://www.usdoj.gov/atr/public/speeches/9536.htm (last visited May 24, 2010).

foundations of antitrust law in the United States and the EU.[3] Thus, whether the EU's *GE/Honeywell* decision is a manifestation of the EU's protectionism or an indication of legitimate differences in the U.S. and EU's antitrust thinking is debatable.

When antitrust authorities in a given jurisdiction evaluate a merger, they analyze whether the merger increases or diminishes competition in their domestic market. Efficiency gains or competitive harm outside the home market are irrelevant. Domestic antitrust laws strive to advance domestic consumer welfare, not global welfare. When evaluating the proposed GE/Honeywell merger, for instance, the EU antitrust authorities did not consider whether the merger's possible efficiencies in the United States would offset its alleged competitive harm within the EU. Similarly, the U.S. antitrust authorities focused on the transaction's consumer welfare effects within the United States, ignoring the effects in the EU. By internalizing only the domestic costs and benefits of a merger and externalizing its foreign effects, national antitrust authorities act within the legitimate boundaries of their domestic antitrust laws. This, however, can lead to a situation whereby a merger that would enhance global welfare is prohibited because the consumer harm it creates in a particular jurisdiction is not offset by efficiencies in that same jurisdiction.

The end result of the multi-jurisdictional antitrust enforcement is that the most stringent antitrust jurisdiction always prevails. If the United States wants to adopt a permissive antitrust policy (e.g., approve the GE/Honeywell merger) and the EU an interventionist policy (e.g., prohibit the GE/Honeywell merger), the EU antitrust policy prevails: the GE/Honeywell transaction is banned. Had GE/Honeywell been able to withdraw from the EU market altogether, it could have avoided EU antitrust review and proceeded with the merger. This, naturally, was not an option, given the importance of the EU market for the merging parties. The *GE/Honeywell* case illustrates how the EU becomes the de facto global antitrust regulator by choosing stringent enforcement policies.

Purely domestic antitrust laws fail to efficiently control cross-border transactions and anticompetitive practices spanning across global markets. Consequently, demands for establishing a comprehensive international antitrust regime have increased.[4] Those fearing antitrust protectionism argue that an international

3. *See generally* Anu Bradford, *International Antitrust Negotiations and the False Hope of the WTO*, 48 HARV. INT'L L.J. 383 (2007).

4. *See, e.g.*, Andrew Guzman, *The Case for International Antitrust*, *in* COMPETITION LAWS IN CONFLICT: ANTITRUST JURISDICTION IN THE GLOBAL ECONOMY 99 (Richard A. Epstein R. & Michael S. Greve eds., 2004); Eleanor M. Fox, *Antitrust and Regulatory Federalism: Races Up, Down, and Sideways*, 75 N.Y.U. L. REV. 1781 (2000); PHILIP MARSDEN, COMPETITION POLICY FOR THE WTO (2003); Leon Brittan, *A Framework for International Competition*, Address at World Competition Forum (Feb. 3, 1992), *reprinted in* 3 INT'L ECON. INSIGHTS 21 (1992); WTO Competition Working Group, *Communication by the*

antitrust regime could restrain and punish such protectionist impulses. Others support international antitrust cooperation on the grounds that it could mitigate coordination problems, reduce transaction costs, and prevent enforcement conflicts by enhancing convergence across jurisdictions.

International antitrust regime, properly designed, can diminish the various problems associated with decentralized antitrust enforcement. However, while the need for enhanced international antitrust cooperation is generally recognized, there is little consensus on the precise content of such cooperation. A group of scholars and some states, including the EU, hold that a legally binding international antitrust agreement ought to be established, perhaps by extending the coverage of the World Trade Organization ("WTO") to antitrust law.[5] Others find a binding international agreement politically infeasible or normatively undesirable.[6] The United States, for instance, is skeptical of a WTO antitrust agreement and calls instead for enhanced voluntary cooperation.

This article focuses on the relative merits of binding and nonbinding international antitrust cooperation. It argues that the primary impediment to international antitrust cooperation is the disagreement over the substance and institutional form of such cooperation. This disagreement has led states to water down the proposed binding international antitrust agreement to the point of severely limiting, if not eliminating, any net benefits. In the end, states have chosen not to spend resources and political capital in negotiating a binding international agreement that fails to generate substantial benefits, preferring to resolve their differences informally on a case-by-case basis.

Irrespective of its normative merits, a binding international antitrust agreement is currently not feasible to negotiate. Yet states do not resort to nonbinding antitrust cooperation as a "second-best" solution to capture limited gains when their first-best regime choice is unavailable. Nonbinding international antitrust

---

European Community and its Member States, WT/WGTCP/W/62, at 12–13 (Mar. 5, 1998); Munich Working Group, Draft International Antitrust Code, 5 WORLD TRADE MATERIALS 126 (Sept. 1993), *reprinted in* 64 ANTITRUST & TRADE REG. REP. (BNA) Special Supp. (July 10, 1993); Ernst-Ulrich Petersmann, *Competition-Oriented Reforms of the WTO World Trade System-Proposals and Trade Options*, *in* TOWARDS WTO COMPETITION RULES 43, 48–49 (Roger Zäch ed., 1999); Robert D. Anderson & Peter Holmes, *Competition Policy and the Future of the Multilateral Trading System*, 5 J. INT'L ECON. L. 531 (2002).

5. *See, e.g.*, Guzman, *supra* note 4. *See also* Julian L. Clarke & Simon J. Evenett, *A Multilateral Framework for Competition Policy? in* THE SINGAPORE ISSUES AND THE WORLD TRADING SYSTEM (Simon J. Evenett ed., 2003) (providing a good overview of the various proposals for including antitrust in the WTO); MARSDEN, *supra* note 4.

6. *See, e.g.*, Paul B. Stephan, *Against International Cooperation*, *in* COMPETITION LAWS IN CONFLICT: ANTITRUST JURISDICTION IN THE GLOBAL ECONOMY, *supra* note 4, at 66; Diane P. Wood, *Cooperation and Convergence in International Antitrust: Why the Light Is Still Yellow?*, *in* COMPETITION LAWS IN CONFLICT: ANTITRUST JURISDICTION IN THE GLOBAL ECONOMY, *supra* note 4, at 177.

cooperation remains preferable even if a binding agreement later becomes feasible. Given the nature of the collective action problem in international antitrust cooperation, binding agreements and formal institutions remain largely unnecessary and undesirable. Thus, this article rebuts the presumed supremacy of a binding international antitrust regime and claims that nonbinding cooperation offers a better path for international antitrust convergence for now and in the foreseeable future.

Part I below briefly reviews the nonbinding international antitrust regime that has emerged in the absence of a binding international antitrust agreement. Part II explains why negotiating binding international antitrust cooperation has been difficult and why such negotiation would yield limited benefits for states. Part III discusses why nonbinding cooperation is more likely to foster international antitrust convergence. Part IV explains why nonbinding cooperation is likely to persist even if the negotiation of a binding international antitrust agreement were to become viable in the future.

I. THE EMERGENCE OF A NONBINDING INTERNATIONAL ANTITRUST REGIME

States have attempted to launch WTO antitrust negotiations on several occasions.[7] However, all attempts to negotiate a binding international antitrust agreement have thus far failed,[8] prompting states to engage in voluntary cooperation instead.[9] Over the past decade, states have concluded a number of bilateral

---

7. *See, e.g.*, MARSDEN, *supra* note 4, at ch. 1; *see also* Nataliya Yacheistova, *The International Competition Regulation—A Short Review of a Long Evolution*, 18 WORLD COMPETITION, LAW AND ECON. 99, 99–110 (1994).

8. Most recently, the WTO negotiations on antitrust were stalled in Cancun in 2003 due to the resistance of the developing countries. *See, e.g.*, Day **5: Conference ends without consensus,** ***available at*** http://www.wto.org/english/thewto_e/minist_e/min03_e/min03_14sept_e.htm (last visited May 24, 2010). On August 1, 2004, the WTO General Council decided to officially drop antitrust policy from the Doha Round negotiation agenda ("July decision"). *See* WTO General Council, *Decision Adopted by the General Council*, WT/L/579 (Aug. 2, 2004).

9. *See generally* Oliver Budzinski, *The International Competition Network: Prospects and Limits on the Road towards International Competition Governance*, 8 COMP. & CHANGE 223–42 (2004); Frederic Jenny, *International Cooperation on Competition: Myth, Reality and Perspective*, 48 ANTITRUST BULL. 973–1003 (2003); Anu Piilola, *Assessing Theories of Global Governance: A Case Study of International Antitrust Regulation*, 39 STAN. J. INT'L L. 207 (2003).

agreements and engaged in active nonbinding multilateral cooperation in order to promote convergence and reduce enforcement conflicts.[10]

Bilateral cooperation occurs on a case-by-case basis. Antitrust authorities exchange nonconfidential market information, assist each other in evidence gathering, coordinate investigations, and negotiate joint remedies.[11] The primary challenge for the case-by-case cooperation is the agencies' inability to exchange confidential business information absent a waiver from the relevant corporations. For this reason, enforcement cooperation tends to be more successful in merger control investigations than in cartel investigations. Corporations seeking to merge often have an incentive to grant a waiver in order to ensure a swift investigation and, consequently, timely consummation of their transaction. In contrast, corporations remain reluctant to facilitate agencies' joint cartel investigations, as consenting to the exchange of confidential information would expose them to additional sanctions in another jurisdiction.[12]

Bilateral cooperation has been particularly successful between the United States and the EU.[13] Frequent interactions between the two antitrust regimes have resulted in significant convergence in their antitrust analysis and enforcement practices. And while intense cooperation does not guarantee identical decisions, as the controversial GE/Honeywell merger demonstrated,[14] enforcement

10. These cooperation arrangements have been extensively described elsewhere in the literature, *See, e.g.,* Bruno Zanetti, Cooperation between Antitrust Agencies at the International Level (2002); *see also* Jenny, *supra* note 9; Budzinski, *supra* note 9.

11. Even though states have concluded formal bilateral agreements, the decision on whether to cooperate remains entirely at the discretion of domestic antitrust authorities. Thus, this form of cooperation is more aptly characterized as nonbinding rather than binding.

12. *Id.* Jenny, *supra* note 9. at 995. *See also* International Chamber of Commerce & Business and Industry Advisory Committee to the OECD, *ICC/BIAC Comments on Report of the U.S. International Competition Policy Advisory Committee (ICPAC)* 8 (June 5, 2000), *available at* http://www.biac.org/statements/comp/00-06-ICC-BIAC_comments_on_ICPAC_report.pdf [hereinafter *ICC/BIAC Comments on Report of the U.S. International Competition Policy Advisory Committee*].

13. *See* Agreement Between the Government of the United States of America and the Commission of the European Communities Regarding the Application of the Competition Law, U.S.–E.C., Sept. 23, 1991, U.S. State Dep't No. 91-216, 30 I.L.M. 1487, 1991 WL 495155; Agreement Between the Government of the United States of America and the European Communities on the Application of Positive Comity Principles in the Enforcement of Their Competition Laws, art. III, U.S.–E.C., June 4, 1998, U.S. State Dep't No. 98-106, 1998 WL 428268. *See also* Press Release, US–EU Merger Working Group, Best Practices on Cooperation in Merger Investigations (Oct. 30, 2002), *available at* http://www.usdoj.gov/atr/public/international/docs/200405.pdf (last visited May 24, 2010).

14. *See supra* note 1.

conflicts between the two agencies are rare in practice.[15] In contrast, cooperation is less frequent between developed countries and developing countries.[16] This might be because developed countries have less to gain from such cooperation. Developed countries would likely be exposed to numerous requests of enforcement assistance from developing countries, as large developed country corporations often achieve a high market share in small developing country markets. In contrast, smaller developing-country corporations rarely trigger an antitrust investigation in large developed-country markets.[17]

Bilateral antitrust cooperation offers only a partial solution for achieving greater coherence across antitrust jurisdictions. Multilateral institutions have complemented the efforts to foster international antitrust cooperation. Since 2001, the most active forum for nonbinding multilateral antitrust cooperation has been the International Competition Network ("ICN"). The ICN is an informal network of antitrust agencies, which seeks to enhance cooperation among the world's antitrust authorities and promote substantive and procedural convergence of antitrust policies on a voluntary basis.[18] The ICN identifies, develops, and publishes policy recommendations and best practices.[19] Such voluntary norms are aimed at enhancing policy convergence, reducing transaction costs, and catalyzing and guiding domestic reforms. The ICN, together with other international institutions, also offers technical assistance to developing countries with the view of strengthening antitrust advocacy, building institutional capacity, and supporting market reforms in those countries.[20] Following the collapse of the WTO antitrust negotiations in 2003, the ICN remains the most influential international regime facilitating multilateral antitrust cooperation today.

---

15. The *GE/Honeywell* decision remains the only merger case in which the U.S. and EU authorities have reached a conflicting decision. The EU also prohibited a proposed merger between DeHavilland and ATR, which was approved by the Canadian authorities. (*See* Commission Decision, Case No. IV/M.053 of October 2, 1991, Aerospatiale-Alenia/de Havilland). Legal uncertainty resulting from multi-jurisdictional merger review is thus unlikely to form as significant of a negative externality as one might imagine. It is, however, difficult to evaluate the costs of the prospect—no matter how unlikely in practice—that any given merger has a higher risk of being prohibited when it must survive multiple regulatory reviews.

16. *See* Jenny, *supra* note 9, at 993, 979.

17. Developed countries are also more often than developing countries able to extend their domestic antitrust laws to regulate the conduct of foreign corporations, further diminishing their need to rely on enforcement assistance. Besides, developed countries might assume that their requests for assistance would never be met in practice due to the limited resources of the developing country antitrust agencies.

18. For more information on the purpose and the functioning of the ICN, see www.internationalcompetitionnetwork.org (last visited May 24, 2010).

19. *See* Budzinski, *supra* note 9, at 228.

20. *See, e.g.*, Jenny, *supra* note 9, at 976–77.

II. THE LIMITED GAINS OF A BINDING INTERNATIONAL ANTITRUST AGREEMENT

A. How States' Divergent Preferences and Capacities Obstruct Cooperation

States agree that competitive markets and antitrust laws are beneficial. However, they disagree on the particular goals and priorities of antitrust enforcement. States also acknowledge the necessity to coordinate antitrust enforcement across jurisdictions but fail to agree on the specifics. These conflicting views on a globally optimal antitrust regime amount to a distributional conflict. A distributional conflict arises when the costs and the benefits of an international antitrust agreement are unevenly distributed among states, and when states therefore cannot agree on the focal point of coordination.[21]

The long-standing distributional conflict between the United States and the EU is one of the principal impediments for a binding international antitrust agreement. Both the United States and the EU acknowledge the efficiencies that international antitrust cooperation could generate, but disagree as to the optimal content, the legal form, and the institutional framework of cooperation.[22]

The U.S.-EU disagreement stems from some key differences that persist between the United States and the EU despite the increasing alignment of their antitrust laws over the last decade.[23] The United States and the EU agree that antitrust laws seek to maximize consumer welfare. However, social considerations, such as promotion of employment or protection of small enterprises, still play a role at the margins of the EU antitrust analysis. The EU also employs its antitrust laws to further European integration. Antitrust laws ensure that anticompetitive practices of private enterprise do not frustrate the efforts to remove trade barriers within the EU. This market integration goal has led to a more interventionist enforcement policy vis-à-vis vertical agreements, in particular territorial restraints that threaten to partition the common market. The EU is also more skeptical of market power and has a lower threshold in bringing cases against dominant companies (*see* decisions against Microsoft and Intel). Similarly, the EU has also historically taken a harsher view towards vertical and conglomerate mergers (*see* GE/Honeywell). While there is increasing convergence between the two key antitrust jurisdictions today, these remaining

---

21. Generally, conflicting state preferences regarding international cooperation on any given issue emanate from many different factors, such as economic disparities, diverse development priorities and market structures, dissimilar enforcement capacities, different legal traditions, and the distinct domestic political equilibrium within each state.

22. *See* Bradford, *supra* note 3, at 522–26 (exploring reasons for the divergence of views between the United States and the EU regarding international antitrust cooperation).

23. *See* Einer Elhauge & Damien Geradin, Global Antitrust Law and Economics 1100, 1100 (2007).

differences have led the United States and the EU to endorse international convergence each toward their respective antitrust laws.[24]

The United States and the EU also disagree on the optimal institutional framework for antitrust cooperation. The EU supports a binding WTO antitrust agreement. This is consistent with the EU's view that antitrust and trade policies are intrinsically linked. The United States, on the other hand, fears that antitrust would lose its exclusive focus on consumer welfare when enmeshed with trade policy considerations in the WTO. Instead, the United States has promoted antitrust cooperation within the ICN, which allows antitrust enforcers to cooperate without interference from the trade community.

In addition to the U.S.-EU controversy, disagreement between developed countries and developing countries regarding the content and the costs of a prospective antitrust agreement has obstructed cooperation efforts.[25] Developed countries want to "level the playing field" by enhancing multinational corporations' ("MNCs") access to the developing-country markets. Developed countries also seek to reduce transaction costs involved in MNCs' cross-border business transactions.[26] In contrast, developing countries are concerned about their inability to control the anticompetitive conduct of MNCs in their markets.[27] Developing countries also resist the idea of a level playing field, maintaining that they need to be able to shield their small domestic corporations from larger MNCs. Developing countries struggling with capacity constraints have also opposed WTO antitrust agreement because of the regulatory burden that new international obligations would impose on them.[28]

Consequently, a critical impediment to antitrust cooperation is the difficulty of overcoming the distributional conflict between the United States and the EU

---

24. *See, e.g.*, Fox, *supra* note 4, at 1799 (explaining how the United States and the EU have actively been exporting their own antitrust laws to developing countries and transition economies in the recent decade in an attempt to expand their preferred regulatory regimes).

25. Bradford, *supra* note 3, at 526–28, 534–37.

26. Bernard M. Hoekman & Kamal Saggi, *International Cooperation on Domestic Policies: Lessons from the WTO Competition Policy Debate*, *in* ECONOMIC DEVELOPMENT AND MULTILATERAL TRADE COOPERATION 439, 446 (Simon J. Evenett & Bernard M. Hoekman eds., 2006).

27. Ajit Singh & Rahule Dhumale, *Competition Policy, Development, and Developing Countries*, *in* WHAT GLOBAL ECONOMIC CRISIS? 122, 127 (Philip Arestis, Michelle Baddeley, & John McCombie eds., 2001). Developing countries are particularly vulnerable to international cartel activity, because their nonexistent or weak antitrust enforcers are unable to prosecute the threat effectively. *See* Margaret Levenstein & Valerie Y. Suslow, *Contemporary International Cartels and Developing Countries: Economic Effects and Implications for Competition Policy*, 71 ANTITRUST L.J. 801, 801–03 (2004).

28. *See* discussion *infra* Part II.C (explaining why an international antitrust agreement would impose high compliance costs).

on one hand, and the developed countries and the developing countries on the other. These distributional tensions have narrowed the scope for any feasible international agreement.

B. How the Distributional Conflicts Would Lead to a Shallow Agreement

Distributional conflicts force states to negotiate compromises that lead to shallow international obligations. A shallow international antitrust agreement would likely exclude all areas of disagreement. The disagreement between the United States and the EU would prevent the inclusion of rules on unilateral conduct by monopolies, vertical and conglomerate mergers, and on vertical territorial restraints. These are the key areas where the U.S. and the EU antitrust thinking differ.[29] The United States would also likely oppose rules banning export cartels, given that it remains the only country that continues to use such exemptions to its domestic antitrust laws widely.[30] Developing countries would also demand significant exceptions to any obligations subjecting their local firms to international competition.[31] However, meaningful rules might be difficult to negotiate, even with respect to issues where broad consensus exists. For instance, all states agree that hard-core cartels are anticompetitive. Yet a commitment to prohibit such cartels would be difficult to agree on in the absence of a consensus regarding the definition of a hard-core cartel or appropriate sanctions that should apply.[32]

The United States has objected to the WTO antitrust agreement precisely on these grounds. It has argued that a binding international agreement would weaken antitrust laws throughout the world. Given the conflicting regulatory priorities, states could only reach a watered-down compromise.[33] At worst, the prospective antitrust agreement would only codify the lowest common denominator among the broad WTO membership.[34]

---

29. *See* ELHAUGE & GERADIN, *supra* note 23, at 1100 (2007).

30. For example, the United States has defended domestic rules that permit the exemption of export cartels before the WTO in 2003 by arguing that these exemptions "were conceived as mechanisms for domestic entities that lacked the resources to engage in effective export activity acting individually." *See* WTO Working Group on the Interaction between Trade and Competition Policy, *Note by the Secretariat: Report on the Meeting of February 20–21, 2003,* 37, WT/WGTCP/M/21 (May 26, 2003).

31. Singh & Dhumale, *supra* note 27, at 127.

32. The United States, for instance, applies criminal sanctions and treble damages to antitrust violations, whereas the EC competition provisions limit remedies to administrative fines.

33. Wood, *supra* note 6, at 186.

34. *See* Roscoe B. Starek, III, Commissioner, Federal Trade Commission, International Aspects of Antitrust Enforcement, Address at the Antitrust 1996 Conference (Sept. 29, 1995), *available at* http://www.ftc.gov/speeches/starek/starekda.htm ("The sticking point is whether agreement can be reached on a sufficiently stringent set of antitrust policies.

As the United States predicted, the proposed antitrust agreement within the WTO grew weaker with every new attempt to agree on the negotiation mandate. In the end, states were forced to strip the agreement of any meaningful content in an effort to accommodate their divergent preferences. The most recent proposal for a WTO antitrust agreement forwent substantive antitrust rules altogether, proposing merely to extend the fundamental yet vague WTO principles of "transparency" or "national treatment" to antitrust matters. Such an agreement would accomplish little in terms of fostering international convergence and would leave states with limited benefits to offset the costs of negotiating the agreement.[35]

Some might argue that even weak antitrust commitments could deepen with time due to the gradual alignment of states' preferences and alleviation of uncertainties surrounding cooperation.[36] As states learn more about the effects of the agreement and gradually reach a consensus on a wider set of issues, they may incrementally adopt deeper obligations. However, even if states were willing to gradually expand their obligations, the WTO—the most likely venue for a binding international agreement—would not lend itself well to frequent revisions of obligations. New, deeper commitments would call for new negotiations, which are slow, cumbersome, and costly. Consequently, states are more likely to resort to the WTO when they are able to agree on meaningful substantive norms at the outset. When the necessary consensus is missing, however, nonbinding agreements outside the WTO are more likely to accomplish effective cooperation.

It is the fear of a "lowest-common-denominator" antitrust code that has made many American policymakers skeptical about pursuing a world code"); *see also* A. Douglas Melamed, Principal Deputy Assistant Attorney General, U.S. Dep't of Justice, Antitrust Enforcement in the Global Economy, Address at the Fordham Corporate Law Institute, 25th Annual Conference on International Antitrust Law and Policy (Oct. 22, 1998), *available at* http://www.usdoj.gov/atr/public/speeches/2043.htm ("[A]ny WTO rules would be lowest-common-denominator rules that would merely serve to justify weak national antitrust enforcement. Third, such lowest-common-denominator rules would serve little purpose").

35. Bernard M. Hoekman & Michel M. Kostecki, The Political Economy of the World Trading System 133–34 (2d ed. 2001).

36. This argument is advanced in particular by the "transformational approach." Transformationalists endorse shallow framework agreements with broadest possible participation and claim that commitments that are that initially shallow deepen with time. For a discussion and critique of transformationalism, see George W. Downs et al., *The Transformational Model of International Regime Design: Triumph of Hope or Experience?*, 38 Colum. J. Transnat'l L. 465 (2000) [hereinafter Downs et al., *Transformational Model*].

C. How a Shallow Agreement Would Offer Limited Net Gains

A shallow WTO antitrust agreement mitigates distributional tensions. However, diluting the substance of the agreement simultaneously lowers its expected benefits. Thus, if an agreement becomes too shallow, it is no longer worth negotiating, because states do not gain any net benefits to offset the costs of negotiating the agreement.

The expected benefits of the WTO antitrust agreement are further reduced by the low-opportunity costs of not cooperating within the WTO. States with existing, well-functioning antitrust regimes are often able to exercise jurisdiction vis-à-vis foreign corporations as long as the foreign anticompetitive conduct has an effect on their domestic market.[37] States' ability to resort to extraterritorial enforcement makes the case for an international agreement less compelling. States can also solve many of the collective action problems through informal cooperation mechanisms that are already in place. Numerous bilateral agreements and nonbinding plurilateral and multilateral antitrust regimes have enhanced convergence and reduced negative externalities caused by decentralized antitrust enforcement. This further diminishes the need for a binding international antitrust regime.[38]

Finally, negotiating a WTO antitrust agreement would be costly, reducing the net benefits from its success. Contracting costs are particularly high when international negotiations involve numerous states, distributional tensions, and burdensome national ratification procedures.[39] The WTO antitrust negotiations would involve 153 governments with heterogeneous preferences, multiple negotiation rounds, and extensive multi-issue bargaining. In addition, domestic ratification would presumably be necessary in most member states. Legislative approval adds to the contracting costs due to the additional negotiations, delays, and risks involved. Contracting costs are further augmented by the WTO enforcement mechanism, which enables member states to enforce potential violations of WTO commitments with sanctions.[40] States are expected to research and

---

37. *See, e.g.*, Hartford Fire Ins. Co. v. California, 509 U.S. 764, 796 (1993); Joined Cases 89, 104, 114, 116, 117 and 125 to 129/85, A. Ahlstrom Osakeyhtio v. Commission ("Wood Pulp"), 1988 E.C.R. 5193 (1988).

38. *See* discussion *infra*, Part IV.B.3.

39. Kenneth W. Abbott & Duncan Snidal, *Hard and Soft Law in International Governance*, 54 INT'L ORG. 421, 434 (2000) [hereinafter Abbott & Snidal, *Hard and Soft Law*].

40. A violation of a binding international agreement can lead to sanctions (including, for instance, bilateral retaliation authorized by the WTO Dispute Settlement Mechanism) or a loss of reputation. While a state might also impose (unauthorized) unilateral trade sanctions, an established framework for retaliation within the WTO makes sanctioning easier, as a state can withdraw an existing concession and benefit from the backing of the international system that approves the retaliation. Sanctions are therefore more likely to be feasible in the case of a breach of a binding WTO commitment. However, loss of reputation can occur when a country breaches a nonbinding agreement just as easily as when

negotiate each provision more cautiously when they know that they will face sanctions if they breach the agreement. This, obviously, entails higher contracting costs than the less rigorous bargaining associated with nonbinding commitments that lack enforcement.

Developing countries' resistance to WTO antitrust negotiations is illustrative of the significance of contracting costs. Developing countries blocked the antitrust talks in the 2003 WTO ministerial meeting in Cancun, partially because of the high contracting costs involved in the negotiations. Already faced with a high burden of regional trade negotiations,[41] developing countries were unwilling to pursue yet another binding agreement, particularly since the negotiations of a WTO antitrust agreement would have required significant resources and technical expertise.[42]

In addition, compliance costs associated with implementing and enforcing international antitrust rules would be high, especially for developing countries that lack the institutional capacity, technical expertise, and financial resources to establish sophisticated antitrust institutions to enforce new laws. The developing countries, in particular, would also incur political costs because their import-competing industries and former state-owned enterprises would resist any reforms that would remove the government protection they enjoy.[43] Even if states already have antitrust agencies, implementation of international antitrust rules involves costs if those rules require states to depart from antitrust laws that would be domestically optimal. New laws might also require retraining of antitrust enforcers or other similar adjustment expenses. Similarly, corporations might incur further costs if they have to revise some of their business practices to comply with new antitrust rules.

---

it breaches a binding agreement. This might be the case with nonbinding international antitrust cooperation, where frequent contacts among antitrust authorities reinforce peer pressure for countries to comply with jointly negotiated norms.

41. While the WTO negotiations were underway, Caribbean and Latin American countries were finalizing their Free Trade Area of Americas (FTAA) Agreement; and African, Caribbean, and Pacific (ACP) countries were still burdened by the aftermath of the Cotonou Agreement negotiations with the EU.

42. Taimoon Stewart, *The Fate of Competition Policy in Cancun: Politics or Substance?*, 31 Legal Issues of Econ. Integration 7, 7 (2004); *see* Editorial, *The Real Lesson of the Cancun Failure*, Fin. Times (London), Sept. 23, 2003, at 16 ("It is absurd to push, as the EU has done, to impose rules in complex areas such as competition and investment on countries so poor that some cannot even afford WTO diplomatic representation.").

43. William E. Kovacic, *Getting Started: Creating New Competition Policy Institutions in Transition Economies*, 23 Brook. J. Int'l L. 403, 404–05 (1997). In contrast, domestic interest groups are not a significant source of resistance to antitrust enforcement in developed countries. Instead, they have been inactive in conveying their support for, or resistance of, international antitrust rules. *See* discussion *infra*, Part IV.B.2.

Consequently, while a binding international antitrust agreement would clearly create some benefits in the form of transactional efficiencies, those benefits are trivial when the substantive provisions of the agreement are watered down to accommodate states' divergent preferences and regulatory capacities. The high costs of cooperation together with the availability of alternatives further reduce the attractiveness of a binding international antitrust agreement. These reasons, taken together, explain why states have abandoned the binding antitrust negotiations within the WTO and have turned to other ways to achieve international antitrust convergence.

III. WHY NONBINDING COOPERATION OFFERS A BETTER PATHWAY TOWARDS CONVERGENCE

Nonbinding cooperation offers a superior alternative for states seeking international antitrust convergence for two primary reasons. First, nonbinding international agreements reduce contracting costs and implementation costs that states incur while pursuing cooperation. Second, while nonbinding agreements do not solve distributional tensions, they permit states to capture some benefits from cooperation by allowing them to cooperate case-by-case in instances where a necessary consensus exists. States are also more willing to enter into nonbinding multilateral agreements, knowing that if they later decide to deviate from the agreement, they can avoid costly sanctions.

Nonbinding international agreements often provide cooperating parties with the benefits of binding agreements at a lower cost.[44] Cooperation within informal networks such as the ICN, or targeted case-specific enforcement cooperation among a small number of antitrust authorities, involves low contracting costs. Negotiations in these venues are more circumscribed and less contentious.[45] The ICN is a largely virtual network that is flexibly organized around working groups. The members of the working groups draft recommendations and guidelines, which are then approved by the Network. As the individual antitrust authorities remain free to decide whether and how to implement the recommendations domestically, the process of approving such recommendations is unlikely to involve rigorous bargaining. Nonbinding recommendations also allow antitrust agencies to seek international convergence without involving the legislators, which diminishes costs and delays embedded in the domestic ratification process.

44. Abbott & Snidal, *Hard and Soft Law*, *supra* note 39, at 434.

45. Anne-Marie Slaughter, *The Accountability of Government Networks*, 8 Ind. L. Global Legal Stud. 347, 347 (2001). Even though the ICN involves multiple parties with divergent preferences, the promulgation of nonbinding norms within the Network can be described as being "fast, flexible, and effective."

However, critics may argue that nonbinding cooperation is more costly than negotiating an antitrust agreement through the WTO. Non-binding antitrust cooperation today consists of numerous bilateral, plurilateral, and multilateral governance instruments, all focusing only on some subset of substantive or procedural antitrust matters. These multiple non-binding instruments, taken together, could be costlier than a single binding international antitrust agreement, provided that such an agreement was feasible to reach.

However, there are a number of reasons a WTO antitrust agreement probably involves higher contracting costs, even when compared to the aggregate costs of negotiating a myraid of nonbinding agreements. For instance, the pursuit of multiple nonbinding agreements has an important advantage of allowing a "cherry-picked" solution, where parties can choose to cooperate only on those issues where the net benefits of cooperation are the greatest. While the absence of (aggregate) net gains can delay or prohibit an entire binding international agreement—including the contemplated WTO antitrust agreement—the multitude of nonbinding agreements renders cooperation possible in those matters and among those parties where the benefits exceed the costs of cooperation.[46] Also, risk-adjusted contracting costs are significantly higher when states pursue a binding, nearly universal agreement. The possibility that the parties will fail to reach an agreement on a specific issue within the ICN, for instance, is less costly than the possibility that the WTO negotiations will fail to successfully conclude after years of intense bargaining. Thus, while the *ex post* costs of a single, all-embracing and successfully concluded binding international antitrust agreement could be lower, states' *ex ante* risk-adjusted perception of those costs is significantly higher.

Compliance costs for developing countries are likely to be significant regardless of whether they enact domestic antitrust laws and set up enforcement mechanisms under binding or nonbinding international agreements. However, nonbinding agreements are likely to be more attractive in that they allow developing countries to adopt only those international norms that involve relatively low compliance costs.[47] Nonbinding cooperation is also likely to reduce political

46. This particular advantage also explains why states have pursued extensive bilateral cooperation. *See* discussion *supra* the chapter, pp.322–324 (Section I).

47. However, developing countries might be able to negotiate flexible provisions even if states choose to pursue a binding agreement under the auspices of the WTO. While the WTO is built on the idea that all its agreements apply equally to all WTO members, the WTO principle of "common but differentiated responsibilities" occasionally permits developing countries to enjoy more limited obligations or more generous implementation timeframes. *See, e.g.*, Christopher D. Stone, *Common but Differentiated Responsibilities in International Law*, 98 Am. J. Int'l L. 276 (2004).

costs stemming from the domestic resistance of international antitrust rules by decreasing the visibility and the prominence of the international commitments.

Nonbinding agreements do not remove distributional tensions among states. However, they often ease bargaining problems by granting more flexibility regarding the manner and the extent to which states implement international antitrust commitments domestically.[48] Pursuing a myriad of nonbinding cooperation agreements allows states to limit cooperation to parties that maintain similar preferences or to issues where consensus exists.

States are also likely to prefer nonbinding agreements because the consequences of a breach are less severe. States with capacity constraints or conflicting preferences have a marginal ability, or willingness, to comply with any negotiated commitments. They are therefore more likely to join a regime under which they can defect without facing sanctions. Thus, by keeping international commitments nonbinding, states are able to capture some gains from international cooperation without relinquishing control over their domestic antitrust laws, or assuming the risk of sanctions if they are ultimately unable or unwilling to comply with their obligations.[49]

IV. DO NONBINDING AGREEMENTS PAVE THE WAY FOR A BINDING INTERNATIONAL ANTITRUST AGREEMENT?

The above discussion has argued that a meaningful binding international antitrust agreement would currently be infeasible to negotiate, and explained why nonbinding agreements can still be effective in fostering cooperation. This Part extends the claim by asserting that even if binding multilateral cooperation were to become more viable in the future (predominantly due to the gradual alignment of state preferences as a result of voluntary cooperation), states will continue to rely on nonbinding cooperation in the near future.

A. Conventional Wisdom: Nonbinding Agreements Form a Second-Best Solution

Among international law scholars, there is often a presumption that binding international agreements, if attainable, would be superior tools to generate regulatory convergence. States are assumed to resort to nonbinding agreements

---

48. *See also* Abbott & Snidal, *Hard and Soft Law, supra* note 39, at 445. Abbott and Snidal suggest that "soft law should be attractive in proportion to the degree of divergence among the preferences and capacities of states."

49. In contrast, the WTO's Dispute Settlement Mechanism would authorize trading partners to retaliate if one party failed to comply with a potential WTO Antitrust Agreement.

when normatively more desirable binding agreements are not available.[50] Many commentators also argue that the greatest virtue of nonbinding agreements is their potential to pave the way for binding cooperation.[51] Under this view, nonbinding agreements are considered to form merely a stepping stone in a gradual process towards the ultimate goal: a binding international agreement.

International cooperation may evolve gradually from lower to higher levels of cooperation.[52] States may initially enter into modest cooperative arrangements that are more viable to negotiate.[53] Those arrangements might then incrementally evolve into binding international agreements, as uncertainty progressively diminishes and consensus among states begins to emerge. Constructivist scholars in particular support this theory of incremental norm formation. They argue that social interaction, diffusion of information, and collective deliberation within nonbinding regimes trigger a "self-reinforcing dynamic," which leads states to pursue deeper and more formal means of cooperation.[54]

Historically, the proponents of a nonbinding international antitrust regime have endorsed such a regime primarily on the grounds that it is more *feasible* to attain than a binding international agreement. Nonbinding cooperation is frequently viewed as the "best available" regime, implying that a binding international agreement would represent the optimal solution, if it were attainable. Diane Wood, one of the leading proponents of nonbinding international antitrust cooperation, has aptly summarized this view by calling a binding international

---

50. Steven R. Ratner, *Does International Law Matter in Preventing Ethnic Conflict?*, 32 N.Y.U. J. INT'L L. & POL. 591, 653 (2000) (noting the implicit assumption that hard law affects state behavior more than soft law); *see also* Jack L. Goldsmith & Eric A. Posner, *International Agreements: A Rational Choice Approach*, 44 VA. J. INT'L L. 113, 114 (2003) (noting that among traditional, positivistic approaches to international law, "nonlegal" instruments are viewed as being of secondary importance).

51. *See, e.g.*, Christine Chinkin, *Normative Development in the International Legal System*, *in* COMMITMENT AND COMPLIANCE: THE ROLE OF NON-BONDING NORMS IN THE INTERNATIONAL LEGAL SYSTEM 21, 32 (Dinah Shelton ed., 2000) (noting that soft law can act as a catalyst for the development of customary international law, which to many commentators is the "*raison d'être* of soft law").

52. *See* Kenneth W. Abbott & Duncan Snidal, *Pathways to International Cooperation*, *in* THE IMPACT OF INTERNATIONAL LAW ON INTERNATIONAL COOPERATION 50, 50 (Eyal Benvenisti & Moshe Hirsch eds., 2004).

53. *See* Kenneth W. Abbott & Duncan Snidal, *Filling in the Folk Theorem: The Role of Gradualism and Legalization in International Cooperation to Combat Corruption* 1–2 (Aug. 30, 2002) (working paper presented at the American Political Science Association annual meeting).

54. *Id.* at 12. *See also* Abbott & Snidal, *Pathways to International Cooperation*, *supra* note 56; Downs et al., *Transformational Model*, *supra* note 36, at 467 n.2 (referring to literature that represents the Transformationalist perspective).

antitrust agreement an "impossible dream."[55] A binding agreement is regarded as the ultimate goal and nonbinding cooperation as a pathway towards that goal.[56] While some independent benefits of nonbinding cooperation have been acknowledged in the debate, most advocates of nonbinding international antitrust law see it only as a second-best, partial, or interim solution.[57]

It is possible that nonbinding antitrust cooperation will pave the way for binding international antitrust rules. Voluntary cooperation facilitates information exchange, learning, and trust-building among antitrust authorities. As a result, state preferences are expected to become more aligned, alleviating the distributional tensions that currently undermine cooperation. In addition, the costs of negotiating a legally binding agreement are prone to diminish, as states would no longer need to adjust their domestic laws significantly (as the domestic equilibrium would be closer to that sought by an international agreement). Such developments would likely remove, or at least mitigate, obstacles to the binding international antitrust agreement.

This view suggests that as binding cooperation becomes more feasible, states may attempt to revive negotiations toward a binding international antitrust agreement, within or outside the WTO framework. This raises the question whether negotiating a binding agreement is indeed the optimal path or whether a nonbinding international antitrust regime is preferable even when the alternative of binding cooperation becomes more viable.

B. Disputing the Presumed Supremacy of Binding Agreements

This article argues that a pathway from nonbinding to binding rules in antitrust cooperation is not inevitable, nor is it even likely. "Nations cooperate without law all the time,"[58] and they do so for a reason. Nonbinding agreements have their own, independent advantages and are sometimes more optimal governance

---

55. Diane P. Wood, *The Impossible Dream: Real International Antitrust*, 1992 U. Chi. Legal F. 277, 300–01 (1992).

56. *See* Wood, *supra* note 6, at 179, 185–185 ("[W]e need to exercise caution before we take a leap into a formal antitrust regime"; "A slower approach . . . was the better way toward our ultimate goal"; and "I believe that harmonization is, at this time, premature").

57. *Id. See also, e.g.,* Spencer Weber Waller, *The Internationalization of Antitrust Enforcement*, 77 B.U. L. Rev. 343, 402 (1997) ("Cooperation is a valuable addition to the antitrust landscape, but not as an alternative to harmonization or a particularly valuable end unto itself."); Wolfgang Kerber & Oliver Budzinski, *Competition of Competition Laws: Mission Impossible?*, *in* Competition Laws in Conflict: Antitrust Jurisdiction in the Global Economy, *supra* note 4, at 31 (supporting nonbinding cooperation on the grounds of retaining flexibility and allowing for parallel experimentation and mutual learning). However, Kerber and Budzinski also endorse supplementing nonbinding cooperation in cross-border antitrust matters with binding international jurisdictional rules.

58. *See* Goldsmith & Posner, *supra* note 54, at 116.

instruments than binding agreements.[59] States choose between binding and nonbinding agreements in accordance with their interest in any given issue, taking into account the constraints imposed by other states and the external environment in which they operate. Nonbinding agreements do not merely "come to the rescue" when legally binding regimes are not attainable.[60] Rather, binding and nonbinding agreements offer distinct benefits, the relative importance of which depends on the strategic situation of the states pursuing cooperation.

Nonbinding international antitrust cooperation avoids the problem of watering down the rules to accommodate divergent preferences. Nonbinding cooperation also offers more flexibility and reduces contracting and implementation costs associated with cooperation. A shift to binding cooperation would cause states to lose those important benefits. In addition, the specific advantages of binding agreements are of no real value to the negotiating parties for three primary reasons. First, assuming that antitrust laws are rarely used opportunistically for protectionist purposes, there is no need to pursue a binding agreement with enforcement provisions. Second, in the absence of coherent interests group support for far-reaching international antitrust cooperation, a binding agreement does not offer political economy gains. Finally, evolving nonbinding regimes are pre-capturing the highest gains of cooperation and thereby gradually decreasing the net benefits from the pursuit of a binding agreement.

1. The Self-Enforcing Nature of Antitrust Cooperation Renders a Binding Agreement Unnecessary The risk of opportunism is one of the key variables that states consider when choosing between binding and nonbinding agreements.[61] Binding international agreements with cautiously negotiated commitments are less susceptible to states' self-serving interpretation.[62] Binding agreements raise the costs of noncompliance; cheating is easier and possibly more prevalent with nonbinding agreements.[63] Thus, binding agreements seem advantageous as "assurance devices" in situations where the potential for costly opportunism is high and cheating is difficult to detect.[64]

---

59. Abbott & Snidal, *Hard and Soft Law*, *supra* note 39, at 423 ("[S]oft law offers many advantages of hard law, avoids some costs of hard law, and has certain advantages of its own"); *id.* at 456 (arguing that soft law is valuable on its own, and not just as a stepping stone to hard law).

60. Jan Klabbers, *The Undesirability of Soft Law*, 67 Nordic J. Int'l Law 381, 384 (1998).

61. Kal Raustiala, *Form and Substance in International Agreements*, 99 Am. J. Int'l L. 581, 593–94 (2005).

62. Abbott & Snidal, *Hard and Soft Law*, *supra* note 39, at 426–27.

63. The costs of reneging can manifest themselves both in the form of reputational costs or actual enforcement costs, for instance, in case of WTO dispute settlement. *See id.* at 427.

64. *Id.* at 429.

Binding agreements make sense in some contexts. For example, binding agreements are required as assurance devices most prominently in the national security domain, where any defection from cooperation would be particularly dangerous. Also, international trade matters are susceptible to opportunism. States seek enhanced market access for their exports but are at the same time tempted to renege on their own commitments to reciprocally open their domestic markets to foreign imports. These types of cooperation problems are characterized as Prisoner's Dilemmas where the central problem is the states' pervasive incentive to defect from any agreement they negotiate. In contrast, when the incentives to defect from the agreed commitments are low, a binding agreement with enforceable commitments is less valuable. This is the case in coordination games where the parties lack the incentives to deviate from the agreement once the focal point of coordination has been established.[65]

I have elsewhere argued that the strategic situation underlying international antitrust cooperation resembles predominantly a coordination game with distributional consequences.[66] States would like to coordinate their antitrust policies but cannot agree on the optimal rules around which to converge.[67] For instance, while the United States would prefer all countries to enforce U.S.-style antitrust laws, the EU would rather see all countries enforce EU-style antitrust laws. This distributional conflict makes international antitrust cooperation difficult. However, if states were to agree on the optimal point of antitrust convergence, the agreement would be self-enforcing, as none of the states would have the incentive to deviate from the agreed rules.[68] This would render the enforcement

---

65. Raustiala, *Form and Substance*, *supra* note 66, at 592–94. *See also* Kenneth W. Abbott, *Modern International Relations Theory: A Prospectus for International Lawyers*, 14 Yale J. Int'l L. 335, 358–62, 371–74 (1989). While the possibility of defection is not entirely absent in coordination situations, any surreptitious cheating at least is unlikely. *See* Lisa L. Martin, *The Rational State Choice of Multilateralism*, *in* Multilateralism Matters: The Theory and Praxis of an Institutional Form 91, 102 (John Gerard Ruggie ed., 1993).

66. *See generally* Bradford, *supra* note 3.

67. The efforts to coordinate merger policies or cartel investigations among antitrust agencies, for instance, are unlikely to involve incentives to engage in noncooperative strategies and cheating. States can generally be expected to benefit from a more effective control of international cartels that adversely affect several markets. Similarly, harmonized merger control procedures enhancing legal certainty and reducing transaction costs and delays should generate aggregate and individual benefits that would only be undermined by choosing noncooperative strategies. For instance, neither the United States nor the EU would benefit from an inconsistent merger review decision between the two agencies, even though both states can be expected to want the other state to reach the same decision that they have reached. *Id.*, pp. 514–16.

68. However, China's first enforcement decisions under its newly adopted antimonopoly law offer some indication that antitrust review could be used as a vehicle for protectionism, possibly calling into question the characterization of international antitrust cooperation as a coordination game (as opposed to a Prisoner's Dilemma). China's

mechanism of any legally binding antitrust agreement less attractive, if not altogether unnecessary.[69]

While deliberate cheating is likely to be rare in the antitrust domain, developing countries' capacity constraints, including a lack of enforcement institutions and antirust expertise, might lead to occasional defections from international commitments. However, to the extent that states' defections can be traced to capacity constraints rather than to an intentional violation of the agreement, a binding agreement with enforcement provisions would be unlikely to bring about greater compliance. Capacity building in the form of technical assistance is likely to yield better results vis-à-vis developing countries whose inadequate regulatory capacities renders compliance with the contemplated agreement difficult. The "managerial model of compliance," which rests on transparency, capacity building, and persuasion, rather than on enforcement and sanctions,[70] seems therefore particularly suitable for ratcheting up antitrust standards in the developing countries.

Consequently, if the major obstacle to an international antitrust agreement is not the difficulty of ensuring compliance, but the difficulty of reaching an agreement in the first place due to the distributional problem, the enforcement benefits of binding agreements are limited. This is likely to cause states to prefer

---

decision to prohibit Coca Cola's proposed acquisition of the Chinese juice company Huyian, for instance, raised suspicions on the motivations behind China's antitrust policy. The possibility of China becoming a major antitrust force that repeatedly applies its antitrust laws strategically to block the market entry of foreign companies might underline the limits of voluntary cooperation. However, it is uncertain whether China's antitrust practices can revive the WTO antitrust negotiations. It is too soon to argue that China's early antitrust enforcement practices have fundamentally amended the strategic situation underlying international antitrust cooperation. It is also unclear whether China's enforcement patterns will prompt the United States and other states currently opposing WTO antitrust rules to change their minds on the benefits of such rules. Second, any WTO antitrust agreement aimed to constrain China's antitrust policies would require China's acquiescence on those new rules, complicating the negotiations.

69. Charles Lipson has argued that the distinction between enforceable and nonenforceable commitments is largely moot in international law, which lacks the enforcement mechanisms comparable to those embedded in domestic legal systems. Contrasting international and domestic enforcement structures does indeed highlight the weaknesses of the international legal system. However, this distinction is somewhat less pronounced with respect to areas of international trade law that are supported by the WTO dispute settlement mechanism. The dispute settlement mechanism provides for multilaterally authorized (yet bilaterally executed) retaliatory measures. Thus, the question of enforcement remains a relevant consideration when states choose between a binding WTO agreement on antitrust and, for instance, nonbinding ICN guidelines and recommendations. *See* discussion in Lipson, *Why Are Some International Agreements Informal?* 45 INT'L ORG. 495, 502–08, 513 (1991).

70. Abraham Chayes & Antonia Handler Chayes, *On Compliance,* 47 INT'L ORG. 175, 197–204 (1993).

nonbinding agreements even in a situation where a binding agreement is assumed to be more feasible to attain.

2. A Binding Agreement Does Not Offer Political Economy Gains The choice between a binding and nonbinding international agreement is also informed by domestic political economy considerations.[71] Binding agreements emerge in areas where domestic interest groups are active. Interest groups that favor international cooperation in a given issue area generally support binding agreements because of their perceived effectiveness.[72] Binding agreements also offer the domestic constituency more opportunities to influence the content of the agreement, as their conclusion generally requires more domestic legislative involvement. In contrast, nonbinding cooperation mechanisms are common in the complex areas of "technocratic cooperation," including antitrust, where domestic interest groups are less active.[73]

There is no evidence that domestic interest groups, including consumers, corporations, or industry organizations, would deem an international antitrust agreement a priority.[74] Consumers, who would be expected to benefit from enhanced international antitrust enforcement, form a fragmented interest group with little agenda-setting capacity.[75] Corporations, on the other hand, have interests that are largely case- and issue-specific, rendering *ex ante* support for any comprehensive international antitrust agreement difficult. For example, a corporation will probably support international cooperation to ensure a smooth clearance of a merger in which it is participating, but may have contrary interests when its competitors are seeking to merge. Similarly, the corporation's support for international cooperation in cartel matters is likely to hinge on whether agencies are seeking to prosecute a cartel in which the corporation itself, or its competitors, are participating.[76] Thus, corporations prefer to choose case-by-case the

---

71. Raustiala, *Form and Substance, supra* note 65, at 582.

72. *Id.* at 600.

73. *Id.*

74. *See, e.g., ICC/BIAC Comments on Report of the U.S. International Competition Policy Advisory Committee, supra* note 12, at 2, 6, 10. While the ICC and the BIAC support some degree of substantive and some procedural harmonization and convergence of domestic merger regimes, "ICC and BIAC agree that the WTO is not an appropriate forum for review of private restraints and that the WTO should not develop new competition laws under its framework at this time."

75. International antitrust cooperation has not been a priority for consumer organizations either, which might be explained by the "technocratic" nature of antitrust law. *See* Raustiala, *Form and Substance, supra* note 65, at 600.

76. In general, while corporations tend to define their interests case-by-case, they are expected to support cooperation in the case of merger reviews, as this would reduce transaction costs and uncertainty. In contrast, corporations often resist rules that facilitate cooperation in cartel cases, out of fear of one day being the target of a cartel investigation. *See* ABA & INT'L BAR ASSOC., A TAX ON MERGERS?: SURVEYING THE TIME AND COSTS TO

issues and instances in which they want antitrust agencies to cooperate among themselves.

In the absence of coherent domestic interest group support, states are able to reap few political gains by pursuing a binding international antitrust agreement.[77] As a result, states prefer to focus on other regulatory priorities, leaving international antitrust cooperation to the domain of antitrust agencies.[78] This has caused international antitrust cooperation to be primarily an agency-driven regulatory process. Most antitrust agencies operate relatively independently from the executive and the legislature. Nonbinding international cooperation further strengthens their independence and expands their regulatory powers.[79] It is therefore not surprising that antitrust agencies have been the principal *norm entrepreneurs* behind the pursuit of international antitrust cooperation.[80] And as long as the demand for international antitrust cooperation continues to stem from the agencies rather than from domestic interests groups or the legislature, nonbinding cooperation is likely to persist.

3. Nonbinding Agreements Reduce the Gains Available from a Binding Agreement Today, a growing number of jurisdictions enforce increasingly

---

Business of Multi-Jurisdictional Merger Reviews 5 (June 2003) (noting that 56 percent of the businesses see scope for improving and harmonizing merger notification processes); *see also ICC/BIAC Comments on Report of the U.S. International Competition Policy Advisory Committee, supra* note 12, at 8.

77. The absence of interest group support is one reason countries have had difficulty negotiating a binding international antitrust agreement. By contrast, countries successfully concluded the WTO Agreement on Trade-Related Aspects of Intellectual Property Rights ("TRIPs") largely as a result of intense lobbying by domestic corporations in the United States, the EU, and Japan. *See* Sylvia Ostry, *Convergence and Sovereignty: Policy Scope for Compromise?*, *in* Coping with Globalization 52, 55–57 (Aseem Prakash & Jeffrey A. Hart eds., 2000); *see also* Bradford, *supra* note 3, at 547–48. (discussing why the prospects for formal cooperation in the case of the TRIPs and antitrust have been different).

78. "States" are in this connection understood as elected officials, including the legislature and the executive.

79. Antitrust enforcers rarely need to consult other government agencies or the legislature when pursuing nonbinding cooperation directly with their counterparts abroad. A nonbinding international regime that exclusively focuses on antitrust matters also empowers antitrust agencies vis-à-vis other government agencies. For example, a binding WTO antitrust agreement would shift powers from the Antitrust Division of the U.S. Department of Justice (DOJ) and the U.S. Federal Trade Commission (FTC) to the U.S. Trade Representative (USTR), whereas cooperation under the auspices of the ICN would allow antitrust agencies to retain all decision-making powers. This is probably one reason the USTR has endorsed incorporating antitrust in the WTO while the DOJ and FTC have opposed it. *See* Spencer Weber Waller, *National Laws and International Markets: Strategies of Cooperation and Harmonization in the Enforcement of Competition Law*, 18 Cardozo L. Rev. 1111, 1122–24 (1996).

80. The attempts to generate cooperation in any international forum—whether in the WTO, ICN, or OECD—have been predominantly driven by antitrust agencies.

consistent antitrust laws. Approximately one hundred states have domestic antitrust laws, all of which were enacted without any binding international obligation to do so.[81] In addition to the rapid proliferation of new antitrust regimes, the existing antitrust laws are moving closer to one another.[82] Antitrust norms and economic theories behind them have diffused rapidly across jurisdictions as countries have emulated more established antitrust regimes.[83]

A large part of this predominantly voluntary adoption of antitrust rules and their increasing alignment may be attributed to the market-based diffusion of neo-liberal economic ideology and increasing domestic support for privatization and liberalization of trade and investment, even in developing countries and transition economies.[84] In addition, existing bilateral cooperation and nonbinding multilateral antitrust norms have accelerated this diffusion of antitrust norms across the globe, further contributing to international antitrust convergence.

While it is difficult to determine the extent to which existing convergence reflects nonbinding international rules on the one hand, and other motivations on the other, the very fact that convergence is taking place has two implications. First, increasing voluntary alignment of domestic antitrust laws ought to alleviate the distributional problem that has thus far undermined any efforts to negotiate a binding international antitrust agreement. Voluntary convergence is also likely to decrease the adjustment cost of cooperation. When domestic antitrust laws increasingly begin to resemble one another, commitments sought by a binding international agreement would not require states to undertake

---

81. *See* http://www.globalcompetitionforum.org (last visited May 24, 2010) (maintaining a list of existing antitrust laws across the world).

82. *See, e.g.*, Fox, *supra* note 4, at 1787 (discussing cross-fertilization of antitrust laws, which has produced "increasingly high levels of common understanding").

83. The existing international convergence has taken place largely around the U.S. or the EU antitrust regimes, resulting in two "clusters" of antitrust systems instead of a single *de facto* harmonized global antitrust regime. While the bipolar antitrust convergence is to some extent the result of a voluntary decision on the part of new antitrust regimes to emulate the two more developed regimes, the existing convergence also reflects a conscious effort by the United States and the EU to actively export their respective antitrust regimes abroad. On market-based harmonization that occurs when countries have an incentive to emulate more established regulatory regimes, see Beth A. Simmons, *The International Politics of Harmonization: The Case of Capital Market Regulation*, 55 Int'l Org. 589 (2001).

84. For the most part, the creation of antitrust laws in developing countries does not appear to reflect an externally induced policy change. However, it is difficult to estimate the extent to which developing countries adopt antitrust laws out of self-interest and the extent to which they are pressured to conform to the preferences of the powerful antitrust regimes. *See, e.g.*, Susan K. Sell, Power and Ideas: North-South Politics of Intellectual Property and Antitrust (1998) (characterizing developing countries' decisions to implement antitrust laws as a "choice within constraints rather than coercion").

substantial new commitments. This would decrease contracting costs and compliance costs alike, and increase the likelihood that even formal cooperation would gradually become net beneficial. The second implication is that the ongoing voluntary convergence is gradually eroding the benefits of binding cooperation. The voluntary alignment of domestic antitrust laws reduces negative externalities embedded in the current system, which decreases the need for binding international rules. In such circumstances, the added value from seeking to codify the status quo becomes questionable.

While it is difficult to predict whether the benefits or the costs of cooperation are likely to fall at a faster rate following voluntary convergence, it is likely that net benefits from cooperation are gradually shrinking. Existing voluntary cooperation focuses on issues where net benefits are the greatest and distributional tensions most manageable; any remaining binding agreement would be left to address a range of issues with lower prospective benefits. As the pursuit of a binding agreement must entail some level of fixed costs (in particular, contracting costs), a dwindling pool of available net benefits will likely reduce the incentive to pursue a binding agreement.

Accordingly, as long as (1) international antitrust cooperation continues to be largely self-enforcing and opportunistic behavior an exception, (2) domestic interest group support for international antirust cooperation continues to be weak, and (3) nonbinding antitrust convergence continues to expand and show progress in mitigating negative externalities, states are likely to continue to rely on nonbinding agreements when pursuing antitrust cooperation. Nonbinding instruments may gradually develop toward binding antitrust commitments, but that is not inevitable. Nor is the move toward a binding international antitrust agreement necessarily a desirable one as long as the fundamental assumptions described above continue to hold.

CONCLUSION

This article has argued that the pursuit of nonbinding international antitrust cooperation represents an optimal choice for states. It is not merely an opportunity to capture limited gains from cooperation while proceeding towards a binding international agreement, as is commonly perceived.

States' conflicting preferences over the optimal content of international antitrust cooperation is the primary impediment for negotiating binding antitrust rules in the WTO. States have sought to accommodate their divergent preferences by removing controversial issues from the negotiation agenda. However, this has led to proposals for watered-down rules that would confer trivial benefits to WTO member states. Because states expect low net benefits from a prospective WTO antitrust agreement, states have abandoned the negotiations to seek case-by-case cooperation and voluntary international guidelines instead.

Nonbinding cooperation has successfully fostered international antitrust convergence. A growing number of states enforce increasingly consistent antitrust rules today without any binding international agreement requiring them to do so. Eventually, successful voluntary convergence could pave the way for binding cooperation. However, this article has argued that nonbinding agreements are likely to persist for three primary reasons. First, as cooperation under nonbinding agreements is largely self-enforcing, the added value of a binding agreement with provisions for monitoring, enforcement, and sanctions is trivial. Second, in the absence of coordinated domestic interest group support for international antitrust cooperation, a binding agreement would not provide states with any domestic political economy rents and therefore will remain a low national priority. Finally, the emerging voluntary convergence will slowly eradicate negative externalities stemming from decentralized antitrust regimes, making the case for a binding international agreement less compelling.

By arguing that nonbinding agreements are preferable to binding agreements, even in situations where binding agreements are feasible, this article disputes the view that nonbinding agreements are second-best instruments for fostering international antitrust convergence. States have not chosen nonbinding agreements because their first-best regime choice has been unavailable. Instead, states have viewed binding agreements as unnecessary and undesirable.

An optimal institutional design must be consistent with state interests to be effective. By acknowledging both the difficulties involved in the pursuit of binding international antitrust cooperation and the ability of nonbinding agreements to mitigate those difficulties, this article raises two critical questions. First, given the obstacles to international antitrust cooperation, how could a binding agreement emerge? And second, assuming that a binding agreement could emerge, what would it add to the existing nonbinding international antitrust regime? Until the proponents of a binding international antitrust agreement can answer those questions, nonbinding cooperation is, and will likely remain, the preferred solution.

17. COMPETITION LAW AND COOPERATION
Possible Strategies

ANDREW GUZMAN

I. INTRODUCTION

In many respects, international competition policy already exists. Overlapping domestic legal regimes create a de facto regime that firms involved in international business must navigate. There are, however, almost no binding international agreements on the topic; there is no overarching institution that applies or enforces laws on competition; and there are no international requirements regarding procedural or substantive rules. Given the state of international competition policy, several questions arise. First, what characterizes the relationship between domestic competition laws and international business activities? Second, to what extent is international cooperation on competition policy likely or possible? Finally, given the answers to the first two questions, what form might international cooperation on competition policy take?

II. DOMESTIC JURISDICTIONS, EXTRATERRITORIALITY, AND INTERNATIONAL COMPETITION

We begin by looking at the de facto regime of international competition policy created by overlapping domestic jurisdictions. This entails a brief examination of the principle of extraterritoriality before describing the competition policy of the United States and the European Union.[1]

A. Extraterritoriality

It is essential to international competition policy to understand how countries apply their laws to activities that take place beyond their borders. Whereas "territoriality" refers to the application of a country's laws to activity in its domestic sphere, "extraterritoriality" describes the application of a country's laws to conduct by firms located in countries abroad.

There is wide variation in the abilities of countries to regulate activity that happens outside of their borders. On one end of the spectrum are countries with

1. I refer to the competition policy of the European Union as "domestic" because its legal policy is established through a formal legislative process and not by a treaty process. This is appropriate in the context of this chapter, despite not being entirely accurate.

a limited ability to govern the behavior of foreign firms because those firms do only a small amount of business in the country and hold few, if any, assets in the country. The only enforcement power these countries have is to deny a firm access to the domestic market. This sort of extreme remedy would impose large costs on the country and may not represent much of a loss for the firm. As a result, a country in this situation has little choice but to limit the reach of its laws to activities that take place within its borders.

At the opposite end of the spectrum are countries where foreign firms hold an abundance of assets in the country or where firms conduct substantial amounts of business within the country. In this situation, a country can effectively sanction a misbehaving firm by levying fines or restricting how the firm does business. In other words, the country has the ability to influence the behavior of the firm through the application of its domestic laws. This allows it to regulate foreign firms, including the foreign activities of these firms, in much the same way it regulates domestic firms.

When states apply their domestic laws to international activity, there is a question of which laws apply to which activities. To answer this question requires an examination of the jurisdictional rules in place in relevant countries. As a practical matter, then, it is the jurisdictional reach of domestic laws that is key to understanding how business activity is regulated. These jurisdictional rules also make up the central policy tool under consideration in any policy discussion of international competition.

B. Extraterritoriality and the United States Position

The United States was the first country to apply its competition laws extraterritorially, and now, along with the European Union, is one of the two most important jurisdictions to be examined.

Justice Holmes's 1909 opinion in *American Banana Co. v. United Fruit Co.* marks the original American jurisdictional rule regarding competition policy.[2] There, Holmes put forward an unambiguously territorial approach, holding that "the character of an act as lawful or unlawful must be determined wholly by the law of the country where the act is done."[3] Since the United Fruit Company's conduct had taken place solely in Panama and Costa Rica, the Court held that the defendant's activity could not be reached by the Sherman Act. Under *American Banana*, geographic borders served to mark the outermost limits of a domestic law's reach, and conduct had to occur within those boundaries in order for domestic laws to apply. Though this purely territorial perspective seems odd to modern lawyers—especially those working in the context of international business—the decision was not remarkable at the time.

---

2. American Banana Co. v. United Fruit Co., 213 U.S. 347 (1909).
3. *Id.* at 356.

The 1945 decision in *United States v. Aluminum Co. of America (Alcoa)* marked the authoritative shift from a series of cases in which the Supreme Court had continually edged away from the territorialist position on jurisdiction taken in *American Banana*.[4] There, the Second Circuit, acting in lieu of the Supreme Court, held that the jurisdiction of American competition law extended beyond the United States' borders for actions that took place outside the borders but had consequences within the United States.[5] Known as the "effects test," Judge Learned Hand in *Alcoa* established the rule that permitted extraterritorial jurisdiction if activities abroad "were intended to affect imports and did affect them."[6]

This decision marked a period of extraterritorial application of American antitrust laws[7] leading up to the reaffirmation of the effects test and the extraterritorial reach of the Sherman Act in the 1993 decision in *Hartford Fire Insurance Co. v. California*.[8] At the outset, this case looked like it would be the Supreme Court's opportunity to determine the application of principles of international comity when there was a conflict of international laws. Nineteen states and several private parties had brought suit against the defendants—including London reinsurers—arguing that they had violated the Sherman Act.[9] In response, the defendants argued that jurisdiction should be declined on the basis of international comity considerations.[10] The jurisdictional conflict was of central concern since the domestic laws of the United Kingdom allowed the conduct in question, but the United States domestic laws prohibited the firm's activities.[11]

In its decision, however, the Supreme Court avoided the comity question altogether by holding that comity considerations apply only when there is a "true conflict" between foreign laws and U.S. laws. A true conflict in this context is defined as a situation in which it is impossible for the affected party to comply

---

4. United States v. Aluminum Co. of America, 148 F.2d 416 (2d Cir. 1945). See *United States v. Sisal Sales Corp.*, 274 U.S. 268 (1927); *Thomsen v. Cayser*, 243 U.S. 66 (1917); and *United States v. Pacific & Arctic Railway Navigation Co.*, 228 U.S. 87 (1913) as examples of holdings that gradually depart from the territorial jurisdiction approach.

5. United States v. Aluminum Co. of America, 148 F.2d at 443.

6. *Id.* at 444. Because of a lack of quorum among Supreme Court Justices, the Second Circuit was acting in lieu of the Supreme Court and had the standing of the Court's jurisprudence. The Supreme Court later adopted the effects test in *Continental Ore Co. v. Union Carbide & Carbon Corp.*, 370 U.S. 690, 704 (1962).

7. Diane P. Wood, *The Impossible Dream: Real International Antitrust*, UNIV. CHI. LEGAL F. 277 (1992).

8. Hartford Fire Ins. Co. v. California, 509 U.S. 764, 796 (1993) (stating that "[T]he Sherman Act applies to foreign conduct that was meant to produce and did in fact produce some substantial effect in the Unites States.").

9. *Id.* at 769.

10. *Id.* at 797.

11. *Id.* at 798–99.

with the laws of both jurisdictions simultaneously. In the *Hartford Fire* case, said the Court, a true conflict was absent because the defendants were able to comply with both sets of laws.[12] On this basis, the Court determined that the *Alcoa* effects test applied.[13]

The decision in *Hartford Fire* exemplifies one of the inherent and crucial tensions in the de facto international competition policy regime. If domestic laws from two jurisdictions apply to the same international activity, then both states may claim jurisdiction. When this happens, however, the stricter of the two legal regimes will always govern in such a situation, regardless of the market share of the state with the stricter regime. As in Hartford Fire, any leniency of the less strict regime will be overcome by the assertion of jurisdiction and subsequent enforcement of the state with stricter anticompetition laws.

C. Extraterritoriality and the European Union Position

Europe was far behind the United States in embracing the extraterritorial application of its laws. It was not until the *Wood Pulp* case in 1985 that the European Union and its member states applied their competition policies in this way.[14] In that case, 41 producers and two trade associations were alleged to have established an illegal agreement to fix prices. In its decision, the European Court of Justice (ECJ) applied, for the first time, what is known as the "implementation test." Under the implementation test, the court examined both the place where the illegal agreement was formed and the place where the anticompetitive agreement or conduct was put into play.[15] The jurisdictional inquiry, found in Article 85, then has two factors: (1) an agreement, decision, or concerted practice entered into by two or more undertakings, and (2) the actual implementation within the EU of that agreement, decision, or concerted practice.[16]

Additionally, Council Regulation 4064 gives the Commission authority to review all concentrations that have any impact on the EU, with impact defined as global combined sales of ECU 5 billion or two companies each having sales of ECU 250 million.[17]

---

12. *Id.* at 799.

13. *Id.* at 796–97. *See also* U.S. Department of Justice and Federal Trade Commission, *Antitrust Enforcement Guidelines for International Operations,* 24 (April 1995) ("[T]he Sherman Act applies to foreign conduct that was meant to produce and did in fact produce some substantial effect in the United States.").

14. *In re* Wood Pulp Cartel, 1985 O.J. (L 85) 1, [1985] 3 C.M.L.R 474 (1985).

15. Evan Briebart, *The Wood Pulp Case: The Application of European Economic Community Competition Law to Foreign-Based Undertakings,* 19 GA. J. INT'L & COMP. L. 149, 173 (1989).

16. *Wood Pulp, supra* note 14.

17. Andre Fiebig, *The Extraterritorial Application of the European Merger Control Regulation,* 5 COLUM. J. EUR. L. 100 (1998). The Commission may also look to supplementary tests to find jurisdiction. Examples of supplementary tests include (1) the combined aggregate worldwide sales of all the undertakings concerned are more than ECU 2.5 billion,

Both the American and European jurisdictional rules focus on features of the affected firms and the domestic economy. They pay no attention to whether and how foreign laws might apply. From a firm's perspective, however, the interaction between the legal regimes is critical. If the laws of both countries (or in some cases, the laws of many countries) apply, the firm must satisfy them all. This means that it is the strictest law that governs or—even worse—the strictest elements from among the various legal regimes that apply, creating a de facto regime that is stricter than any single domestic system.

D. Implications of the De Facto Regime

1. **Overregulation** The de facto international regime created by the extraterritorial reach of domestic anticompetition laws, creates an increased burden on businesses that conduct activities in states with extraterritorial jurisdiction. As noted above, a firm doing business in states that apply their laws extraterritorially must face an increased regulatory burden because they are subject to the most strict dimension of the states' anticompetition laws.

An example is helpful. Consider, for instance, a firm that conducts business in countries A and B and that is subject to the regulatory laws of each country. If Country A has more restrictive policies than Country B with regard to horizontal restraints on trade, but more lenient anticompetition laws with regard to vertical restraints, the firm will be restricted in its horizontal conduct by the laws of country A. Now imagine that Country B has more restrictive laws than Country A in terms of vertical restraints, but is more lenient in terms of horizontal restraints. The firm is subject to the more restrictive vertical restraints of Country B. Assuming that both countries think their policies are the optimal competition policies, the firm is still subject to the more restrictive dimension of both countries' policies within the de facto international regime. We can confidently call this an example of overregulation because it creates a legal system that is more burdensome than that selected by any single country.

Mergers are another context in which firms face overregulation in the de facto international regime. Take, for example, the proposed merger of two or more firms that conduct business in both the United States and the European Union. The firms are thus subject to merger review in both jurisdictions.[18] The merger can therefore proceed only if approved in both jurisdictions. Even if the substantive

(2) in each of at least three Member States, the combined aggregate sales of all the undertakings concerned are more than ECU 100 million, (3) in each of these Member States, the aggregate sales of each of at least two of the undertakings concerned are more than ECU 25 million, and (4) the aggregate Community-wide sales of at least two of the undertakings concerned are more than ECU 100 million.

18. In the United States, both the Sherman and Clayton Acts apply to companies proposing mergers as do the U.S. Department of Justice and Federal Trade Commission

rules are the same—which makes it likely that both the U.S. and EU authorities would approve the merger—there is no promise that both sets of authorities will reach the same decision. Innumerable factors—including differences in culture, politics, guiding assumptions, and biases—can yield different results despite substantive agreement in the rules. Thus, even if the rules in the two systems are identical, the merger must be approved twice, doubling the chances for a denial.

2. Underregulation The de facto international regime also creates problems of underregulation. The above discussion details the implications stemming from extraterritorial application of domestic anticompetition laws as they apply to firms conducting business activities in those states. Yet, there are many countries that either lack effective anticompetition policies or do not apply their laws extraterritorially. The most persuasive explanation for a country's lack of extraterritorial application is pragmatic—either a state does not have the power to enforce its laws beyond its borders, or it does not have the ability to pursue conduct that took place extraterritorially. Most developing countries are of this type. For firms that do business in these states, the de facto regime is more haphazard and has different implications than doing business in the United States and the EU.

One implication of this fact is that for states that do not apply their laws beyond their borders, their competition policy is unaffected by the presence of imports. Since the state does not or cannot enforce its competition laws extraterritorially, it cannot control conduct of foreign companies that serves to reduce competition. Therefore, policy makers in those states can only take domestic production into account when crafting the country's competition policies. The optimal competition policy, then, is the same as if the country had no imports at all, since the country cannot influence the anticompetitive behavior of firms operating outside of its borders.

Given that antitrust laws impact consumers and producers alike, as long as at least some domestic production is manufactured for export, the state has an incentive to allow more anticompetitive behavior than if it had a closed economy. The benefits of more stringent policies are enjoyed by consumers, and if some percentage of those consumers live abroad, the state has no reason to take their interests into account. The state, then, factors only a portion of the benefits of stricter policies into its competition policy while taking the whole of the benefits derived from more permissive policies into the calculation. The result is a more permissive regime as a whole. The lack of small states with substantial antitrust policies and the fact that when the EU began to enforce its competition laws extraterritorially its policies became more restrictive is consistent with the

Horizontal Merger Guidelines (1992). The companies would also be subject to Council Regulation 4064/89 (called the Merger Control Regulation) in the European Union.

expectation that smaller states and states without extraterritorial application will have less restrictive policies.

It is true that without extraterritorial reach, some firms are able to free ride on the policies of states that do apply their competition laws beyond their borders. Imagine, for example, two firms that wish to merge and that do business in the United States, the EU, and several other states. Because both places apply their laws extraterritorially, the merger is subject to review in both jurisdictions.

States that are unable to apply their laws beyond their borders cannot regulate the activities of these firms unless at least one of the firms operates within the borders of the state. But if, as in the example, the firms are doing business in both the United States and the EU, the decision of either of those regimes to block or allow the merger will still have implications for the state that cannot reach the firms through extraterritorial application of its laws. From the perspective of a state that does not apply its laws extraterritorially, an action by, say, the EU to prevent the merger may serve to protect the former's consumers.

Free riding, however, is no replacement for a state's own competition policy regime. Different countries have different cost-benefit analyses; free riding is only possible if the firms conduct business activities in the United States or the EU (or some other state that applies its laws extraterritorially), and even then the United States or the EU might not choose to assert its jurisdiction over a merger that bears only marginally to their domestic situation, or might approve a merger that is harmful to the free riding state.[19]

In sum, the application of myriad domestic competition laws—some applied extraterritorially, some not—yields a de facto international competition policy regime. Problems of overregulation and underregulation, however, reveal that the de facto regime is far from optimal from a global perspective. International cooperation would be necessary to optimize competition regulation. While there do exist some limited forms of international cooperation on this issue, there also exist serious obstacles to a true international cooperative regime on competition policy.

III. BARRIERS TO INTERNATIONAL COOPERATION: A THEORETICAL ANALYSIS

The existence of international trade introduces several distortions in the way states create their competition policy. Several theoretical examples serve to show

---

19. *See* M.C. Levenstein & V. Suslow, *Private International Cartels and the Effect on Developing Countries*, Background paper for the *World Development Report 2001*, Washington, D.C.: World Bank (2001); JOHN M. O'CONNOR, GLOBAL PRICE FIXING: OUR CUSTOMERS ARE THE ENEMY (2001); Lawrence J. White, *Lysine and Price Fixing: How Long? How Severe?* 18 REV. OF INDUS. ORG. 23 (2001); Christopher Sprigman, FIX PRICES GLOBALLY, GET SUED LOCALLY? U.S. JURISDICTION OVER INTERNATIONAL CARTELS, 72 U. CHI. L. REV. 265 (2005).

the impediments to international cooperation in the absence of a supranational body to oversee regulation. Such analysis requires the assumption that each state attempts to maximize its own interests without regard to other states' interests. The distortions arise as each state tries to externalize costs and internalize the benefits of market power as it extends across borders.

First, take the example of a country that exports almost all of its production.[20] Only consumers living in other states feel the implications of anticompetitive behavior of domestic firms, and the domestic firms enjoy the full benefits of the anticompetitive behavior. For domestic policy makers concerned only with local costs and benefits, only the benefits accrued by the firms will be considered, since the costs to consumers are only felt abroad. Here, the domestic policy maker would favor the producers over the consumers. It is the presence of international trade that influences the decision. Since most of the products of the domestic firms are exported, only the domestic benefits are considered, which is a much different analysis were it not for international trade.

For policy makers and governments that want to favor local producers over consumers abroad, one of the simplest methods is the export cartel exemption. Here, when firms present in a certain country export almost all of their goods, a domestic legal exemption to regulations on anticompetitive behavior by those firms allows the state to maximize domestic benefit while externalizing the costs on consumers abroad. Industry exemptions serve the same function. For example, in the United States, international aviation, international energy, international ocean shipping, and international communications all enjoy certain exemptions to competition regulation laws that serve to favor U.S. domestic firms over their foreign competition.[21] This tool works best only if most of a domestic firm's products are exported. Another option is to alter substantive laws. As in the example above, a state that primarily exports goods could make all of its anticompetitive laws more permissive, thereby giving an advantage to domestic firms while still keeping some regulatory control to give protection to local consumers.

---

20. Here we consider only imperfectly competitive industries. With regard to antitrust, firms in competitive industries do not present a problem.

21. The United States has a long history of export cartel exemptions. The Webb-Pomerene Act, 15 U.S.C. §§ 61–66 (1994) of 1918 created an exemption from the Sherman Act and also from Section 7 of the Clayton Act for export associations that are created for the purpose of engaging in export trade and actually engaged solely in such export trade. These export associations are required to register with the FTC. The Act does not protect activity that has an anticompetitive effect within the United Sates, although there are other restrictions on its application. *See* A. Paul Victor, *Export Cartels: An Idea Whose Time Has Passed*, 60 Antitrust L.J. 572 (1991). In 1992, Congress enacted the Export Trading Company Act, 15 U.S.C. §§ 4001–4016 (2000), and the Foreign Trade Antitrust Improvements Act, 15 U.S.C. § 6a (2000), in response to the fact that the Webb-Pomerene Act had fallen out of use and was no longer effective.

Next, consider the distortion caused by imports in the context of international trade. In the case of states that have the ability to apply competition laws extraterritorially, there is a strong incentive to increase the strength of its competition policy with regard to imported goods that are manufactured in imperfectly competitive markets. Here, only a fraction of the benefit to domestic firms is considered in the policy analysis, whereas the full amount of harm that local consumers experience is captured. With the assumption that states will act to maximize their domestic interests, it is easy to predict distortion caused by imports.

The above analysis shows that, given the assumption that states will act rationally, once the extent of a state's trade of goods in an imperfectly competitive international market is known, its competition policy behavior is predictable in comparison to its behavior were it in a closed economy. Put in more formal terms, imagine that domestic firms within a certain country produce x percent of the global production of certain goods in an imperfectly competitive market, and that those firms benefit from x percent of the monopoly gains that come from the sale of those same goods. In considering its competition policy, the government of that state will consider x percent of the producer surplus that a change in its competition policies would yield. So if the country made its competition laws more permissive, the firms might enjoy greater producer surplus, and the government would choose not to calculate the portion of surplus allocated outside of its borders.

Additionally, assume that the consumers living in that country make up y percent of consumption of those goods sold in imperfectly competitive markets worldwide. The government would then calculate y percent of the global effects were it to change its competition policies.

It follows that that the ratio of a country's global share of production to its global share of consumption of imperfectly competitive goods yields the net effect of trade. The baseline is a closed economy in which the ratio of production to consumption of goods is equal. In formal terms, a closed economy is represented by ($x = 100 = y$). A country whose share of global production is greater than its share of global consumption is a net exporter, and can be represented by the formula ($x > y$). A country that is a net exporter will devise a competition policy that places more emphasis on the policy's impact on producers than its impact on consumers. Measured against the baseline of a closed economy, a country that is a net exporter will create a more permissive competition policy that is in the interests of producers.

Alternately, a country that consumes a greater global share of goods than its export share—a net importer represented in formal terms by ($x < y$)—will craft a strict competition policy that reflects the country's interest in protecting its consumers. As the model predicts, the patterns of international trade, production, and consumption in imperfectly competitive markets cause predictable distortions in the domestic competition policy of a state relative to what it would do in a closed economy.[22] The distortions caused by international trade are one form of cost from the perspective of an optimal global perspective on international trade. There are, however, other costs stemming from noncooperation.

IV. COSTS OF NONCOOPERATION

As the above theoretical explanation shows, attempts to regulate international trade creates costs and benefits that are not fully accounted for in the domestic policy decisions of states. Transaction costs and bias stand out as two prominent costs of the de facto regime.

Since regulatory bodies exist in many different countries, and since some of those bodies apply their laws extraterritorially, firms that conduct business on a global scale must contend with increased and duplicative costs. In order to operate in accord with regulatory policies in many different countries, firms must retain legal counsel in multiple states in order to satisfy jurisdictional differences in reporting and disclosure requirements. This is slow, burdensome, and expensive for the firms, while it also increases costs carried by the various regulatory agencies. Because regulatory bodies in different states all act independently, from the perspective of global efficiency, the regulatory bodies are expending duplicative energy in reviewing the same activities.

In the context of international trade under the de facto international competition policy regime, firms operating in multiple states are subject to multiple regulatory reviews. As already noted, this overregulation is costly in terms of duplicative work on the part of both firms and regulatory states, but it also introduces yet another cost of noncooperation in the form of bias. A regulatory agency has the temptation to be more lenient when reviewing activities by local firms and potentially more restrictive when reviewing activities by foreign firms.

From the point of view of the firms, even if regulatory activities by states are unbiased, it might appear that unfavorable rulings stem from bias. Perception, in this case, is important because the way firms perceive regulatory actions or regulatory policies by states has implications for the way firms conduct their business activities. Furthermore, states might perceive the regulatory activities of other states on their firms as biased or even as punitive regulatory activity, which potentially drives a wedge between any possibility of interstate regulatory cooperation. Bias is more apparent in the choice of which cases to pursue, rather than in statutory language, but nevertheless, the presence of export cartel exemptions is the most ready example of substantial evidence that points to state bias in regulatory activity. Again, as mentioned above, the United States reveals its

---

22. See Andrew T. Guzman, *Is International Antitrust Possible?*, 73 N.Y.U. L. REV. 1501 (1998) for a more extensive explication of this theory.

bias in exemptions for firms operating in the international markets in aviation, energy, ocean shipping, and communications.

In the above analysis, it is assumed that states pursue domestic welfare by acting rationally and thereby create competition policies that are optimal in the domestic sphere but suboptimal if one takes a global view. While domestically these policies seek to externalize costs while maximizing benefits, in the context of international trade, costs and benefits on a global scale are left out of the calculation.

If one posits a different governmental model based on public choice, international trade will cause competition policies to veer away from what would exist under a closed economic policy. It may or may not be the case that the proposed shift in policy moves closer to the optimal global policy. If one assumes that there is general agreement across states on what would constitute the ends and means of an optimal competition policy in a closed economy, then states would be able to reach agreement on an international policy in the absence of transaction costs. Although net importers would still adopt more strict policies if they are able to apply their laws extraterritorially, and net exporters' policies will still be more permissive, states could still agree on an optimal global policy. This follows from standard federalism theories that hold that the responsibility for making decisions should be allocated to the lowest level of government that is able to internalize economic externalities.[23]

In a world in which there is a wide array of ideas regarding the optimal policy and in which transaction costs are potent, the model must be finessed. If transaction costs are still held to be zero, but ideas regarding optimal policy are allowed to deviate, international dialogue might eventually yield an optimal global competition policy. Even if states differ with regard to preferences of policy, sharing information through international agreement will not bring about a shared global policy. An optimal global policy, however, is not entirely out of reach if such preferences could be overcome through a system by which one state compensates another for agreeing on a policy that deviates from its preferences. This method would work, as well, for distortions that arise through international trade. In such a model, states could agree to a globally optimal competition policy, and states that benefit from such a policy could make transfer payments to those states that incur losses as a result of the global policy.

Ultimately, transaction costs are the biggest stumbling block to an optimal global competition policy. Since net importers and net exporters have differing policy interests, true and substantive cooperation can only be realized through a system that allows transfer payments by those states that would gain from the optimal global policy and those states that would incur a loss.

---

23. *See, e.g.*, Robert P. Inman & Daniel L. Rubinfeld, *Rethinking Federalism*, 11 J. of Econ. Persp. 45 (1997).

V. THE COSTS OF COOPERATION

It is clear from the presence of the de facto regime, the numerous transaction costs, and the existence of bias in the context of international trade that the absence of cooperation results in costs for both firms and regulatory states. Yet, not all cooperation reduces costs. Rather, some forms of cooperation also introduce costs on the actors involved.

In general, no matter the form cooperation takes, the higher the administrative level on which cooperation takes place, the greater the amount of resulting costs. As cooperation increases, decisions are made further and further away from the domestic realm of policy decisions and democratic process and are governed more and more by domestic or international bureaucracies.

Such cooperation also raises problems of enforcement. States might not choose or be able to fully comply with their commitments to cooperation. Additionally, enforcement on a global scale might require the creation of an intrastate enforcement body that does not currently exist. The upkeep of an international cooperation regime is costly because it not only requires negotiation in the formation of the rules and institutions, but also requires the ongoing process of negotiation to gain agreement to regulations or changes in the rules or institutions that comprise the regime. Such inertia of an international cooperative regime has yet another cost in that it might not be flexible enough to adapt to changes in the world market, and might thereby introduce new inefficiencies as international trade patterns and business activities change over time.

These costs need to be avoided, and thus states would need to institute cooperation at the lowest level possible, while avoiding the numerous costs of non-cooperation discussed above. There are three forms of cooperation that could be implemented with regard to competition policy—information sharing, agreement on choice of law rules, and cooperation in terms of substantive rules.

A. Information Sharing

Information sharing is the current status quo with regard to international competition policy—current efforts at cooperation are mostly voluntary agreements of this sort. Continued growth in international business activity has prompted domestic competition policy makers to adopt a minimal amount of cooperation. Information sharing is the minimal amount of cooperation that allows states to maintain their authority and enforcement powers of conducting international business. Without agreements to facilitate the sharing of information, firms could reside abroad, conduct meetings abroad, and store certain documents regarding prohibited activity offshore and out of the hands of prosecutors. Cooperation regarding information, then, is essential, at a minimum, for the purposes of enforcement.

To date, cooperation has most often taken the form of information sharing agreements.[24] Such agreements most often entail sharing of information between enforcement authorities when the actions of regulators in one state would influence the interests of another state.[25] The agreements also include provisions that call for consultation, if needed, to resolve disputes among states, that call upon countries to cooperate in enforcement when possible, and that urge states to consider the implications of their regulatory activities for other states. While following this final principle would significantly address many of the costs associated with the current de facto regime, existing agreements do not provide guidelines for how this consideration should be given. Nor do any current agreements provide sanctions or means to impose sanctions for a state that fails to consider the impact of its proposed regulatory activities on the interests of another state. Finally, no guidelines are given as to how other state's interests should be taken into account when crafting domestic policy.

While information sharing agreements are surely necessary, they do not solve the various problems associated with international cooperation, nor are they a substitute for a truly international competition policy regime. Information sharing agreements do not address coordination of substantive laws or suggest minimum standards for states, nor do they shape what form compromise with regard to domestic control should take.[26] Ultimately, individual states may refuse cooperation when they want to and are free to consider only their individual interests when choosing to refuse to cooperate.

---

24. Eleanor M. Fox, *Antitrust and Regulatory Federalism: Races Up, Down, and Sideways*, 75 N.Y.U. L. Rev. 1785, 1785–88 (2000). *See also* Charles W. Smitherman III, *The Future of Global Competition Governance: Lessons From the Transatlantic*, 19 Am. U. Int'l L. Rev. 769 (2004).

25. *See, e.g.*, Agreement Between the Government of the United States of America and the Government of Canada Regarding the Application of Their Competition and Deceptive Marketing Practices Laws, Aug. 3, 1995, U.S.-Can., in Trade Regulation Reporter (CCH) 4, ¶ 13,503. *See also* Agreement Between the Government of the United States of America and the Government of the Federal Republic of Germany Relating to Mutual Cooperation Regarding Restrictive Business Practices, June 23, 1976, in Trade Regulation Reporter (CCH) 4, ¶ 13, 501. The United States also has similar information sharing agreements with Australia, the European Communities, Israel, Japan, Brazil, and Mexico. *See* John J. Parisi, *Enforcement Cooperation among Antitrust Authorities*, 12 Int'l Q. 691 (2000). See also Spencer Weber Waller, *The Internationalization of Antitrust Enforcement*, 77 B.U. L. Rev. 343 (1997) for a more detailed discussion.

26. Two exceptions to this last point must be noted. Canada and the United States entered into the Treaty on Mutual Legal Assistance in Criminal Matters, Mar. 18, 1985, Can.-U.S., 24 I.L.M. 1092 (1985). This agreement provides for the use of compulsory power to collect evidence for criminal antitrust cases and allows for the exchange of compulsory information. Also, the United States and Australia entered into agreement under the International Antitrust Enforcement Act of 1994, P.L. No. 103-438, codified at 15 U.S.C. §§ 6201–6212.

"Soft cooperation" in the form of information sharing has been the subject of aspirational documents issued by the Organisation for Economic Co-operation and Development (OECD).[27] Yet again, these documents do not impose any obligations on states and are intended to facilitate communication among states on issues related to cooperation and competition. The International Competition Network (ICN) is another entity that tries to facilitate cooperation, and along with the OECD guidelines, may have some effect at harmonizing substantive competition laws. But any level of harmonization that has occurred is probably not much more than what one could expect from rationally acting states attempting to maintain their own interests and influence.[28] Information sharing gives over no authority while still allowing states and their administrative enforcement agencies to continue their regulative activities. As a whole, information sharing does serve some of the goals of regulators, but it fails to address either under- or overregulation in the international context.

B. Choice of Law

Another option would allow states to retain significant amounts of domestic control while implementing a slightly higher level of cooperation through a system of choice of law rules regarding competition policy. For example, such a regime could include some rather standard factors for determining the appropriate law, such as the location of the anticompetitive conduct, the location of the most important effects, or the principle place of business of the firm engaged in anticompetitive practices. Cooperating states would face decisions about whether the goal would be to assign jurisdiction to one particular state or several, and despite problems attaching to each factor noted above, some anticompetitive activities could be governed through an agreement on choice of law rules.

An agreement of choice of law rules, however, cannot by itself solve the problems associated with over- and underregulation. If the choice of law system allows overlapping jurisdiction of states, then the problems of overregulation will still exist. For example, firms that do business in the United States and the EU would still be subject to excessive regulation as long as both bodies continued to exercise jurisdiction over the conduct of these firms.

On the contrary, if states agree to a choice of laws system that assigns jurisdiction to one single state, then the problems of underregulation will still be present. A choice of law agreement also cannot affect the distortions on international trade that are caused by local favoritism or substantive domestic policies.

In theory, the problem of underregulation in states that cannot apply their competition laws extraterritorially could be addressed through a choice of law

27. *See, e.g.*, OECD Guidelines for Multinational Enterprises: Ministerial Booklet (Paris, OECD, 2000), *available at* http://www.oecd.org/document/28/0,3343,en_2649_34889_2397532_1_1_1_1,00.html (last visited May 24, 2010).

28. *See* Parisi, *supra* note 25.

system that would grant standing to plaintiffs if the corresponding firm activity took place within the jurisdiction, even if the injuries occurred abroad. Even more aggressively, a rule could grant standing to a plaintiff no matter where the conduct took place. Under such a rule, injured plaintiffs would have a remedy against the actions of foreign firms that target states whose laws do not apply beyond their borders, as long as the conduct in question was within a state with effective anticompetition laws. A rule of this type would ensure, at a bare minimum, that western firms were faced with some regulation when conducting activities in states without extraterritorial capacity. The rationale for such a rule is the same as disposing of the export cartel exemption—states would be required to regulate some anticompetitive behavior, even when it benefits local firms and harms foreign consumers. Implementing this type of rule would be a serious change of course from the status quo and would therefore face many problems. Such a rule is most likely unrealistic given the current state of affairs, and speaks to the fact that a deeper form of cooperation is necessary.

C. Substantive Cooperation

If information sharing as the status quo is ultimately ineffective, and if agreement on a choice of law system is unrealistic, then we are led to consider a third possibility for cooperation. If international competition is to be regulated in a realistic and effective manner, substantive cooperation—that is, cooperation that deals with the content of actual antitrust rules governing transactions—is required.

Substantive cooperation as discussed does not necessarily entail the harmonization of domestic competition laws. It is possible to have forms of cooperation that fall short of harmonization, but it is true that almost all forms of cooperation will require states to let go of some level of domestic control. For example, if we imagine that the United States and the EU were to enter into an agreement that placed the obligation on enforcement authorities to share information with one another under certain conditions, it would make it easier for, say, the EU authorities to pursue cases against firms in the United States. This amounts to a de facto increase in the regulatory burden on those American firms, where the agreement is less than a rule of harmonization, but results in an increase in the reach of both sets of laws. In fact, for firms subject to laws in both jurisdictions, there is a de facto harmonization because they face potential regulation by both regulatory systems no matter where they are located.

Once one accepts the proposition that substantive cooperation is needed, the question becomes how to achieve it. The history of attempts at cooperation, as well as the theory of international cooperation proposed above, tells us that achieving cooperation on substantive issues is difficult.[29] The transaction costs

29. *See* Guzman, *supra* note 22.

are quite high—differences in priorities, perceptions, and legal culture across countries, and different positions of the potentially cooperative states make negotiation and agreement difficult. As discussed above, the domestic policies chosen by states, and the global policies preferred by states, depend on the pattern of trade in imperfectly competitive markets. Net importers of these goods would rather have a strict competition policy, and states that are net exporters would prefer a more permissive policy, relative to what each state would choose were this distortion not present. Given this problem, the best approach to cooperation is to start small. Again, harmonization of laws need not be the end goal, because states might conclude that policy differences across regimes are desirable, but it would require negotiation regarding a substantive policy in a forum where transfer payments are available.

The most plausible area in which agreement might be reached is a nondiscrimination principle, including both national treatment and most favored nation elements.[30] A national treatment obligation squares with our notion of fairness, is consistent with the spirit of already existing WTO obligations, and could also address export cartel exemptions. A national treatment obligation might even be useful in addressing discrimination application, though its success is debatable. Although a national treatment obligation could eliminate explicit discrimination, it would not be as successful at addressing the problem of discrimination in application and enforcement. In the context of trade, discrimination against an imported product is fairly easy to see by comparing the treatment of one product with the treatment of a similar product. This is much more difficult in the antitrust context because prosecution turns on a unique set of facts, and a lack of closely analogous sets of facts will often prevent comparisons.

Additionally, other areas subject to nondiscrimination requirements are not always policed effectively, and the national treatment obligation is often more of a *de jure* rather than de facto standard, especially in areas where fact-specific analysis is required. A national treatment obligation is useful, therefore, primarily in preventing the use of export cartel exemptions or in constraining particular flagrant types of de facto discrimination. It still does not stop regulators from being biased toward local firms in the day-to-day administration of the laws, nor does it solve the problems that come with the domestic adoption and enforcement of rules to govern international activity, as in the case of the strategic choice of domestic laws by states engaged in trade.

---

30. *See* John O. McGinnis, *The Political Economy of International Antitrust Harmonization*, *in* Competition Laws in Conflict: Antitrust Jurisdiction in the Global Economy (Michael S. Greve & Richard A. Epstein eds., 2004). *See also* Michael Trebilcock & Edward Iacobbucci, *National Treatment and Extraterritoriality: Defining the Domains of Trade and Antitrust Policy*, *in* Competition Laws in Conflict, *supra*; Andrew T. Guzman, *Antitrust and International Regulatory Federalism*, 76 N.Y.U. L. Rev. 1142, 1142–63 (2002).

Beyond a nondiscrimination agreement, states could consider the WTO's proposed "core principles that include transparency, non-discrimination and procedural fairness and provisions on hardcore cartels; [and] modalities for voluntary cooperation."[31] Though appearing more ambitious, it is still a fairly modest set of proposals and rests on issues that enjoy widespread agreement. Eventually, other types of cooperation may emerge, such as mandatory information sharing agreements, streamlining cooperation in international merger review, and jurisdictional agreements that at a minimum commit states to decline jurisdiction if the impact of a measure on their own citizens is sufficiently small. This type of cooperation is difficult to achieve, but is the only way to reach realistic competition in the globalized world.

Whatever form of cooperation is pursued, there remains the question of the institutional context in which negotiation takes place. This is no insignificant detail—the forum in which negotiations take place is likely to affect the possibility of reaching agreement. I have argued that the WTO provides the most proper forum for these negotiations,[32] whereas others argue that WTO business and antitrust policy negotiations should not be mixed.[33] Still others argue that the failure to reach agreement at the Doha round and the withdrawal of competition policy from the WTO's negotiating agenda because of strong opposition from developing countries at Cancun in 2001 reveal that the WTO is not the best forum for negotiating competition.[34]

Nevertheless, negotiating at the WTO has the advantage that several issues can be negotiated at once, and allows for concessions in one area in exchange for agreement in another. Such ability to negotiate across a wide range of topics is essential to achieving cooperation. It reduces transaction costs, which in turn increases the chance that parties will reach an optimal policy outcome. Furthermore, the presence of the WTO's dispute settlement system is also a significant advantage. If there is no recourse to enforcement, parties to an agreement have very little incentive to abide by the agreement. Finally, the WTO offers the advantages of universal membership, relatively transparent procedures, and experience managing negotiation and implementation of international agreements.

---

31. WTO Ministerial Declaration, Doha Ministerial Conference Fourth Session, WTO Doc. WT/MIN(01)/DEC/1 (Nov. 20, 2001), ¶ 25.

32. Andrew T. Guzman, *International Antitrust and the WTO: The Lesson from Intellectual Property*, 43 VA. J. INT'L L. 933 (2003).

33. Fox, *supra* note 24. *See also* Daniel K. Tarullo, *Norms and Institutions in Global Competition Policy*, 94 AM. J. INT'L L. 478 (2000).

34. Trebilcock & Iacobbucci, *supra* note 30.

VI. CONCLUSION

While international competition policy does already exist, it is present in a de facto form. This regime, created by overlapping domestic jurisdictions, in which some states can and do apply their competition laws extraterritorially and others do not, is rife with distortions and transaction costs for firms and states alike. In order to reach an optimal global policy, international cooperation—beyond what minimum levels already exist—is needed. Such cooperation must take place in a form that allows distortions to be minimized and transaction costs kept at a minimum.

INDEX

A

B

C

H

I

J

K

L

M

CPSIA information can be obtained
at www.ICGtesting.com
Printed in the USA
BVOW06*1059081217
502133BV00006B/32/P

9 780195 387704